Research and Development on Genetic Resources

National implementation of the Convention on Biological Diversity (CBD) provisions has yielded plenty of challenges for providers and users of genetic resources and associated traditional knowledge alike. The Nagoya Protocol brings novel ideas for resolving the challenges plaguing the access and benefit-sharing (ABS) process in general and non-commercial research in particular.

This is one of the first books to address research cooperation and facilitated access for non-commercial biodiversity research. It uniquely offers concrete and practicable solutions based on the experiences of researchers and administrative officials with ABS, as well as on the interpretation of the Nagoya Protocol, which offers solutions for ensuring free and lively taxonomic research while also observing the commitment of obtaining prior informed consent and sharing of benefits.

This book will be useful to students of international environmental law, international biodiversity law, intellectual property law, climate law, and law of indigenous populations.

Evanson Chege Kamau is Senior Researcher in the Research Centre for European Environmental Law (FEU) at the University of Bremen, Germany.

Gerd Winter is Co-Director of the Research Centre for European Environmental Law (FEU) at the University of Bremen, Germany.

Peter-Tobias Stoll is Professor of Public International Law in the Institute for International Law and European Law, Department for International Economic Law and Environmental Law, at the Georg-August-Universität Göttingen, Germany.

Routledge Research in International Environmental Law

Research and Development on Genetic Resources
Public Domain Approaches to Implementing the Nagoya Protocol
Edited by Evanson Chege Kamau, Gerd Winter and Peter-Tobias Stoll

Forthcoming titles in this series

International Liability Regime for Biodiversity Damage
The Nagoya-Kuala Lumpur Supplementary Protocol
Akiho Shibata

Culture and International Economic Law
Valentia Vadi and Bruno de Witte

Climate Change and Forest Governance
Lessons from Indonesia
Simon Butt, Rosemary Lyster & Tim Stephens

Climate Change and Human Rights
An International and Comparative Law Perspective
Ottavio Quirico and Mouloud Boumghar

Ecological Restoration in International Environmental Law
Afshin Akhtarkhavari, An Cliquet, and Anastasia Telesetsky

Law and Practice on Public Participation in Environmental Matters
The Nigerian Example in Transnational Comparative Perspective
Uzuazo Etemire

Natural Resources Law, Investment and Sustainability
Shawkat Alam, Jahid Hossain Bhuiyan, Carmen Gonzalez, and Jona Razzaque

Sustainable Development Principles in the Decisions of International Courts and Tribunals
1992-2012
Marie-Claire Cordonier Segger and Yolanda Saito

Research and Development on Genetic Resources

Public domain approaches in implementing the Nagoya Protocol

Edited by Evanson Chege Kamau, Gerd Winter, and Peter-Tobias Stoll

LONDON AND NEW YORK

First published 2015 by Routledge

2 Park Square, Milton Park, Abingdon, Oxon OX14 4RN
711 Third Avenue, New York, NY 10017, USA

Routledge is an imprint of the Taylor & Francis Group, an informa business

First issued in paperback 2017

British Library Cataloguing in Publication Data
A catalogue record for this book is available from the British Library

Library of Congress Cataloging-in-Publication Data
Research and development on genetic resources : public domain
   approaches in implementing the Nagoya Protocol / edited by Evanson
   Chege Kamau, Gerd Winter, and Peter-Tobias Stoll
      pages cm
   Includes bibliographical references and index.
  1. Biodiversity conservation—Law and legislation.   2. Convention on
Biological Diversity (1992 June 5). Protocols, etc. (2010 October 29)
3. Renewable natural resources—Law and legislation.   4. Nature
conservation—Law and legislation.   I. Kamau, Evanson C., editor.
II. Winter, Gerd, editor.   III. Stoll, Peter-Tobias, editor.
   K3488.R47 2015
   333.95072—dc23
   2014048374

ISBN: 978-1-138-85861-9 (hbk)
ISBN: 978-1-138-74360-1 (pbk)

Typeset in Goudy
by Apex CoVantage, LLC

Contents

Contributors

Erwin H. Beck, professor emeritus at the University of Bayreuth, was promoted to Dr. rer. nat. in 1963 (University of Munich, Germany) with a thesis in plant taxonomy and appointed full professor for plant physiology at the University of Bayreuth (Germany), where he chaired the Department of Plant Physiology from 1975 until 2006. He taught plant science while performing research projects combining laboratory and field work. His publications cover subjects from plant molecular biology to plant ecology, with a focus on tropical plants and ecosystems. He supervised the doctoral theses of numerous students from several tropical countries. (erwin.beck@uni-bayreuth.de)

Susette Biber-Klemm graduated in 1992 as a doctor in international law of environment and conservation of biological resources at the University of Basel and holds a postgraduate master's degree in applied ethics. Her research focuses on genetic resources at the interface with property rights, international trade and access and benefit sharing, as well as on land-rights and land-use systems. She is associated with sustainability research at the University of Basel, where she has been teaching interdisciplinary courses in environmental law and international and national law of sustainable development. Since 2003, she has led the program on ABS for academic research at the Swiss Academy of Sciences. Her expertise enabled her to defend the interests of academic research in the Nagoya negotiations. (susette.biber-klemm@unibas.ch)

Hamadi Iddi Boga is a professor of microbiology at Jomo Kenyatta University of Agriculture and Technology (JKUAT) and the principal of Taita Taveta University College in Voi, Kenya. Has a BSc in botany/zoology, an MSc in microbiology from Kenyatta University and a PhD in microbial ecology/microbiology from University of Konstanz, Germany. He teaches microbiology/microbial ecology and carries out research on termites, soda lakes and other ecosystems. He is a fellow of the Humboldt Foundation and was a board member of the World Federation of Culture Collections (2010–2013) and secretary of the Kenya Society of Microbiology (2002–2010). He has produced over 40 publications and has supervised over 40 postgraduate students. (hamadiboga@ttuc.ac.ke or hamadiboga@yahoo.com)

Arianna Broggiato, LLM in environmental law and PhD in international law. She recently finished three years as a post-doctoral researcher at the Biodiversity Governance (BIOGOV) Unit, Universitè Catholique de Louvain (Belgium). She and the whole team have been drafting the Micro B3 Agreement on Access to Marine Microorganisms and Benefit Sharing, the legal work package of the EU 7FP project Micro B3 (marine microbial biodiversity, bioinformatics, biotechnology, www.microb3.eu). Her research focuses on the law of the environment and the law of the sea, with emphasis on the legal regimes of genetic resources. (arianna@broggiato.it)

Gemedo Dalle holds a PhD in rangeland ecology (agricultural sciences), an MSc in botanical sciences (biology) and a BSc in biology. He is director general of the Ethiopian Biodiversity Institute. He served in different capacities in the same institute in the past, including as director of the Genetic Resources Transfer and Regulation Directorate and head of the Forest Genetic Resources Department. He is also CBD and ITPGRFA National Primary Focal Point. Dr. Dalle served as chair of the CBD SBSTTA from November 2012 to October 2014. His professional focus is on biodiversity conservation, ecosystem management and vegetation ecology. (gemedod@yahoo.com)

Manuela da Silva holds a PhD in food science (microbiology) at UNICAMP in Brazil. She works at the Food and Drug Administration – National Center for Toxicological Research (FDA-NCTR) in the United States and at FIOCRUZ – Fundação Oswaldo Cruz as advisor to the vice president of Research and Reference Laboratories and as coordinator of the Fiocruz Biological Collections. She is also professor of the postgraduate program in health surveillance at the National Institute for Health Quality Control (INCQS/FIOCRUZ). Her studies are focused on microbiology (fungal taxonomy and biodegradation) and her practice and experience is in biological collections and access and benefit-sharing legislation. (manueladasilva@fiocruz.br)

Kate Davis is a consultant on ABS issues and is an ABS advisor to Botanic Gardens Conservation International. She holds degrees in natural sciences from Duke University (MS) and Oxford University (BA Hons). She was previously the CBD Implementation Officer at the Royal Botanic Gardens, Kew. Her work has centered on helping scientists, horticulturists and policymakers to understand how ABS relates to *ex situ* collections and biodiversity research. Consultancies have included a European Union–Brazil project to facilitate collections-based research cooperation and the development for botanic gardens of an online tool to explain the Nagoya Protocol. (kathrynkdavis1@gmail.com)

Tom Dedeurwaerdere is director of the Biodiversity Governance Unit of the Centre for the Philosophy of Law (http://biogov.cpdr.ucl.ac.be/) and professor at the Faculty of Philosophy, Université Catholique de Louvain. He is a graduate in engineering and philosophy, with a PhD in the philosophy of science. (tom.dedeurwaerdere@uclouvain.be)

Dagmar Fritze, PhD. Since 1987 employed at DSMZ; until 2005 responsible for the patent strain depositary (IDA) and curator for the aerobic endospore forming bacteria; since 2005 responsible for collection-related policies and regulatory matters; 1996–2000 vice president of the WFCC; 2004–2010 president of the ECCO; 2004–2006 member of the OECD-Task Force on BRCs; 2008–2011 executive secretary of the Demonstration Project for a Global Biological Resource Centre Network (GBRCN); 2012–2013 coordinator of the ESFRI Preparatory Phase Project MIRRI. Lectures and publications on taxonomic- and collection-related technical, managerial and regulatory matters. Consultancies in the past to the Brazilian and Vietnamese Patent Offices on IDA practice, presently to German ministries on CBD/ABS matters. (dfr@dsmz.de)

Laurent Gautier received his PhD in tropical botany in 1992 at the University of Geneva after three years of fieldwork in Côte d'Ivoire. He has participated in research projects in floristics, systematics, vegetation studies and monitoring deforestation in Africa and Madagascar. He is a specialist in systematics of the plant family Saptaceae and is currently head of the flowering plants herbarium at Conservatoire et Jardin Botanique de la Ville Genève, Switzerland. He teaches tropical botany at the University of Geneva and pursues his research and capacity-building activities in Madagascar. (laurent.gautier@ville-ge.ch)

Fabian Haas, FRES, currently freelance lecturer and photographer with a focus on Africa. He holds a PhD in biology (1998) and has worked on CBD-related issues and with ICIPE in Nairobi, Kenya, for several years. Previously, he was head of the Biosystematic Support Unit, in charge of material exchange and identification of organisms (2006–2012); head of German National Focal Point of CBD Global Taxonomy Initiative in Germany (2003–2006); and biology lecturer, University of Ulm (1999–2003). His publications focus on the exchange of biocontrol agents and the role of the CBD-ABS regime. His major publications are in biodiversity and insect systematics. Dr. Haas has done consultancies for mining companies to monitor water quality using biological organisms and trained local people and members of nature clubs in Kenya using the same technology. (fabianhaas2@gmx.net)

Evanson Chege Kamau is senior research fellow in law at the Research Centre for European Environmental Law (FEU), University of Bremen, Germany. He holds a Doctor of Laws and a master's degree in European and international law. His current research focuses on genetic resources, environment, development, and intellectual property issues. He has done several legal consultancies in ABS, including for the African Union, and has published widely in the area. (echege@uni-bremen.de)

Michael Kiehn is the director of the Botanical Garden and an associate professor of botany at the University of Vienna (Austria). He holds a PhD and habilitation in biology/botany, University of Vienna. Short studies, e.g. at the RBG Kew (UK) and the Smithsonian Institutions, Washington, DC (USA). Research associate, National Tropical Botanical Garden, Kauai, USA;

associate in science, Bishop Museum, Honolulu, USA. Member, Austrian Bio-diversity Commission; senior vice president, International Association of Botanic Gardens (IABG); member, European Botanic Gardens Consortium; chair, International Plant Exchange Network (IPEN) Task Force. Research and teaching foci include plant phylogeny, evolution and radiation on islands; nature conservancy issues; and history, tasks and strategic planning of botanic gardens. (michael.kiehn@univie.ac.at)

Veronica Kimutai holds a bachelor's and a master's degree in wildlife management from Moi University. She has worked as a senior standards officer with the National Environment Management Authority (NEMA) and was responsible for issuing access permits from 2008–2014. (vkimutai@yahoo.com)

Wolfram Lorenz studied at Humboldt University and Free University of Berlin. He holds a master's degree (MA) in Southeast Asian science. He works for the University of Göttingen as coordinator for research collaboration in Central Sulawesi and recently in Sumatra, Indonesia. His work location is at the Bogor Agricultural University in Bogor, where an important part of his responsibilities includes handling permit-related issues and ensuring that all research activities are implemented in line with the CBD and Nagoya Protocol. His research interests focus on the impact of the NP on research management in international cooperation. (wlorenz@uni-goettingen.de)

Sylvia I. Martínez is science coordinator in the Department of Environmental Sciences at the University of Basel (Switzerland) and manages the Swiss Plant Science Web – the network of all plant scientists at Swiss universities. Since 1997, she has been a scientific adviser for the Swiss Federal Office for the Environment (FOEN) and a member of the Swiss delegation in the meetings of the Convention on Biological Diversity (CBD SBSTTA & COP). She was involved in the Nagoya Protocol negotiations and has coauthored several publications on ABS and non-commercial academic research. (sylvia.martinez@unibas.ch)

Edwardina O. Ndhine, PhD, holds masters of science degrees in applied physiology from Makerere University and in cellular biology from University of Nairobi, and a bachelor's degree in chemistry, botany and zoology from University of Jabalpur, India. She is head of Biological Sciences Schedule at the National Commission for Science, Technology and Innovation (NACOSTI), Kenya, and board member, National Biosafety Authority Kenya. (edwardinaotieno@yahoo.com)

Carlos Alberto Pittaluga Niederauer holds a PhD in industrial engineering (2002) from the Federal University of Santa Catarina, Brazil. He is an analyst in science and technology at the National Council for Scientific and Technological Development (CNPq), a federal agency of the Brazilian Ministry of Science, Technology and Innovation, and was responsible for the design and implementation of the CNPq electronic access authorization system. He is a member of CGEN, within the Ministry of Environment, since 2011. The council is responsible for managing the implementation of the Brazilian access and benefit-sharing regime. (carlos.niederauer@cnpq.br)

Maria Victoria Cabrera Ormaza is a PhD candidate at the Institute for International and European Law, University of Göttingen. She obtained her LLM from the University of Chile and the University of Heidelberg (2009) and was admitted to legal practice in Ecuador since 2007 and in Chile since 2009. Her previous publications focused on the situation of indigenous peoples under international law. Her main research interest centers on the recognition and application of international norms. She also provides consultation for indigenous peoples in issues affecting them directly. (m.cabrera@stud.uni-goettingen.de)

André Oumard, PhD. Since 2012 employed at DSMZ; 1991–1998 studies of biology at the Technical University of Braunschweig, Germany; 1998–2001 PhD thesis at GBF in Braunschweig (in molecular and cell biology); 2001–2009 researcher at Helmholtz Centre for Infection Research (HZI), Braunschweig (on cell-line development); 2009–2011 project manager for the Graduate School of the HZI, Braunschweig; since 2012 project manager for the EC-financed ESFRI project MIRRI at DSMZ. (andre.oumard@dsmz.de)

Mónica Ribadeneira Sarmiento is an Ecuadorian doctor in law. She holds a bachelor's degree in political and social sciences and two master's degrees in environmental law and management and in administration of protected areas (PA). She has undertaken studies in Ecuador, Spain, Sweden, Germany and the United States in different fields. As researcher and consultant, she has been working on CBD issues, originally in PA and later on access to genetic resources and benefit sharing. She is an author and a coauthor of publications on the management of PA, monitoring legal compliance and genetic resources. (mrib adeneira@gmail.com)

Peter-Tobias Stoll is a professor of public law and public international law at the Georg-August-University of Göttingen. He is the director of the Institute for International Law and European Law. He earned his PhD in Kiel in 1993 and habilitation in Heidelberg, 2001. He is a junior researcher at the Walther Schücking Institute in Kiel and a senior research fellow at the Max-Planck-Institute for Foreign, Public and International Law in Heidelberg. He provided legal consultancy to German delegations in CBD and FAO negotiations. He has released publications in the area of international environmental and economic law. (pt.stoll@jur.uni-goettingen.de)

Aiyen Tjoa is senior academic staff at the Agriculture Faculty of the Tadulako University in Palu, Central Sulawesi. She obtained her PhD in plant nutrition from University of Hohenheim in Germany and has published several articles on phytomining and plant nutrition status. Currently, she serves as technical advisor to the governor of Central Sulawesi and regional coordinator for the University Forum on Climate Change. In the last 10 years, she has been responsible for the research management of international collaborations at her university and coordinator of several EU- and UN-funded projects. (aiyen@ untad.ac.id)

Caroline von Kries, LLM, is the head of the Department of Social Law at German Caritas Association. Law studies at universities of Montpellier, Konstanz, Freiburg/Br., Lund (Sweden). 1999: First state exam. 2000: LLM European Law (Lund). 2002: Law assessor. 2002–2005: German representative at a transborder consulting desk (D,F,CH)/Regierungspräsidium Freiburg. 2005–2007: Appointed lawyer at a law firm, 2007–2014 stand-alone advocate. Various research projects on nature protection in the marine realm, water law and Natura 2000 issues. 2012–2014: Research assistant at the University of Bremen in the project "Micro B3." (caroline.v.kries@gmx.de)

Mukonyi Kavaka Watai holds a BSc degree from Kenyatta University and an MSc degree from the University of Botswana. He also has certificates in biodiversity and law and intellectual property management. He works with Kenya Wildlife Service as the head of bioprospecting in Kenyan protected areas. He is the chair of the National Technical Committee on ABS, a member of the African Union Technical Experts on ABS, a consultant on ABS and technology transfer and the lead scientist in many bioprospecting projects. Kavaka Watai represents Kenya in COP ABS meetings as a national technical expert. He is also a visiting scientist at ICIPE. (mwatai@kws.go.ke)

Gerd Winter is research professor of public law and the sociology of law at the University of Bremen. He is director of the Research Centre for European Environmental Law (FEU) (www.feu.uni-bremen.de). The focus of his teaching, research and publications is on administrative and environmental law in comparative and international perspectives. He has also worked as legal consultant in various countries concerning administrative and environmental law development. For further information see his personal website at www-user. uni-bremen.de/~gwinter/. (gwinter@uni-bremen.de)

Foreword

As the international community grapples with a multitude of environmental challenges, the role of information on biodiversity has never been more important. We cannot achieve the conservation and sustainable use of biodiversity without knowing what it is we are trying to protect. The Convention on Biological Diversity (CBD) recognizes the importance of biodiversity information and works continuously towards building our understanding of biodiversity through such means as scientific and technical cooperation and the Global Taxonomy Initiative.

In many cases, biodiversity research requires access to genetic resources. Such access – and its concomitant requirements for benefit sharing – is the third objective of the CBD and has been one of its more challenging aspects for countries to implement. Calls for more clarity and legal certainty ultimately led to the adoption, in 2010, of the *Nagoya Protocol on Access to Genetic Resources and the Fair and Equitable Sharing of Benefits Arising from their Utilization.*

The importance of basic biodiversity research or non-commercial research was discussed extensively during the negotiation of the Nagoya Protocol. Researchers reported difficulties in obtaining the permits they needed to carry out their projects due to restrictive, burdensome, or ill-defined access and benefit-sharing regimes. They described how such systems hindered research, ultimately to the detriment of biodiversity itself. On the other hand, many countries expressed concerns about the ease with which non-commercial intent can switch to commercial activity and the challenges they face in monitoring the use of their genetic resources to ensure compliance with the conditions on which access was granted.

As a result, the Protocol addresses the need for conditions that encourage research, including simplified measures on access for non-commercial research purposes, taking into account the need to address a change of intent for such research. The Protocol also encourages the development of model contractual clauses, codes of conduct, guidelines and best practices and standards on access and benefit sharing and suggests that mutually agreed terms include provisions on changes of intent on the use of genetic resources.

With the entry into force of the Protocol on 12 October 2014, the focus now turns to implementation. As this volume illustrates, the role of trust is critical in the creation of effective access and benefit-sharing systems. Countries that establish clear and straightforward access procedures for non-commercial research will be well-placed to benefit from research on their biodiversity. Similarly, the research community needs to recognize the history that has led to the requirements for access and benefit sharing. Rather than approaching access and benefit sharing as a problem to be overcome, it should be seen as an opportunity to work with partners in countries providing access to genetic resources, to increase the impact of the research being undertaken and, ultimately, to exercise the principles of equity and fairness. Through the development of such trust, we will be in a better position to access genetic resources, perform research on these genetic resources and share the benefits from such research to contribute to the conservation and sustainable use of biodiversity.

This book can assist countries in designing their access and benefit-sharing systems to take into account the special considerations posed by non-commercial research. It brings together a variety of experiences from both the government and research sectors to offer good practices, lessons learned and constructive options on how to approach access and benefit sharing for non-commercial research. The insights that it presents will be a valuable resource in exploring, understanding and implementing the Nagoya Protocol.

Braulio Ferreira de Souza Dias,
Executive Secretary, CBD

Preface

In about a year following the adoption of the Nagoya Protocol, the University of Göttingen and the University of Bremen together conceived a project on research cooperation and facilitated access to genetic resources and traditional knowledge. With particular interest on Article 8 (a) of the Nagoya Protocol, the project aimed at searching for ways of achieving simplified measures for gaining access to genetic resources and associated traditional knowledge for non-commercial research, easing and enhancing the activities of collections and promoting observance of provider countries' access and benefit-sharing rules, as well as effecting the measures. In order to encourage a balanced discourse of both providers and users (in the traditional usage of the terms), the partners decided to bring together a number of ABS focal points and experts from African, Asian and Latin American countries, researchers engaged in biological field work and representatives of scientific collections. This led to the hosting of an international interdisciplinary conference at the University of Göttingen on the 20th to 21st of January 2012. The conference was also attended by one representative of the European Commission and one of the German Ministry of Environment – all acting in their private capacity. The conference was either the first or among the first of such endeavors after the adoption of the Nagoya Protocol on 29 October 2010. The project and the conference were funded by the German Research Foundation (DFG) which we hereby acknowledge.

More than half of this book is based on the results and further research endeavors of the participants of the abovementioned conference. We hereby thank all contributors who worked hard and patiently to bring this work to a good end. The book has also benefitted a lot from invited contributions which form almost half of the entire content. Many of the invited authors were approached at a very late stage to fill some of the visible gaps, and all were either self-sponsored or depended on funding from their own research projects. In spite of short notices and tight timelines, they all managed to deliver their contributions on time. We hereby acknowledge you specially! We also thank Antje Spalink (secretary, FEU) for taking up most of the formatting work and our student assistant, Max Schwartz, for doing most of the language editing.

We appreciate the fact that ABS efforts are currently focusing on how best to operationalize the Nagoya Protocol in order to ultimately realize the third objective of the CBD (which is captured in the Nagoya Protocol under Article 1, with an innovative idea to enhance conservation and sustainable use of biological diversity). This book is a contribution to that end and hence we hope that it will provide some assistance in finding reasonable solutions.

Evanson Chege Kamau, Peter-Tobias
Stoll and Gerd Winter
Bremen and Göttingen, 8 October 2014

Abbreviations and acronyms

ABNJ	Areas Beyond National Jurisdiction
ABS CH	ABS Clearing-House
ABS	Access and Benefit-Sharing
AHWG	Ad Hoc Working Group
Art.	Article
ATK	Associated Traditional Knowledge
BBRAC	Biosciences and Biosecurity Research Authorization Committee
BCCM	Belgian Co-ordinated Collections of Micro-Organisms
BDI	Biodiversity Institute
BGCI	Botanical Gardens Conservation International
BHL	Biodiversity Heritage Library
BIO	Biotechnology Industry Organization
BPG	Best Practice Guidelines
BRCs	Biological Resource Centres
BS	Benefit-Sharing
CABRI	Common Access to Biological Resources and Information
CAN	Community of the Andean Nations
CBD	Convention on Biological Diversity
CBOL	Consortium for the Barcode of Life
CC	Creative Commons
CETAF	Consortium of European Taxonomic Facilities
CGEN	Genetic Heritage Management Council
CGRFA	Commission on Genetic Resources for Food and Agriculture
CITES	Convention on International Trade of Endangered Species
CNA	Competent National Authority(ies)
CNPq	National Council for Scientific and Technological Development
COAPG	Coordination of the System of Authorization for the Access to Genetic Heritage
CoC	Code of Conduct
CONAGEBIO	National Commission for the Management of Biodiversity
COP	Conference of the Parties

COP/MOP	Conference of the Parties serving as the Meeting of the Parties
CPA	Counterpart Agreement
CRC	Collaborative Research Centre
CV	Curriculum Vitae
DAAD	German Academic Exchange Service
DDBJ	DNA Data Bank of Japan
DFG	German Research Foundation (Deutsche Forschungsgemeinschaft)
DGHE	Directorate General for Higher Education
DNA	Deoxyribonucleic Acid
DOI	Digital Object Identifier
DSMZ	Leibniz-Institut DSMZ-Deutsche Sammlung von Mikroorganismen und Zellkulturen (German Collection of Microorganisms and Cell Cultures)
DVS	Department of Veterinary Services
EARO	Ethiopian Agricultural Research Organization
EBI	Ethiopian Biodiversity Institute
ECCO	European Culture Collections' Organisation
ED	Executive Directive
EESC	European Economic and Social Committee
EEZ	Exclusive Economic Zone
EMbaRC	European Consortium of Microbial Resources Centres
EMBL	European Molecular Biology Laboratory
EMCA	Environment Management and Coordination Act
EoL	Encyclopedia of Life
ESFRI	European Strategy Forum on Research Infrastructures
ETI	Expert Center for Taxonomic Identification
EU	European Union
FAO	(UN) Food and Agriculture Organization
Fiocruz	Oswaldo Cruz Foundation
FRP	Foreign Research Permit
FTA	Free Trade Agreement
FUNAI	National Indian Foundation
GBIF	Global Biodiversity Information Facility
GBRCN	Global Biological Resource Centre Network
GDP	Gross Domestic Product
GMBSM	Global Multilateral Benefit-sharing Mechanism
GOK	Government of Kenya
GR(s)	Genetic Resources(s)
GRFA	Genetic Resources for Food and Agriculture
GTI	Global Taxonomy Initiative
GTLE	Group of Technical and Legal Experts
GUID	Globally Unique Identifier
IAS	Invasive Alien Species

Ibama	Brazilian Institute for the Environment and Renewable Natural Resources
iBOL	International Barcode of Life project
ICNP	Intergovernmental Committee for the Nagoya Protocol
ICNP	Open-ended Ad Hoc Intergovernmental Committee for the Nagoya Protocol
IDA	International Depositary Authority
IFPMA	International Federation of Pharmaceutical Manufacturers and Associations
IGC	Intellectual Property and Genetic Resources, Traditional Knowledge and Folklore
IGO	Intergovernmental Organisation
IJSB	International Journal of Systematic Bacteriology
IJSEM	International Journal of Systematic and Evolutionary Microbiology
ILCs	Indigenous and Local Communities
INBIO	National Biodiversity Institute
IP	Intellectual Property
IPB	Institut Pertanian Bogor (Bogor Agricultural University)
IPEN	International Plant Exchange Network
IPHAN	Institute of National Historical and Artistic Heritage
IPR(s)	Intellectual Property Rights
ISE	International Society of Ethnobiology
ITPGRFA	International Treaty on Plant Genetic Resources for Food and Agriculture
JKUAT	Jomo Kenyatta University of Agriculture and Technology
KEMRI	Kenya Medical Research Institute
KEPHIS	Kenya Plant Health Inspectorate Service
KEPRES	Keputusan President (Presidential Decision)
KESBANGPOL	Kesatuan Bangsa dan Politik (National Unity and Community Protection)
KFS	Kenya Forestry Service
KWS	Kenyan Wildlife Service
LA	Lead Agency
LAC	Latin America and the Caribbean
LIPI	Lembaga Ilmu Pengetahuan Indonesia (Indonesian Institute of Science)
MA	Model Agreement
MAA	Model Access Agreement
MAT	Mutually Agreed Terms
MEA(s)	Multilateral Environmental Agreement(s)
MENRISTEK	Kementerian Riset dan Teknologi (Ministry of Research and Technology)
MGRs	Microbial Genetic Resources

Micro B3	EU project on Marine Microbial Biodiversity, Bioinformatics and Biotechnology
MINAET	Ministry of Environment, Energy and Telecommunications
MIRRI	Microbial Resource Research Infrastructure
MLS	Multilateral System (of the ITPGRFA)
MMA	Ministry of the Environment
MoA	Memorandum of Arrangement
MOSAICC	Micro-Organisms Sustainable use and Access regulation International Code of Conduct
MoU	Memorandum of Understanding
MP	Medida Provisória 2186/ Provisional Act 2186
MRC	Microbial Resource Centre
MSA	Material Supply Agreement
MSc	Master of Science
MTA(s)	Material Transfer Agreement(s)
NACOSTI	National Commission for Science, Technology and Innovation
NCBI	National Center for Biotechnology Information
NCST	National Council for Science and Technology
NEMA	National Environment Management Authority
NFP	National Focal Point
NGO	Non-governmental Organisation
nm	Nautical Miles
NMK	National Museums of Kenya
NP	Nagoya Protocol
OECD	Organisation for Economic Co-operation and Development
OFC	Overseas Field Committee
PCPC	Personal Care Products Council
PDE	Protocol of Data Exchange
PGRFA	Plant Genetic Resources for Food and Agriculture
PhD	Doctor of Philosophy
PIC	Prior (and) Informed Consent
QM	Quality Management
R&D	Research and Development
RUFORUM	Regional Universities Forum for Capacity Building in Agriculture
SBSTTA	Subsidiary Body on Scientific, Technical and Technological Advice
SCNAT	Swiss Academy of Sciences
SEB	Society for Economic Botany
Sect./sect(s)	Section(s)
SENESCYT	Ecuadorian National Secretariat for Higher Education, Science and Technology
SfAA	Society for Applied Anthropology

SINAC	National System of Conservation Areas
TD	Technological Development
TK	Traditional Knowledge
UK	United Kingdom
UN	United Nations
UNCLOS	United Nations Convention on the Law of the Sea
UNEP	United Nations Environmental Programme
UNEP-GEF	UNEP Global Environment Facility
UNESCO	United Nations Educational, Scientific and Cultural Organization
UPOV	International Union for the Protection of New Varieties of Plants
VicRes	Lake Victoria Research Initiative
WDCM	World Data Centre for Microorganisms
WFCC	World Federation for Culture Collections
WG-ABS	Ad Hoc Open-Ended Working Group on Access and Benefit-Sharing
WIPO	World Intellectual Property Organization
WRTI	Wildlife Research and Training Institute
WTO TRIPS	World Trade Organization Agreement on Trade-Related Aspects of Intellectual Property Rights

1 Unbound R&D and bound benefit sharing

Introduction, synthesis and conclusions

Evanson Chege Kamau and Gerd Winter

Introduction

The global discussion on access to genetic resources and benefit sharing (ABS) seems to be entering a third phase: After a period of designing the international legal regime through the Convention on Biological Diversity (CBD) of 1992 and its Nagoya Protocol (NP) of 2010 and a period of interpreting – and unendingly questioning the solutions found – the discourse is now focusing on how to implement the international provisions at the national level. One outstanding concern is how common research and development processes are affected by ABS provisions. On the one hand, overly stringent requirements have been experienced as strangling free research and development (R&D), but on the other hand, the legitimate expectations of fair benefit sharing must be accommodated. The present collection of contributions is focused on this dilemma. Arranged in a certain order the contributions aim at:

- ascertaining the international legal framework (Part I)
- presenting and evaluating exemplary national ABS legislation (Part II)
- reporting on experiences made by researchers seeking access to genetic resources (GR) and associated traditional knowledge (ATK; Part III)
- describing and assessing self-regulation by guidelines and model access agreements of individual and institutional actors, as well as considering and recommending points for national legal frameworks of provider and user states (Part IV).

Individual contributions will be summarized below. Some overall conclusions will be drawn at the closing of this introductory chapter.

Summaries of contributions

Part I: The international legal framework

Before studying the implementation of the CBD and NP provisions on research and development, the content of these provisions should be clarified. Chapter 2 aims to do this. Given the importance of core terms – non-commercial and commercial R&D – for the regulatory instruments, the definition of these terms is discussed in Chapter 3. While ABS issues are normally related to territorial GR and ATK, the vast marine resources should be kept in mind. Insofar as these are concerned, two access regimes apply and are compared in Chapter 4: UN Convention on the Law of the Sea (UNCLOS) and the CBD/NP.

In Chapter 2, titled "Research and development under the Convention on Biological Diversity and the Nagoya Protocol," Evanson Chege Kamau ascertains the access and benefit-sharing (ABS) framework of the CBD and its Nagoya Protocol. The focus is on the rights and obligations created by these instruments and how the implementation of the relevant provisions impacts biodiversity-based research and development. Kamau first shows that the governance/regulation of R&D on genetic resources and traditional knowledge associated with such resources crosscuts several international legal instruments. He goes on to ask what R&D is in the context of the CBD and the NP and identifies references to it in these instruments. He notes that the CBD and the NP do not define R&D, although its definition exists in other legal contexts. In line with Article 31 (1) of the Vienna Convention on the Law of Treaties, the interpretation of the term in the context of the CBD and the NP is to be made based on the ordinary meaning of the term in light of these instruments' object and purpose. He concludes that, taking the definition of "utilization" in Article 2 (c) of the NP, R&D in the context of the CBD and the NP may include all types of systematic work on the genetic or biochemical composition of genetic resources aimed to discover potentially interesting properties and to devise practical applications of such discoveries. It is noted that the CBD and its NP seldom refer directly to R&D on genetic resources and associated traditional knowledge. They instead often talk of the utilization of genetic resources and ATK which is defined as "research and development on [. . .]." The definition of utilization has untied a difficult knot in ABS because it helps to sort out what is subject to prior informed consent (PIC) and what is not. The next important task, he states, is to define the terms "non-commercial" and "commercial" research, because the intent of the research to be undertaken is what determines the rights and obligations attached to corresponding activities. Further, Kamau looks at the regulation of R&D on genetic resources and ATK under the CBD and the NP. The discourse follows the access and benefit-sharing three-pillar pattern: access (A), benefit sharing (B) and compliance (C). With an analysis of the implementation of the relevant ABS provisions, Kamau notes that under the CBD, provider access measures were highly restrictive and benefit-sharing and compliance measures were lacking or completely missing in user countries, the result being that biodiversity-based R&D was greatly hampered. Without ignoring lingering ABS challenges, the anticipated situation with the adoption and entry into force of the Nagoya Protocol is presented with hope. He believes that the various innovative ideas and mechanisms introduced by the NP in different provisions and at different levels have the potential to counter the challenges faced under the CBD. They lead to the creation of measures to facilitate access and benefit sharing, as well as to effect compliance.

In Chapter 3, titled "Defining commercial and non-commercial research and development under the Nagoya Protocol and in other contexts," Caroline von Kries and Gerd Winter address the distinction between non-commercial and commercial research which is crucial for a number of aspects of ABS regimes, such as the obligation to simplify access to genetic resources, the determination by access agreement of allowed utilizations of genetic resources and the kinds of benefits that qualify for sharing. The authors explore the terminology used in various legal frameworks to treat different kinds of research differently, such as industry and university based, basic and applied, of market or use value, etc. Summarizing the approaches, the authors distinguish between terms and definitions relating to the institutional setting, the content, the market value and the function of research. Applying these options to the terms non-commercial and commercial as used in the ABS context and considering that definitions should reflect the purpose of the term used, they reject the institutional definition because both private and public research organizations conduct private and public research in the functional sense. Likewise, the content-related definition which points to the difference between basic and applied, or nonmarketable and marketable, research is rejected because the distinction has become blurred in such modern developments as genomics research. For the purposes of the ABS regime, the functional definition is proposed which points to the difference between the submission of research results to the public domain and the proprietary use of research results. It is shown that this definition is compatible with the relevant provisions of the Nagoya Protocol and even helps to solve some terminological riddles posed by some of its provisions.

The distinction between public domain and proprietary research is also crucial for understanding differences between the CBD/NP regime on the one side and the UN Convention on the Law of the Sea regime on the other. Access and benefit sharing was already part of the law of the sea before it was introduced as part of the law on biodiversity protection. This leads to an overlap of regulation insofar as genetic resources are taken from the marine realm.

In Chapter 4, titled "Harmonizing ABS conditions for research and development under UNCLOS and CBD/NP," Caroline von Kries and Gerd Winter examine in what respects the two international regimes converge or differ from each other. Their focus is on how research and development on marine genetic resources are affected by the respective regulations. The authors discuss how the UNCLOS distinction between marine scientific research and research relevant for the exploration and exploitation of marine resources relates to the NP distinction between non-commercial and commercial research, drawing on the functional definition proposed in Chapter 3. The authors then examine the convergences and differences of the two regimes in relation to the preconditions of access, obligations to provide legal certainty, duties to share benefits, duties to ensure compliance and encouragement of good practices, taking into consideration variations according to the maritime zone where the genetic resources are accessed and focussing on the different treatment of public domain and proprietary research. The chapter shows that the existing differences between the two regimes can be bridged by harmonising interpretation, the mutual filling of gaps and the taking of the CBD/NP as implementing convention, in the sense of UNCLOS's Article 243.

Part II: Exemplary national legal frameworks

In Part II, five national ABS systems are presented, including those of Brazil, Kenya, Ethiopia, Costa Rica and Ecuador. In addition, the Andean Community is described as an example of regional harmonization of national systems. The studies focus on how research and development activities are treated. The common story told by the case studies is that the first generation of ABS systems tended to erect bureaucratic hurdles for access to ensure benefit sharing and that the new generation is now providing mechanisms of simplified access, at least for non-commercial research.

In chapter 5, titled "Research on genetic resources in the framework of the Brazilian ABS law," Carlos Alberto Pittaluga Niederauer and Manuela da Silva present the framework regulating access to genetic resources and ATK for R&D and benefit sharing in Brazil. The main legal act regulating ABS in Brazil is the Provisional Act (Medida Provisória, MP) 2186 of 23 August 2001 which has been revised 16 times since it was first drafted in 2000. The often-hasty revisions resulted in too many ABS requirements and unclear definitions which led to divergent interpretations. The MP establishes who may access Brazilian genetic resources, under what conditions and which requirements must be fulfilled prior to the export of material abroad. One notable condition for qualification for an access permit is that the applicant, whether local or foreign, must be a legal entity (research institution), not an individual researcher. Besides that, a foreign institution must work with a local collaborating institution which assumes any responsibility related to access. All types of research – scientific (non-commercial), bioprospecting and technological development (commercial) – are subject to the prior informed consent of the so-called Genetic Heritage Management Council (CGEN), which the MP established as the competent national authority (CNA) responsible for the management of the ABS process. Concerning the two latter types of research, the PIC of public and private providers is required in addition and mutually agreed terms (MAT) must be established if there is a commercial potential. The MP was implemented by five decrees, some of which establish additional rules on access and use of genetic resources. Pittaluga Niederauer and da Silva explain that CGEN has undertaken several measures in order to tackle varying ABS challenges. To enhance its capacity to manage the ABS system, CGEN accredited other institutions to grant permits. These include the National Council for Scientific and Technological Development (CNPq) which is charged with issuing permits. Through numerous resolutions and technical orientations, CGEN has also managed to deal with specific hardship aspects, as well as terminological ambiguity. For example, it eliminated the contradictions in the meaning of the term "access" which could be interpreted as "using" (i.e. conducting an activity on genetic resources with the intent to isolate, identify or use the information of genetic origin or molecules and substances derived from the metabolism of living beings and extracts from those organisms) and "collecting." Constant streamlining of the Brazilian ABS regime has gradually eased the access procedure to the benefit of commercial and non-commercial research. Specifically of benefit to scientific research is the exclusion by CGEN of certain activities from the concept of access. In addition, through the electronic system of application and issuing permits designed and operated by CNPq, it takes approximately two weeks to issue a permit for non-commercial research purposes. The efficiency of the system is testified by the steady rise of permits issued.

In Chapter 6, titled "Research on genetic resources and indigenous knowledge in the framework of the Kenyan ABS law: Experiences and opportunities," Mukonyi K. Watai, Veronica Kimutai and Edwardina O. Ndhine present the framework for the management of biological resources in Kenya. They note that the constitution of Kenya contains provisions to protect genetic resources and biological diversity and expresses the will of the citizens concerning the governance of their biodiversity. ABS in Kenya is regulated by approximately seven different pieces of legislation and subsidiary legislation. The Environmental Management and Coordination Act (EMCA) No. 8 of 1999 domesticated the CBD and established the National Environment Management Authority (NEMA) with a statutory mandate to oversee the coordinated management of the environment. NEMA enacted ABS regulations in 2006 which entered into force in 2008. These regulations subject access to PIC, the establishment of MAT, the conclusion of material transfer agreements (MTAs) and the sharing of benefits. Permits for access are granted by NEMA. Before an access permit can be granted by NEMA, the applicant must obtain clearance for research from the National Council for Science and Technology (established by the Science and Technology Act) after fulfilling a number of requirements and obtaining the PIC from the relevant stakeholder, depending on the area or site of the physical access. To that effect, the various government institutions established by different acts have their own procedures and requirements for granting PIC. If access is to be conducted in areas or sites under the jurisdiction of several such institutions, then the applicant must obtain PIC from all of them after fulfilling all of their conditions. The same applies when mandates of two or more institutions overlap. In addition, the PIC of indigenous and local communities must be obtained if the genetic resource sought is located in a territory occupied by such a community or if access involves their traditional knowledge associated with genetic resources. The current regime is thus very fragmented and leads to confusion as to which institution is competent to grant PIC, long durations for processing applications and issuing permits, high transaction costs and legal uncertainty. Permits are issued for a period of one year and may be renewed for a further period of one year upon payment of the prescribed fee. Watai, Kimutai and Ndhine note that most affected by the current ABS regime are students on split programmes but they likewise concur that there have been no applications for commercial and bioprospecting research since the ABS regulations entered into force. However, there are reliable indications that all types of research based on Kenyan genetic resources are still being carried out locally and abroad. This suggests that the procedures and requirements are so cumbersome that researchers opt to circumvent them or that they are too ambiguous to be accomplished diligently. The regime also does not differentiate the procedure for commercial and non-commercial research. The authors claim that nondifferentiation is compelled by past experiences with non-commercial research which often acts as a channel of abuse and biopiracy and a lack of compliance measures in most user countries. Clear and transparent ABS systems in both provider and user countries are crucial for ensuring facilitated access. The authors admit that most applicants would like to comply with access rules and procedures, but they lack guidance. Also, some desk officers are not knowledgeable enough about the laws governing ABS regimes. The authors report that there are ongoing processes at different levels to improve the current situation, including the revision of the current ABS legislation and the creation of a one-stop shop for ABS.

In Chapter 7, titled "Research on genetic resources and indigenous knowledge in the framework of the Ethiopian ABS law," Gemedo Dalle discusses the regulation of access to genetic resources and ATK (referred to as community knowledge) and benefit sharing in Ethiopia. The Ethiopian legislation regulating ABS consists of the Access to Genetic Resources and Community Knowledge, and Community Rights Proclamation (Proclamation No. 482/2006) and a Regulation (No. 169/2009) which were enacted to ensure that the country and its communities obtain a fair and equitable share of the benefits that arise out of the use of genetic resources and thereby promote the conservation and sustainable utilization of the country's biodiversity resources. The legislation subjects access to PIC and MAT and establishes a competent national authority, the Ethiopian Biodiversity Institute (EBI), with the mandate to issue access and export permits. Ownership of genetic resources is vested on the state and the people of Ethiopia; therefore any access to genetic resources is subject to the PIC of EBI. Local communities only give PIC for access to their knowledge. However, EBI negotiates and concludes access agreements, including those for access to ATK (based on PIC and MAT). Apart from PIC and MAT, Dalle lists other requirements of the legislation for access to Ethiopian genetic resources and ATK, which include collaboration with national institutions designated by the EBI, as well as the condition that the research is conducted in Ethiopia, unless the hosting institution abroad issues a written statement guaranteeing the observation of access obligations. Violation of the access procedure and contractual obligations (including change of intent without seeking new consent from EBI), provision of false information in the access application, etc., are punishable by law and, depending on the gravity of the violation, may result in imprisonment of up to five years. The proclamation is clear concerning the formula for sharing benefits: Communities obtain 50 percent of the monetary benefits received from the utilization of any genetic resource accessed from their area and 100 percent of the shared benefit arising from their associated traditional knowledge. Dalle states that the Ethiopian legislation provides a clear and transparent ABS legal system. It is notable that the procedure created by the ABS regime is somewhat streamlined, with the EBI acting as a one-stop shop, eliminating the uncertainty of accessing ATK and, to a certain degree, setting clear criteria for access/PIC and hence, Dalle states, the Ethiopian

ABS regime ". . . promotes facilitated access as far as the users are transparent and fulfil the identified minimal requirements." In addition, he says, the legislation differentiates between commercial and non-commercial research and thus varies the requirements for access – access for non-commercial research can be issued in less than an hour, as long as the applicant has submitted all required documents. This status was achieved even before the Nagoya Protocol was adopted in October 2010. In spite of the abovementioned progressive steps, Dalle concludes that effective and sustainable implementation of ABS still faces practical challenges, including the hardship of clearly demarcating commercial and non-commercial research, the lack of capacity and effective mechanisms for downstream enforcement of ABS obligations.

In Chapter 8, titled "Research on genetic resources in Latin America and the Caribbean (LAC): Perspectives for facilitated access," Mónica Ribadeneira Sarmiento presents two case studies of regulation of access and benefit sharing in the LAC region in an attempt to examine whether non-commercial research is afforded access facilitation. The case studies focus on Andean Decision 391 and Costa Rica and therefore only intend to give a general regional perspective rather than a detailed country-by-country analysis, as the title may suggest. She points out that Decision 391 of the Andean Community regarding the Common Access Regime to Genetic Resources (1996) and the Costa Rican ABS regime are the region's standard references on the topic of ABS. Decision 391 is binding on and directly applicable in the member states of the Andean Community of Nations (CAN)[1] but need some additional organizational provisions to be enacted at the national level. The Andean Decision establishes a two-stage access process: presentation and evaluation of the application and negotiation of the access contract. An interesting phenomenon is the so-called *"contracto marco"* (framework contract). Such a contract is concluded between government and research centres and universities. It facilitates access, for instance, by allowing R&D on genetic resources that are not precisely predetermined. Decision 391 also created a regional notification mechanism for contracts involving transboundary resources. There is an ongoing process in the region to bring Decision 391 into compliance with the Nagoya Protocol. Further, the author discusses the Costa Rican ABS system. The country adopted General Norms for the Access to Genetic and Biochemical Resources and Elements of Biodiversity and Protection of the Associated Knowledge of 2003 and the Regulations for Access to Genetic and Biochemical Resources and Elements of Biodiversity in Ex-Situ Conditions of 2007. The Biodiversity Law of 1994 establishes a competent national authority, the National Commission for the Management of Biodiversity (CONAGEBIO). Although the general norms of 2003 define three types of access permits (basic research, bioprospection and commercial use), this does not create a special procedure for basic research. What is interesting in this regard, however, is that the biodiversity law recognizes the autonomy of universities in biodiversity-related teaching and research activities, as long as these are not carried out for commercial purposes.

1 The current member states are Bolivia, Colombia, Ecuador and Peru.

Thus, the University of Costa Rica set up its own ABS regulatory framework, the so-called parasystem. Hence it enjoys a form of facilitated access in that research permits granted under the parasystem are not reviewed or registered by CON-AGEBIO or any other authority, unless access requires sampling in protected areas. In general, Ribadeneira Sarmiento considers the clarity offered by the Costa Rican ABS regime and a reasonably fast permit processing and issuing duration as *de facto* support for scientific research, but acknowledges that there is room for improvement. An outstanding issue is the unwillingness of foreign researchers to comply with national prerequisites for access, for example, to appoint an in-country representative to act as a spokesperson during the authorization process and project execution. At the end, she offers some recommendations for LAC region-wide implementation of facilitation mechanisms for scientific research.

In Chapter 9, titled "Research on genetic resources in the framework of the Ecuadorian ABS law: Legal issues preventing the current system from being effective," Maria Victoria Cabrera Ormaza discusses the regulation of access to GR and ATK and benefit sharing in Ecuador. Ecuador has been a member of the Andean Community of Nations since its creation in 1996. Consequently, Decision 391 applies directly in Ecuador in matters of ABS. Like most members of the CAN, Ecuador additionally enacted its national ABS rules, Executive Decree No. 905 (ED) of 2011, in order to operationalize Decision 391. It is notable that this took place only recently. The author indicates that Decision 391 was not successful in operationalizing the third objective of the CBD, although that was its original purpose. Its failure, she says, is its strong emphasis on control which seems to hinder rather than foster the attainment of its purpose. Hence, the late enactment of Executive Decree No. 905 came as a corrective measure. Before that, Ecuador had only included ABS elements of Decision 391 in the constitution of 2008. The Ecuadorian ABS regime thus consists of the three legal instruments, with the following hierarchical order of supremacy: the Constitution, Decision 391 and Executive Decree No. 905 – with the latter two being complementary in regard to procedures. Decision 391 and the constitution proclaim the sovereignty of states over their genetic resources, which are regarded as public property, and acknowledge the rights of indigenous communities over the traditional practices/knowledge associated with genetic resources. Decision 391 and the ED subject access to genetic resources to PIC and benefit sharing from utilization based on MAT for both commercial and non-commercial research. In Ecuador, the Minister of Environment acts as the competent national authority with power to grant PIC. The ED aims to promote access and use of genetic resources for scientific and technological capacity development in line with the state's commitment towards the same, as well as creating conditions for fair and equitable benefit sharing from such resources and their derivatives. Cabrera Ormaza, however, criticizes the ED's failure to achieve this based on a number of substantive and procedural flaws, some of which were inherited from Decision 391. In regard to the former, she in particular mentions the extensive rights of the state's sovereign rights over genetic resources resulting from the extremely broad definition of "genetic resources." This, she says, creates the assumption that the State has absolute property rights over the discovered genetic content and, thereby, an unlimited ability to utilize and restrict the use of such information, and thus disregards the researchers' moral and economic interests connected to their findings. Another issue is the uncertainty that exists as to whether derivatives are implied in the permission for access, based on the fact that Decision 391 extends states' sovereign rights to derivatives which are recognized in the ED but not recognized by the constitution. She also criticizes the ED's approach of attempting to deal with ATK issues in isolation from genetic resources issues, whereas the constitution sees the two as intertwined. These flaws suggest a need for harmonization of the legal instruments. Concerning procedural flaws, she criticizes the overly bureaucratic procedure created by the ED and the unlimited ability of the state to unilaterally suspend access agreements on grounds which are neither concretely spelled out nor their extent defined in law. On a positive note, she applauds the clear guidance provided by the ED concerning the prerequisites and steps to follow for access, the possibility to use a framework contract for non-commercial scientific research (an idea adopted from Decision 391 as explained in the preceding chapter), which consists of research that falls under the scope of activities listed in Article 2.4 of the Executive Directive. The advantage of using a framework contract lies in the fact that the applicant does not have to follow the usual full procedure and also has the possibility of transferring genetic resources abroad, as long as a sample is deposited in a local repository approved by the competent authority.

Part III: Experiences of research projects for non-commercial purposes with ABS

The presentation of national legal ABS requirements in Part II is contrasted with the practical experiences of researchers with access to genetic resources in various countries, including Nepal, Kenya, Ethiopia, Ecuador and Indonesia. Most authors report about difficulties in obtaining PIC, MAT and MTA. Most important is the fact that such complaints are not only made by researchers from foreign countries but also by domestic researchers, because in most national legal systems they too are subject to access requirements. The authors ask for more legal certainty and simplification, for example, through a one-stop-shop procedure. They also stress, however, the importance of mutual trust relationships and of cooperative research involving researchers from user and provider countries.

In Chapter 10, titled "Experiences in international ecological/biological research," Erwin H. Beck reports on the experiences of German biologists in four collaborative research projects in South Asia (Nepal), East Africa (Kenya and Ethiopia) and South America (Ecuador), in which the author participated as well as headed. These research projects cover a wide time spectrum of about 35 years between the start of the first project and the conclusion of the most recent one. This time period begins many years before the CBD and ends recently after the NP was adopted. In Kenya, for example, numerous projects have been conducted since 1975 when no CBD-related regulations for access existed, while others were concluded several years after the CBD. In Ethiopia, the first projects began shortly after the CBD had entered into force with the most current being concluded after the NP was adopted. In Nepal and Ecuador, on the other hand, the projects started after the CBD had been adopted with some being concluded in 2010 – the same year the NP was adopted. The reports show that getting clearance and permission to conduct research was achieved with relative ease prior to the CBD, except, for example, for delays caused by procedures, for instance in Kenya. Carrying out field work did not present much difficulty, as the researchers were accompanied by assistants and colleagues from collaborating local institutions, but the language barrier and cultural and social structures presented some hitches, as in Ethiopia. The execution of projects also occasionally faced logistical problems, as was the case in Kenya and Ecuador. In Ecuador, for example, the cause was particularly related to language hitches, as collaborators were often hesitant or unable to communicate in any language other than Spanish. Export of biological material even for bioprospecting purposes was not difficult prior to the CBD as long as it was brought to Germany by a host country scientist for personal analytical work. Beck indicates that Kenyan partners, for example, could do that without an export permit and take the material back at the conclusion of the research without getting into trouble with the authorities in Kenya. He notes that the situation has been gradually worsening since the CBD and in particular after the NP. Negotiations with national authorities have become more complicated and regulations for import and export of biological material are very complex. However, Beck shows that the positive impact created by the joint venture kind of collaboration between the German scientists and local scientists of these countries, including capacity building, the training of students and technology transfer, concurrently helped to ameliorate the treatment accorded to their projects. Although no special access facilitation measures were provided, except the use of a framework contract in Ecuador (described in Chs. 8 and 9 of this volume), permits were always granted and no demands were made to conclude contracts. Beck even claims that authorities asked for as many investigations as possible to be conducted in local universities. Therefore, he underlines the importance of *inter alia* trust building, obeying the host country's regulations and accepting each other as full partners in collaboration projects, irrespective of individual contributions.

In Chapter 11, titled "Experiences in accessing biological resources for noncommercial research: Results of an informal survey in Switzerland," Susette Biber-Klemm and Sylvia I. Martinez report on a survey conducted in 2009 with the Swiss academic research community on the topic of access and benefit sharing. Ten researchers of varying research disciplines who had carried out projects in 15 countries on 4 different continents – Africa (7 countries), the Americas (5 countries), Asia (1 country) and Europe (2 countries) – were involved. All were knowledgeable in ABS principles. Accessed material was used in different scientific activities which are representative of biodiversity research in general. Questions presented to the interviewees covered questions on negotiation partners, the mode of negotiations including types of contract and permits, time and costs involved and the level of satisfaction with the outcome. The objectives of the survey were to help in further developing the national ABS program, to feed into

Nagoya Protocol negotiations and to search for ways of facilitating international research cooperation. The authors report that researchers complained about the difficulties that non-commercial academic research faces as a result of ABS regimes: additional formalities and different types of permits to be sought. Some of the projects had several negotiation partners and most of the foreign researchers depended on their partners in regard to understanding the local administrative processes. Negotiations were time-consuming and expensive, and on average it took up to one year to get a permit. Also, not all projects succeeded in getting an export permit. In half of the countries, the fees were too high, to the extent that one of the projects was abandoned as a result. According to Biber-Klemm and Martinez, some scientists pointed to the rising costs for permits, notwithstanding the fact that permits are granted for short durations and need to be renewed and new fees paid. In a few cases, the foreign partners did not understand the contracts as they were negotiated by their local collaborators and the documents were issued in national languages. At times, the researcher was required to travel to the provider country to personally accomplish the access process, but there was no certainty that access would be granted in spite of the incurred travel time and expenses. Occasionally trips had to be made to competent offices or villages without certainty that the responsible persons would be available. These and other challenges made the activities of non-commercial academic research increasingly difficult and at times impossible in spite of the fact that all projects shared benefits – in most cases non-monetary, but in some also monetary. The researchers graded their level of satisfaction with access procedures and ABS negotiations rather poorly. The results are considered as confirming findings of earlier studies by the authors and other scholars. The survey also found out, however, that the restrictions instilled by national authorities in provider countries are partly due to their mistrust of scientific, non-commercial research as a channel of misuse and even biopiracy, as well as to the fact that scientific research – its goals, methods and products – is difficult for nonscientists to understand. The situation can be aggravated by a researcher's failure to observe the regulations of the provider due to difficulties in finding information on the right requirements and procedures. To foster scientific, non-commercial research, the authors suggest the creation of simple and clear procedures based on existing procedures, government structures and an adapted research permit that clearly defines the ABS-relevant obligations, rather than the establishment of new procedures and drafting new documents. To change providers' perceptions of scientific, non-commercial research, researchers are encouraged to *inter alia* engage more in trust building, specifically through joint venture activities and making the benefits of non-commercial research and its benefit-sharing practices visible.

In Chapter 12, titled "Local scientist's experience with bioscience research authorization process in Kenya: Need for facilitation," Hamadi Iddi Boga describes the authorization process for accessing biological materials in Kenya prior to and after the implementation of the access and benefit-sharing (ABS) framework of the Convention on Biological Diversity (CBD) and the challenges the latter has created for scientific research that is dependent on such materials.

Due to its rich and unique biodiversity, Kenya is a popular research destination for researchers from all over the world. Studies conducted to date based on Kenyan biological material have generated knowledge that is critical for understanding species and ecosystems and for the management and conservation of plants and animals. Until the CBD ABS regulations were introduced, such activities by local and foreign researchers operated without difficulties, with researchers being able to obtain research and export permits for a biological specimen in about a month. Access to biological research samples required only a permit from the National Council for Science and Technology and, if the specimen was to be collected from national parks or the wild, the prior informed consent of the Kenya Wildlife Service. The task of the Convention on International Trade of Endangered Species (CITES) was just to confirm that the specimen was not on its list (of endangered species). The CBD was domesticated in Kenya through the enactment of the Environment Management and Coordination Act 1999 and, in 2006, the competent national authority established by the Act, NEMA (National Environment Management Authority), published regulations for ABS. Things changed from that time with procedures becoming complicated and the processing time for access permits increasing considerably. The most challenging issue seems to be the large number of state agencies a scientist has to engage with before securing authorization for research. From Boga's experience, there are at least five such agencies that a scientist might have to visit for PIC, depending on the research area or site and the specimen being accessed, not forgetting NEMA that is responsible for scrutinizing the complete application and issuing the permit. The process of authorization is not coordinated between these agencies; each agency bases its action on a mandate derived from law, thus causing a sort of interagency competition and conflict. This situation results in confusion and uncertainty for scientists. In addition, the researcher is tasked with obtaining the PIC of host communities especially around sensitive ecosystems, for example, the soda lakes of Kenya. Holding meetings with such communities and their chiefs and explaining, as well as justifying, complicated science to them in local languages is cumbersome. Likewise, meeting some of their demands, for example, immediate benefits to solve their pressing needs, may be unachievable for an academic researcher, especially a student. According to Boga's experience, it can take up to a minimum of six months to get all the necessary documents. The waiting period has been estimated to take even longer by some scholars and other local scientists. The costs are also very high and at times unmanageable, especially for students. Foreign researchers have to travel to Kenya at times to personally pursue their applications without any guarantee of securing research authorization. Boga sees the many challenges faced by researchers as a big handicap to the management and conservation of Kenya's ecosystems and the development of technologies to support the growth of a bioeconomy. He notes, however, that there are a few reasons why non-commercial research is scrutinized rigorously in Kenya, one of them due to the perception that it facilitates biopiracy. Even local researchers are not exempted from the long and restrictive procedure, although the law indicates that they are not subject to such a procedure when conducting research locally. No differentiation is made between commercial and non-commercial research and, hence, even research without any chances of producing a commercial potential must abide by the strict rules. The author therefore sees the imminent need for *inter alia* local and international researchers to engage in trust building, including by trying to understand and fulfil existing access requirements, honouring reporting requirements, regularly sharing their findings in workshops, conferences, etc., and helping to build the capacities of authorization agencies and local research, even as lobbying for facilitation by researchers continues. Currently, there is an ongoing process to streamline access procedures, as well as to create a kind of one-stop shop, as likewise mentioned in Chapter 6 of this volume.

In Chapter 13, titled "Researcher's experiences in ecosystem research: A case study of Indonesia," Wolfram Lorenz and Aiyen Tjoa report on a non-commercial Collaborative Research Centre (CRC 552) project involving two German and two Indonesian universities. The project was conducted in Indonesia, near Lore Lindu National Park in Central Sulawesi, by German scientists in collaboration with Indonesian partners between 2000 and 2009 and was funded by the German Research Foundation (DFG). The research team, comprised of more than 100 scientists divided into four project groups, worked on 15 projects within the abovementioned period. The theme of the project was "Stability of Rainforest Margins in Indonesia," and it aimed to study the interactions between socioeconomic development, rainforest conversion and biodiversity in Indonesia through an assessment and analysis of different factors and processes that contribute to the stability of rainforest margins. Essentially, the project was a pure scientific venture. CRC 552 was established after the CBD but prior to the publication of the DFG guidelines for funding proposals concerning research projects within the scope of the CBD and the adoption of the Nagoya Protocol. However, based on existing cooperation agreements between Germany and Indonesia, some legal basis was laid to support the project based on a Memorandum of Arrangement; Agreement on Intellectual Property Rights; Protocol of Data Exchange (PDE); and a Material Transfer Agreement. Such documents, however, do not exempt the foreign partners from the already established requirements and regulations concerning research projects, but they may form part of the documents necessary for application of a permit. In their report, Lorenz and Tjoa depict phases of fluctuations in the authorization process before the 1990s, around 1993 shortly after the CBD was adopted and after 2007 after Law 41/2006 came into force. At first, ambiguity reigned concerning the right procedure as institutions could independently issue permits and universities were granted the right to collaborate directly with partners abroad. This continued even after the Indonesian Institute of Science (LIPI) was put in charge of all research permit matters for foreigners through a presidential decision of 1993 (KEPRES 100/1993) and eventually became the sole institution issuing research permits. LIPI professionalized its performance and service for scientists and developed an efficient and transparent online application system in 2005. With the coming into force of Law 41/2006, the procedure was made more complex, as the authority to issue research permits was moved to the Ministry of

Research and Technology (MENRISTEK). MENRISTEK coordinates the permit process through a team consisting of about 30 governmental institutions, and the number of reviewers/departments required depends on the research theme. Since all involved institutions have a veto power, it is often hard to conclude the permit process due to frequent postponements and rejections that is often the result of a failure to involve relevant local partners. The procedure for foreign researchers, however, still follows the regulations laid down by the presidential decision of 1993. Accordingly, the researcher has to fulfil numerous pre- and post-arrival requirements. The pre-arrival process for research approval and visa takes two to three months. This time period is not sufficient to begin research upon arrival in Indonesia, as further permits and permissions have to be obtained, including those from representatives of villages located far from the central administration in Jakarta, and additional administrative work may be required. Permits involving working with biological material, sample taking and sending are subject to separate regulations. Approximately two more months are required for the post-arrival process. The authors lament that a researcher without a local partner or assistance from a service office would either fail to accomplish the procedures or lose much time on other activities than those intended – research. This, they note, also contradicts one of the goals of research permit procedures in Indonesia, which is to ensure that the partner institutions benefit from the research collaboration. Local partnering institutions and villages have benefitted immensely from the CRC 552 project, thanks to the heavy investments realized through their foreign partners. The authors conclude that to encourage more of such research activities in Indonesia, including by researchers without such a strong infrastructure as the CRC 552 project, researchers need to be provided with easily understandable and simplified time-saving procedures – ideally through a one-stop shop.

Part IV: Good practice and legislative options

In Part IV, a normative approach is taken. Most of the contributions discuss the self-regulatory good practices which emerged prior to the NP and are now being adapted to new legal expectations and practical experiences. Guidelines adopted and practiced for collecting plants and microbes, creating databases and developing research networks are presented in Chapters 14, 15, 16 and 18. Model access agreements, which are core instruments for coping with ABS regulations, are examined and proposed in Chapters 17 and 20, with the latter presenting an elaborated example with commentary. The last chapter, 19, draws experiences and international requirements together by advising how to draft a national ABS law that aims at bridging the dilemma of free R&D with the obligation to share benefits arising from it.

Non-commercial, academic biodiversity research is essential in generating information needed for the conservation and sustainable use of biological diversity. *Ex situ* collections are important instruments to this end. Biodiversity research relies on scientists having free access to the stored resources and on the exchange of resources between them. However, the forming of such common pools by repositories has been challenged by the bilateral approach underlying the ABS regime which entitles the country providing genetic resources to ask for benefit sharing in exchange. Chapter 14, titled *"Ex situ* collections of plants and how they adjust to ABS conditions,"* by Susette Biber-Klemm, Kate Davis, Laurent Gautier, Michael Kiehn and Sylvia I. Martinez gives an overview of how collections of plants have reacted to this challenge. It concentrates on two policies of networks of botanical gardens: the principles of the International Plant Exchange Network (IPEN) and the Principles on Access to Genetic Resources and Benefit-Sharing of the Botanical Gardens Conservation International (BGCI) as implemented by the UK Kew Gardens. While IPEN has a tradition as an infrastructure for non-commercial research, Kew and its network has had a longer practice of also providing commercial development on genetic resources. The chapter describes the principles and practices that participating collections apply to comply with ABS requirements at the stages of receiving, utilizing and transferring genetic resources. It shows how they "clear" the ABS status of the specimen provided to them, how they keep their research within the limits of any mutually agreed terms, how they transfer the terms to third parties receiving material from them and how they monitor the implementation of their rules. It appears that previous differences of approach of IPEN and the Kew network have somehow converged. This is also true for the two weak points the authors have identified: The impossibility of collections to take responsibility for the compliance with the access conditions by receivers of material and the difficulty to distinguish between non-commercial and commercial research and obtain consent for a change of intent. The authors conclude by explaining how under the new EU regulation 511/2014, collections can achieve the status of a trusted collection which somehow alleviates the burden of administrative supervision.

In Chapter 15, titled *"Ex situ* collections of microbes and how they adjust to ABS conditions,"* Dagmar Fritze and André Oumard show that microbial collections face a similar dilemma to that of plant collections. They aim at facilitating free research but are bound to respect ABS conditions which may restrict the research process and even deter research on genetic resources found in countries operating a strict access regime. Specific characteristics of microbes, however, also pose a peculiar challenge for ABS regulations, such as their enormous variety, their ubiquitous occurrence, the vast number of unknown species and the fact that interesting species are found not only in developing but also in industrialized countries, such as microbes adapted to polluted conditions. The authors show how ABS concerns are integrated into the broader scope of rules operated by collections such as the German Collection of Micro-organisms and Cell Cultures (DSZM), including rules on biosafety, biosecurity, quality of the material and scientific aspects. The rules concerning ABS include the request from depositors of information on the country of origin and on prior informed consent of the sample, the assignation of an individual accession number to each sample and the obligation in material transfer agreements of recipients of samples not to pass them on to third parties and to contact the provider country in case of change of intent from non-commercial to commercial use. In view of the thousands of accessions and supplies of samples, the authors warn that huge up-front costs might emerge on all sides if – for any sampling, isolation, deposit, or exchange of biological material – detailed agreements have to be formulated which try to foresee any potential use and theoretical benefit without knowing whether any economic success can be expected from it. Fritze and Oumard strongly recommend that common standards be developed. One way to facilitate the operations of collections is the registration as a trusted collection under EU Regulation 511/2014. The authors find it impossible, however, to fulfil the requirement that collections may supply genetic resources to third persons only with documentation providing evidence that the genetic resources were accessed in accordance with ABS requirements of provider states. The chapter concludes by drawing attention to the ongoing process of developing a pan-European Microbial Resource Research Infrastructure (MIRRI) which also addresses ABS issues.

While the two previous chapters are concerned with material collections, Fabian Haas in Chapter 16, titled "Biodiversity knowledge commons and sharing of research results with providers in East Africa," looks at data collections. He strongly advocates common pools of data as an infrastructure for biodiversity protection and human welfare. The open access to the data is normally enabled by the Creative Commons License with regards to intellectual property rights and the Open Source License with regards to software. The author describes a number of global common pools of biodiversity-related knowledge. He starts with the Global Biodiversity Information Facility (GBIF) with its focus on biodiversity occurrence data. The system holds the submitter of data responsible for their being made accessible to the public. Any restrictions of use travel with the data in the user chain. GBIF cannot, however, control whether the rights status of the data was correctly declared and that users abide by any restrictions, for example, concerning commercial purposes. The specimen to which the data refer remains with its owner, but it is traceable. Other common data pools presented in this chapter include the Encyclopedia of Life (EoL), which aims at compiling all available information about a species, the Biodiversity Heritage Library (BHL), which digitizes old literature on biological species, and the International Barcode of Life (iBOL), which makes species identifiable by the sequence of one typical gene and collects such denominators in its data base. All of these databases or portals have become accessible for developing countries to use for their own research and applications, notably in the context of biodiversity protection. They can also contribute to the enrichment of the databases and portals and create their own national subsidiaries. According to Haas, participation in pools is the major benefit that developing countries such as Kenya, Tanzania and Uganda have experienced. From that perspective, it would be counterproductive to erect hurdles hindering access to genetic resources and subsequent research on them. Therefore, a commons approach should be envisaged concerning ABS rights of provider states. He adds, however, that biodiversity informatics is not bioinformatics or genomics, suggesting that ABS may be seen differently with regard to the use of genomic data for genetic technology.

Provider and user dissatisfaction with the malfunction of the ABS system is based on genuine concerns for both sides. These concerns arise from a myriad of flaws which cannot be easily fixed by one instrument. Apart from good legislation and its thorough implementation, auxiliary tools can play a monumental role towards the operationalization of the ABS regime. It is interesting to observe that even the Nagoya Protocol requires each party to encourage, as appropriate, the development, update and use of model contractual clauses for MAT (Article 19) and voluntary codes of conduct, guidelines and best practices and/or standards in relation to access and benefit sharing (Article 20).

In Chapter 17, titled "Model agreements on ABS for non-commercial research and development," Evanson Chege Kamau discusses the potential of ABS model agreements/contracts in confronting provider–user challenges in accessing genetic resources and ATK for R&D and benefit sharing. He believes that ABS agreements are able tools for solving many of the challenges faced by providers and users in an equitable manner. The focus is mainly on non-commercial biodiversity research. After highlighting the historical grievances of users of biological material for non-commercial research and providers of such material, the author presents the main provisions of an ABS agreement/contract in a tabular form and shows some of the issues they aim to address and who, between the provider and the user, receives the greatest relief. Although the provider alone is depicted as receiving the greatest advantages in some sections, it should be noted that the user likewise benefits when relevant issues are regulated clearly in a contract. For example, ambiguity and uncertainty are eliminated in regard to the user if the terms of "use of material" and "third party transfer" are regulated contractually from the onset. Kamau then discusses the importance of the different sections of a normal full-fledged ABS agreement/contract and gives guidance on the most important points that parties should consider when deciding which clauses they should include in such an agreement/contract. Focus on the concerns of both the provider and user is maintained as much as possible in regard to the different issues, and options are offered intermittently. In the last section, the author gives advice on how an ABS model agreement/contract can be used: as a *vade mecum*, i.e. a kind of pocket reference; blueprint, i.e. an assessment copy of the agreement presented by the provider; or a fallback text which a researcher can present as a possible text for the agreement in case of inertia. He concludes that well-designed ABS agreements/contracts can *inter alia* raise legal certainty, improve transparency and lower transaction costs, and thus serve as an incentive for R&D on genetic resources and ATK.

The perspective on self-regulatory mechanisms of actors in the field of ABS is further enhanced by Peter-Tobias Stoll in Chapter 18, titled "Guidelines for ABS and their potential to implement the Nagoya Protocol." The chapter presents a choice of guidelines found on the CBD secretariat's website. It covers guidelines of networks and associations of individuals and organizations in the fields of ethnobiological research; bioprospection by the biotech, pharmaceutical and cosmetics industries; microbial research; plant collections; and research-funding organizations. Some of the guidelines have grown out of intrinsic needs of the networks, such as the commitment of ethnobiology to indigenous communities, some are based on the CBD and some reflect the more specific provisions of the NP. Common themes of the guidelines are, among others, prior informed consent to access, focus on genetic resources or traditional knowledge, practices as to obtaining intellectual property rights (IPR) protection, models for access and material transfer agreements, cooperation with provider states and the sharing of research results and of monetary benefits. Most of the guidelines are voluntary documents, but some – such as the IPEN guidelines – are binding, although no formal sanctions apply except the possible exclusion from the network. Being not formal but informal law, the guidelines serve, as the author summarizes, the following purposes: They aim at assisting and guiding their members in view of their ABS-related activities, thereby seeking to build confidence *vis-à-vis* providers and clarifying their joint positions in public discourse at the international or national level. The author concludes by relating the guidelines to Article 20 NP which encourages the introduction of such informal mechanisms. While collections have pioneered in the adoption of such documents, Stoll believes that more should be done by the networks and organizations of basic research and commercial R&D. In particular, he recommends that the provider side should be more systematically consulted in the development of new guidelines.

The book returns to the formal level of national legislation in Chapter 19 by Gerd Winter, titled "Points to consider for national legislation on access to genetic resources and benefit sharing." The author advises lawmakers on what to consider when elaborating national legislation on ABS issues. Taking a practical perspective, he presents options and suggests solutions on the major issues the envisaged national ABS law should address. A general part of the law should include its objectives, definitions of terms, and its geographical, temporal and material scope. The second part of the law should establish a regime concerning the state's internal genetic resources and traditional knowledge, laying down rules on material and procedural requirements of access to genetic resources and ATK, on allowed R&D activities and on obligations to share benefits. The third part should be concerned with R&D on genetic resources and ATK imported from other states, introducing obligations and administrative checking to ensure compliance with the provider state's access and benefit-sharing legislation. The chapter also attempts to solve some of the definitional and substantive riddles the NP has left open. For instance, it is suggested what legal status should be given to genetic resources and ATK, what areas should be left out of the scope of ABS requirements, what simplification of PIC procedures are imaginable and practicable, how PIC for ATK and landraces should be obtained, if the contribution of accessed genetic resources or ATK can be exhausted in the valorization chain, how provider states should frame the ABS obligations in order to make user state monitoring effective and how user states should specify their obligations to ensure compliance with provider state conditions.

Chapter 20, "Micro B3 model agreement on access to marine microorganisms and benefit-sharing. Text and commentary," contains a model access agreement that was elaborated and commented on by Caroline von Kries, Arianna Broggiato,

Tom Dedeurwaerdere and Gerd Winter for Micro B3. Micro B3 is an international and interdisciplinary project funded by the EU Commission that studies marine microbes from biodiversity, bioinformatics and biotechnology perspectives. As samples were planned to be taken from the marine areas of many coastal states, the CBD provisions on ABS had to be respected. The model agreement was developed to be at hand if a coastal state required PIC, MAT and MTAs and did not yet use its own models. In reality, the Micro B3 was hardly used, because the coastal states, most of which were European, either did not operate an ABS regime or did not apply it because the samples were taken by their own research teams. The authors anticipated this and designed the model agreement so that it can be used for purposes beyond the concrete project. The agreement is applicable for proprietary and public domain research. It contains the following provisions: preamble, objective, definition of terms, access conditions, conditions for the utilization of the genetic resources, transfer of material and data to third persons, dissemination of knowledge, acknowledging the contribution of the provider state, recording and reporting, sharing of knowledge, scientific collaboration with the provider state and capacity building, benefit sharing in case of utilization for proprietary purposes, other laws to be respected, duration of the agreement, applicable law, dispute settlement and termination of the agreement. Some innovative solutions have been proposed that may be highlighted: the precise genetic resource to be utilized can be specified at a later stage in the R&D process, a provision for change of intent not only on the side of the user but also on the provider side and a viral clause for the case of material transfer. Much effort was spent concerning data management, such as by extending the viral clause to data users and – in a qualified way – even to databases, the obligations to share non-monetary benefits are specified in various ways, the duty to share benefits is extended to cases where benefits were generated against PIC conditions, and formulas are suggested on how an agreement for sharing monetary benefits can be reached.

Towards better implementation of the international ABS regime. Synthesis and conclusions

This book takes the perspective of research and development on genetic resources and associated traditional knowledge and asks how this chain of utilization of resources is affected by the international and national ABS regimes. The ABS regime can be understood as framing the utilization chain by both enabling and restricting it through establishing property and use rights. This relationship is illustrated in Figure 1.1. The utilization process starts with the sampling of GR or ATK and proceeds with R&D activities which lead to results on two levels: the level of material (maintenance, breeding, biotechnological modification of the organism under investigation) and information (databases, publication of GR and ATK). The process may end in the public domain (collections, public media) or generate marketable products and information. The access phase is subject to the jurisdiction of the provider state, while the utilization and commercialization

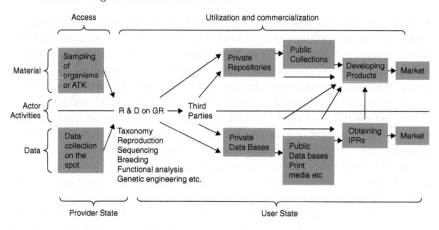

Figure 1.1 Process of access to and utilization of GR and ATK

stages escape its jurisdiction if the GR or TK is transferred to and utilized in another state.

The provider state can only use the access situation as a lever for controlling these processes. Even if it does so, it will have *de facto* difficulties in monitoring the utilization chain, more so the longer and the more variable the chain becomes. In that situation, the provider state will be tempted to severely restrict the allowed utilization.

Whether this is true in fact and what can be done to alleviate the burden for R&D without neglecting legitimate expectations of benefit sharing is the subject of this collection of contributions. Summing them up and adding more considerations to them, the following observations can be highlighted:

- There is evidence from our case studies that access to genetic resources has in various countries been hampered by national ABS requirements. The causes were ambiguous and fragmented legislation, unclear competences of authorities, multiplication of PICs under different laws, the long duration of procedures, and restrictive conditions for PIC, MAT and MTAs. Often there is also a lack of differentiation between access for taxonomic biological research which aims at understanding and protecting biodiversity on the one side and bioprospection for commercial purposes on the other.
- Following the demands of the NP, in particular those pertaining to legal certainty and simplification, some states have introduced new rules to this effect. They treat non-commercial research in privileged ways, such as in Brazil, where PIC for basic research is applied for and delivered electronically, and in Costa Rica, where a framework PIC is provided for basic research by scientific institutions if they guarantee to supervise their own research in certain ways. Some shortcomings remain, such as when domestic and foreign researchers are treated differently. It is also important that,

by differentiating between non-commercial and commercial research, national legislation does not forget to provide legal certainty also for commercial research. For instance, a one-stop shop procedure is recommendable that includes all permits required under non-ABS legislation, such as laws concerning general research policy, nature protection, indigenous communities, etc.

- One effective means of reducing the burden of obtaining PIC, MAT and MTA is the cooperation of provider states with trusted institutions. They could be freed from individual PIC requirements through framework agreements or the granting of a generalized PIC, provided they operate an ABS regime by themselves. For instance, Costa Rica has concluded framework agreements with the University of Costa Rica and previously with a pharmaceutical company, hence for non-commercial and commercial research respectively. Collections of plant material are other candidates for such facilitation of procedures. Some networks of collections such as IPEN have been quite active in developing their own ABS rules. These rules require that the collection shall, on the input side, ask providers of material to clear its ABS status, ensure the traceability of the origin of the received organisms when maintaining and reproducing them, and, on the output side, bind the receiver of material to any conditions attached to the original PIC for access. While they generally only allow R&D for non-commercial purposes, commercial use is not excluded if the receiver promises to seek prior consent from the provider state. Admittedly, however, the effectiveness of self-regulation has its limits. As for the collections, for instance, they cannot take responsibility for the ABS clearance declaration being true or the user keeping their promise to come back to the provider state in case of change of intent from non-commercial to commercial. Therefore, some kind of supervision by public authorities must be retained.

- As in many respects the distinction between non-commercial and commercial research is of consequence, the book proposes a definition of the terms that refers to whether the R&D results shall enter the public domain or be kept proprietary. It is also suggested that even the development step in R&D can be aimed at the public or private domain.

- An issue that has up to now widely escaped the attention of stakeholders is data management in the utilization process. While there is agreement that the patenting of knowledge associated with GR and ATK is subject to ABS legislation allowing, for instance, the provider state to exclude patenting or ask for a share in any revenue from the patent, it is not clear how the patented information can be traced back to its original accessed organism or piece of ATK. Research results on the original GR or ATK can easily be lost in the intermediate process of dissemination, e.g. through publication media and databases. Therefore, the question arises if databases should also develop their rules on input clearance, tracking and output conditions as the material collections do. The Micro B3 model agreement suggests a moderate solution in that regard (see von Kries et al., Ch. 20 in this volume). Of course, such reorientation of databases would also help tracing products through the utilization chain back to sources.

- Another way to assist provider states in tracking their GR or ATK through the utilization chain is reinforcing the obligations of user states to monitor and enforce compliance with provider state requirements. This is one of the major innovations the Nagoya Protocol brought about. The EU has pioneered the implementation of these obligations through its Regulation 511/2014. Researchers and developers of GR or ATK have a duty of due diligence to ascertain that the GR and ATK were accessed in compliance with provider state requirements and benefits are shared. They have to declare to comply with these duties at two stages: when they receive research funding and when they finally develop a marketable product. Public authorities are called to supervise these duties. Still, some issues are still to be solved, such as: Does the declaration of due diligence involve the proof of effective PIC or only the effort that steps were taken to obtain it? Does the proof only relate to whether PIC was obtained, or also whether the utilization complies with the PIC conditions concerning allowed research, publication and even benefit sharing? What precise duties of tracing products back to GR and ATK exist at the marketing stage when, due to long and complex intermediate steps, information about origins was lost? Should a concept of exhaustion of provider state rights apply when the original trait is not discernible any more in the final product because so many other traits were added to it? We believe that practicable answers must and can be found to these questions.

- As a general conclusion, the book shows that it is difficult but feasible to implement the bilateral approach proposed by the CBD/NP regime. However, an even better way would be to strive for common pool solutions wherever they are possible and fair, especially in relation to the legitimate interests of the provider states. Concerning non-commercial research, it is suggested to invite researchers from the provider state to participate in the projects, include an element of capacity building, strive for co-publication, transfer R&D know-how, etc. Likewise, projects with a commercial intention could be formed as joint ventures with participation of provider state personnel and business. Such pools would provide for the sharing of non-monetary benefits. The implied development of R&D capacity would often reap more benefits for the country than if they just transfer their GR or ATK and wait for monetary benefits to emerge in a user state. Many more examples of well-functioning common pools have been documented, to which we refer.[2]

2　See Kamau, EC, Winter, G (eds) (2013) *Common pools of genetic resources. Equity and innovation in international biodiversity law.* London: Earthscan/Routledge.

To sum up, many states are now overhauling their ABS laws or developing new ones that reflect the experiences made in the phase of implementing the CBD. While the NP reacted to the restrictive policies of provider states by strengthening the monitoring duties of user states, thus trying to build trust, provider states are now striving to find less-restrictive solutions. The outcome of these endeavours will be something that can be called second-generation ABS legislation. We hope that this book provides some assistance to find reasonable solutions.

Part I

The international legal framework

Part I

The international legal framework

2 Research and development under the Convention on Biological Diversity and the Nagoya Protocol

Evanson Chege Kamau

Introduction

The Convention on Biological Diversity[1] and its Nagoya Protocol[2] are the main international legal instruments governing research and development on genetic resources and traditional knowledge associated with such resources. Due to various reasons, however, the governance/regulation of R&D on genetic resources and traditional knowledge associated with such resources crosscuts several international legal instruments, *inter alia*, the International Treaty on Plant Genetic Resources for Food and Agriculture (ITPGRFA, Treaty), the United Nations Convention on the Law of the Sea (UNCLOS) and the World Trade Organization Agreement on Trade-Related Aspects of Intellectual Property Rights (WTO TRIPS).

The ITPGRFA (2001) regulates access and benefit sharing of plant genetic resources for food and agriculture, comprising 35 food crops and 29 forage genera of global importance. These make up 64 crops that the Treaty lists in Annex I and makes them the subject of a common pool in order to ensure their continual availability. The Treaty operates in line with the objectives of the Convention on Biological Diversity (CBD) and therefore, according to the Nagoya Protocol (NP), it consists of a specialized international instrument for access and benefit sharing (ABS) of these genetic resources. As a result, the 64 crops are exempted from the ABS regulations of the CBD and its Nagoya Protocol (Article 4.4 NP).

Access and benefit sharing of resources that are located in areas beyond national jurisdiction (ABNJ) are regulated by the UNCLOS (1982). It is important to note that UNCLOS does not use the term (marine) genetic resources, but only "resources", which it defines in Article 133(a) as "all solid, liquid or gaseous mineral resources *in situ* in the Area at or beneath the seabed, including

---

1 The Convention on Biological Diversity was adopted in 1992 in Rio de Janeiro and entered into force on 29 December 1993.
2 In full: The Nagoya Protocol on Access to Genetic Resources and the Fair and Equitable Sharing of Benefits Arising from their Utilization to the Convention on Biological Diversity. It was adopted on 29 October 2010 in Nagoya, Japan, and entered into force on 12 October 2014.

polymetallic nodules", which are nonliving resources. We therefore do not make an authoritative statement concerning the regulation of marine genetic resources in ABNJ but a careful comment that, if at all, ABS for such resources can only be examined currently from the perspective of UNCLOS. There is ongoing work to investigate how ABS of marine genetic resources in ABNJ can be executed and therefore we choose to refrain from further comments as this process is still in its early stage.

The TRIPS Agreement (1994) introduces global minimum standards for protecting and enforcing nearly all forms of intellectual property rights (IPR), including those for patents. The relevant question in regard to ABS is how to ensure that the TRIPS Agreement and the CBD are supportive of each other, e.g. in checking and regulating the commercial use of traditional knowledge and genetic material when these are the subject of patent applications. Parties to the TRIPS Agreement have tried to fumble with understanding the "practical and operational context" of the existing patent mechanisms for disclosing the origins of genetic material and any associated traditional knowledge (ATK) used in inventions.[3] In the Doha debate,[4] different groups of countries made divergent suggestions on how the problem could be dealt with, which include:

- making disclosure a TRIPS obligation, including by amending the TRIPS Agreement so that patent applicants are required to disclose the country of origin of genetic resources and traditional knowledge used in the inventions, evidence that they received prior informed consent (PIC) and evidence of fair and equitable benefit sharing;
- regulating disclosure through the World Intellectual Property Organization (WIPO) by amending the regulations of WIPO's Patent Cooperation Treaty (and, by reference, WIPO's Patent Law Treaty) so that domestic laws may require inventors to disclose the source of genetic resources and traditional knowledge when they apply for patents; failure to meet the requirement of which could stop a patent from being granted or, when done with fraudulent intent, could entail a granted patent being invalidated;
- regulating disclosure by requiring that all patent applicants disclose the source or origin of genetic material and with legal consequences for not meeting this requirement, but outside patent law; and
- using national legislation, including contracts rather than a disclosure obligation.

Negotiations on an international legal instrument on intellectual property (IP) issues related to genetic resources are taking place in the WIPO

---

3 See www.wto.org/english/tratop_e/trips_e/art27_3b_e.htm (accessed 28 October 2014).
4 See ibid.

Intergovernmental Committee on Intellectual Property and Genetic Resources, Traditional Knowledge and Folklore (IGC).[5] Issues under discussion include:[6]

- The prevention of erroneously granted patents. It is generally considered that the granting of patents for inventions based on or developed using genetic resources and ATK which do not fulfil the existing requirements of novelty and inventiveness should be prevented. To help patent examiners find relevant "prior art" and avoid the granting of erroneous patents, WIPO has improved its own search tools and patent classification systems, and it is proposed that databases and information systems related to genetic resources be created to address this issue.
- Ensuring and tracking compliance with access and benefit-sharing frameworks. Disclosure requirements are one of the proposals to address this issue. Disclosure requirements mean patent (and perhaps also other forms of IP) applicants should disclose several categories of information concerning genetic resources, such as their source or origin and evidence of PIC and benefit sharing, when these genetic resources are used in developing the innovation claimed in a patent application.

Another issue of paramount importance that lacks concrete solutions to date is how traditional knowledge and its subject matter can be defined. This needs to be addressed in order to find out which forms of IP can be used to protect ATK.

In tune with the overall focus of the book, this chapter limits its discussion to the question of research and development (R&D) under the access and benefit-sharing conditions of the Convention on Biological Diversity and its Nagoya Protocol.

The organization of ABS has a big influence on the success of the entire process of R&D on genetic resources. On the one hand, the organization of compliance in the downstream chain of R&D would define the success of benefit sharing and determine how relaxed access can become. On the other hand, the organization of access will influence the demand for genetic resources and ATK and the urge of scientific research and industry to use them in R&D activities. The three elements, access (A), benefit sharing (B) and compliance (C), hence shape the discourse in this chapter. They are often referred to as the ABC of ABS and comprise the three pillars of ABS (see Figure 2.1). The discourse in this chapter will only give an overview of the rights and obligations that arise to parties in the access and utilization of genetic resources and ATK in R&D as portrayed in the CBD and the NP.

5 www.wipo.int/tk/en/genetic/ (accessed 30 October 2014).
6 Ibid.

R&D on genetic resources and ATK in the context of the CBD and the NP

What is research and development?

Research and development is defined in the OECD (Organisation for Economic Co-operation and Development) glossary of statistical terms as "any creative sys-tematic activity undertaken in order to increase the stock of knowledge, including knowledge of man, culture and society, and the use of this knowledge to devise new applications" and "includes fundamental research, applied research in such fields as agriculture, medicine, industrial chemistry, and experimental develop-ment work leading to new devices, products or processes".[7] "Fundamental research" is at times referred to as "basic research", also in the OECD glossary, and the two terms are hence synonymous and often used interchangeably. The CBD and the Nagoya Protocol do not define the term "research and development". How then should the content of these terms be determined in the context of these instruments? According to Article 31(1) of the Vienna Convention on the Law of Treaties, the general rule of interpretation in international law is that, in the absence of a special meaning, terms used in a treaty are to be interpreted in good faith with the ordinary meaning to be given to the terms in their context and in light of the treaty's object and purpose (see also Greiber et al., 2012, 62; Morgera, Tsioumani, & Buck, 2014). Therefore, in line with the ordinary usage of the term, in the context of the CBD and NP "research" according to the Oxford dictionary means "the systematic investigation into and study of materials and sources in order to establish facts and reach new conclusions" (Greiber et al., 2012, 65; Morgera et al., 2014). According to the ordinary meaning of "research and devel-opment", Encyclopædia Britannica refers, in the context of the NP, to two inti-mately related processes intended to create new products and new forms of old products through technological innovation when "research" is used in combina-tion with "development" (Morgera et al., 2014). Considering the definition of "utilization" in Article 2 (c) of the NP, this may include all types of systematic work on the genetic or biochemical composition of genetic resources aimed to discover potentially interesting properties and to devise practical applications of such discoveries (Morgera et al., 2014).

The CBD and the NP do not seem to operate according to a strict dividing definition of research or research and development, and often it is evident that their provisions concurrently address a whole range of activities spanning from basic or applied research to development and commercialization. What seems to matter for these instruments is hence the intent of accessing genetic resources and ATK – i.e. whether they are intended for commercial or non-commercial purposes – because that is what determines the rights and obligations they attach to corre-sponding activities. This is especially evident in the NP. We therefore consider the inquiry to the use of the terms "commercial research" and "non-commercial

---

7 See UNESCO Statistical Yearbook, UNESCO, Paris, 68 and 65, Chapter 5.

research" as the task worth more investigation. This is done by von Kries and Winter in Chapter 3 of this volume, and hence this chapter will not proceed with that discourse. Otherwise the use of the term R&D in this chapter indiscriminately covers basic research, applied research and experimental development.

Reference to R&D on genetic resources and ATK in CBD and NP

Nowhere does the CBD directly mention access to or use/utilization of genetic resources and/or ATK for research and development. A few times, access to or use/utilization of genetic resources is mentioned for

- *environmentally sound uses* in Article 15.2,[8] whereby no clarification is given as to what kind of uses those are, although obviously this is a prerequisite for all types of research
- *scientific research* in Article 15.6[9]
- *biotechnological research* in Article 19.1.[10]

Research on genetic resources is mentioned very indirectly in Article 9 (b).[11] In regard to R&D, the CBD only says in Article 15.7 that "Each Party shall take . . . measures . . . with the aim of sharing in a fair and equitable way the *results of research and development*", whereas concerning the sharing of benefits, it expressly says ". . . benefits arising from the *commercial and other utilization of genetic resources*". Likewise in Article 8 (j) it precisely says benefits arising from the utilization of ATK. Did the CBD intend to separate R&D from other uses so that from the former only "results" are shared and from the latter "benefits"? Did it wish to leave it open for Parties to share even R&D results that are not based on genetic resources? Or is it another "Tower of Babel" language episode?

Indeed, the Article seems a little mixed up. It depicts R&D and utilization, for example, as complete strangers, whereas the former also often entails utilization. This has been made clear in the definition of "utilization of genetic resources" in Article 2 (c), as can be seen below. By logic, however, it implies R&D on genetic resources provided by a Contracting Party. In any case, R&D is also subsumed in

8 "Each Contracting Party shall endeavour to create conditions to facilitate *access to genetic resources for environmentally sound uses*."
9 "Each Contracting Party shall endeavour to develop and carry out *scientific research based on genetic resources* provided by other Contracting Parties . . ."
10 "Each Contracting Party shall take legislative, administrative or policy measures, as appropriate, to provide for the effective participation in *biotechnological research* activities by those Contracting Parties, especially developing countries, which *provide the genetic resources for such research*, and where feasible in such Contracting Parties."
11 "Each Contracting Party shall, as far as possible and as appropriate, and predominantly for the purpose of complementing in-situ measures: Establish and maintain facilities for ex-situ conservation of and *research on plants, animals and micro-organisms*, preferably *in the country of origin of genetic resources*."

"environmentally sound uses" of genetic resources, as long as it is environmentally sound. We are therefore of the opinion that Article 15.7 CBD also encompasses R&D on genetic resources and Article 8 (j), R&D on associated traditional knowledge. We also consider results of R&D as being a benefit.

The Nagoya Protocol makes direct reference to R&D on the *genetic composition of genetic resources* and R&D on the *biochemical composition of genetic resources* in the definition of "utilization" under Article 2 (c). Through the extension of this definition in subparagraph (d), it also includes *R&D on derivatives*. Indirect reference is made in Article 23 where it talks of collaboration and cooperation in *technical and scientific research and development* programmes, including *biotechnological research* activities. Elsewhere it only mentions R&D in reference to benefits (Annex, 2 (a) and (b)).

Regulation of R&D on genetic resources and ATK under the CBD

The third objective of the CBD[12] is the genesis of the rights and obligations that arise in connection to R&D on genetic resources and ATK. According to Article 1 CBD, the third objective foresees ". . . the fair and equitable sharing of the benefits arising from the utilization of genetic resources, including by appropriate access to genetic resources and by appropriate transfer of relevant technologies, taking into account all rights over those resources and to technologies, and by appropriate funding". The CBD only established *quasi* basic rules for operationalizing this objective, the core ones falling under Articles 15 and 8(j). They form the ABS legal framework which embraces the three ABC elements (Figure 2.1). The idea behind

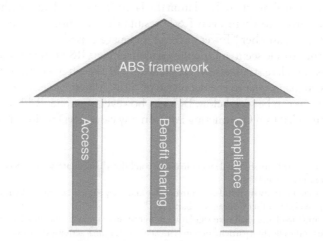

Figure 2.1   The ABC of ABS

Source: Own illustration

12 According to Article 1 CBD, its two other objectives are the conservation of biological diversity and the sustainable use of its components.

this is to facilitate access to genetic resources and ATK for R&D by users while acknowledging the authority of the provider to determine the terms and conditions of access (pillar A) based on the sovereign rights over its natural resources and subject to national legislation. In return, the user is obliged to share the benefits arising from utilization with the provider (pillar B). The state where the genetic resources and ATK are utilized is obliged to put measures in place to ensure that the rules of the provider state are obeyed and benefits are shared with the provider (pillar C).

Access

The rules of access to genetic resources are established by the provider state[13] in line with Article 15.2–5 and Article 8 (j). Accordingly, access to genetic resources is subject to the PIC of the CBD Contracting Party providing such genetic resources, unless that party determines otherwise, and to the establishment of mutually agreed terms (Articles 15 (5), 15 (4)). Access to traditional knowledge associated with genetic resources is subject to the PIC or approval and involvement of indigenous and local communities that hold such knowledge (Article 8 (j)).

The concept of PIC is based on the principle that prior to potential users gaining access to genetic resources, those affected and those authorized to make decisions should be informed about the potential uses so that they can make a decision to either allow or disallow access with full knowledge of the matter (Greiber et al., 2012, 9). In the context of ABS, PIC requires that the provider who makes the genetic resources and/or TK available gives consent through an affirmative act based on information provided prior to the actual decision by the potential user of the genetic resources (Greiber et al., 2012, 9). The practice of requesting PIC by the potential user of genetic resources and its granting by the party providing them is the norm *unless the latter waives that requirement* (Glowka, Burhenne-Guilmin, Synge, McNeely, & Gündling, 1994, 81; Greiber et al., 2012, 282).

This does not imply though that the authority of the provider is limitless, or that it should be exercised without reason. Some checks are thus built into Article 15. First, access is conditioned on the establishment of mutually agreed terms (MAT) between the Party providing the genetic resources and the potential user, e.g. an individual, a company, or an institution (Greiber et al., 2012, 8 f.). MAT therefore implies a negotiation between the parties, although obviously the bargaining power can never be equal. Whereas the provider might have an upper hand, e.g. concerning the conditions of access and use, the user might have an upper hand, e.g. in deciding which benefits to share with the provider and to what extent. But, of course, each party will normally use its strength to bargain for its interests. Anyway, if MAT are established successfully, they lead to the conclusion of and form the core part of an access agreement – sometimes called an ABS agreement, material transfer agreement, research agreement, or contract (see

13 Provider State can also be a user State, see Kamau (2014), fn 100, p. 161.

Kamau, Ch. 17 in this volume; see also Greiber et al., 2012, 9). Second, in exercising its authority, the provider should not impose restrictions that run counter to the conservation and sustainable use objectives of the CBD, but rather endeavour to facilitate access (Article 15.2 CBD), e.g. by taking relevant measures in their legal systems (Glowka et al., 1994, 81; Kamau & Winter, 2009, 371ff.).

It should also be noted that a Contracting Party should only subject access to genetic resources to the CBD rules if:

- The request for access is *for a genetic resource* and *not a biological resource*. Under Article 2, the CBD defines "genetic resources" as "genetic material of actual or potential value" whereby "genetic material" is defined as "any material of plant, animal, microbial or other origin containing functional units of heredity". On the other hand, "biological resources" are defined as including "genetic resources, organisms or parts thereof, populations, or any other biotic component of ecosystems with actual or potential use or value for humanity". These definitions were meant to separate cases where access to a biological resource is subject to PIC and MAT under ABS rules and where it is not. Does the requested material contain functional units of heredity or is it being requested with the intention to access such? Then this would fall under the ABS regime. Is it being requested for consumption, to be used as an ornamental plant or as any other commodity or good in trade? Then this would fall outside the scope of the ABS regime. This distinction was hard to apply in practice and therefore some national ABS legislations subject access to biological resources in general to ABS requirements. This ambiguity caused legal uncertainty for providers and users alike. The Nagoya Protocol tries to resolve this conundrum by defining the term "utilization" as discussed below.
- If it is either the country of origin of such resources, or if it has acquired them in accordance with the CBD (Article 15.3 CBD).[14] The most relevant question for our discussion relates to the second condition or qualification because it involves the discussion on *temporal scope*. Does the CBD affect R&D in regard to genetic resources that were accessed prior to its entry into force? Can its rules apply retroactively?

Generally, law forbids retroactive or *ex post facto* laws. The principle of nonretroactivity of law has its roots in the criminal law principle that there is no crime or punishment except in accordance with law. Brief and to the point: "No law, made after a fact done, can make it a crime . . . For before the law, there is no transgression of the law" (Hobbes, 1651).[15] This principle gradually permeated other areas of law and it applies equally to international treaties and hence to the CBD. Therefore, the provider cannot subject genetic resources and ATK used in

---

14 For a discussion on the concept of "country of origin" see Glowka et al. (1994), p. 77ff.; Greiber et al. (2012), p. 98; Kamau and Winter (2013b), p. 110f.

15 *Leviathan*, Chapters 27–28, as quoted in Williams (1961), p. 580.

R&D to access and benefit-sharing requirements of the CBD if they were taken prior to its entry into force.

The question of temporal scope is critical mostly for countries that were traditionally considered as providers, because many resources were taken prior to the Convention and are lying in *ex situ* collections abroad; some of these are still accessed for new uses while others have continuing uses. The question hence has been whether the benefits from the new uses and continuing uses should not be shared; even if they do not go to a specific entity but are shared through a multilateral system of benefit sharing – such as the global multilateral benefit-sharing mechanism (GMBSM) proposed under Article 10 NP (see below) – and used for conservation and sustainable use purposes. This question was not resolved under the CBD and became one of the core and controversial issues during the negotiations for an international ABS regime (Kamau, Fedder, & Winter, 2010, 249f.).

The national implementation of the access provisions of the CBD proved a nightmare for users of genetic resources and ATK. Instead of facilitating access for R&D as initially envisaged, the restrictive approach of most ABS legislations became a hindrance. This has gradually led to a general decline in the demand and use of genetic resources and ATK in R&D, a race to the bottom, high transaction costs, etc. and consequently to fewer benefits that can be shared from R&D (Kamau, 2014, 152ff.).

Benefit sharing

The benefit-sharing obligation is spelled out in Article 15.7 for genetic resources and Article 8 (j) for ATK. The former states that

> Each Contracting Party shall take legislative, administrative or policy measures, as appropriate, and in accordance with Articles 16 and 19 and, where necessary, through the financial mechanism established by Articles 20 and 21 with the aim of sharing in a fair and equitable way the results of research and development and the benefits arising from the commercial and other utilization of genetic resources with the Contracting Party providing such resources. Such sharing shall be upon mutually agreed terms.

The latter states that

> Each Contracting Party shall, as far as possible and as appropriate: Subject to its national legislation . . . encourage the equitable sharing of the benefits arising from the utilization of such knowledge, innovations and practices.

Though shallow and vague, Article 15.7 tries to describe the benefits to be shared and the measures to be undertaken to achieve the benefit-sharing result. In regard to ATK, Article 8 (j) simply talks of benefits arising from utilization without specifying the types. It does not say how the sharing should be achieved and leaves this to national legislation. We shall now focus on benefits and come back to measures below under compliance.

Article 15.7 and its reference to articles 16 and 19 envisage the following benefits that may be shared for using genetic resources:

- Results of research and development (Art. 15.7)
- Benefits of commercial and other utilization (Art. 15.7)
- Access to and transfer of technology (Art. 16.3)
- Participation in biotechnological research activities (Art. 19.1)
- Priority access to the results and benefits arising from biotechnologies (Art. 19.2)

As shown in Table 2.1, the formula for sharing most of the benefits listed above is mainly based on mutually agreed terms. In addition to MAT, fair and equitable sharing is merely aimed at in regard to two types of benefits. In regard to one, neither fair and equitable sharing nor mutually agreed terms are mentioned.

As Glowka et al. (1994, 82f.) suggest, Article 15.7 is mindful of what and how the provider can demand in terms of benefits because most of the benefits contemplated in this proviso are within the private sector. It therefore frames benefit sharing as an aim rather than an express obligation and, in addition, subjects it to mutual agreement between the provider and the user of genetic resources.

The types of non-monetary and monetary benefits that can be shared were elaborated in the Bonn Guidelines[16] and their nonexhaustive list is now annexed

Table 2.1 Benefits and formula of sharing

Proviso	Benefits	Fair & Equitable Sharing	Based on Mutually Agreed Terms
Art. 15.7	Results of R&D	X	X
Art. 15.7	Of commercial & other utilization	X	X
Art. 16.3	Technology transfer	–	X
Art. 19.1	Participation in biotech. research	–	–
Art. 19.2	Access to results & benefits of biotechnologies	X	X

Source: *Own illustration*

X: Mentioned in the provision
–: Not mentioned in the provision

16 Bonn Guidelines on Access to Genetic Resources and Fair and Equitable Sharing of the Benefits Arising out of their Utilization, in Report of the Sixth Meeting of the Conference of the Parties to the Convention on Biological Diversity, UN Doc. UNEP/CBD/COP/6/20 (2002).

to the Nagoya Protocol. These and other benefits can be shared as appropriate with providers of genetic resources and ATK.

Whereas benefit sharing is conditioned on achieving mutually agreed terms under Article 15.4 (i.e. during negotiation for physical access), it might be impossible (and perhaps unwise) to specify the benefits to be shared and the modalities to be employed to facilitate their sharing *a priori* due to the varying circumstances and situations surrounding the use of genetic resources (Glowka et al., 1994, 83). Considerations should be made on a case-by-case basis, for example concerning the use or potential use of genetic resources – which is also dependent on the sector using them – and the investment contemplated for research and development thereon, e.g. in terms of monetary and human capital and technical input, the risks and chances of success, etc. This would also be useful in assessing the value of the genetic resource, as well as in determining what share of benefits can be regarded as fair and equitable (Glowka et al., 1994, 83). Although the CBD did not foresee situations which might require the renegotiation of terms down the value chain of R&D, the practice of including come-back clauses in agreements developed with time because many circumstances and outcomes might not be known at the onset.

There are benefits, however, that can be agreed without necessarily basing negotiations on such considerations such as technology transfer, results of research and development, involvement of providers in research projects and capacity building. In addition, the CBD's financial mechanisms under Articles 20 and 21, which are linked to Article 15.7, can be invoked to, e.g. finance the agreed full incremental cost of sharing the results of R&D if the Conference of the Parties deems such activities eligible for funding (Glowka et al., 1994, 83).

Except for maybe a handful of cases and the notable generic Merck-INBio case,[17] there are barely any fascinating cases of benefit sharing from R&D undertakings involving the use of genetic resources and ATK under the CBD.

Compliance

Article 15.7 is also the provision in the CBD that forms the basis for compliance measures. It requires Contracting Parties to take legislative, administrative or policy measures as appropriate in this regard. Although the CBD is silent concerning compliance measures for ATK, these measures should be seen as serving that purpose too. The CBD proviso nonetheless limits the aim of such measures to ensuring that benefits from the use of genetic resources are shared. There is no direction concerning consequences for noncompliance with the provider measures or any obligation to undertake measures to facilitate access to justice, or on recognition and enforcement of foreign judgements and arbitral awards. Likewise, there are no measures to support compliance, e.g. a requirement for downstream monitoring and tracking.

Apart from the narrow material scope of foreseen measures and the mortifying failure of most user countries to put benefit-sharing measures in place, the limited

17 See http://www1.american.edu/ted/MERCK.HTM (accessed 30 October 2014).

ones taken by a handful of user countries were just a deceptive gesture of compliance (Kamau & Winter, 2009). With that, R&D on genetic resources and ATK could proceed without the provider's knowledge of the uses being made thereon and/or the benefits arising therefrom (Kamau, 2014).

Fate of R&D and benefit sharing under the CBD: An upshot

The main intention of instituting the ABS regime was to achieve the fair and equitable distribution of the benefits arising from the utilization of genetic resources and ATK between providers and users. The ABS regime under the CBD to date has achieved little in that direction. There are two major reasons for its failure. First, national measures implementing the ABS framework in provider states are often so restrictive. Hence, they serve as a disincentive for R&D on genetic resources and ATK. Second, user states have hardly any measures to ensure that provider measures are obeyed within their jurisdictions and that users share benefits with providers. The result of these flaws is that there has been a gradual decline in demand for genetic resources and ATK for R&D (Kamau, 2014, 152ff.), and there are scarcely any examples of benefit-sharing successes as well.

Regulation of R&D on genetic resources and ATK under the NP

The Nagoya Protocol is the instrument implementing the third objective of the CBD. Its objective therefore, as stated in Article 1, is a verbatim repetition of the third objective of the CBD, except that it further develops it to ensure that benefit sharing underpins the other two objectives of the CBD, the conservation of biological diversity and the sustainable use of its components. The clause, "thereby contributing to the conservation of biological diversity and the sustainable use of its components", is hence the only new thing added to the objective. Being a protocol to the Convention, the NP does not aim to create a new ABS regime but to operationalize the ABS provisions of the CBD. However, it comes with a number of innovative approaches for access, benefit sharing and compliance which are expected to resolve many hurdles under the CBD. These innovations are expected to go a long way in easing – if not eliminating – challenges that are faced by researchers and industry.

The Nagoya Protocol entered into force on 12 October 2014. Now its provisions are binding ". . . for a State or regional economic integration organization that ratifies, accepts or approves this Protocol or accedes thereto . . ." (Article 33.2 NP). In the following, we shall look at the ABC of ABS under the NP and how it could affect R&D on genetic resources and ATK.

Access

Access is regulated under Articles 6, 7, 8, 13 and partially 12. Other relevant Articles are Article 2 (because of the definition of "Utilization", "Biotechnology" and "Derivative") and Article 14.

Prior informed consent and mutually agreed terms

The NP reaffirms the sovereign rights of States over their natural resources according to the provisions of the CBD in the preamble paragraph 3 and defines its scope under Article 3 in line with the scope of Article 15 CBD and Article 8 (j), albeit it does not mention the latter – it only says "This Protocol shall also apply to traditional knowledge associated with genetic resources within the scope of the Convention and to the benefits arising from the utilization of such knowledge." Access to genetic resources is subject to the PIC of the ". . . country of origin of such resources or a Party that has acquired the genetic resources in accordance with the Convention, unless otherwise determined by that Party", according to Article 6.1, which is a combination of paragraphs 1, 3 and 5 of Article 15 CBD. Although one of the core elements of Article 15 CBD is not integrated in Article 6.1, i.e. the requirement that access is granted subject to the establishment of MAT (paragraph 4), this is implied in Article 6.3 (e) which requires evidence that these were established.

New, concerning access to genetic resources, is the introduction in Article 6.2 of the right of indigenous and local communities (ILCs) to grant access where they have the established right to do so. In such cases, each Party is required to take measures in accordance with domestic law with the aim of ensuring that the PIC of such communities is obtained, or ensuring their approval and involvement. The same concerns ATK and, in addition, ensuring that mutually agreed terms are established (Article 7) and that consideration is taken concerning ILCs' customary laws, community protocols and procedures (Article 12).

So the parties on the provider side that must be involved in giving consent and agreeing on mutual terms include the provider state itself and the ILCs where they have the established right to grant access to genetic resources and if they hold ATK. Private landowners are not mentioned in the NP, but State practice shows that domestic law may recognize them as owners of genetic resources and therefore as having the right to be involved in granting PIC and establishing MAT. The Kenyan ABS legislation explicitly does so under Section 9 (2) in combination with Schedule 2.0 (g) (Kamau & Winter, 2013b, 111).

Whereas the PIC requirement may be waived under Article 6.1, Articles 6.2 and 7 are silent concerning the possibility of such a waiver. That does not tie the hands of the ILCs if they wish to waive it, e.g. if they undertook a joint venture activity with a company to develop a drug based on their genetic resources and/ or ATK.[18] Likewise, nothing hinders them from taking measures themselves with the aim of ensuring that their PIC is obtained, or approval and involvement and

---

18 This seems to be the case in the collaboration on traditional medicinal plants between Laboratoire de Pharmacognosie (Porto Novo, Benin) and Université Catholique de Louvain (Belgium). The collaboration involves not only the two parties but also many local traditional herbal practitioners whose partnership is subsumed under the laboratory, which acts as their representative or spokesperson. This information is not based on an official statement but on a personal assessment as made during an excursion organized by the GIZ ABS-Initiative team on 12 March 2014 during the 8th Pan-African ABS Workshop (10–14 March 2014) in Cotonou, Benin, to the laboratory and its botanical garden in Porto Novo.

MAT are established should they have the capacity to do so (Kamau & Winter, 2013b, 112). If the provider requires PIC, then a number of obligations are triggered under Article 6.3 as discussed below.

Access subject to PIC: Differentiation

But it is probably important to clarify first when access to genetic resources is subject to PIC before looking at the consequences of its subjection to PIC. According to Article 6.1, access to genetic resources is subject to PIC when genetic resources are accessed for utilization purposes. The term "utilization" was not defined under the CBD, albeit Article 15.7 foresaw it as a trigger for benefit sharing.

The Nagoya Protocol defines the term under Article 2 (c) according to which "Utilization of genetic resources means to conduct research and development on the genetic and/or biochemical composition of genetic resources, including through the application of biotechnology." By the definition of "biotechnology"[19] and "derivative"[20] under Article 2 (d) and (e), respectively, utilization is extended to the use of derivatives of biological systems or living organisms to make or modify products or processes for specific use through any biotechnological application, even when these do not contain functional units of heredity, as required by the CBD. That means, unlike access under the CBD where some state practice defined genetic resources so broadly so as to include biological resources in general and thus subject them to PIC, only access to genetic resources for their utilization is subject to PIC under the NP. In order to make this clearer, Winter (Ch. 19 in this volume) suggests that the term "consumption of a biological resource" should be introduced in order to further clarify what is not meant by R&D. Unlike genetic resources for utilization, derivatives can only be subject to PIC if the intention to use them exists and is declared at the early stage of physical access to genetic resources, otherwise their latter use would trigger the benefit-sharing obligation and the need to establish mutually agreed terms on how such benefits should be shared.

Due to the lack of a definition of the term "access" in both the CBD and the NP, some questions arise concerning the status of genetic resources initially taken for bulk uses. When would access for utilization be deemed to have taken place? How can a provider's prerogative of PIC be exercised in such circumstances?

Most of the articles of the NP that make reference to the term "access" infer an action that takes place within the jurisdiction of the party providing genetic

---

19 "Biotechnology" as defined in Article 2 of the Convention means any technological application that uses biological systems, living organisms, or derivatives thereof, to make or modify products or processes for specific use.

20 "Derivative" means a naturally occurring biochemical compound resulting from the genetic expression or metabolism of biological or genetic resources, even if it does not contain functional units of heredity. Winter (Ch. 19 in this volume) suggests that States should further clarify this definition while developing ABS legislation by distinguishing derivatives from compounds that are not biochemical but just chemical (such as crystallized coral reefs or shells) and proposes an addition to the effect that "chemicals which were separated from the organic cycle of an organism (such as crystallized corals or shells of snakes) are not considered biochemicals".

resources (see Table 2.2) and that may consist of collecting biological material in the wild; obtaining samples of genetic resources or biochemicals from gene banks, research institutions or the private sector; or, arguably, obtaining digitalized information about genetic resources and their genetic or biochemical composition (Morgera et al., 2014). However, some articles also indicate an action that may take place after the genetic resource has left the jurisdiction of the party that provided it (see Table 2.2) which consists of a post-physical access activity involving R&D on the genetic and/or biochemical composition of the genetic resource. These two scenarios seem to suggest that in the context of the NP, currently, "access" can be defined as *collecting/taking*, as well as *utilizing* genetic resources (Greiber et al., 2012, 97). That would imply that "access for utilization" can be established either:

- Through a prior declaratory statement by the recipient at the point of physical access to the effect that the genetic resource being requested is meant for utilization, or
- Through actual post-access utilization activity that can also be determined by a preceding intent (see Kamau, Ch. 17 and von Kries et al., Ch. 20 (MicroB3 model agreement, Article 4.4) in this volume).

This makes sense because the latter complements the former where the purpose to utilize was not declared or could not be established *ab initio*. Such cases may include where:

- A discovery phase preceding commercialization is permitted, for instance according to the practice in the South African ABS regime.[21] If the commercial potential is discovered later, then a need to seek new prior informed consent and renegotiate MAT will be triggered.
- Genetic resources are collected for non-commercial purposes, but a commercial intent arises later. A change of intent will trigger the need for new prior informed consent and renegotiation of MAT.
- Biological material is taken for bulk uses, but later its genetic and/or biochemical composition is utilized or the intent to use it arises. PIC and MAT requirements will be triggered.

The most common technique to counteract violation after the discovery phase or a change of intent from non-commercial to commercial R&D is the use of the so-called "come-back" clauses in ABS contracts. This technique can be used likewise in other laws, e.g. forests, wildlife and fisheries Acts to deal with the case of

---

21 See South African National Environmental Management: Biodiversity Act No. 10, 2004, Government Gazette Vol. 467 Cape Town 7 June 2004 No. 26436 (http://ship.mrc.ac.za/biodiversity.pdf); and Bioprospecting, access and benefit-sharing regulations (http://cer.org.za/wp-content/uploads/2014/02/10-OF-2004-NATIONAL-ENVIRONMENTAL-MANAGE-MENT-BIODIVERSITY-ACT_Regs-GNR-138_1-Apr-2008-to-date.pdf) (accessed online 11 November 2014).

Table 2.2 Provisions making reference to access to genetic resources in the Nagoya Protocol

Provision	Text	Comments/observations
Preamble § 8	*Acknowledging* the linkage between **access to genetic resources** and the fair and equitable sharing of benefits arising from the **utilization of such resources**	Indicates two acts: **taking** and **using**. If access was synonymous to using, the use of the term "utilization" would be superfluous. Otherwise the text would read: ". . . **access to genetic resources** and the fair and equitable sharing of benefits arising from such access".
Art. 6	1. In the exercise of sovereign rights over natural resources, and subject to domestic access and benefit-sharing legislation or regulatory requirements, **access to genetic resources** *for their utilization* shall be subject to the prior informed consent of the Party providing such resources . . . 2. In accordance with domestic law, each Party shall take measures, as appropriate, with the aim of ensuring that the **prior informed consent or approval and involvement** of indigenous and local communities is obtained **for access to genetic resources** where they have the established right to grant access to such resources	Paragraph 1 indicates two acts: **taking** and **using**. If access was synonymous to using, the use of the term "utilization" would be superfluous. In paragraph 2, the act of **taking**, or **requirements that must be fulfilled or activities that must take place before** the genetic resources leave the territory of the Party providing them, are implied. That also applies to paragraph 1.
Art. 6.3	Pursuant to paragraph 1 above, each Party requiring prior informed consent shall take the necessary legislative, administrative or policy measures, as appropriate, to: (b) Provide for fair and non-arbitrary **rules and procedures on accessing genetic resources;** (e) Provide for the issuance **at the time of access** of a permit or its equivalent as evidence . . . (f) Where applicable, and subject to domestic legislation, set out **criteria and/or processes for obtaining prior informed consent or approval and involvement** of indigenous and local communities **for access to genetic resources**	The act of **taking** and **prior requisites** (before the genetic resources leave the territory of the Party providing them) are implied.

Art. 8	In the development and implementation of its access and benefit-sharing legislation or regulatory requirements, each Party shall: (a) Create conditions to promote and encourage research which contributes to the conservation and sustainable use of biological diversity, particularly in developing countries, including through **simplified measures on access** for non-commercial research purposes, . . . (b) Pay due regard to cases of present or imminent emergencies that threaten or damage human, animal or plant health, as determined nationally or internationally. Parties may take into consideration the need for **expeditious access to genetic resources** . . .	The act of **taking, or activities that take place before** the genetic resources leave the territory of the Party providing them, are implied.
Art. 13.1	Each Party shall designate a national focal point on access and benefit-sharing. The national focal point shall make information available as follows: (a) For applicants **seeking access to genetic resources,** . . .	The act of **taking** is implied.
Art. 13.2	. . . Competent national authorities shall, in accordance with applicable national legislative, administrative or policy measures, be responsible for **granting access** . . .	**Permission to take** is implied.
Art. 14.2	. . . The information shall include:(c) Permits or their equivalent issued **at the time of access** as evidence of the decision . . .	Time/**moment of taking** is implied.
Art. 17.3	An internationally recognized certificate of compliance shall serve as **evidence that the genetic resource which it covers has been accessed** in accordance with prior informed consent and that mutually agreed terms have been established . . .	The act of **taking** is implied.
Art. 15.1	Each Party shall take appropriate, effective and proportionate legislative, administrative or policy measures to provide that **genetic resources utilized** within	Two situations are imaginable here: 1) That access to **(taking)** genetic resources took place in accordance with prior informed consent

(Continued)

Table 2.2 (Continued)

Provision	Text	Comments/observations
	its jurisdiction **have been accessed** in accordance with prior informed consent . . .	**before they left the territory** of the Party providing them. 2) That "access" to genetic resources took place in accordance with **prior informed consent** by seeking such PIC after they have left the territory of the Party that provided them. The latter situation would mean that the permission to utilize genetic resources was sought *ex post facto* (afterwards) and not necessarily that the term access has changed meaning. Such a situation would arise, for example, in cases of a change of intent or use of the genetic and/or biochemical composition of material initially accessed for bulk uses. The obligation of Parties is not to control when prior informed consent was granted but rather whether it exists for or before utilization of genetic resources within their territories.
Art. 21	Each Party shall take measures to raise awareness of the importance of genetic resources . . . , and related **access** and benefit-sharing **issues**. Such measures may include, *inter alia*:(g) Education and training of users and providers of genetic resources . . . about their access and benefit-sharing obligations	Access (issues) here may be interpreted widely to encompass obligations related to **taking** and **ensuing activities, including utilization.**
Art. 22.5	Measures . . . may include, *inter alia*:(j) Special measures to increase the capacity of indigenous and local communities with emphasis on enhancing the **capacity of women** within those communities **in relation to access to genetic resources** . . .	The act of **taking**, or **activities that take place before** the genetic resources leave the territory of the Party providing them, are implied. It is doubtful that the Protocol meant enhancing capacity for R&D.
Annex	1. Monetary benefits may include, but not be limited to:(a) **Access fees/fee per sample collected or otherwise acquired;**	Implies a fee for **taking/ collecting** and indicates an **act that takes place before** the resource leaves the territory of the Party providing it.

Source: *Own illustration*

access to the genetic potential of material accessed for bulk uses. A come-back clause obliges the recipient to seek new consent from the provider and to renegotiate MAT before using any material that was accessed under non-commercial use terms for commercial purposes (see Kamau, Ch. 17 and von Kries et al., Ch. 20 (MicroB3 model agreement, Article 4.4) in this volume). If used in other laws, the come-back clause should oblige the recipient to seek the PIC of the provider, as well as establish MAT under the ABS regime. But probably the most effective way of realizing the provider's PIC prerogative in all three cases is through the new compliance and monitoring measures of the NP (discussed below), a view which confirms that without user measures, provider measures are essentially impotent.

Facilitation

ACCESS TO GENETIC RESOURCES FOR R&D
SUBJECT TO PIC (ARTICLE 6.3)

According to Article 6.3, if a Party subjects access to genetic resources to a PIC requirement, then it ". . . shall take the necessary legislative, administrative or policy measures, as appropriate to" provide procedural facilitation of access. The procedural facilitation that is foreseen is quite elaborate and entails *inter alia* the obligation to provide for legal certainty, clarity, and transparency of domestic ABS legislation; fair and nonarbitrary rules and procedures on accessing genetic resources; information on how to apply for prior informed consent; clear, cost-effective and timely decision making; and evidence of the decision to grant PIC and the establishment of MAT in the form of a permit or its equivalent. The ABS Clearing-House established under Article 14 shall be notified about the permit or its equivalent. In addition, such a Party shall establish clear rules and procedures for requiring and establishing MAT which may include a dispute settlement clause; terms on benefit sharing, including in relation to intellectual property rights; terms on subsequent third-party use, if any; and terms on changes of intent, where applicable, among others. Where PIC of the ILCs for access to genetic resources is involved, it shall also set out criteria and/or processes for obtaining their PIC or approval and involvement. Kamau and Winter (2013b, 112) are of the opinion that the NP also places the burden of establishing MAT for access to genetic resources of the ILCs and ATK on the State, as implied by Articles 5.2 and 5, if they do not have the capacity to organize that process.

FURTHER FACILITATION FOR SPECIFIC SECTORS (ARTICLE 8)

The Nagoya Protocol included an additional stand-alone obligation under Article 8 for further facilitation of access for some sectors: non-commercial biodiversity research, health and food, and agriculture. These sectors are considered to be of paramount importance to conservation and sustainable use of biological diversity; the control and suppression of human, animal and plant health pandemics; and food security, respectively, but they are readily hindered by ABS requirements.

(i) Non-commercial biodiversity research sector

The distinct needs of non-commercial biodiversity research are addressed under Article 8 (a). It requires each Party, in developing and implementing its ABS legislation or regulatory requirements, to

> Create conditions to promote and encourage research which contributes to the conservation and sustainable use of biological diversity, particularly in developing countries, including through simplified measures on access for non-commercial research purposes, taking into account the need to address a change of intent for such research.

Some of the reasons why non-commercial biodiversity research is easily hindered by ABS requirements and why providers struggle with the idea of facilitating it – one of the reasons is that the results of non-commercial research can be used for commercial R&D – are discussed in Chapter 17 of this volume and comprise both the concerns and controversies of parties during negotiations. The deal reached between the providers and the users envisages facilitation against an obligation to address a change of intent which means a deviation from the mutually agreed terms at the time of access, that triggers a need for renegotiation of terms. Such a situation could be addressed by inserting a clause in the material transfer agreement, often referred to as a "come-back clause", that obliges the user to seek a new prior informed consent from the provider for the newly proposed uses and to renegotiate the mutually agreed terms.

(ii) Health sector

A provision on simplified procedures for expeditious access to genetic resources (especially pathogens) in cases of emergency was also included under Article 8 (b).[22] It calls upon each Party, in developing and implementing its access and benefit-sharing legislation or regulatory requirements, to

> Pay due regard to cases of present or imminent emergencies that threaten or damage human, animal or plant health, as determined nationally or internationally [and to] take into consideration the need for expeditious access to genetic resources and expeditious fair and equitable sharing of benefits arising out of the use of such genetic resources, including access to affordable treatments by those in need, especially in developing countries.

Access and benefit sharing related to pathogens are crucial in addressing human, animal and plant health in a responsible, fair and equitable way (Greiber et al., 2012, 117). It is therefore critical that genetic resources required for the production of medicines and also for building vaccine stocks in preparedness of pandemic outbreaks are made available either expeditiously or with ease

---

22 For controversies that dominated the negotiations in this regard see Wilke (2013), p. 315, note 18.

depending on the emergency. While most virus samples with a pandemic potential are found in developing countries, which are likewise dependent on and keen to support global efforts to combat pandemics by sharing needed virus strains, they have found themselves excluded from the benefits of that process in the past (Wilke, 2013). This is because most R&D activities are located and conducted in Europe and North America. Countries in these regions at times place a large number of advanced-purchase agreements on vaccines in order to guarantee priority treatment in case of an emergency, resulting in high prices and strong competition for the limited resources which bar developing countries from purchasing needed treatments.[23] Therefore, while seeking to maintain and ensure the supply of such genetic resources, the provision sought to balance the ABS equation by ensuring that their providers also benefit from the process. The *quid pro quo* deal reached therefore envisages expeditious access to genetic resources in exchange for expeditious fair and equitable sharing of benefits arising out of the use of such genetic resources.

(iii) Food and agriculture sector

The food and agriculture sector, with a strong representation in the name of the United Nations Food and Agriculture Organization (FAO), was also very much engaged in the negotiations in order to protect the interests of the sector. Its special needs are addressed under Article 8 (c) which requires each Party, in developing and implementing its access and benefit-sharing legislation or regulatory requirements, to

> Consider the importance of genetic resources for food and agriculture and their special role for food security.

The availability, simplified access and exchange of genetic resources for food and agriculture is core to food production in view of meeting the human food and nutrition supply demand, ensuring food security and coping with the impacts of climatic stress resulting from global warming and other forms of climatic change: in other words, climate adaptation. In the absence of a special regime for such genetic resources, ABS procedures can negatively impact this sector. Parties, recognizing the interdependence of all countries with regard to GRFA, their special nature and importance for achieving food security worldwide and for sustainable development of agriculture in the context of poverty alleviation and climate change (see preamble § 16 NP), agreed on the above text.

The clause does not seem to reflect a win-win situation in terms of facilitation of access and permission to use such genetic resources, on the one hand, and sharing of benefits, on the other hand. However, the understanding should be that all countries depend on genetic resources for food and agriculture and all countries are interdependent in terms of their supply. In other words, in the end, everyone

---

23 Wilke (2013) discusses this problem in detail, highlighting the case of Indonesia.

benefits from their availability for R&D. Of course, benefits of proprietary uses should be shared when the results of R&D are not put in the public domain.

In implementing this obligation, the national legislation may take two situations into consideration:

1   Relating to all PGRFA included in Annex I of the International Treaty on Plant Genetic Resources for Food and Agriculture (ITPGRFA). The Treaty makes these PGRFA the subject of a common pool – widely referred to as the multilateral system of the Treaty – in line with an agreement reached by the Contracting Parties of the Treaty to establish a special ABS regime of expeditious access by restraining themselves from exercising their sovereign right to subject them to PIC requirement for specific non-commercial uses.[24] The Treaty deals with eventualities of uses not envisaged in the Treaty for PGRFA that were initially accessed under the MLS rules.[25] It comprises the specialized international ABS instrument for the Treaty Annex I PGRFA, making these exempt from the CBD/NP ABS rules in line with Article 4.4 NP.[26] Concerning the PGRFA, a provision should be inserted in the legislation clearly waiving the PIC requirement for their access.

2   Relating to all other GRFA, i.e. those that are not covered by Annex I of the Treaty. Other GRFA are equally important for food security and nutrition, climate adaptation, etc. Currently, there is ongoing work within the FAO Commission on Genetic Resources for Food and Agriculture (CGRFA) to identify such resources and to reflect on possibilities of creating a specialised regime to address their ABS needs. The list of identified GRFA is comprized of animal, forest, aquatic and microbial genetic resources and biochemical agents (see Greiber et al., 2012, 124).[27] According to Article

24 I.e. solely for the purpose of conservation for research, breeding, and training for food and agriculture in line with Article 12 (3) (a) of the Treaty. See also Kamau and Winter (2013b), p. 117ff. For an in-depth discussion on how the multilateral system of the ITPGRFA functions see Chiarolla and Jungcurt (2011), www.evb.ch/cm_data/ITPGR_ABS_Study_1.pdf (accessed 23 January 2013); Kamau and Winter (eds) (2013a), pp. 343–372.

25 Article 13 (d) (ii) of the Treaty requires users of the material of the MLS to share monetary benefits if they make a product from it, but do not make the product available, and commercialize it.

26 Article 4.4 NP states that: "This Protocol is the instrument for the implementation of the access and benefit-sharing provisions of the Convention. Where a specialized international access and benefit-sharing instrument applies that is consistent with, and does not run counter to the objectives of the Convention and this Protocol, this Protocol does not apply for the Party or Parties to the specialized instrument in respect of the specific genetic resource covered by and for the purpose of the specialized instrument."

27 The report of the sixth meeting of the AHWG (UNEP/CBD/COP/9/6) recommended that animal genetic resources for food and agriculture are accorded special consideration. In Decision IX/12 of the ninth meeting of the Conference of the Parties to the CBD, a clause was adopted requiring special consideration for "[g]enetic resources within the remit of the FAO Commission on Genetic Resources for Food and Agriculture" in addition to genetic resources for food and agriculture covered by the ITPGRFA and animal genetic resources. See also background study papers at www.fao.org/nr/cgrfa/cgrfa-back/en/?no_cache=1 (accessed 30 October 2014).

4.2 NP, Parties may create other specialized ABS instruments provided that they do not run counter to the objectives of the CBD. Although no specialized ABS instrument exists yet for those resources, Parties may still consider how to develop or implement their ABS legislation or regulatory requirements in a manner that pays due regard to the ongoing work in accordance with Article 4.3 NP.[28] To the extent that a multilateral system such as the Treaty MLS exists, parties thereto may consider exempting genetic resources for food and agriculture covered by such a system from the ABS requirements of the CBD and its Nagoya Protocol.

FACILITATION IN REGARD TO INSTITUTIONAL AND
ADMINISTRATIVE ARRANGEMENTS (ARTICLE 13)

One of the challenges users often face in access is the lack of clarity as to which authorities are responsible for authorization and which authority has which function. The NP tries to create clarity under Article 13 on national focal points and competent national authorities.[29] Accordingly, each party is obliged to designate a national focal point (NFP) on access and benefit sharing (Article 13 (1)) and one or more competent national authorities (CNA) on access and benefit sharing (Article 13 (2)). The NFP is more or less an information agency. It is responsible for providing information on procedures for obtaining PIC and establishing MAT, the national authority, the relevant indigenous and local communities and other relevant stakeholders (Article 13 (1) (a)–(c)). The CNA, on the other hand, is responsible for authorizing access, issuing access permits and advising on applicable procedures and requirements for obtaining PIC and entering into MAT (Article 13 (2)). A Party that designates more than one CNA must provide information as to which competent authority is responsible for the genetic resources sought (Article 13 (4)). A single authority may be designated with power to fulfil all the above functions (Article 13 (3)). If this approach is adopted, such an authority will serve as an NFP and CNA at the same time.

Information

Another challenge for users has been the lack of an international portal where relevant information on provider access and benefit-sharing legislations, administrative and policy measures, national authorities and their competences, access procedures and requirements, etc. could be accessed without the need to travel abroad. The NP has established an ABS Clearing-House (ABS CH) under Article

---

28 Article 4.3 NP states that: "This Protocol shall be implemented in a mutually supportive manner with other international instruments relevant to this Protocol. Due regard should be paid to useful and relevant ongoing work or practices under such international instruments and relevant international organizations, provided that they are supportive of and do not run counter to the objectives of the Convention and this Protocol."
29 For a detailed explanation see Greiber et al. (2012), p. 144 ff.

14 which will serve as a hub of such information. In this regard, each party is obliged to notify all relevant access and benefit-sharing information to the Secretariat of the CBD (Articles 13 (4), 14 (2), (3)) through its NFP (which is responsible for liaising with the Secretariat (Article 13 (1)). The Secretariat will make the information available through the ABS CH (Article 13 (5)). Such information will be decisive, e.g. for an applicant who wishes to access genetic resources and would like to ascertain which authority is mandated to grant PIC and/or issue an access permit.

Benefit sharing

Benefit sharing from utilization of genetic resources and ATK accessed under PIC conditions

Benefit sharing is regulated under Article 5 of the Nagoya Protocol. Accordingly, each Party is required to take legislative, administrative or policy measures with the aim of ensuring that benefits arising from the utilization of genetic resources and ATK are shared in a fair and equitable way with their providers based on mutually agreed terms. The benefits to be shared include, but are not limited to, the monetary and non-monetary benefits listed in the Annex.

Additionally, the Protocol prescribes collaboration and cooperation in technical and scientific R&D programmes, which preferably take place in and with participation of provider parties, including by encouraging access to technology by, and transfer of technology to, developing country parties (Article 23). Finally, the Protocol introduces extensive measures on improving capacities (Article 22), which is one of the core benefits under the Protocol (Annex, 2 (g)–(j)), and the obligation for parties to cooperate in capacity building, capacity development, and the strengthening of human resources and institutional capacities (Article 22.1). Therefore, developing country parties should conduct capacity self-assessments to identify their national needs and priorities (Article 22.3). Key areas identified by the Protocol that require capacity building include implementation of the Protocol, negotiation of MAT, development and enforcement of domestic legislation, and endogenous research capabilities (Article 22.4 and 5).

The NP introduces some innovations concerning benefit sharing. First, it requires that benefits not only from the utilization of genetic resources are shared with the Party providing such resources, but also from subsequent applications and commercialization. This was a major victory for providers, because immense benefits of R&D accrue in these latter phases of development of products and processes and, therefore, benefit sharing can only be effective if it extends to these stages (Greiber et al., 2012, 85). Second, it clarified which measures should be taken to effect the sharing of benefits from R&D on ATK namely, legislative, administrative or policy measures. The CBD is mute concerning this.

But the NP flaws the benefit-sharing obligation *vis-à-vis* the ILCs by failing to expressly mention that the benefits from subsequent applications and commercialization are also to be shared with such communities if they provided genetic resources and ATK for utilization. Should it be assumed that this requirement applies equally for this category of genetic resources and ATK? The contrary would be a big blow to the ILCs in terms of the lost opportunity to share such benefits. Of course, national legislation is free to require that such benefits are shared in these circumstances, hence allowing mutually agreed terms to be established during negotiation for access. However, the Conference of the Parties serving as the Meeting of the Parties (COP/MOP) would do well to clarify this uncertainty for the sake of easing negotiations between providers and users, as well as of raising legal certainty and clarity.

Benefit sharing from utilization of genetic resources
and ATK accessed without PIC

Cases of benefit sharing from the utilization of genetic resources and ATK accessed without PIC[30] are dealt with under Article 10. The article aims to enable benefits of R&D based on genetic resources and ATK that *occur in transboundary situations* or for which it is *impossible to grant or obtain PIC*. Towards this aim, it requires Parties to consider the need for and modalities of a global multilateral benefit-sharing mechanism (GMBSM).

What are transboundary situations or situations for which it is not possible to grant or obtain PIC? How Article 10 should be construed and operationalized has been a subject of discussion, mostly of the second and third meetings of the Open-ended Ad Hoc Intergovernmental Committee for the Nagoya Protocol (ICNP)[31] following the adoption of the NP in October 2010 and an online discussion, convened by the Executive Secretary of the CBD through the ABS CH from 8 April to 25 May 2013 at the request of COP-11, to conduct a broad consultation on this issue.[32] The recommendations of ICNP-2 were adopted by COP-11 (8–19 October 2012) in Hyderabad, India, and included in Annex I of Decision XI/1.[33] COP-11 decided to reconvene the ICNP for a third meeting to address outstanding issues, in preparation for the first meeting of the COP/MOP.[34]

---

30 It should be noted that this discussion does not deal with access undertaken in violation of the CBD.
31 The ICNP was established by COP-10 in accordance to Decision X/1 to serve as an interim governing body for the Nagoya Protocol until the first meeting of the Parties to the Protocol, at which time it will cease to exist. It was planned to meet twice during the intersessional period and was mandated to undertake, with the support of the Executive Secretary, the preparations necessary for the first meeting of the Parties to the Protocol.
32 The full text of the online discussions is available on the ABS Clearing-House at http://absch.cbd.int/Art10_groups.shtml (accessed 30 October 2014). The revised synthesis document UNEP/CBD/ICNP/3/INF/4 is available at www.cbd.int/doc/meetings/abs/icnp-03/information/icnp-03-inf-04-en.pdf (accessed 30 October 2014).
33 See www.cbd.int/cop/cop-11/doc/2012–10–24-advanced-unedited-cop-11-decisions-en.pdf (accessed 30 October 2014).
34 Ibid. The first meeting of the COP/MOP took place from 13–17 October 2014 in Pyeongchang, Republic of Korea.

The synthesis of the online discussions document UNEP/CBD/ICNP/3/INF/4 and the report of the expert meeting on Article 10 (Pyeongchang, Republic of Korea, 24–28 February 2014) which reviewed the synthesis of the online discussions indicate that there are still very many areas needing further examination.[35] Therefore, we do not wish to explore those results *vis-à-vis* the two questions raised, as reference can be made to the synthesis and the report. The only comments we would like to make concern the article's indication that such a mechanism might be useful in

- addressing the issue of benefit sharing from utilization of genetic resources and/or ATK that were accessed prior to the entry into force of the CBD. This would be a possible solution to the question of temporal scope, e.g. *vis-à-vis ex situ* collections in regard to new and continuing uses, an objective which was strongly supported by the African group at the negotiations leading to the NP;
- resolving access issues concerning a certain group of ubiquitous genetic organisms, e.g. microbes and benefit sharing from their utilization (see Fritze and Oumard, Ch. 15 in this volume).

Genetic resources and ATK requiring transboundary cooperation under Article 11 cannot simply or automatically be thrown into the same pot with those referred to under Article 10. That is because the sovereignty of States and the power to invoke that right in order to subject them to PIC and MAT and benefit-sharing requirements is not taken away and is implied by "genetic resources are found *in situ* within the territory of more than one Party" and ATK shared by one or more ILCs "in several Parties". These cannot be equated, e.g. to genetic resources and ATK in *ex situ* collections of unknown origin, or genetic resources in ABNJ. States within the territory of which such genetic resources are found may decide to exercise that right corporately or opt to do so individually. To encroach on their right to do so would not only be derogatory to the principle of sovereign rights of states over their natural resources, but also a departure from an important cornerstone of the CBD, the concept of bilateralism. Even the Nagoya Protocol is careful of what it can ask in its formulation of Article 11 and therefore only requires Parties to "endeavour to cooperate". What is probably novel in this regard is that the Protocol gives leeway for common pools' endeavours at different points (Kamau & Winter, 2013b, 121), including at a regional level.

Compliance

Compliance measures are found in Articles 15–18, but alongside these, Article 14 is also relevant.

---

35 See UNEP/CBD/ICNP/3/5, available at www.cbd.int/doc/meetings/abs/icnp-03/official/icnp-03-05-en.pdf (accessed 30 October 2014).

Measures for compliance with domestic
ABS requirements

The duty to ensure compliance with the domestic legislation or regulatory requirements on ABS is anchored in Articles 15 and 16 for both genetic resources and
ATK, respectively. Accordingly, each Party is required to take legislative, administrative or policy measures to provide that genetic resources and ATK utilized
within its jurisdiction have been accessed in accordance with PIC and that MAT
have been established as required by the domestic ABS legislation or administrative requirements. In addition, Articles 15 and 16 require each Party to take
measures to address situations of noncompliance with adopted measures and also
call upon Parties to cooperate in cases of alleged violation of domestic ABS
requirements.

Measures for compliance with MAT

Measures for compliance with mutually agreed terms are found in Article 18. The
Article addresses three issues:

1   Specific focus on MAT covering dispute resolution (Article 18.1). It requires
    each Party to encourage providers and users of genetic resources and ATK to
    include MAT on dispute resolution while implementing Article 6.3 (g) (i)
    and Article 7. Such MAT, according to subparagraph 1 (a)–(c), may include:
    • The jurisdiction to which they will subject any dispute resolution
      process;
    • The applicable law; and/or
    • Options for alternative dispute resolution, such as mediation or
      arbitration.
2   Obligation for each Party to ensure the availability of the opportunity to
    seek recourse under its legal system in cases of disputes arising from MAT,
    consistent with applicable jurisdictional requirements (Article 18.2).
3   Obligation for each Party to take measures regarding access to justice and
    the utilization of mechanisms regarding mutual recognition and enforcement
    of foreign judgements and arbitral awards (Article 18.3 (a), (b)).

The Protocol foresees a review of the effectiveness of this article (Article 8.4)
by the COP/MOP four years after its entry into force and thereafter at intervals
determined by it in accordance with Article 31.

Measures to support compliance with domestic
ABS requirements and MAT

Article 17 contains measures for supporting compliance with domestic measures
as envisaged in Articles 15 and 16. They aim to create a mechanism of monitoring
the utilization of genetic resources in the downstream chain of R&D. Such

measures will also be critical in providing institutional assistance in relation to breaches of MAT under Article 18 (Kamau & Winter, 2013b, 119).

According to the chapeau of Article 17 (1), the measures envisaged aim not only to *monitor* but also to *enhance transparency* about the utilization of genetic resources by each Party. They aim to address four main issues: What agency should be in charge of monitoring/checking; at what point in the valorization stream of genetic resources shall checking occur; what substantive issue shall be checked; and what documents shall count as evidence of compliance (Kamau, Fedder, & Winter 2010, 256). Thus the measures should achieve the following results:

- Designation of one or more checkpoints that will collect and receive relevant information related to PIC, source of the genetic resource, establishment of MAT and/or utilization of genetic resources (Article 17.1 (a) (i)). Such checkpoints must be effective and their functions must be relevant to the implementation of the mandates as spelled out above and to the utilization of genetic resources, or to the collection of ". . . relevant information at, *inter alia*, any stage of research, development, innovation, precommercialization or commercialization" (Article 17.1 (a) (iv));
- Compulsion of users of genetic resources to provide the information mentioned in bullet point 1 to designated checkpoints and to address situations of noncompliance (Article 17.1 (a) (ii));
- Provision of the information mentioned in bullet point 1, including from internationally recognized certificates of compliance,[36] to relevant national authorities and to the Party providing PIC and to the ABS CH, without prejudice to the protection of confidential information (Article 17.1 (a) (iii));
- Encouragement of users and providers of genetic resources to include provisions in mutually agreed terms to share information on the implementation of such terms, including through reporting requirements (Article 17.1 (b)); and
- Encouragement of the use of cost-effective communication tools and systems (Article 17.1 (c)).

Critique on compliance measures

Some authors have criticized the compliance measures of the Nagoya Protocol. We only wish to reiterate two critiques by Kamau and Winter (2013b, 119ff.). The first concerns monitoring of the utilization of ATK and the second the scope of user obligations.

MONITORING OF THE UTILIZATION OF ATK

Article 16 on compliance with domestic legislation and regulatory requirements requires each Party to take legislative, administrative or policy measures to

---

36 According to Article 17.2 and 3, a permit issued by the provider in accordance with Article 6.3
   (e) and notified to the ABS CH comprises an internationally recognized certificate of compliance
   and serves as evidence that the genetic resource it covers has been accessed according to PIC and
   MAT as required by the domestic ABS legislation or regulatory requirements.

provide that ATK utilized within its jurisdiction has been accessed in accordance with PIC or approval and involvement of ILCs and that MAT have been established as required by the domestic ABS legislation or administrative requirements. It would have been expected that a clause is inserted accordingly under Article 17 to require that its utilization is monitored, but this was not done. It is unclear why ATK is not covered. That, however, does not hinder the insertion of such a requirement during the establishment of mutually agreed terms in line with Article 7, as well as requiring checkpoints to collect or receive information related to PIC of or approval and involvement of ILCs and the utilization of ATK.

SCOPE OF USER OBLIGATIONS

The main problem according to Kamau and Winter (2013b, 120f.) lies in the scope of user obligations for which the user state shall ensure compliance and the measures the user state shall take to this effect. The Protocol envisages two kinds of measures: authoritative enforcement, as assumed in Article 15.2, and the availability of recourse in case of disputes about MATs (Article 18.2).

The reading advocated by EU negotiators (Buck & Hamilton 2011) and also by the IUCN explanatory guide (Greiber et al., 2012, 163) is that authoritative enforcement is only obligatory in relation to whether PIC was obtained for access to genetic resources and MAT established. Cases where the utilization of an accessed genetic resource is against permit or contractual conditions are regarded to fall in the scope of Article 18. Article 15 does not apply to these cases because, as it has been alleged, the clause ". . . , as required by the domestic access and benefit-sharing legislation or regulatory requirements of the other Party" in Article 15.1 refers to the general legislation/regulation but not to the specific conditions in the concrete case. This is indicated by the comma before the cited clause. The narrow reading also excludes from enforcement cases in which a user does not fulfil benefit-sharing obligations that may be required by provider state legislation, the reason being that Article 15 only speaks of the utilization of genetic resources which is defined as research and development, but not benefit sharing. In other words, there is no specified obligation for user states to ensure benefit sharing, thus leaving the enforcement of benefit-sharing duties to contractual means as before, with all the difficulties of forum, litigation costs, and prosecution of titles (Kamau et al.,2010, 257). The fact that the Protocol does not go further in that direction constitutes a major disappointment for the provider side.

It is submitted that a more extensive understanding is also possible. This stems from an observation on some embarrassing effects of the ruling opinion: assuming that the monitoring state authority is informed that a user did obtain a provider state permit but clearly performed commercial R&D though the permit only allows non-commercial R&D, shall it really stick to confirming that the access utilization was in compliance with the PIC requirement and disregard the blunt violation of the permit? Assuming further that the user in this case has obtained various non-monetary or monetary benefits from the utilization but never shared any of those with the provider state, though the permit so required, shall the user state authority still confirm compliance and ignore the breach of law? Should the user state authority not have to order the user to comply with the provider state law and the permit issued on its basis?

As a temporary solution, it could be suggested that in such cases the user state authority should at least be obliged to inform the provider state of the case. Such obligation could be based on Article 17.1 (a) (iii). But this offers little help because the enforcement powers of the provider state do not reach into the jurisdictional realm of the user state.

Legal arguments for extending user state enforcement to breaches of permit conditions related to utilizations and of legal requirements concerning benefit sharing include the following:

- The above cited clause "as required . . ." can also be understood to refer to the individual permit whenever the provider state legislation requires that the permit shall specify the permissible utilization, and it can be understood to refer to any precise benefit-sharing requirement established by the same legislation or regulation.
- It would be illogical to extend the monitoring to the utilization of genetic resources but refuse to draw consequences from that information.
- Article 15.1, when stating that "each Party shall take [. . .] measures to provide that genetic resources utilized within its jurisdiction have been accessed in accordance with prior informed consent," can be understood to mean that genetic resources utilized in breach of permit conditions were not accessed "in accordance with prior informed consent".
- The duty to ensure compliance with the benefit-sharing obligation can already be derived from Article 5 NP. Article 5 NP refers to Article 15.7 CBD, which clearly addresses an obligation to ensure benefit sharing both to the provider and user state. Article 5.3 NP, reading "To implement paragraph 1 above, each Party shall take legislative, administrative or policy measures, as appropriate," can be understood as asking for enforcement measures by the user state.

Information on compliance

As already seen above, Article 14 establishes an ABS CH as a mechanism for sharing information related to ABS.[37] We consider this mechanism to be a vital tool in supporting compliance. One of the practical examples is that a Party (checkpoint) can use the information on a permit or its equivalent – which, when notified to the ABS CH, comprises an internationally recognized certificate of compliance – to establish whether a user complied with PIC and MAT as required by the domestic ABS legislation or regulatory requirements, or on methods and tools developed to monitor genetic resources to assess the effectiveness of a

37 For the kind of information that Parties should or may make available to the ABS CH see Greiber et al. (2012), Table 5 (p. 156f.).

checkpoint. The ABS CH will now also be an important source of any relevant information for the newly established committee on compliance.[38]

Chances of R&D and benefit sharing under the NP: An upshot

The Nagoya Protocol has gone a long way to offer solutions for unravelling the ABS maze. It introduces novel measures to counter the many challenges that users faced in accessing genetic resources and ATK and providers faced in monitoring the flow of genetic resources and ATK through the value chain, as well as in enforcing their PIC and MAT requirements in user countries. These measures aim to make the ABS regime functional and thus enhance R&D on genetic resources and ATK, as well as facilitate the sharing of benefits from such activities. This is also expected to have a positive impact on the conservation and sustainable use of biological diversity as Parties are required to "... encourage users and providers to direct benefits arising from the utilization of genetic resources towards [. . .]" that course (Article 9). What the Nagoya Protocol can achieve will depend on how effectively the positive elements of the Nagoya Protocol are implemented and how much of its shortcomings can be rectified (Kamau, 2014, 173). There is a legitimate need, therefore, to apply diligence in developing the new generation of national legislations, taking the concerns of providers and research and industry or users into consideration (see Winter, Ch. 19 in this volume).

Conclusion

The access and benefit-sharing framework of the Convention on Biological Diversity and its Nagoya Protocol envisages a *quid pro quo* arrangement between providers and users of genetic resources and ATK. Providers are required to facilitate access to genetic resources and ATK for R&D purposes and users are required to share the benefits that arise from the utilization of such resources and knowledge. To achieve this purpose, Contracting Parties to the CBD and NP are required to transpose the relevant provisions of these instruments into national law. National implementation to date depicts results that are far from achieving that aim. ABS regimes are often not sufficiently clear and thus do not provide the necessary legal certainty and clarity either for users or providers of genetic resources. This has often prevented ABS from becoming a fully functional system for R&D of genetic resources and ATK (Morgera et al., 2014).

The Nagoya Protocol has brought some novel ideas aimed at rectifying this situation. In particular, it introduces innovative measures to counter the many challenges that users face in accessing genetic resources. They aim to provide legal certainty, ease access procedures, facilitate access for non-commercial research

---

38 See Annex IV of the advance unedited version of the combined decisions of COP-11, at www. cbd.int/cop/cop-11/doc/2012–10–24-advanced-unedited-cop-11-decisions-en.pdf (accessed 30 October 2014).

purposes, enable easy accessibility to relevant information, etc. This is expected to enhance access for researchers and companies to quality samples of genetic resources, based on predictable access decisions at reasonably low transaction costs and thus create new opportunities for nature-based R&D (Morgera et al., 2014). It is also expected to lead to the creation of innovative goods and services that help to meet societal challenges (Morgera et al., 2014). The Nagoya Protocol introduces innovative measures to curb the challenges faced by providers by *inter alia* enhancing compliance with domestic legislation or regulatory requirements on ABS. It is hoped that these measures will help to limit abuse and violations by users and increase the benefits to be shared with providers. All these innovations should change the current crummy ABS atmosphere, if the NP is implemented effectively and outstanding issues are clarified as well as remaining challenges eliminated.

References

Buck, M, Hamilton, C (2011) "The Nagoya Protocol on Access to Genetic Resources and the Fair and Equitable Sharing of Benefits Arising from their Utilization to the Convention on Biological Resources", 20, *Review of European Community and International Environmental Law*, pp. 47–61.

Chiarolla, C, Jungcurt, S (2011) *Outstanding issues on access and benefit sharing under the multilateral system of the International Treaty on Plant Genetic Resources for Food and Agriculture*, a background study paper by the Berne Declaration and the Development Fund, www.evb.ch/cm_data/ITPGR_ABS_Study_1.pdf (accessed 23 January 2013).

Glowka, L, Burhenne-Guilmin, F, Synge, H, McNeely, JA, Gündling, L (1994) *A Guide to the Convention on Biological Diversity*, Gland, Switzerland: IUCN.

Greiber, T, Peña Moreno, S, Åhrén, M, Nieto Carrasco, J, Kamau, EC, Cabrera Medaglia, J, Oliva, MJ, Perron-Welch, F, in cooperation with Ali, N, Williams, C (2012) *An explanatory guide to the Nagoya Protocol on access and benefit-sharing*, Gland, Switzerland: IUCN.

Kamau, EC (2013) "The multilateral system of the International Treaty on Plant Genetic Resources for Food and Agriculture: Lessons and room for further development" in: Kamau, EC, Winter, G (eds) *Common pools of genetic resources. Equity and innovation in international biodiversity law*, London: Routledge, pp. 343–372.

Kamau, EC (2014) "Valorisation of genetic resources, benefit sharing and conservation of biological diversity: What role for the ABS regime?" in: Dilling, O, Markus, T (eds) *Ex Rerum Natura Ius? – Sachzwang und Problemwahrnehmung im Umweltrecht*, Baden Baden: Nomos, pp. 143–173.

Kamau, EC, Fedder, B, Winter, G (2010) "The Nagoya Protocol on access to genetic resources and benefit sharing: What is new and what are the implications for provider and user countries and the scientific community?", *Law, Environment and Development Journal* 6(3), pp. 246–262, Available online at www.lead-journal.org/current_issue.htm (accessed 30 October 2014).

Kamau, EC, Winter, G (eds) (2009) *Genetic resources, traditional knowledge and the law: Solutions for access and benefit sharing*, London: Earthscan/Routledge.

Kamau, EC, Winter, G (eds) (2013a) *Common pools of genetic resources. Equity and innovation in international biodiversity law*, London: Earthscan/Routledge.

Kamau, EC, Winter, G (2013b) "An introduction to the international ABS regime and a comment on its transposition by the EU", *Law, Environment and Development Journal* 9(2), pp. 106–126, Available online at www.lead-journal.org/content/13106.pdf (accessed 30 October 2014).

Morgera, E, Tsioumani, E, Buck, M (2014) *Unraveling the Nagoya Protocol. A commentary on the Nagoya Protocol on access and benefit-sharing to the Convention on Biological Diversity*, Leiden: Brill/Martinus Nijhoff.

Wilke, M (2013) "The World Health Organization's Pandemic Influenza Preparedness Framework as a public health resources pool" in: Kamau, EC, Winter, G (eds) *Common pools of genetic resources. Equity and innovation in international biodiversity law*, London: Routledge, pp. 315–342.

Williams, G (1961) *Criminal law, the general part*, 2nd ed., London: Stevens & Sons.

3 Defining commercial and non-commercial research and development under the Nagoya Protocol and in other contexts

Caroline von Kries and Gerd Winter

Introduction

There are many ways to define criteria for the categorization of research and development (R&D) activities as they are applied to the study and further elaboration of genetic resources (GR). Also, in other contexts it seems difficult to develop a consistent classification of research, although it is of relevance in different areas of science (biotechnology, biology, chemistry) and in different areas of application of the knowledge resulting from the research (pharmacy, agriculture, engineering). This may be due to the fact that a number of factors influence and are influenced by research classification: the flow of benefits to the provider of research material, the allocation of funding to the researcher, the application of intellectual property rights on the resulting knowledge, the different possible actors using the classification, the extent to which research output shall or shall not be published, and any privileged protection of research through basic rights.[1]

The following study will start by analyzing the contextual use of the various terms that are related to the distinction between non-commercial and commercial. In a second section, the explored terminological variants shall be the starting point for interpreting the terms commercial/non-commercial as they are used in the Nagoya Protocol. Finally, the proposed interpretation shall be tested in view of the relevant provisions of the Nagoya Protocol, followed by a short summary of the main results of the study.

Categorization in different contexts

When discussing the definition of terms, some basic considerations should be kept in mind:

- a definition does not objectively exist but is a convention that is first of all informed by the context and the goal in and for which the term is used and that may regularly be adapted if social developments challenge the nature of research

---

1 On the European level: Art. 13 Charta of Fundamental Rights of the European Union; on the national level: p.ex. Article 5.3 of the German Grundgesetz.

- the lawmaker is largely free to define a term he/she uses in a given law
- when a definition concerns two opposite terms (like black and white), there are often clear cases belonging to one or the other side (black or white), but there are also often overlapping "grey" cases; in the legal sphere, however, grey cases should be avoided if different legal consequences are tied to the opposite terms.

Terms related to the organization conducting research

A possible categorization of research is related to the entity that executes the research activity or that finances a research project. This may be called the *institutional approach*. On the one hand there is the public sector, such as universities and other public research institutions. They are mainly funded by public budgets. The choice of project objectives and content is generally at the discretion of the individual researcher. The research results are normally published. On the other hand there is the private sector, meaning private enterprises and private research institutions. The research is mainly funded by private budgets. The choice of project objectives and content are rather determined by potential commercial gains. Research results are kept secret if this is required in view of commercialization. But there are also "grey" cases, such as private non-profit entities, private entities conducting basic research, public entities which are partly funded by private sources, as well as public–private partnerships.

Terms related to the content of research

Another possible categorization is related to the research activity as it unfolds in the chain of research and development; it may be called the *content-related approach*.

Basic/applied research

Research is often categorized as basic (or fundamental/pure) and applied research. The OECD's *Frascati Manual*, for instance, distinguishes between basic research, applied research, and experimental development. It serves as a standard for R&D surveys and data collection. According to the manual,

> basic research is "experimental or theoretical work undertaken primarily to acquire new knowledge of the underlying foundation of phenomena and observable facts without any particular application or use in view",
> applied research is "also experimental or theoretical work undertaken primarily to acquire new knowledge but it is directed primarily towards a specific practical aim or objective",
> experimental development is "systematic work drawing on existing knowledge gained from research and/or practical experience which is directed to

producing new materials, products or devices, to installing new processes, systems and services or to improving substantially those already produced or installed".

(OECD 2002, 23)

Other terms are also in use characterizing the content of research. For instance, concerning state aid control, the European Commission, in a paper on the legality of state aid for research and development, which was regulated in Article 87 of the pre-Lisbon EEC Treaty (EU Commission 1986), differentiated between fundamental research,[2] industrial basic research[3] and applied research and development.[4] The Commission ruled that state aid for fundamental research goes beyond the scope of the application of Article 87 of the EEC Treaty and thus the control of the Commission. Rather, "the control of state aid must be had to the need for resources to be channelled to the industries contributing to improved European competitiveness" (EU Commission 1986, 5). This content-related distinction thus serves to draw a line between the scope of the Commission's competence to monitor competition-related measures and the unlimited competence of the Member States to regulate matters of (fundamental) scientific research.

The difference between fundamental and applied research is also brought forward to solve a constitutional problem: the question whether and to what extent applied/industrial research should be protected by constitutional basic rights. Research is, for instance, constitutionally protected by Article 13 of the CFR and Article 5.3 of the German Grundgesetz. The German Federal Constitutional Court takes a restrictive view, declaring: "The guarantee of scientific freedom is justified by the consideration that it is the science which is detached from ambitions of social benefits and political usefulness that serves state and society best."[5] Likewise some authors hold that only basic research deserves special constitutional protection because economic motives might impair scientific standards (Dickert 1991, 85; Blankenagel 2001, 44). Other authors argue that industry also carries out research which is neither manipulated nor unqualified and shall thus be protected under constitutional law (Kamp 2004, 70; Bernstorff 2011, 270).

Research/development

"Research" is often connected to "development", such as in the common abbreviation R&D. For instance, in an opinion on the "European Research Area", the

---

2 ". . . enlargement of scientific or technical knowledge not linked to industrial or commercial objectives".
3 ". . . original theoretical or experimental work whose objective is to achieve better understanding of the laws of science or engineering as they might apply to an industrial sector or a particular undertaking".
4 ". . . investigation or experimental work based on the results of basic industrial research to acquire new knowledge to facilitate the attainment of specific practical objectives such as the creation of new products, production processes or services".
5 Judgement of 1 March 1978, BVerfGE 47, 327 (370).

European Economic and Social Committee distinguished basic research, application-oriented research, "encyclopaedic" research (e.g. "to complete our knowledge about substance properties, new substances, active substances, etc."), technological development and product and process development (EESC 2000, para 7.1).

Terms related to the economic yield from research

There are various terms indicating whether research is or is not aimed at economic gain. They are closely related to the distinction between basic and applied research but differ because they are concerned with exchange value while the latter looks at use value. The categorization listed here can be called *yield-related approach*.

Precompetitive/competitive

Research is sometimes qualified as precompetitive or competitive, such as in European documents on the enhancement and support of research and innovation (p.ex. EESC 2000).

"Precompetitive/competitive" is sometimes synonymously used with "fundamental/applied" or "non-commercial/commercial". Research is considered precompetitive when it is "of unknown and/or unlikely value", whereas it is competitive if it is "of known commercial value" (DOW MicroB3 2011).

The said distinction was introduced in order to better target the funding of appropriate kinds of research. For instance, a proposal by the EU Commission concerning an initiative for innovative medicines (EU Commission 2007), which observes bottlenecks in drug development, suggests supporting precompetitive pharmaceutical research and development. It states that "in this context 'precompetitive pharmaceutical research and development' should be understood as research on the tools and methodologies used in the drug development process." In the pharmaceutical sector in general, an emerging interdependency between "competitive and precompetitive knowledge" in drug discovery is observed (Collaborative Drug Discovery (CDD) 2012).

Precompetitive research is seen as a necessary step before moving on to competitive development, regardless of which institution carries it out (EESC 2007 on Lisbon Strategy, 4; EU Commission 2011, 34; EU Commission 2008, 588). The European Economic and Social Committee stated that "in many particularly relevant areas of research, costly infrastructure and a large apparatus are essential to securing fundamentally new findings and technological progress, and they provide technological development (at the precompetitive stage) with novel options for improvements and innovation. Such infrastructures are the basis and catalyst for top-level research" (EESC 2008, 1).

Scientific/significant for commercial purposes

Another term looks more specifically at the way research results can be used. For instance, in UNCLOS, Part XII, on marine scientific research, a distinction is drawn between "marine scientific research" and "marine scientific research with direct significance for the exploration and exploitation of natural resources" (Article 246.1 and 246.5 (a) UNCLOS). The former activity shall be carried out "exclusively for peaceful purposes" and "in order to increase the benefit of all mankind" (Article 246.3 UNCLOS).

The meaning of "with direct significance" is further explained in a guidance paper by the United Nations Division for Ocean Affairs and the Law of the Sea. It suggests that "direct" should be understood as meaning that a project "can reasonably be expected to produce results enabling resources to be located, assessed and monitored with respect to their status and availability for commercial exploitation" (Secretary General 2005, 10).

Yielding non-monetary/monetary benefits

According to Article 5.1 Nagoya Protocol, "benefits arising from the utilization of genetic resources as well as subsequent applications and commercialization shall be shared in a fair and equitable way with the Party providing such resources." Article 5.2 classifies benefits to include monetary and non-monetary ones, and the Annex to the Nagoya Protocol further specifies different kinds of the two classes. The list indicates that monetary benefits involve the payment of money, while non-monetary involve benefits in kind. To be more precise, some of the listed benefits do not arise "from" the utilization of the genetic resources (as, for instance, payments of royalties and R&D results), but rather as an exchange "for" the consent of their utilization, such as up-front payments, research funding, collaboration in research activities and participation in product development.

Notwithstanding this fact, the Protocol notes that benefits do accrue in the process and from the results of utilizing genetic resources, and it is interesting to note that the Protocol suggests categorizing them. The purpose of introducing the distinction is however not to attach any legal effect to it. It appears to simply alert contracting parties of the fact that there can be multiple benefits, and that providers and users should be aware of that when negotiating mutually agreed terms of benefit sharing.

Terms related to the availability of research results

The categorization of research in terms of availability of research results can be called the *functional approach*. The most common distinction is that between keeping knowledge under one's private disposition and making it publicly available.

There is a wealth of legal documents which mention the distinction between private and public availability of research results, both on the national and international levels. To name just one international example, Article 244 UNCLOS asks states and international organizations to "make available by publication and dissemination through appropriate channels [. . .] knowledge resulting from marine scientific research". By contrast, research which is "of direct significance for the exploration and exploitation of natural resources" must not be regarded as subject to the publication requirement.[6] The coastal state can however require publication as a precondition for granting its research consent.

Privatization of knowledge can be searched and ensured by various legal mechanisms: The form of the knowledge may be protected by copyright, which excludes its publication by others. The content of the knowledge (if it is an invention, new and commercially applicable) may be protected by patent rights. Privatization is also obtainable through the protection of trade secrets. Inversely, an author may waive his/her copyright and allow further publication of his/her work by introducing it into the public domain. Concerning patent rights, he/she may desist from applying for such rights or provide use licenses at no or low royalties.

Interpreting commercial/non-commercial in the context of the Nagoya Protocol

Against the background of the various terms and definitions, we will now explore what the Nagoya Protocol might mean when it employs, in Article 8 (a), the distinction between commercial and non-commercial research. As a starting point for suggesting an interpretation, the objectives of the access and benefit-sharing concept in the CBD and NP should be identified. These objectives are that providers shall have a share in the benefits drawn from genetic resources (GR) and traditional knowledge (TK), and that they can use their sovereign rights of regulating access to GR and TK in order to ensure *ex ante* that benefit sharing takes place. On the other hand, users shall be allowed to accede to and work on GR and TK. The distinction between commercial and non-commercial is introduced for the sake of structuring the modalities of access regulation, benefit sharing, compliance enforcement and monitoring. It should help, in particular, to distinguish between facilitated and normal access conditions, between non-monetary and monetary benefits, between different kinds of monitoring (such as reporting duties and checkpoints), and between different instruments of ensuring compliance in effect (such as through administrative supervision or the enforcement of contracts).

It may be noted that several States have indeed introduced national ABS legislation recognizing simplified measures for non-commercial research according to Article 8 NP, such as Brazil, Indonesia, Australia, Ethiopia and Ecuador (see table in IUCN 2012, 120/121).

Applying first the *institutional approach*, "non-commercial/commercial" could be defined as to mean research by public or private institutions. However, as already pointed out, the private or public institutional setting may often indicate but does not per se determine what kind of research (basic or applied, of economic value or not) will be conducted and what kinds of benefits (non-monetary/monetary) will accrue. Therefore, in view of the objectives of the terms, the institutional approach is not appropriate.

Better suited seems to be the *content-related approach* and the *yield-related approach*, which are based on the distinction of the term "basic" (or fundamental/

6 See von Kries and Winter on "Harmonizing ABS conditions under UNCLOS and CBD/NP", Ch. 4 in this volume.

applied, research/development, precompetitive/competitive, scientific/commercial and non-monetary/monetary). They would perceive the working on GR and TK as a process from basic research via the development of products to their patenting and marketing. This perception has well characterized R&D in the past. However, with the advent of genomics and the extension of the intellectual property concept to nature-forms, the "old" distinction has been blurred (Kamp 2004, 63, 64). Already at the stage of analyzing the genome, their functions (and thus applicability of uses) may be identified. A gene and its function can be patented and thus made a source of royalty payments. The synthesis of the gene and the gene itself can be offered as marketable services and products. Inversely, a researcher whose final purpose is application and commercialization may, as a first step, be willing to do research for the pure gain of new knowledge and share this freely with the research community (Kamp 2004, 54). There is, of course, still a wide array of "basic" research in the sense that its results do not yet have a commercial value, such as biological research on organisms and ecosystems, but economic value nowadays emerges at earlier stages than before. The early phase of fundamental research can thus not automatically be associated with non-commercial research. Hence, the distinction between commercial and non-commercial should not be attached to the traditional sequence of steps of R&D.

We are thus left with the fourth option – the *functional approach*. It appears indeed to be the most appropriate. The potential economic value of a genetic resource should not be determinative, but rather the intention, whether that value be realized or not. Arico and Salpin (2005, 33) also suggest the functionality criterion when they conclude that "the difference of regime lies in the treatment of research results". The UN Secretary-General stresses that "the difference between MSR and bioprospecting therefore seems to lie in the use of knowledge and results of such activities, rather than in the practical nature of the activities themselves" (Secretary General 2005, para. 202; also Treves 2008, 1).

Distinguishing between the public domain on the one hand and privatization for capitalization on the other, the functional definition captures benefits whenever they emerge. If the benefits are in the public realm – most often these will be non-monetary benefits – access is open to the public, providers being free to make use of them like anybody else. Provider states may feel that this is not sufficient reward for them. But then they may demand to somewhat restrict the publication of results or ask for privileged access to the public domain. In contrast, if the benefits are in the private realm – they will normally be monetary benefits – the provider must secure a share bilaterally by way of setting conditions in the access permit and contract.

Testing the functional definition in the Nagoya Protocol

We will now discuss whether the functional definition of commercial/non-commercial research is compatible with the relevant provisions of the Nagoya Protocol. We will in turn examine the regulation of access, the sharing of benefits, the assurance of compliance, and monitoring.

Regulation of access

In relation to the regulation of access, Article 8 NP is relevant which states:

> In the development and implementation of its access and benefit-sharing legislation or regulatory requirements, each Party shall:
>   (a) Create conditions to promote and encourage research which contributes to the conservation and sustainable use of biological diversity, particularly in developing countries, including through simplified measures on access for *non-commercial* [emphasis added] research purposes, taking into account the need to address a change of intent for such research; . . .

The terms "non-commercial research" and, by implication, "commercial research" are used here at the stage of acceding to GR (and, incidentally, also TK). The aim of the paragraph is to simplify the regulatory regime of access if non-commercial research is envisaged.

It should be noted that Art. 8 (a) NP has research in mind that "contributes to the conservation and sustainable use of biological diversity". This corresponds to the system of objectives of the CBD. The sharing of benefits from the utilization of genetic resources is not an absolute right but is contextualized by the two other objectives, the conservation of biodiversity and sustainable use (Art. 1 CBD). Likewise, the sovereign rights of states over their natural resources as recognized by Art. 15.1 is immediately followed by the duty enshrined in Art. 15.2 to "endeavour to create conditions to facilitate access to genetic resources for environmentally sound uses". This means that facilitation of access is strongly related to the objective that knowledge should be generated which helps to conserve and sustainably use the resources. Such knowledge can best serve these goals if it is publicly available. Thus, it appears to be public domain research which is meant by "non-commercial" in Art. 8 (a) NP.

As said earlier, "to conduct . . . development" (*viz.* of products) can also be non-commercial. Although Art. 8 (a) NP only refers to research, states should nevertheless consider simplifying access also for activities aiming at the "development" of products, the use of which is publicly available and free.

Looking from the provider state perspective it may not always be attractive to just be part of the general public and have as such free access to the knowledge and products. After all, it was its resources that were provided to the public. However, by appropriate clauses in the access consent and/or agreement the provider state may ask for special conditions, like prior information on knowledge to be published, duties of users to explain results, inclusion of personnel in the research, etc.

There is a risk, however, that published knowledge will result in products and monetary benefit drawn from them without the provider state being able to track this down to the GR/TK provided by it. In order to cope with this risk, the provider state may require the user to transfer come-back clauses to third parties that use knowledge from the public domain. As this is difficult to implement, the provider state may alternatively ask the user to keep the knowledge private for both the provider and the user, based on trade secret protection or even joint patenting.

All these variants of provider strategies are still related to the functional definition, notwithstanding whether the provider opts for the public domain or the privatization of knowledge. Thus, the functional definition appears to be the most suitable concerning the access regime.

This result is also supported by the suggestion of the ABS-Working Group of Legal and Technical Experts on Concepts, Terms, Working Definitions and Sectoral Approaches (WG-ABS 2008). The non-commercial research was characterized by this group as follows:

a)   willingness to disclose the scope and methods of research projects,
b)   eagerness to engage provider country research institutions and researchers in projects,
c)   willingness to provide access to research results to the provider country and international research community,
d)   interest in providing training and technical assistance to provider countries with the goal of building their national research capacities,
e)   commitment to transparency and open sharing of benefits, without proprietary ownership of any potential commercial benefits stemming from the research, and
f)   explicit agreement to a default benefit-sharing arrangement for unanticipated commercial benefits, or willingness to inform provider countries if any unanticipated potential commercial benefits are uncovered and to renegotiate the ABS agreement to include a new benefit-sharing arrangement for commercial intellectual property rights.

In conclusion, we propose that the terms "non-commercial" and "commercial" be understood in the functional sense, i.e. by looking at whether the GR material and knowledge are to be publicized or privatized. This means that a provider state should require in its PIC and MAT that the researcher promises to submit any research results to the public domain. If this is the case, the provider state does not need to precisely circumscribe and restrict the allowed kinds of research. For instance, traditional taxonomy as well as modern genomics would be part of the allowed research activities. Moreover, it would be of no concern if access is sought by public or private research institutions or financed through public or private sources. Of course, a come-back clause would have to be included for cases of change of intent from public domain to privatization.

It is, in the opinion of the authors, also sufficient to rely solely on the functional criterion. Greiber et al. (2012) however suggest adding a content-related criterion to it. In this view commercial research

• is normally designed to produce at least some results and benefits that will have real or potential commercial value, and
• creates benefits that are held privately rather than entered into the public domain and are restricted in different forms (Greiber et al. 2012, 118).

While the second attribute circumscribes the functionality discussed above, the first recurs to the substantive approach that relates to the content of the research activity. We do not consider this necessary because (1) public domain research also produces results with potential (financial) value, since it is inherent in the object of research ("genetic resources" are genetic material of actual or potential value); (2) commercial research can also be "basic" as a first step producing "only" non-monetary benefits; and (3) the formulation is rather imprecise in using vague terms such as "normally" (what are the exceptions?), "at least some results" (how many to fulfil this criterion?), "will have . . . value" (no precise time period). The application of this attribute is thus difficult to handle.

Benefit sharing

Concerning the regulation of benefit sharing Article 5.1 NP is relevant which says:

> In accordance with Article 15, paragraphs 3 and 7 of the Convention, benefits arising from the utilization of genetic resources as well as subsequent applications and *commercialization* [emphasis added] shall be shared in a fair and equitable way with the Party providing such resources that is the country of origin of such resources or a Party that has acquired the genetic resources in accordance with the Convention. Such sharing shall be upon mutually agreed terms.

The provision introduces the obligation to share benefits resulting from GR. The activities generating benefits are the utilization and subsequent applications and commercialization. (Subsequent) commercialization is here juxtaposed to utilization (i.e. according to Article 2 NP, any research and development including biotechnology) and (subsequent) application. This appears to indicate that the substantial definition which refers to the valorization chain of GR is the one meant in this paragraph.

However, this would imply that benefits from earlier phases in the valorization chain cannot be "commercial". For instance, patents on genes identified in the course of basic research that yield license money would not qualify as commercial benefits. Though they would still be subject to the benefit-sharing obligation, the terminology would be very confusing because these clearly monetary benefits would qualify as non-commercial. This would be understandable with regard to access fees, fees to be paid to trust funds, and research funding (Annex to the NP No. 1 a), f) and h)), because such payments should cover the costs of research, collections, data banks, etc. and are thus elements of managing the public domain. But the patenting of genes etc. is a business operation that should be captured by the term "commercial". It is therefore more appropriate to employ the functional definition also in the realm of Article 5. This would mean that the words "as well as subsequent applications and commercialization" is only to be understood as a reminder and even emphasis that the "subsequent" steps in the valorization sequence are also included, but that it is not excluded that commercialisation may also occur at the stage of fundamental research.

The adoption of the functional definition would also help to solve a riddle posed by paragraphs 2 and 5 of Article 5. These paragraphs are concerned with genetic resources held by indigenous and local communities (ILCs) as well as with TK of ILCs. They extend the obligation to share benefits from these particular resources only for the utilization of GR and TK (i.e. R&D including biotechnology) but do not – other than in paragraph 1 – mention the stages of subsequent application and commercialization. The omission may be explained by the difficulty the negotiating parties expected concerning the tracing of benefits back to local GR and TK, but this does not justify cutting back the sharing obligation to benefits from non-applied basic R&D. This shortcoming can be solved if the functional definition is applied. It would allow regarding benefits capitalizing on the utilization of local GR and TK (i.e. R&D plus biotechnology) as commercial and thus also subject to the benefit-sharing obligation. Moreover, it would also allow including the "subsequent application and commercialization" into the notion of utilization. This would be perfectly in line with the mother convention of the NP, the CBD, because its Article 15.7 extends the benefit-sharing obligation to "the benefits arising from the commercial and other utilization of genetic resources". Likewise, Article 8 (f) CBD refers to benefits from any "utilization" meaning that also commercial utilization is covered. It is hardly imaginable that within the Nagoya negotiations the resource states were willing to retire from a position they had already seized under the CBD. Thus, the cited provisions of the CBD remain intact, complementing the somewhat amputated provisions of the NP and supporting the making use of the functional definition of commercial/non-commercial.

Duty to ensure compliance

Concerning the duty to ensure compliance, the relevant provision is Article 15.1 NP which says:

> Each Party shall take appropriate, effective and proportionate legislative, administrative or policy measures to provide that genetic resources utilized within its jurisdiction have been accessed in accordance with prior informed consent and that mutually agreed terms have been established, as required by the domestic access and benefit-sharing legislation or regulatory requirements of the other Party.

Article 15 does not explicitly make use of the terms commercial & non-commercial. It may however be considered as implicitly doing this because other than in Article 5.1 NP it does not mention "subsequent applications and commercialization". This is widely understood to mean that the obligation of user states to ensure compliance in effect (and not just by monitoring) only extends to non-commercial utilization (i.e. R&D plus biotechnology) (Buck & Hamilton 2011; cf. Kamau, Fedder & Winter 2010). The same would be true in relation to TK of ILCs because the pertinent Article 16 NP also does not refer to "subsequent applications and commercialization".[7]

This interpretation unduly privileges the capitalization of GR and TK. It would mean that the user state is only required to supervise R&D processes but not the patenting and marketing of products derived from them. In consequence, the duty to ensure benefit sharing would exclude from its realm precisely those benefits which are the most sought after by provider states, i.e. monetary benefits from the placing of R&D results on the market. This may be seen as a negotiation success of user states, but it is one that is one-sided and likely to create mistrust among provider states.

Against this, the application of the functional definition would provide a more equitable solution. Its beneficial role already probed in relation to Article 5 (1) NP could be extended to Article 15. In other words, the material duty to share benefits (Article 5) and the enforcement duty to ensure benefit sharing (Article 15) would run parallel and relate to both the phase of R&D and "subsequent application and commercialization", because any capitalization, be it early or late in the valorization sequence, would be covered. In conclusion, user states are obliged to ensure compliance with provider state access legislation in relation not only to R&D but also to the obtaining of property rights and the placing on the market of R&D results.

That this solution is being accepted by state practice shows the EU Regulation No. 511/2014/EU which in Article 7 (2) provides that "at the stage of final development of a product developed via the utilization of genetic resources or traditional knowledge associated with such resources, users shall declare to the competent authorities . . . that they have fulfilled the obligations under Article 4," which are to comply with provider state access requirements.

Duty to monitor

The duty to monitor is regulated by Article 17.1 NP which lays out:

> To support compliance, each Party shall take measures, as appropriate, to monitor and to enhance transparency about the utilization of genetic resources. Such measures shall include:
>
> (a) The designation of one or more checkpoints, as follows:
> (i) Designated checkpoints would collect or receive, as appropriate, relevant information related to prior informed consent, to the source of the genetic resource, to the establishment of mutually agreed terms, and/or to the utilization of genetic resources, as appropriate;

---

7 Special attention was not paid to GR of ILCs by Articles 15 to 18 NP. This means that Article 15.1 is applicable, requiring that user states see to compliance with any provider state requirements, but that they do not bear a self-standing duty to ensure benefit sharing with ILCs.

    (ii)   – (iii) . . .

    (iv)   Checkpoints must be effective and should have functions relevant to implementation of this subparagraph (a). They should be relevant to the utilization of genetic resources, or to the collection of relevant information at, *inter alia*, any stage of research, development, innovation, pre-commercialization or commercialization.

The provision asks for monitoring by states – and notably by user states – through the designation of checkpoints. These checkpoints shall collect information *inter alia* concerning the utilization of GR (i) and, more specifically, information at any stage of research, development, innovation, pre-commercialization and commercialization (iv). By alluding to the sequence of steps it appears that this provision once more uses the content-related definition of "commercial/ non-commercial". But it would certainly not exclude that commercialization can already occur at earlier steps. It is therefore suggested that the functional definition should also command Article 17 NP. This implies that the mentioning of "pre-commercialization" and "commercialization" is not constitutive of the term but only a reminder and emphasis that all aspects of the utilization of GR, and in particular the last steps, shall be covered by the monitoring.

    A beneficial implication of this suggestion is that it gives subparagraph (i) a useful effect which would otherwise be missing. For if one understood the words "pre-commercialization" and "commercialization" in the substantial sense, this would mean that information on them, while still having to be collected, would be of no avail because there was no corresponding duty to ensure compliance in effect for which the information could be used. The information would, so to

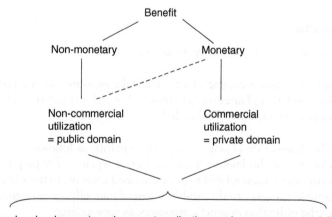

Figure 3.1 Overview of terminology

Source: *Own illustration*

speak, hang in the air. In contrast, with the functional definition such information would be about commercial utilization and thus be valuable for enforcing compliance, related also to later stages of the valorization chain.

Conclusion

It is an impossible task to develop an abstract categorization of research without respecting the objectives of the special field of research and research policy. This is due to inconsistent terminology in the legal texts, different approaches to research classification within and between research disciplines, and a different understanding of the dimension of the freedom of research on the European and national levels.

Classifying the types of research and development according to the functional approach will, as we have seen, best solve the tension between non-commercial and commercial utilization of GR as regulated by the Nagoya Protocol. It is the intention to release R&D results to the public domain or keep them proprietary which predetermines (a) if access shall be simplified or not, (b) if non-monetary or monetary benefits shall be provided to the provider state, (c) to which extent states shall ensure compliance and (d) to which extent states have a duty to monitor.

References

Arico, S, Salpin, C (2005) *Bioprospecting of genetic resources in the deep seabed: Scientific, legal and policy aspects*, UNU-IAS Report, http://i.unu.edu/media/unu.edu/publication/28370/DeepSeabed1.pdf (accessed 4 November 2014).

Bernsdorff, N (2011) "Article 11" in: Meyer, J (ed.) *Kommentar zur Charta der Grundrechte*, 3rd ed., Baden-Baden: Nomos, pp. 270 *et seq.*

Blankenagel, M (2001) *Wissenschaft zwischen Information und Geheimhaltung – über einen blinden Fleck in den Lehren zu Art. 5 Abs. 3 GG*, Sinzheim: Pro Universität Verlag.

Buck, M, Hamilton, C (2011) 'The Nagoya Protocol on Access to Genetic Resources and the Fair and Equitable Sharing of Benefits Arising from their Utilization to the Convention on Biological Diversity', *Review of European Community and International Environmental Law* 20(1), pp. 47–61.

CBD WG-ABS, 2008, Report of the Meeting of the Group of Legal and Technical Experts on Concepts, Terms, Working Definitions and Sectoral Approaches, UNEP/CBD/WG-ABS/7/2.

Collaborative Drug Discovery (CDD), 2012, Announcement of World Pharma Innovation Congress, accessible at www.collaborativedrug.com/buzz/2011/11/30/world-pharma-innovation-congress-2012.

Dickert, T (1991) *Naturwissenschaften und Forschungsfreiheit*, Berlin: Duncker & Humblot.

DOW MicroB3 (2011) Description of Work of workpackage 8, accessible at www.microb3.eu/work-packages/wp8 (accessed 3 November 2014).

EU Commission (1986) "Framework on state aids for research and development", *Official Journal*, C 83/02, p. 5.

EU Commission (2007) Proposal for a Council Regulation setting up the Innovative Medicines Initiative Joint Undertaking, COM(2007) 0241 final.

EU Commission (2008) Communication to the Council and the European Parliament – A strategic European framework for international science and technology cooperation, COM(2008) 0588 final.

EU Commission (2011) Proposal for a Regulation of the European Parliament and of the Council establishing Horizon 2020 – The Framework Programme for Research and Innovation (2014–2020), COM(2011) 809 final.

European Economic and Social Committee (EESC) (2000) Opinion on the "Communication from the Commission to the Council, the European Parliament, the Economic and Social Committee and the Committee of the Regions – Towards a European Research Area", 2000/C 204/16.

European Economic and Social Committee (EESC) (2007) Opinion on Investment in Knowledge and Innovation (Lisbon Strategy), 2007/C 256/04.

European Economic and Social Committee (EESC) (2008) "Opinion on the 'Green Paper on the European Research Area – New Perspectives" COM(2007) 161 final, *Official Journal* C044/01, 16/02/2008, pp. 01–11.

Greiber, T et al. (2012) *An explanatory guide to the Nagoya Protocol on access and benefit-sharing*, Gland, Switzerland: IUCN.

Kamau, EC, Fedder, B, Winter, G (2010) "The Nagoya Protocol on access to genetic resources and benefit sharing: What is new and what are the implications for provider and user countries and the scientific community?", *Law, Environment and Development Journal* 6(3), pp. 248–263.

Kamp, M (2004) *Forschungsfreiheit*, Berlin: Duncker & Humblot.

OECD (2002) Frascati Manual, Proposed Standard Practice for Surveys on Research and Experimental Development, 6th edition, 23 and 50 et seq. (cited "Frascati 2002"). Available at www.oecd-ilibrary.org/science-and-technology/frascati-manual-2002_9789264199040-en (accessed 13 October 2014).

Regulation (EU) No 511/2014 of the European Parliament and of the Council of 16 April 2014 on compliance measures for users from the Nagoya Protocol on Access to Genetic Resources and the Fair and Equitable Sharing of Benefits Arising from their Utilization in the Union, OJ L 150, p. 59.

Secretary General (2005) Conservation and sustainable use of marine biological diversity, A/60/63/Add.1.

Treves, T (2008) Marine scientific research, www.wsi.uni-kiel.de/de/lehre/vorlesungen/matz-lueck/seerecht/materialien/reading-assignment-no.-9 (accessed 4 September 2013).

United Nations (Division for Ocean Affairs and the Law of the Sea) (2010) *The law of the sea. Marine scientific research – A revised guide to the implementation of the relevant provisions of the United Nations Convention on the Law of the Sea*, New York: Author.

4 Harmonizing ABS conditions for research and development under UNCLOS and CBD/NP

Caroline von Kries and Gerd Winter

Introduction

When introducing national legislation on access and benefit sharing (ABS) concerning marine genetic resources, provider and user states must comply with the provisions of two international regimes, the Convention on Biological Diversity (CBD), including its Protocol of Nagoya (NP), and the United Nations Convention on the Law of the Seas (UNCLOS). Neither of these regimes actually oblige provider states to introduce such legislation: They can decide to allow free access to and free utilization of their genetic resources.[1] If a provider state did establish ABS legislation, user states may be obliged to regulate their research and development (R&D) on genetic resources accessed in the provider state. Our focus will be whether and in what respect the two regimes differ concerning provider and user state rights and obligations or allow for harmonized solutions.

We will start with a general characterization of the two regimes in relation to R&D on marine genetic resources. As the question is crucial on where to draw a line between two categories of R&D activities, one being concerned with commercialization and the other not, we will define the two categories and compare the rules applicable to them in relation to access and benefit-sharing requirements, taking differences related to different maritime zones into account.

Overview of UNCLOS and CBD/NP

UNCLOS

The UNCLOS establishes a comprehensive set of rules for all activities that may occur in the marine realm. Its objective is not only to contribute to the maintenance of peace and justice in the ocean space, but also to promote the equitable utilization of ocean resources and the protection and preservation of the environment (UNCLOS, preamble, paras 1, 4). It thus introduces a delicate balance

---

1 Regulation of access may however be obligatory under environmental protection regimes such as the Convention on International Trade in Endangered Species (CITES).

between the principle of state sovereignty over natural resources and the principle of common concern and use.

Within its substantive scope of application, the UNCLOS covers on the one hand the exploration and exploitation of non-living and living natural resources which also comprise genetic resources (Dux 2011, 97) and other economic activities, such as the production of wind energy. On the other hand, the UNCLOS creates a special legal order for marine scientific research (MSR) reflecting the importance of marine science "for eradicating poverty, contributing to food security, conserving the world's marine environment and resources, helping to understand, predict and respond to natural events and promoting the sustainable development of the oceans and seas" (UN 2010, at (iii)).

The regulatory regime is geographically divided into different maritime zones: the territorial sea and the contiguous zone, the exclusive economic zone (EEZ), the continental shelf, and the area beyond national jurisdiction (ABNJ) which comprises the high seas and the "Area".

The nearer a maritime zone is to the coast, the stronger the rights of the coastal state to regulate access to marine genetic resources. Whereas the coastal state has full national sovereignty over its territorial sea, it has less regulatory power regarding its EEZ and even less regarding the part of the continental shelf which lies beyond the EEZ. The ABNJ is open for free use from any state except for the Area with its common property regime which however does not (yet) apply to uses of genetic resources. In all maritime zones, use rights are in certain ways subject to general obligations to allow for common marine R&D.

CBD/Nagoya Protocol

The CBD introduces a global regulatory mechanism for the conservation and sustainable use of biological diversity without addressing a special part of the earth mass. As it thus covers the marine realm as well, its geographical scope of application overlaps with the UNCLOS.

While the UNCLOS deals with non-living and living (marine) resources, the CBD focusses on biological (marine and terrestrial) resources. Thus, both conventions address uses of marine biological resources.

While the UNCLOS is primarily concerned with the fair allocation of resource uses to different states and humanity in general, the CBD primarily establishes obligations to protect the resources. However, insofar as genetic resources are concerned, the CBD and – more elaborately – the NP also have the fair allocation of resource use in mind. Thus, there is overlap not only of scope but also of basic approach.

Concerning the geographical variation of provisions the CBD/NP also know distinctions, albeit less sophisticated than the UNCLOS. Sovereign rights of coastal states on genetic resources are acknowledged in the territorial sea and the exclusive economic zone (Art. 4.1, Art. 15.1 CBD), but not in the ABNJ. On the other hand, obligations to undertake cooperative research and share research results are applicable in relation to all areas. Thus, there is also considerable similarity between the UNCLOS and the CBD/NP concerning the geographical differentiation of their provisions.

Conflicts between the UNCLOS and CBD/NP regimes

In cases of conflicting rules, Art. 22 CBD applies, which reads:

1   The provisions of this Convention shall not affect the rights and obligations of any Contracting Party deriving from any existing international agreement, except where the exercise of those rights and obligations would cause a serious damage or threat to biological diversity.
2   Contracting Parties shall implement this Convention with respect to the marine environment consistently with the rights and obligations of States under the law of the sea.

While in relation to other conventions the CBD reserves priority if "serious damage or threat to biological diversity" is caused, there is no such reserve in relation to the UNCLOS. This deference to the UNCLOS has become more and more outdated with the increasing decline of biodiversity. The preservation of the natural conditions of life must have priority over the rights of exploitation of the same.

A way out in this situation is to have a closer look at whether there is a conflict at all, or, in other words, to rather search for ways of mutual concordance of interpretation and filling in of regulatory gaps. In addition, concerning MSR, the UNCLOS itself encourages contracting parties to enter into international agreements which facilitate research (Art. 243 UNCLOS). Could the CBD and the NP be considered as such agreement? We will come back to this question later in the chapter.

Categories of R&D on genetic resources

As said, both regimes regulate marine R&D but attach different rules to two categories of R&D which shall – not yet using the terms of the two conventions – be called public domain and proprietary.

Marine scientific research under the UNCLOS

The UNCLOS has a chapter on marine scientific research (MSR) (Articles 238 et seq.), but does not define the term. MSR is commonly regarded as an "activity that involves collection and analysis of information, data or samples aimed at increasing mankind's knowledge of the environment, and is not undertaken with the intent of economic gain" (UNEP/CBD/SBSTTA/8/INF/3/Rev.1, para 47). These criteria are also reflected in Article 246.3 UNCLOS which obliges the coastal state to give its consent to MSR if it is carried out, *inter alia*, "in order to increase scientific knowledge of the marine environment for the benefit of all mankind". It is obvious that the benefit for all mankind can only be achieved if data and research results are disseminated through the public domain and may thus freely circulate (Vitzthum 2006, 235).

Albeit the interest of the global community in public domain MSR might be high, special rules with a more restrictive approach are reserved for MSR "of direct significance for the exploration and exploitation of natural resources" (Article 246.5 (a) UNCLOS). Although the terms exploration and exploitation are not defined in the Convention, it is evident from the rules that are attached to them (Articles 56, 77 UNCLOS) that the regulated activity essentially focuses on the commercial use of the collected resources. The coastal state wishes to preserve its rights to explore and exploit the resource on its own.

Yet, it must still be clarified what the words "of direct significance" for exploration and exploitation mean. Significance is the importance of something, especially when it has an effect on what happens in the future. It appears that it "objectively" refers to the content of the research rather than "subjectively" to the intention of the researcher. Concerning the word "direct", the United Nations Division for Ocean Affairs and the Law of the Sea suggests in a guidance paper that this should be understood to mean that a project "can reasonably be expected to produce results enabling resources to be located, assessed and monitored with respect to their status and availability for commercial exploitation" (UN 2010, 10).

While this objective understanding is perfectly appropriate for bulk uses of marine resources, such as fish for consumption and oil for energy production, it is problematic with regard to genetic resources. Even basic research on the functions of genes could then be considered as being of "direct significance for the exploration and exploitation" of the genetic resource. This would mean that modern genomics research would be fully grasped by the sovereign rights of the coastal state. Such understanding would largely render the principle of free MSR void. In order to pay tribute to this principle, we suggest that a subjective element should be added to the objective reading. This would be that "direct significance" is understood to also refer to the intentions of the researchers: If the researcher does not intend to commercialize her research results, her research is not of direct significance for the exploration and exploitation of genetic resources.

As discussed in Chapter 3 of this volume (von Kries and Winter), commercialization is only possible if the asset that shall be sold for money is first of all removed from the public. It must be kept private before it can be sold. Assets which are already in the public domain cannot once again be sold to the public because nobody would spend money on something he or she already possesses. Therefore, commercialization can be equated to making something proprietary, or privatizing it.

In conclusion, normal MSR on marine genetic resources in the sense of Art. 238 UNCLOS should be understood to be research intended to submit results to the public domain, and MSR "of direct significance for the exploration and exploitation of natural resources" should be understood to be research, the content of which is of commercial value and the intention of which is to realize that value. As such, commercialization presupposes the privatization of the research results (such as through patent rights or private property in resulting products) and the relevant MSR can be termed proprietary.

Utilisation and research for non-commercial purposes under the NP

In Article 2 NP (use of terms) "utilization of genetic resources" is defined as "conducting R&D on the genetic and/or biochemical composition of genetic resources, including through the application of biotechnology". The Protocol does not contain a list of the kinds of R&D, as was envisaged in prior deliberations (Kamau, Fedder, & Winter 2010, 251).

While there is a discussion if commercialization activities are also covered by the term utilization, it is sufficient for the purpose of our study to state that the term utilization does include intentions to commercialize at the stage of R&D (see further von Kries and Winter in Ch. 3 of this volume). Thus, "utilization" includes R&D activities for commercial as well as for non-commercial purposes. "Utilization" in this sense is subject to the standard access conditions established by the NP, in particular PIC and MAT. For non-commercial research, however, a special provision was introduced requiring provider states to simplify access conditions (Article 8 (a) NP). This means that for non-commercial research different rules might apply. This necessitates to define what commercial/non-commercial research means.

The NP is silent on a definition of these terms. As mentioned above, we suggest defining non-commercial and commercial following the intention of the researcher to submit the research results to the public domain or use them for proprietary purposes (von Kries and Winter in Ch. 3 of this volume; CBD Group of Technical and Legal Experts (GTLE) information document (2008)). This has also won support in the literature and political practice. For instance, Arico/Salpin (2005, 33) conclude that "the difference of regimes lies in the treatment of research results." The UN Secretary-General likewise argues that "the difference between MSR and bioprospecting therefore seems to lie in the use of knowledge and results of such activities, rather than in the practical nature of the activities themselves" (Secretary General 2005, para. 202; Treves 2008).

By implication we suggest that also "development" activities on genetic resources can aim for the public domain. Therefore, although Art. 8 (a) NP only speaks of non-commercial research, it should be kept in mind that there can also be non-commercial "development" (von Kries and Winter in Ch. 3 of this volume). It is not covered by the obligation under Art. 8 (a) to simplify access, but provider states should consider to extend such simplified conditions to non-proprietary development.

Distinguishing between putting the research results in the public domain on the one hand and privatization of the results for capitalization on the other captures benefits whenever they emerge. If the benefits are in the public realm – most often these will be non-monetary benefits – access is free and open to the public, providers being able to make use of them like anybody else. If the benefits are in the private realm – they will normally be monetary benefits – the provider must secure a share bilaterally by way of setting conditions in the access permit and contract.

Unforeseen use (change of intent to commercial use) or disclosure or transfer to third (commercial) parties may nevertheless pose a problem even in application of the functional distinction. This can however be solved by concluding in the ABS agreement that the user must come back to the provider for renegotiation of the contractual conditions for use and of respective rules for eventual obligations of third parties (see further Kamau in Ch. 17 of this volume).

Comparison

From the above analysis of the terminology which the two conventions use with regard to scientific research on marine genetic resources, it can be concluded: The difficulty to decide if an activity falls under the one or the other category can in both cases be mastered with the functional definition – regardless of the differences in terms the two conventions use. "Marine scientific research" (UNCLOS) and non-commercial research (NP) both aim at increasing the knowledge of all mankind and sharing the benefits (i.e. the research results) with the global community. In contrast, "exploration/exploitation" (UNCLOS) and "commercial" utilization (NP) aim at increasing the proprietary knowledge of the user or third parties and reserving for them the benefits of their proprietary sphere. Concerning MSR with direct significance for exploration/exploitation, we suggest categorizing this as proprietary research and development (R&D), assuming that the results will normally be held in the private domain.

Legal effects attached to the categories of R&D

Having in mind how the terminology of UNCLOS and CBD/NP can be harmonized, we will now examine their regulation of the entire R&D process, including support principles, access requirements, R&D conduct standards, and benefit-sharing obligations. As said before, the focus will be on provider and user state rights and obligations.

Right to and support of research

According to UNCLOS, Arts. 2 and 56, provider states have sovereign rights over their genetic resources. These rights include also the regulation of R&D. This is specified in Part XIII of the UNCLOS as follows: In relation to their territorial sea coastal states,

> in the exercise of their sovereignty, have the exclusive right to regulate, authorise and conduct marine scientific research [. . .].
>
> (Art. 245 UNCLOS)

In relation to their EEZ and the continental shelf coastal states,

> in the exercise of their jurisdiction, have the right to regulate, authorise and conduct marine scientific research [. . .] in accordance with the relevant provisions of this Convention.
>
> (Art. 246 UNCLOS)[2]

The sovereign rights to regulate R&D are however not without limitations. These are, among others, set out in other provisions of the UNCLOS, as expressly stated in Art. 246 UNCLOS ("in accordance with the relevant provisions of the Convention") and implied in the structure of the UNCLOS which balances rights and obligations.

Such other provisions include Art. 239 UNCLOS which obliges the coastal state to "promote and facilitate the conduct of marine scientific research". In areas beyond the territorial sea states shall "endeavour to adopt reasonable rules, regulations and procedures to promote and facilitate marine scientific research" (Art. 255 UNCLOS). Moreover, according to Art. 238 UNCLOS, states, including other states, and international organizations have the right to conduct MSR. This right is qualified by the clause that it is "subject to the rights and duties of the coastal state", which means that not only its right to regulate R&D but also its obligation of facilitation is to be considered (UN 2010, 7).

The CBD/NP regime does not have explicit provisions on sovereign rights of coastal states to regulate R&D. But such rights are implicit in their sovereign rights on their biological resources (Art. 15.1 CBD) and somewhat more detailed by specifying these rights in relation to access to the genetic resources and benefit sharing (Art. 15.1 CBD and Arts. 5 and 6 NP). The rights are limited by the duty to "facilitate access to genetic resources for environmentally sound uses" (Art. 15.2 CBD) and "to promote and encourage research which contributes to the conservation and sustainable use of biological diversity" (Art. 8(a) NP). In addition there is an overall obligation for states to "monitor, through sampling and other techniques, the components of biodiversity . . ." (Article 7 CBD).

In conclusion, it can be said that both regimes, while recognizing sovereign rights of coastal states over their genetic resources, put an obligation on these states to support marine research. The UNCLOS goes a bit further by framing this obligation as a right of third countries. But such right could by appropriate interpretation also be derived from the objective obligation under the CBD.

---

2 See also Art. 56 UNCLOS which reads: "In the exclusive economic zone, the coastal State has: [. . .] (b) jurisdiction as provided for in the relevant provisions of this Convention with regard to: [. . .] (ii) marine scientific research; [. . .] 2. In exercising its rights and performing its duties under this Convention in the exclusive economic zone, the coastal State shall have due regard to the rights and duties of other States and shall act in a manner compatible with the provisions of this Convention."

Access requirements

Regarding the access conditions, the coastal state can require prior informed consent under both the UNCLOS and the CBD/NP, regardless of the maritime zone (except ABNJ) in which the sampling shall take place. Yet, the UNCLOS establishes a more differentiated consent system than the NP.

As said before, in the territorial sea the coastal state enjoys "the exclusive right to regulate, authorize and conduct full sovereignty" (Art. 245 UNCLOS). More specifically,

> Marine scientific research therein shall be conducted only with the express consent of and under the conditions set forth by the coastal State.
>
> (Art. 245 sentence 2 UNCLOS)

This means that the coastal state has full discretion to allow or not to allow any envisaged project (Rothwell, Stephens, 2010, 75, 327). The reasons for denying access can be very diverse, including environmental protection, participation of domestic researchers in the R&D activities, ensuring benefit sharing, and even the reservation of any R&D for its own research institutions. Reinforcing this right, Article 19.2 (j) UNCLOS stipulates that passage through the territorial sea becomes non-innocent if it involves any unpermitted research or survey activities. Of course, the coastal state is not obliged to introduce such restrictions, but it is entitled to do so. It is true that there are, as said above, limiting provisions but these appear to be very generally framed so that violations in concrete cases are hardly imaginable (Fedder 2013, 81). For instance, if a third state wishes to have access to genetic resources of a provider state arguing that the provider state is under duty to "promote and support marine scientific research" (Art. 239 UNCLOS), then this state could normally answer that it fulfils this duty by its own marine R&D.

Concerning access to genetic resources in the EEZ and on the continental shelf, the coastal state has the right to require prior consent (Art. 246.2 UNCLOS) but is, more than concerning the territorial sea, under duties to provide its consent. Here, the difference between public domain and proprietary research comes into play. The consent is obligatory "under normal circumstances" if the project "is carried out for peaceful purposes and is intended to increase scientific knowledge of the marine environment for the benefit of all mankind" (Art. 246.3 UNCLOS). The consent is discretionary if the project is "of direct significance for the exploration or exploitation of non-living or living natural resources" (Art. 245.5 UNCLOS), which is proprietary research according to the terminology proposed above.

This shows that a researcher in the EEZ/on the continental shelf conducting a project for the public domain should be given privileged material and procedural requirements as compared to the territorial sea (cf. Martínez Gutiérrez 2011, 168).

In the NP, the respective PIC clause is contained in Art. 6.1. It implements Article 15.1 CBD and stipulates that a state may require prior consent for access to its genetic resources, notwithstanding whether these are found in the territorial sea, in the EEZ, or on the continental shelf.

Like Article 239 UNCLOS, the NP puts an obligation on provider states to create conditions to promote and encourage research with non-commercial purposes through simplified measures (Article 8 (a) NP). As we have seen above, the most appropriate criterion to distinguish non-commercial from commercial is the intention of the researcher: If the results of R&D are intended to be placed in the public realm, then Article 8 (a) NP applies with the conditions and consequences provided therein.

It is not defined what is meant by "simplified measures on access" in Article 8(a) NP. Some scientific experts at the COP-10 meeting proposed that the user state should be exempted from PIC or that a simple notification of the intended research project could be sufficient (CBD (COP 10 information document (2010)), but this did not win the support of provider states. The provider is thus under a general duty to simplify access but not under a precise obligation on how to provide it.

In comparison, the UNCLOS and the CBD/NP access regimes equally allow for free discretion of provider states concerning proprietary R&D in both geographic areas, they largely equally[3] limit the discretion of provider states concerning public domain research in the EEZ/on the continental shelf, but they vary somewhat concerning public domain research in the territorial sea: Whereas the UNCLOS acknowledges free discretion, the CBD/NP obliges to simplify access in that respect (Salpin 2013, 158).

We suggest that this difference can be bridged. The duties to simplify access according to Art. 15.2 CBD and Art. 8 (a) NP should be read as provisions of multilateral conventions that are binding on coastal states according to Art. 243 UNCLOS. Thus, a provider state which is party to both the UNCLOS and CBD/NP regimes would breach its international obligation if reserving full discretion to consent to public domain research in its territorial sea.

Table 4.1 Provider state rights and duties according to areas, research type and conventions (differences in italics)

	access for public domain R&D	access for proprietary R&D
Territorial sea	UNCLOS: discretion *CBD/NP: duty to simplify*	UNCLOS: discretion CBD/NP: discretion
EEZ/Cont. Shelf	*UNCLOS: duty to consent* *CBD/NP: duty to simplify*	UNCLOS: discretion CBD/NP: discretion

Source: Own illustration

3 The duty to simplify appears to be weaker than the duty to give access, but this will not make much difference in effect considering that the duty under Art. 246 para 3 UNCLOS is subject to "normal circumstances".

In conclusion, the UNCLOS and the CBD/NP regimes can be read to have equal rules on the right of provider states to require PIC and the limitations of this right in relation both to public domain and proprietary research.

Legal certainty

Both the UNCLOS and the CBD/NP regimes have rules that structure the form of access for the sake of legal certainty. These rules apply both to public domain and proprietary R&D.

The UNCLOS approach is to list the minimal information the user state has to submit in order to obtain the PIC of the provider state (Art. 248 UNCLOS). If within four months the provider state did not react, the consent is considered to be implied. The access is allowed after two more months (Art. 252 UNCLOS). The user must however notify the provider state of any change of intent. The CBD/NP regime does not specify what information must be submitted and does not provide for implied consent. However, this does not hinder the provider state to introduce an implied consent track. Inversely, a conflict arises when the provider state wants to introduce an explicit consent requirement in every case. This is allowed under the CBD/NP system but not under the UNCLOS system. We suggest that in this case the CBD/NP should once more be regarded as prevalent because it is a more specific convention in the sense of Art. 243 UNCLOS.

Some more conditions are aimed at legal certainty. While the UNCLOS only asks the provider state to decide without delay (Art. 246 para 3 sentence 2), the NP introduces several additional rules. According to its Arts. 6.3 and 13 provider states shall

- provide for legal certainty, clarity and transparency in domestic ABS legislation
- provide for fair and non-arbitrary rules and procedures on accessing genetic resources
- provide information on how to apply for prior informed consent (PIC)
- provide clear, cost-effective and timely decision making and recognition of a permit or its equivalence as evidence of PIC
- provide criteria and procedures for the involvement of indigenous and local communities
- establish clear rules and procedures for requiring and establishing mutually agreed terms
- designate a national clearing house which i.a. informs users about access conditions, and designate national authorities that i.a. are competent to issue access permits

In comparison, the UNCLOS leaves more leeway in the formal dimension. But the discretionary margin can be interpreted to be structured by the more specific NP.

Benefit Sharing

According to Art. 5 NP,

> benefits arising from the utilisation of genetic resources as well as subsequent applications and commercialisation shall be shared in a fair and equitable way with the Party providing such resources.

Benefits can be non-monetary and monetary, as listed in the Annex to the NP. The UNCLOS contains obligations to share benefits although in a less-prominent way and with less attention to monetary benefits.

As neither convention prescribes priorities, the parties are free to agree on the benefits that are most suitable in exchange for the granting of access. We suggest they should take case studies into account which show that provider states reap greater advantage from participation in research, technology transfer and professional exchanges than from expecting monetary payments (Hayes 2007, 700; contributions by Beck in Ch. 10 and Lorenz and Tjoa in Ch. 13 in this volume).

Collaboration with national scientists

The collaboration with scientists from the provider state is explicitly required in Article 23 NP as an associated obligation to technology transfer. The states shall "collaborate and cooperate in technical and scientific research and development programmes, including biotechnological research activities", and "undertake to promote and encourage access to technology by, and transfer of technology to, developing country Parties". The states may also specify similar obligations by PIC and MAT under Article 6.3 (g) (iii) NP.

Within UNCLOS there is, on the one hand, a rather broad requirement to promote international cooperation between states (Art. 242.1 UNCLOS), on the basis of "mutual benefit". On the other hand, the specific right is conferred on the coastal state to participate in public MSR projects in the EEZ on the continental shelf, including being represented on board research vessels (Art. 249.1 UNCLOS). In return, the coastal states shall facilitate access to their harbours and promote assistance for marine scientific research vessels (Art. 255 UNCLOS).

A full chapter is dedicated to technology transfer and capacity building (Articles 266 et seq. UNCLOS). It can be read to also cover biotechnology. It is separated from the chapter on MSR, so these duties are not in mutual relationship to the exercise of marine scientific research. They suggest, for instance, "the development of human resources through training and education of nationals of developing States and countries and especially the nationals of the least developed among them" (Article 268 (d) UNCLOS).

The sharing of research results with the provider

In the framework of the NP, a duty to share research results with the coastal state can be established by consent conditions and mutually agreed terms (Art. 5 NP). The UNCLOS makes a difference between the territorial sea, where the sharing of research results may be required at the discretion of the coastal state, and the EEZ and the continental shelf, where results from public MSR shall be delivered and explained to the coastal state (Article 249.1 (b–d) UNCLOS). Whether explicitly backed by international provisions or not, the provider state can in any case require by consent condition that it shall be informed about the research results.

Publication of results

The obligation to publish research results through open access forums is in principle implied in the notion of research for non-commercial purposes under Article 8(a) NP; an active duty is however not explicitly foreseen.

In the UNCLOS, there is a general obligation to publish research results from public domain research but again only for research on resources from the EEZ and the continental shelf (Art. 249.1 (e) UNCLOS). Interestingly, the right of the coastal state to veto publication in the case of proprietary R&D is explicitly laid down (Art. 249.2 UNCLOS), though this right is already part of the general discretionary power of the coastal state to regulate the MSR concerning its economic interests. This and the other listed benefit-sharing commitments in the article may thus be seen as a kind of negotiation material for determining the conditions for proprietary use (Gorina-Ysern 2003, 2).

Sharing of monetary benefits

As already mentioned, the NP foresees the duty to share monetary benefits with the provider state (Article 5 NP), which may consist of access fees, upfront payment or license fees in case of commercialization (annex to the NP). They may be specified by PIC and MAT.

The UNCLOS does not prescribe an explicit duty to share monetary benefits. The message of Articles 249.2 and 253.2 UNCLOS however implicitly indicates that the coastal state has much leeway to introduce in its national legislation an obligation for the commercial researcher to share benefits. According to these provisions, the coastal state may forbid the distribution of information which may be economically relevant and has the right to require the cessation of activities if they amount to major changes in the project.

Art. 241 UNCLOS appears to even go further by stipulating that research activities "shall not constitute the legal basis for any claim of any part of the marine environment or its resources" (Article 241 UNCLOS). This provision might be interpreted to be an obstacle for commercial research that aims at keeping results confidential or having them protected by intellectual property rights. In fact, the clause must be understood to exclude exclusive rights at least on the collected genetic resources as such, if not also on products and procedures developed on their basis. Yet, the clause implies that such claims can be subject to negotiation (Gorina-Ysern 2003, 2). It is, for instance, imaginable that the coastal state gives the user state its consent to the proprietary use of the genetic resources under condition of ownership sharing.

In conclusion, although there are differences in detail, the two regimes largely converge in enabling provider states to condition their PIC on the sharing of benefits. In particular, provider and user states are encouraged to share non-monetary benefits such as joint participation in the research activities and the sharing of research results.

Ensuring compliance

One of the primary objectives of the NP is to impose obligations on user states to ensure compliance with the provider state's access conditions. The relevant duties are specified by Arts. 13, 15–18 NP. Their core is that user states shall monitor if genetic resources utilized within their jurisdiction have been accessed in accordance with provider state law, and that they shall correct any breaches of the same. They shall also provide dispute settlement institutions enabling provider states to enforce mutually agreed terms, especially concerning any conditions on the sharing of benefits.

The UNCLOS does not establish specific obligations of user states to ensure compliance, but a general duty to respect the sovereign rights and their legal emanations of provider states is implied in the binding character of the convention. For the rest, the more specific rules of the NP can be applied in the UNCLOS context as filling in a regulatory gap of the UNCLOS. Considering that Art. 243 UNCLOS refers to the creation of "favourable conditions for the conduct of marine scientific research in the marine environment" it can be argued that such favourable conditions include both provider and user state obligations.

In addition to these user state obligations, the NP introduces a multilateral mechanism of compliance control, the international clearing house. It has been established at the CBD secretariat and shall, according to Art. 14 NP, collect and disseminate information on access and benefit sharing in general as well as on individual cases. Such multilateral mechanism is not foreseen in the UNCLOS. But the NP mechanism can be regarded as filling in a gap within UNCLOS (Salpin 2013, 161).

Model clauses and codes of conduct

By default of any further precision of the Protocol's access regulation, the states are encouraged to develop contractual model clauses and ABS codes of conduct (Articles 19, 20 NP) which may then, along with national access and benefit-sharing legislation, be distributed among the States through the Clearing-House Mechanism (Article 14 NP). This includes the CBD Clearing-House[4] – an agency that brings together seekers and providers of goods, services, or information, thus matching demand with supply – and a network of national clearing-houses.

---

4 www.cbd.int/chm/default.shtml

A provision similar to Articles 19 and 20 NP is also laid down in the chapter on MSR within UNCLOS. According to its Article 251, the states "shall seek to promote through competent international organizations the establishment of general criteria and guidelines to assist States in ascertaining the nature and implications of marine scientific research". In both conventions we therefore have a multilateral and institutional approach concerning the exchange and establishment of common criteria for scientific research on genetic resources.

Conclusion

In summary, both the UNCLOS and the CBD/NP regimes establish comprehensive rules that balance the interests of the players concerned. The provisions give the contracting Parties the necessary tools at hand to produce well-designed PIC and ABS agreements.

Although the conventions use different terminology, both the NP and the UNCLOS differentiate the regulatory regimes along two kinds of research: public domain and proprietary. In both conventions, the decisive criterion for distinguishing the regimes is not the content of the research but the intention to keep R&D results private or make them public.

Both regimes oblige to promote research, and both of them allow provider states to establish a PIC requirement. In relation to proprietary research, both regimes give the provider state full discretion to provide or not to provide its PIC. The CBD/NP regime demands to simplify access for research for the public domain. The UNCLOS does about the same concerning the EEZ and the continental shelf, but reserves more discretion concerning the territorial sea of the coastal state. This gain of sovereign rights should however be interpreted to be dissolved by the more specific CBD/NP.

The UNCLOS, unlike the NP, stresses peaceful aims in the conduct of research. It also puts emphasis on the duty to cooperate, especially with developing states. This duty is also present in the NP, although less specific. The sharing of results from public research with the Provider is an important obligation in both conventions, in the NP as part of the duty to share non-monetary benefits and in the UNCLOS by explicit provision in Art. 249.1.

The publication of results is implied in the notion of non-commercial research (Article 8 NP), but there is no active duty to publish, whereas in UNCLOS there is a general obligation to publish results of research in the EEZ/on the continental shelf. In the case of proprietary research the coastal state has the right to veto publication (Article 249.2 UNCLOS).

Monetary benefits shall, under the NP, be shared according to mutually agreed terms. In UNCLOS, there is no general duty to oblige the recipient to share monetary benefits; nevertheless, the coastal state is free to require them via PIC conditions. The adoption of come-back clauses in cases of change of intent is foreseen under the NP (for public domain research) and under the UNCLOS (for any R&D). Under UNCLOS, the coastal state may, in the case of unlawful research, require the suspension or cessation of activities (and renegotiate); this is not explicitly foreseen by the NP but may be laid down in PIC conditions and MATs.

Both conventions oblige provider and user states to ensure legal certainty concerning ABS conditions in various ways.

Summing up, while UNCLOS and CBD/NP start with different basic philosophies – the first aiming at a balance between the sovereign rights of the coastal state and the general interest in free marine research, the sharing of benefits being of minor importance (Wolfrum & Matz 2000, 458), and the other introducing a clear *do ut des* system – the two conventions do not, in effect, differ very much. Where differences exist they can be bridged by mutually concordant interpretation, or regulative gaps can be filled by reference to the other regime, or else, if a conflict does appear, the CBD/NP with its focus on the genetic potential of living resources can be regarded as *lex specialis* as acknowledged by Art. 243 UNCLOS. There is no need to recur to the conflict resolution provision under Art. 22 CBD that would give the UNCLOS priority over the CBD/NP regime.

As a practical consequence, national access and benefit-sharing legislation can cover both, terrestrial and marine genetic resources, without having to create special regulations for the marine realm.

References

Arico, S, Salpin, C (2005) Bioprospecting of genetic resources in the deep seabed: Scientific, legal and policy aspects, UNU-IAS Report, http://i.unu.edu/media/unu.edu/publication/28370/DeepSeabed1.pdf (accessed 4 November 2014).

Dux, T (2011) *Specially protected areas in the exclusive economic zone (EEZ): The regime for the protection of specific areas of the EEZ for environmental reasons under international law*, Berlin: LIT Verlag.

Fedder, B (2013) *Access and benefit-sharing in the marine realm*, London: Routledge.

Gorina-Ysern, M (2003) Legal issues raised by profitable biotechnology development through marine scientific research, *American Society of International Law*, www.asil.org/insigh116.cfm (accessed 8 October 2013).

Hayes, M (2007) "Charismatic microfauna: Marine genetic resources and the law of the sea" in: Nordquist, M et al. (eds.), *Law, science and ocean management*, International Law E-Books online, pp. 683–700.

Kamau, EC, Fedder, B, Winter, G (2010) "The Nagoya Protocol on access to genetic resources and benefit sharing: What is new and what are the implications for provider and user countries and the scientific community?", *Law, Environment and Development Journal* 6(3), pp. 248–263.

Martínez Gutiérrez, NA (2011) *Limitation of liability in international maritime conventions*, London: Routledge Chapman & Hall.

Rothwell, D, Stephens, T (2010) *The international law of the sea*, Oxford: Hart.

Salpin, C (2013) "The law of the sea, a before and an after Nagoya?" in: Morgera, E et al. (eds), *The 2010 Nagoya Protocol on access and benefit-sharing in perspective*, Leiden: Martinus Nijhoff, pp. 149–184.

Treves, T (2008) Marine scientific research, www.wsi.uni-kiel.de/de/lehre/vorlesungen/matzlueck/seerecht/materialien/reading-assignment-no.-9 (accessed 4 September 2013).

United Nations (Division for Ocean Affairs and the Law of the Sea) (2010) *The law of the sea. Marine scientific research – A revised guide to the implementation of the relevant provisions of the United Nations Convention on the Law of the Sea*, New York: Author.

Vitzthum, WG (2006) *Handbuch des Seerechts*, Munich: C.H.Beck.

Wolfrum, R, Matz, N (2000) "The interplay of the United Nations Convention on the Law of the Sea and the Convention on Biological Diversity" in: Frowein, JA, Wolfrum R (eds), *Max Planck Yearbook of United Nations Law*, Den Haag: Kluwer Law, pp. 445–480.

Legal Acts and Documents

CBD COP 10 information document (2010) Report of a scientific experts meeting on access and benefit sharing in non-commercial biodiversity research, UNEP/CBD/COP/10/INF/43.

CBD Group of Technical and Legal Experts (GTLE) information document (2008) Concepts, Terms, Working Definitions and Sectoral Approaches Relating to the International Regime on Access and Benefit Sharing, UNEP/CBD/ABS/GTLE/1/INF/2.

Secretary General (United Nations Division for Oceans Affairs and the Law of the Sea) (2005) Conservation and sustainable use of marine biological diversity A/60/63/Add.1.

Part II

Exemplary national legal frameworks

5 Research on genetic resources in the framework of the Brazilian ABS law*

Carlos Alberto Pittaluga Niederauer
and Manuela da Silva

The law regulating ABS in Brazil

The historical context

Access to genetic resources and benefit sharing in Brazil is regulated by Provisional Act 2186–16 of August 23, 2001 (Medida Provisória 2186, MP) (Brasil 2001a). In the Brazilian legal system, provisional acts are normative acts with legal force and can be adopted by the president of the republic in cases of relevance and urgency. The MP was edited for the first time in June 2000 and re-edited 16 times until a constitutional amendment was issued, resulting in the current version.

What led Brazil to regulate access to genetic resources by means of a provisional act was an episode considered as biopiracy that occurred in May 2000, one month before its first publication. That episode was the conclusion of a contract between the Swiss pharmaceutical company Novartis Pharma AG and "Bioamazonia", a social organization created by the Brazilian government, according to which Novartis would finance equipment acquisition and collecting, isolation and characterization of microorganisms on a large scale from the Amazonian region. In return, Bioamazonia would transfer to Novartis the rights of access and exclusive use of these microorganisms for the development of pharmaceutical products (Peña-Neira, Dieperink, & Addink 2002). The agreement had a negative impact on public opinion and was considered detrimental to Brazilian interests (Azevedo 2005; Filoche 2012). Based on this, the Brazilian government edited the MP hastily, ignoring law proposals that had been at the National Congress since 1995 (Guedes & Sampaio 2000), and the contract between Novartis and Bioamazonia was cancelled (Azevedo 2005; Filoche 2012).

The outcome of this revision of the MP was a piece of legislation with too many requirements and unclear definitions, resulting in diverging interpretations. Accordingly, academia and the productive sectors have been highly critical of this development (Colli 2003; Morales 2010; Barreto 2012).

---

* The information and views presented in this chapter are those of the authors and do not necessarily reflect the official opinion of CNPq, Fiocruz, or even CGEN/MMA.

The main features of Provisional Act 2186

In accordance with the Convention on Biological Diversity (CBD), mainly its articles 8j and 15, and with the Brazilian Federal Constitution, the MP regulates:

a) access to genetic heritage;[1]
b) the protection and access to associated traditional knowledge;
c) benefit sharing; and
d) access to technology and technology transfer for the conservation and sustainable use of biological diversity.

The MP also regulates the shipment abroad of the genetic resource being accessed.

One of the main devices of the MP is Article 16, as it determines who can access Brazilian genetic resources and what the requirements are prior to the authorization of access. This Article also determines that the authorization may only be granted to Brazilian institutions with the infrastructure and qualified staff to perform research and development in the biological sector and related areas. This means that authorizations are granted to the legal entity, not to its researchers. On the other hand, foreign institutions can only access Brazilian biodiversity in partnership with a Brazilian institution that, for all legal purposes, will be responsible for the activities of access to genetic resources.

Concerning the location of the genetic resource, Article 16 establishes that the authorization of access and shipment shall be granted with the prior consent of:

a) the indigenous community involved, after consulting the official Indian affairs body (National Indian Foundation – FUNAI), when the access occurs in indigenous lands;
b) the environmental competent body, when access occurs in an environmental protected area;
c) the owner of the private area, when the access occurs there;
d) the National Defense Council, when the access takes place in an area essential for national security; and
e) the maritime authority, when the access takes place in Brazilian jurisdictional waters, on the continental shelf and in the exclusive economic zone.

The MP established the Genetic Heritage Management Council (CGEN) within the Ministry of the Environment as the competent national authority for ABS. It also established the necessity of prior authorization by CGEN for access to genetic resources and associated traditional knowledge for the purpose of

---

1 MP uses the term "genetic heritage" instead of "genetic resources" due to the Brazilian Federal Constitution, which states the need "to preserve the diversity and the integrity of the genetic heritage of the country and supervise the entities dedicated to research and handling of the genetic material" (item II, § 1°, Article 225, Federal Constitution).

scientific research (non-commercial research), bioprospecting and technological development (commercial research), as well as its shipment abroad.

In the case of bioprospecting and technological development, the prior informed consent (PIC) of public and private providers is required, including from indigenous and local communities, for access to genetic resources and traditional knowledge associated with genetic resources. When there is potential for economic gain from the use of products and processes resulting from access to genetic resources and associated traditional knowledge, mutually agreed terms (MAT) must be signed by the provider and the user to ensure the fair and equitable sharing of benefits. Both PIC and MAT, along with the detailed research project on access (including introduction, justification, objectives, methodology, expected results of access, identification of the involved institutions, schedule of milestones, sources of funding, etc.), must be submitted to CGEN. If the research project, PIC and MAT demonstrate coherence and the MAT follows the MP requirements, CGEN endorses MAT and access can be performed.

The MP was implemented and regulated by five decrees.[2] Two of them are essential: Decree 3945 of September 28, 2001 (Brasil, 2001b), and Decree 5759 of June 7, 2005 (Brasil, 2005). Decree 3945 outlines additional rules for accessing and using genetic resources and defines the composition of CGEN, which is constituted by representatives from nine ministries and ten federal organizations, including federal research institutions and organizations that represent traditional communities. The Decree also establishes CGEN attributions and provides regulations for its operation.

Regarding the misappropriation or misuse of genetic resources, Decree 5459 imposes disciplinary sanctions against practices and damaging activities to the genetic resources and/or to the associated traditional knowledge (Brasil 2005).

Since its establishment in April 2002, CGEN has made 40 Resolutions and 8 Technical Orientations in order to deal with specific aspects, as well as clarify inconsistencies and poorly defined terms and promote the implementation of the legislation.[3] Four of them must be mentioned: Technical Orientations 1, 4 and 6 and Resolution n° 21. They will be discussed in the next section.

Differentiation of commercial and non-commercial research and procedures

Differentiation of commercial and non-commercial research

Before looking at how commercial research is differentiated from non-commercial research in the Brazilian legislation, it is necessary to understand its definitions of "genetic resources" and "access to genetic resources".

2 The decrees establish norms for CGEN to work based on the regulation of several articles from the MP that deal with access to genetic resources, benefit sharing, etc.
3 The legislation is available on the website of the Ministry of the Environment at www.mma.gov. br/patrimonio-genetico/conselho-de-gestao-do-patrimonio-genetico/normas-sobre-acesso.

The MP defines genetic resources as

> information of genetic origin, contained in samples of all or part of a plant, fungal, microbial or animal species, in the form of molecules and substances originating in the metabolism of these living beings, and in extracts obtained from *in situ* conditions, including domesticated, or kept in *ex situ* collections, if collected from *in situ* conditions, within the Brazilian territory, on the continental shelf or in the exclusive economic zone.
>
> (item I, Article 7°, MP)

While access to genetic resources is defined as

> acquisition of samples of genetic heritage components for the purpose of scientific research, technological development, or bioprospecting, with a view to its industrial or other application.
>
> (item IV, Article 7°, MP)

On the other hand, Article 16 of the MP states: "Access to genetic heritage components . . . shall be had by collection of samples and information . . ." This formulation of the definition of access to genetic resources resulted in the interpretation that access would also comprise the collecting of genetic material, and it would therefore also need the prior authorization by CGEN. However, this authorization was already the responsibility of another environmental body and, consequently, the collecting would be subject to a second authorization. For this reason, CGEN edited Technical Orientation 1 in 2003 that defined the acquisition of samples of genetic heritage as activity conducted on the genetic heritage with the aim of isolating, identifying or using the information of genetic origin or molecules and substances derived from the metabolism of living beings and extracts from those organisms. Therefore, this Technical Orientation clarified the concept of access to genetic resources, distinguishing it from the act of collecting biological material. Essentially, it indicated that collecting is a field activity and access is a laboratorial activity.[4]

Furthermore, activities that did not imply the handling of the genetic material in the laboratory, such as morphological taxonomy, were still under the exigency of prior consent from CGEN. Thus, after pressure by academia, in 2006 Resolution 21 excluded some research and scientific activities from the concept of access to genetic resources. These included taxonomy, phylogeny and epidemiology, for the reason that they do not have the potential to provide commercial products or processes, therefore with no effect on benefit sharing, one of the three fundamental pillars of the CBD (see Kamau, Ch. 2 in this volume).

---

4 It is worth mentioning that the Brazilian and European definitions of "access" are fundamentally different. In Brazilian legislation, the term "access" means the same as the term "use" adopted by the European ABS framework and the term "utilization" by the Nagoya Protocol (Davis, Marinoni, & Fontes, 2013).

The research and activities listed in the Resolution n° 21 are:

I – research that aims to elucidate the evolutionary history of a species or taxonomic group from the identification of species or specimens, the evaluation of phylogenetic relationships, the assessment of the genetic diversity of the population or the relationship of living beings with each other or with the environment;

II – paternity tests, sexing techniques and karyotype analyses intended to identify a species or specimen;

III – epidemiological research or research that aims to identify the etiologic agents of diseases, as well as measurement of the concentration of known substances whose relative quantities in the body indicate disease or physiological state; and

IV – research intended to build DNA, tissues, germplasm, blood or serum collections.[5]

With the exception of the above activities, any other research that seeks knowledge without economic objective when accessing the genetic resource is defined as "scientific research", and thus not regarded as industrial or commercial activity.

Other two categories of research are regarded as commercial:

a) Bioprospecting: defined as an exploratory activity that aims to identify genetic heritage components and information on associated traditional knowledge, with potential for commercial use (item VI, Art. 7°, MP).

b) Technological development: defined as the systematic research, based on already existing knowledge, that aims at the production of specific innovation, the elaboration or modification of already existing products and processes, with economical application (Technical Orientation n° 4, May 27, 2004).

Bioprospecting was the only research category defined by the MP and it always caused controversy and concern among the scientific community because it was not clear how "potential for commercial use" should be understood. In principle, every study on chemical and/or biochemical components and their biological activity might have this potential (Palma & Palma 2012). Based on this understanding, many academic researchers would be discouraged because of great complications to obtain PIC and MAT, reinforced by the low probability of attaining products and processes with commercial interest.

Because of this situation, CGEN published Technical Orientation 6 in 2008 that considers the "potential of commercial use" of a determined component of the genetic resource to have been identified when the exploring activity confirms the viability of industrial or commercial production of a product or a process from

---

5 The English version of Resolution 21 is available in Davis, Marinoni, & Fontes 2013.

a functional attribute of this component. This, for example, is the case of investigations that start on the laboratory scale and then move to the industrial scale
when it is confirmed that a product or process could be explored economically,
allowing technological development (Filoche 2012).

Procedure for non-commercial and commercial research

To increase the CGEN's capacity to manage the ABS system, the council accredited other institutions to issue permits for access to genetic resources. The institutions are the Brazilian Institute for the Environment and Renewable Natural
Resources (Ibama) from the Ministry of the Environment, accredited in 2003, and
the National Council for Scientific and Technological Development (CNPq)
from the Ministry of Science, Technology and Innovation, accredited in 2009.
More recently, in 2011, the Institute of National Historical and Artistic Heritage
(IPHAN) from the Ministry of Culture was accredited for issuing permits for
access to associated traditional knowledge. Since IPHAN does not deal directly
with genetic resources, it will not be included in this discussion.

The permits for access to genetic resources are issued by the following organizations regarding each research category:

a)   Scientific research: Ibama and CNPq
b)   Bioprospecting and technological development (TD): CGEN and CNPq
c)   Scientific research, bioprospecting, or TD with associated traditional knowl-
     edge: only CGEN

The procedure for permit application from CGEN was regulated for the first
time in 2003, one year after CGEN had started its activities. In 2011, by means
of the Resolution 37, the process was modified. Essentially, the user has to fill out
a paper form; attach a detailed research project (description) highlighting the
activities and proposed research, the PIC and MAT (in the case of bioprospecting
and TD) and other documents; and send them by post to the Executive Secretariat
of CGEN. When the documents arrive, a protocol number is generated and sent
by e-mail to the applicant. Following the analysis of an eventual requirement for
confidentiality, the application for the permit is published in the Official Journal
of the Federal Government and on the webpage of CGEN. Only after this stage
does the Executive Secretariat evaluate if the documentation is complete and
whether it complies with the MP requirements. Otherwise, the applicant is given
a deadline of 60 days, extendable for an equal period of time, to solve the pending
issues. Next, the process proceeds to the ad hoc consultants. Following the evaluation, it is ready to be analyzed by CGEN. Eventually the permit is granted and
published in the Official Journal of the Federal Government.[6]

6 More details can be found at www.mma.gov.br/estruturas/222/_arquivos/res37_222.pdf.

When associated traditional knowledge is involved, the procedure is the same as described above, with the additional requirements of previous consent by the indigenous people or local communities and an independent anthropological report. For indigenous communities, the admission to their land must first be approved by the National Indian Foundation (FUNAI).

Ibama works in a similar way to CGEN in regard to scientific research. It also uses a paper form that has to be filled out and sent back to Ibama by post with a detailed research project (description) and other documents attached; in return, a paper permit is issued.[7]

CNPq has an electronic system for issuing permits that is simple, straightforward and fast; it will be discussed in detail below. Procedures and requirements for the permit application under the electronic system are established by CNPq Resolution 3 of 2012.[8]

Other than these authorizations granted for individual projects, which are defined as "simple", there is another category known as "special authorization". In this case, one single authorization is issued for a group of research projects developed by the same institution. Thus, a portfolio of the institution's projects is presented following the same requirements as for simple authorizations (see below). When there is a new project, it can be added to the already approved portfolio. However, this type of authorization is not valid for technological development.

The two categories of permit, simple and special, require two sets of documents: one specifically about the institution and another about the project. An advantage is that the institution has its documentation approved just once. It does not need to send it again, as is the case with the simple authorization. CNPq solved this limitation of the simple authorizations by creating an electronic form to record the institution data in a particular database. Thus, when a permit is requested, the information provided is automatically linked to the institution data in the database. Most of the authorizations granted by Ibama are special, making up around 95 per cent of all the permits granted by it.[9]

Additionally, the Brazilian ABS legislation has a specific regulation dealing with *ex situ* collections. A representative subsample of the accessed genetic resource shall be deposited in *ex situ* condition at a Brazilian public institution accredited by CGEN as trustee, in accordance with Article 11 and Article 16 of the MP and complementary legislation. Each collection must go through the accreditation process by CGEN to be recognized as a Trusted Depository Collection, even though the institution where it is located has already been accredited as trustee, and the same institution might have several *ex situ* collections.

7 More details can be found at www.ibama.gov.br/servicos/acesso-e-remessa-ao-patrimonio-genetico.

8 The Resolution n° 3 of CNPq is available at www.cnpq.br/web/guest/view/-/journal_content/56_INSTANCE_0oED/10157/551633 and more details can be found on www.cnpq.br/web/guest/acesso-ao-patrimonio-genetic.

9 More details can be found at www.ibama.gov.br/servicos/acesso-e-remessa-ao-patrimonio-genetico.

The deposit of subsamples has several objectives, among others the conservation and the traceability of the biological material. For instance, when a researcher accesses Brazil's genetic resources in Brazil or abroad, as allowed by the MP, a subsample of the genetic resource must be deposited in a Trusted Depository Collection before being shipped overseas.

The collection to be accredited has to prove the availability of infrastructure, technical capacity and funding for the conservation activities. At the end of 2013, CGEN had accredited 358 Trusted Depository Collections within 70 public institutions, most of them in universities.

Design and functioning of the CNPq online application

The time spent by CGEN for issuing authorizations has been criticized and is a huge drawback – some of them exceeding one year, mainly in cases when the purpose for access is bioprospecting or TD.

This delay prevents the celerity needed for the execution of scientific research and, mainly, for the technological development by enterprises that have to react quickly to a changing marketplace and to new scientific information and developments (Damond 2013). When Ibama was accredited in 2003, the possibility to accredit CNPq was also suggested. However, this took place only in 2009 after pressure from the scientific community.

CNPq was accredited with the challenge to issue authorizations faster and in a simpler, less-bureaucratic way. CNPq has the tradition of dealing with researchers, and the majority of authorizations are for non-commercial purposes with research being conducted mainly by universities and public research institutions. After the accreditation, the Executive Board of Directors of CNPq established two guidelines:

a) to create a sector to manage the authorization requests for the access to genetic resources; and
b) to process the requests and to grant authorizations electronically, avoiding the need of sending any document on paper, as it already happens with the projects financed by CNPq.

Therefore, the Coordination of the System of Authorization for the Access to Genetic Heritage (COAPG) was created with the mission to administrate the requests of access authorizations.

The System of Authorization for the Access to Genetic Heritage

A specific system was developed in order to allow the entire process to be conducted online and electronically, avoiding the need of sending any document on paper. Additional documents, such as the research project, the PIC and the MAT can be attached electronically to the proposal in specific fields. The authorization is also issued electronically.

Technically, the System of Authorization for the Access to Genetic Heritage is a functionality added to the Carlos Chagas Platform[10] of CNPq. The platform is the computerized management system of CNPq that has personalized *locus* according to the profile of each user. The users can be external or internal. Researchers, ad hoc consultants, advisory committees and directors of science and technology institutions are the external users. The internal users are the analysts and Executive Board of Directors of CNPq. For example, researchers can send and follow the progress of the application for project grants, sign electronically the term of grant and attach technical reports regarding the projects, since each request generates an electronic process with a specific code. The advisory committees work with an electronic spreadsheet which contains the whole process of a certain action of CNPq – postgraduate scholarship, for example. These spreadsheets contain links to the proposals, to the ad hoc consultant's evaluation and to the technical analysis. Internally, the technical and operative staff analyses are also performed with the Carlos Chagas Platform.

The System of Authorization for the Access to Genetic Heritage is subdivided in four modules. The first one is comprised of two online forms and is restricted to the legal representatives[11] for registration of their institutions and for the approval of authorization requests to access genetic resources. This stage is necessary because Decree 3.495 states that the authorization must be institutional. The basic requirement is that the institution must prove that it conducts research and technological development in biological areas and that it has adequate infrastructure for these activities.

The second module is used by the researchers and is comprised of four online forms for authorization request, one of them for requesting access for scientific research purposes, another for bioprospecting or technological development (TD) purposes. The last two are for the regularization of scientific studies executed without previous authorization, one of which is for finished research and the other for ongoing research. The regularization of activities regarding access to genetic resources and associated traditional knowledge is possible by means of Resolution 35 of 2011.

The third module is internal, for CNPq staff and its Executive Board of Directors. This module has three further online forms: one for a technical evaluation by the analysts, another for deliberation of the COAPG coordinator and the third for the decision of the Board.

---

10 The name of the platform is a tribute to the Brazilian physician and parasitologist who described, in 1909, the disease that carries his name, Chagas Disease, and identified its etiologic agent (*Trypanosoma cruzi*) and its insect vector (*hematophagous triatomine*). The discovery and the studies of the Chagas Disease were very important contributions to the knowledge and the international scientific debate on tropical diseases (www.museudavida.fiocruz.br/media/cartilha_chagas_portugues_site.pdf).

11 The legal representative is a person who can legally answer in the name of the institution before Justice, government, and others. At universities, for example, the legal representative is the dean or other person specifically designated by the university for this role.

The last module is external and is used exclusively by researchers who are CNPq ad hoc consultants and who receive the authorization request along with the evaluation of CNPq analysts.

To be able to use the electronic forms or any other service within the Carlos Chagas Platform, there is one basic requirement (for both external and internal users): to have an electronic *curriculum vitae* registered on Lattes Platform,[12] also of CNPq, known as the Lattes CV. This platform integrates into a single system of information the database of *curricula*, research groups, and science and technology institutions. In December 2013, the Lattes Platform held 2.8 million *curricula*, 33,000 research groups and 24,000 institutions.

Lattes CV became indispensable for students and researchers. It has been adopted by all Brazilian funding agencies, several universities and research institutes. It has become mandatory for analyzing the merit of any project proposal. Lattes CV is integrated with bibliographic databases (Scopus®, ISI Web of Knowledge℠, CrossRef®, SciELO) and to the patent database of the National Institute of Intellectual Property. Lattes CV is also used in eight other countries, in customized versions according to the characteristics of each. Four other countries are also interested in using the platform. Access http://lattes.cnpq.br/ to learn more about it.

Online forms for authorizations and regularization requests

The system, as described above, has four forms:

a)   Authorization for scientific research;
b)   Authorization for bioprospecting and/or TD;
c)   Regularization of scientific research in course; and
d)   Regularization of scientific research completed.

The forms are very similar and most of the fields are the same in all of them. The fields are:

a)   Coordinator of the project (linked to Lattes CV);
b)   Legal representative of the institution (recovered from the database of the institutions);
c)   Lattes CV of the research team (electronic address of the *curricula* if somebody does not have a Lattes CV);
d)   Project (title, objective, unclassified summary, keywords, project duration);
e)   Institutions (the ones conducting the access, service provider, partner);

12 The name of the platform is a tribute to the Brazilian physicist Cesar Lattes, who was part of the group that discovered the pi-meson, a subatomic particle that ensures the cohesion of the atom. The discovery marked the beginning of the physics of elementary particles or high-energy physics (www.cnpq.br/web/portal-lattes/cesare-giulio-lattes).

f) Attached documents: (i) detailed research project; (ii) permit for collecting, (iii) PIC and MAT (exclusive to bioprospecting and TD); and (iv) other documents (material transfer agreement, for example);

g) Complementary information (genetic resource to be accessed, geographic location of biological material, type and quantity of samples to be collected);

h) Provider of genetic resources (specific to bioprospecting and TD);

i) Trusted Depository Collection;

j) Sources of financing (funding agencies, private funding etc.); and

k) Declaration (ensuring the knowledge of the legislation and the veracity of the documents attached to the form).

CNPq has decided to include on the online form data judged essential for performing the analysis and that provide for generating a variety of reports. Thus, it is possible to relate all the authorizations from the same institution and to list others that participate in the projects, as well as to identify places of collecting biological material and the Trusted Depository Collections in which the samples are being preserved.

Several of these data are also required when presenting research projects to funding agencies (except items h, i and k, as well as PIC and MAT). Until the end of December 2013, CNPq had issued 223 authorizations for scientific research, of which 83.4 per cent were supported by Brazilian funding agencies. Therefore, researchers interested in obtaining the authorization replicate the data already given to the agencies, which means doing the same work twice. It is also clear that the information is of an academic nature; nevertheless, replicating the data is worthwhile for companies afraid to expose certain information considered strategic, such as the *curriculum* of their research. Although the legislation foresees the secrecy of some information, the conclusion is that a great deal of the information is of questionable utility and it should be distinguished between academia and enterprises.

Flow of requests, analyses and issue of authorizations

The request of authorization to access genetic resources, its analysis and the grant decision, can be summarized in six steps as explained below and shown in Figure 5.1.

Step 1: The researcher coordinating the project
for accessing genetic resources

The researcher responsible for coordinating the project for access to genetic resources logs onto the Carlos Chagas Platform and chooses the appropriate form – scientific research, for example – and attaches the detailed access project in a specific field, as well as other documents. If the purpose is bioprospecting or TD, there is an appropriate field to attach the PIC and MAT.

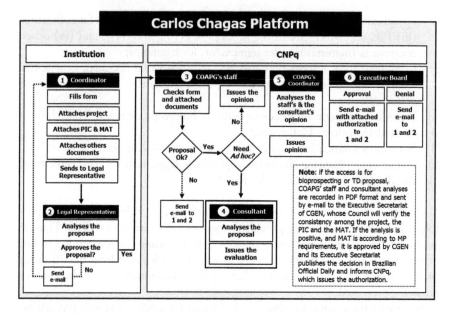

Figure 5.1 Flow of requests, analyses and issue of authorizations by Carlos Chagas Platform

Source: *Carlos Alberto Pittaluga Niederauer*

When the filling of the form is finalized, the researcher request becomes available to the legal representative of the researcher's institution and an electronic receipt is sent to the researcher with information on how to follow the request, and concurrently the electronic process is generated.

Step 2: Legal representative

If the legal representative disagrees with any information, the request is closed and the researcher is informed about the denial. If the legal representative agrees with the process, the request is sent to CNPq.

Step 3: Analysts of CNPq

In the case of scientific research, the analysis is just a mere document check – an evaluation from a specialist (Step 4) is rarely needed. However, when there is a commercial purpose, which is the case with bioprospecting or TD, more precautions are taken due to the benefit sharing with the provider of the genetic resource. This means the need to provide at least two additional documents: the PIC and the MAT. Both documents must be consistent with the research project. For this reason, a more accurate analysis is needed, including the evaluation of ad hoc specialists. For both scientific research and bioprospecting and TD, if there is any mistake/error or missing data/information on the electronic form, the analyst registers rejection. This is communicated to the project coordinator and to the legal representative by an automatically generated e-mail.

Step 4: Ad hoc Consultants

In case the analyst considers it necessary to obtain the opinion of specialists, a selection of consultants in the CNPq ad hoc database is undertaken. As they already have Lattes CVs, the system cross-references the information of the request with the ad hoc database, and selects those who have an affinity with the project. The system also excludes the ones who belong to the institution of the project coordinator, those who are in the project team and, even, those who by chance could have published in partnership with the coordinator of the project.

After the consultants are selected, they receive a standard e-mail informing them that the project refers to access to genetic resources. The consultant has two options: refuse the analysis (a justification is required) or accept it. In the first case, the project returns to the analyst in order to select a new consultant. Alternatively, when the acceptance is registered, a link to the proposal appears, and the consultant gains access to the full process in order to evaluate it; in the end, the evaluation can be registered in a specific electronic form.

Step 5: Coordinator of COAPG

In this step, the COAPG coordinator has the prerogative to disagree with the analyst's opinion and/or with the consultant's evaluation. If the decision is to overrule the request, the procedure is similar to the one conducted by the analyst (Step 3). If approved, the process follows to the decision of the Executive Board of Directors of CNPq.

Step 6: Executive Board of Directors of CNPq

In this stage, the Board is already in possession of the evaluations of the analyst, the consultants and the COPAG coordinator. If favourable, the authorization is signed digitally by the Life of Sciences director and becomes available to the project coordinator and to the legal representative on the Carlos Chagas Platform, and they are informed of this by e-mail automatically generated by the system.

Note: If the access is for bioprospecting or TD, the analyses conducted by the analysts and consultants of CNPq are recorded in PDF format and sent by e-mail to the Executive Secretariat of CGEN in order to verify the consistency among the detailed research project, PIC and MAT and whether the MAT follows the MP requirements. Only after these verifications are made can CGEN analyze the process. If the request is approved, the Executive Secretariat publishes the decision in the Official Journal of the Federal Government and informs CNPq, which issues the authorization. The Executive Secretariat of CGEN does not have an electronic system yet, but it is under development. When the system is ready,

CNPq intends to link it with the Carlos Chagas Platform, so that the Executive Secretariat and the members of CGEN can use the Carlos Chagas Platform facilities in order to accelerate the authorization process.

Issuing authorizations

The authorizations have a standard text with spaces to be filled by the system. There are two types of authorization, one for scientific research and one for bioprospection and TD. In general, both authorizations contain the following information: (i) data of the institution; (ii) data from the researcher who will coordinate access; (iii) the project team; (iv) project title; (v) specification, quantity, and geographic location of genetic material; (vi) trusted depository collection; and (vii) duration of the authorization. In addition to these data, the authorization brings critical information: deadlines for submission of reports of activities and rules to be observed for the shipment of biological material abroad. If during the study the possibility of industrial scale production is confirmed, authorization cancellation must be requested and a new authorization for bioprospection and TD has to be applied for. In this case, it is necessary to add data from the provider of genetic material and submit PIC and MAT.

In case of rejection, an e-mail is sent to the legal representative and to the project coordinator with details of the evaluation. Regarding system performance, the average time of issuing authorizations for scientific research has fallen every year. In the beginning, in 2010, it took 14 days and more recently, in 2013, it had fallen to 9 days. The average time is calculated after the legal representative forwards the authorization request to CNPq. It is still not possible to estimate the average time to issue permits for bioprospecting or TD due to the fact that CNPq was only recently authorized to deal with this. Therefore, there are very few of such requests, also due to the external step, the MAT analysis, conducted by CGEN.

The new modules of the system

The system still has three other modules under development:

- Technical Report: analyses and release of partial and final technical reports;
- Changes in the authorization: the inclusion, exclusion or modification of information in the authorization process, for example, including a new researcher to the project team or excluding a collecting site; and
- Extension of authorization deadline: in case of approval, CNPq issues another authorization with a new deadline. Otherwise, the researcher is communicated the denial.

These modules are essential to complete the system. There is still another module, a subsystem in fact, devoted to generating management and strategic reports. The reports have already been designed and will be built after the three modules described above are finalized.

Evaluation of the authorization process by CNPq

CNPq was accredited by CGEN in August 2009 and launched its system in March 2010. In May of that year, CNPq issued its first authorization. From then until the end of December 2013, 223 authorizations for scientific research were issued. In 2010, only 9 permits were issued; in 2011, 26; rising to 61 in 2012; and reaching 127 permits in 2013.

As was expected, the beginning was shy, mainly due to the unawareness of the existence of the system. Another reason might be that some institutions have chosen to continue using the special authorization from Ibama. Nonetheless, the researchers gradually realized the benefits of the CNPq system.

Data obtained from 223 permits show a high concentration – 96.9 per cent – of authorizations were issued to universities and public institutes of research and development. Still, 83.4 per cent of the 223 authorized projects received funding from agencies that support science and technology, and one of the MP requirements to receive the authorization is to inform the source of funding of the project. These numbers are not surprising because scientific research in Brazil is largely conducted by universities and public institutions that are funded primarily by public agencies.

According to preliminary data of the Executive Secretariat of CGEN, the number of authorizations issued by CGEN and its accredited institutions since 2003 is close to 900. Therefore, CNPq issued 25 per cent of the authorizations in the four years from 2010 to 2013.

Remaining challenges for non-commercial research and suggestions (or ideas) for further facilitation

Despite improvements within the current Brazilian ABS framework, there are still many challenges. There is a collective agreement on the need of a new ABS legislation with clear, simple and straightforward rules with less-bureaucratic approaches, able to establish an environment of tranquillity and safety for biodiversity users. In this way, allowing the creation of fair and sustainable use of the Brazilian genetic resources will ultimately lead to the effective conservation of biodiversity (Vélez 2010; Barreto 2012).

Other important challenges for the new legislation is to accommodate the different interests of the distinct segments affected by the current legislation, which include the government, the scientific community, the business sector and local and traditional communities. In addition, it should provide concrete instruments in order to stimulate research and technological development; monitor research activities without compromising celerity, which is essential for academia and the productive sector; and protect traditional knowledge, as well as the knowledge generated by academia and the productive sector.

Furthermore, taking into account that Brazil is a mega-diverse country, yet knows very little of this heritage, it also has the challenge to acquire the maximum knowledge of this biodiversity in the shortest length of time to use it in a sustainable way and protect it.

Since the establishment of CGEN, there were several initiatives to replace the MP. Currently, a new legal framework is under discussion that is intended to better reflect the reality of non-commercial and commercial research. One important change to which government, researchers and the business sector all agree is that prior authorization for non-commercial research should be replaced by a simple registration of the research. Therefore, the idea is to develop an electronic registration system for the intended research with basic information regarding it, which can be any study related to Brazilian biodiversity, including those listed in Resolution 21. Instead of a permit, the researcher will receive an automatically generated registration number after completing the registration form.

Under this scenario, the CNPq system can play a very important role, since its electronic forms can be easily adapted to register the research from universities, research institutions or enterprises. This can lead to a powerful database on all research conducted on the Brazilian biodiversity, allowing the monitoring of its utilization, which is strategic for Brazil, and to orient public policy formulation for biodiversity.

Conclusion

After almost 13 years of the current ABS legislation, it has improved thanks to norms that clarified terms and inconsistencies and promoted a better implementation of the legislation. Another fundamental positive factor was the accreditation of CNPq for granting permits and its simplified electronic system.

Nevertheless, it is evident that the Brazilian ABS framework urgently needs to be updated. It is unanimous among all sectors involved that the MP is complex, ambiguous and difficult to comprehend, leading to legal uncertainty. In addition, there is excessive bureaucracy and demand of information of questionable utility. The result of this situation is the discouragement of scientific research, technological development and innovation.

Although the tendency of the MP to protect content may be understandable, since it is meant to prevent biopiracy, the major criticism towards it might be of a strategic nature. Brazil has huge biodiversity, yet very restricted knowledge of this treasure. Therefore, we understand that the biggest challenge of the new legislation is to have clear and consistent rules associated with devices for stimulating scientific research, technological development and innovation, including aspects to attract foreign enterprises. This would boost, on the one side, the generation of a huge amount of knowledge in a short length of time and, on the other, would allow knowledge appropriation by the productive sector, generating income to the country, as the Brazilian agribusiness has been doing consistently. In this way, considering the CBD principles, the new ABS framework must target a sector that is viewed as the new industrial era – the bioeconomy.

Brazil already has laws that offer incentives for innovation and technological development, which should be lined up with the future genetic resources legislation. Besides being strategic for the country, this is an issue of sovereignty.

References

Azevedo, CMA (2005) "Regulation to access genetic resources and associated traditional knowledge in Brazil", *Biota Neotropica* 5(1), pp. 19–27.

Barreto, DW (2012) "Patrimônio genético brasileiro: protegê-lo ou aproveitá-lo comercialmente?", *Journal of the Brazilian Chemical* 23(2), pp. 194–196.

Brasil (2001a) Provisional Act No 2,186–16 dated 23 August 2001, www.mma.gov.br/estruturas/sbf_dpg/_arquivos/mp2186i.pdf (accessed 4 November 2014).

Brasil (2001b) Decreto n. 3.945 dated 28 September 2001, www.planalto.gov.br/ccivil_03/decreto/2001/d3945.htm (accessed 4 November 2014).

Brasil (2005) Decreto n. 5.459, dated 7 June 2005, www.planalto.gov.br/ccivil_03/_Ato2004–2006/2005/Decreto/D5459.htm (accessed 4 November 2014).

Colli, W (2003) "A lei de proteção ao patrimônio genético", *Ciência e Cultura* 55(3), pp. 44–46.

Damond, J (2013) Proposal for reform of Brazil's bioprospecting and genetic resources regulations, Biotechnology Industry Organization, www.bio.org/sites/default/files/BIO per cent-20Brazil per cent20Bioprospecting per cent20& per cent20Genetic per cent20Resources per cent20FINAL.pdf (accessed 4 November 2014).

Davis, K, Marinoni, L, Fontes, E (2013) Report on the workshop 'The role to be played by biological collections under the Nagoya Protocol' as part of the Project under the 6th EU/Brazil Sectorial Dialogue Support Facility, Brasilia http://sectordialogues.org/sites/default/files/acoes/documentos/relatorio_2a_oficina.pdf (accessed 4 November 2014).

Filoche, G (2012) "Biodiversity fetishism and biotechnology promises in Brazil: From policy contradictions to legal adjustments", *The Journal of World Intellectual Property* 15(2), pp. 133–154.

Guedes, AC, Sampaio, MJ (2000) Genetic resources and traditional knowledge in Brazil, UNCTAD Expert Meeting on Systems and National Experiences for Protecting Traditional Knowledge, Innovations and Practices, Geneva, http://r0.unctad.org/trade_env/docs/brazil.pdf (accessed 4 November 2014).

Morales, AP (2010) "Bioprospecção: Burocracia ainda emperra acesso ao patrimônio genético nacional", *Ciência e Cultura* 62(3), pp. 8–10.

Palma, CM, Palma, MS (2012) "Bioprospecção no Brasil: Análise crítica de alguns conceitos", *Ciência e Cultura* 64(3), pp. 22–26.

Peña-Neira, S, Dieperink, C, Addink, H (2002) "Equitably sharing benefits from the utilization of natural genetic resources: The Brazilian interpretation of the Convention on Biological Diversity", *Electronic Journal of Comparative Law* 6.3, www.ejcl.org/63/abs63-2.html (accessed 4 November 2014).

Vélez, E (2010) Brazil's practical experience with access and benefit sharing and the protection of traditional knowledge, International Centre for Trade and Sustainable Development, Policy Brief Number 8, http://ictsd.org/i/publications/79880/?view=document (accessed 4 November 2014).

6 Research on genetic resources and indigenous knowledge in the framework of the Kenyan ABS law

Experiences and opportunities

Mukonyi K. Watai, Veronica Kimutai, and Edwardina O. Ndhine

Introduction

Kenya is one of the richest mega-biodiverse countries in the world (Kenya Wildlife Service 2011). The country's unique landscapes and ecosystems offer a wide range of biodiversity that makes it one of the best destinations for non-commercial and commercial local and international researchers. The need for sustainable management of the world's biodiversity is critical for the survival of mankind, as well as for continued access of both biological and genetic resources for various uses. Among the various threats to biodiversity, the cost of conservation has been noted as a major challenge by provider countries. This calls for all countries to work together in order to ensure species survival. Initially biological specimens were viewed as freely accessible for all, but after the CBD, it is the sovereign right of each state to determine how access is conducted and to grant access.

To ensure effective conservation and sustainable utilization of the country's resources, the country has enacted various legislative acts on biodiversity management and continues to review them where it is possible to enhance clarity and legal certainty. Effective legislation increases compliance and enforcement and at the same time serves as an incentive for investments for conservation enhancement and livelihood improvement. Kenya has ratified various multilateral environmental agreements (MEAs) that are relevant to access and benefit-sharing regimes. This includes, among others, the CBD, Nagoya Protocol, ITPGRFA, International Union for the Protection of New Varieties of Plants (UPOV), CITES and WIPO treaties on intellectual property (IP). According to the Constitution of Kenya, any MEAs to which the country is party forms part of the country's laws. Its Chapter 1 Article 2 (5) states that "[T]he general rules of the international law shall form part of the law of Kenya" and Chapter 1 Article 2 (6) further states that "[A]ny treaty or convention ratified by Kenya shall form part of the law of Kenya under this Constitution." This means all MEAs relevant to ABS to which Kenya is party apply under the Kenyan law and have to be interpreted accordingly. Therefore, with the entry into force of the Nagoya

Protocol[1] (NP), which Kenya ratified on 1 May 2014, it forms part of the country's laws. The entry into force of the NP will significantly shape the access regime governing both genetic resources and associated traditional knowledge (ATK) in addition to the sharing of the resulting benefits. It is to be noted that the NP must be interpreted alongside the CBD.

According to Articles 5, 6, 7 and 8 of the NP and Article 15 of the CBD, access to genetic resources is subject to the prior informed consent of the Party providing such resources. Parties are obliged to put in place legislation and take administrative or policy measures, and in accordance with the Convention's Articles 16 and 19 as well as through the financial mechanisms established by Articles 20 and 21, with the aim of sharing in a fair and equitable way the results of research and development and the benefits arising from the commercial and other utilization of genetic resources with the providing Party.[2]

Whereas many provider countries have put in place access and benefit-sharing legislation, very few user countries have ABS systems in place. Those that have ABS legislations have not yet realigned them to the Nagoya Protocol of the Convention. For effective realization of the third objective of the CBD there is need for all countries globally to be party to the CBD and the Nagoya Protocol. Development of effective legislation covering both user and provider obligations through appropriate institutional arrangements and mechanisms will lead to effective conservation, sustainable use and equitable sharing and enjoyment by all of the global biodiversity. Unlike other treaties, such as WTO-TRIPS based on the IP regime and CITES, among others, a similar level of enforcement and compliance with strong support of both developed and developing countries has yet to be developed for ABS systems to guarantee maximum benefits to providers of genetic resources and ATK.

The Kenyan Constitution of 2010 emphasizes the need to promote sustainable exploitation, utilization, management and conservation of the environment and natural resources and ensure the equitable sharing of the accruing benefits. The Constitution further commits to protecting and enhancing IP on and indigenous knowledge of biodiversity and genetic resources. While there is need for facilitated access for basic and other types of non-commercial research, the dilemma is how to ensure that, after access has been granted, the exploitation of any natural resource of Kenya is undertaken in a sustainable manner, the environment is conserved and benefits arising from these activities are shared fairly and equitably with the people of Kenya as required by the Constitution (GOK 2010, Art. 69 (1) (a), (c), (h)).

Since 2006, the Kenyan government has domesticated the Bonn guidelines under the CBD through the enactment of the Environmental Management and

---

1 In full: Nagoya Protocol on Access to Genetic Resources and the Fair and Equitable Sharing of Benefits Arising from their Utilization to the Convention on Biological Diversity. The Nagoya Protocol entered into force on 12 October 2014.
2 For a detailed discussion on the international ABS framework see Kamau, Ch. 2 in this volume.

Coordination (Conservation of Biological Diversity and Resources, Access to Genetic Resources and Benefit Sharing) Regulations, 2006, which control access to biological and genetic resources including associated traditional knowledge. Access to biological material and associated knowledge is governed by prior informed consent (PIC), mutually agreed terms (MAT), material transfer agreements (MTA), and permits from the national competent authorities and lead agencies, in addition to other legal requirements. Practice shows that for the last few years, the applicants that have faced the most challenges are students on split programmes and applicants from countries that do not have ABS regimes in place. Some of the challenges have been on IP elements and aspects of specimen depository, compliance enforcement, monitoring and evaluation. The country's experience shows that clear systems of ABS between providers and users will facilitate both commercial and non-commercial research activities. Therefore, capacity building for both users and providers on ABS aspects is core.

Framework for management of biological resources

Constitution

In recognition of biological diversity and the traditional indigenous and local knowledge of communities on biodiversity, the Government of Kenya is not only committed to the protection of genetic resources and biological diversity but also emphasizes that it is every person's duty to cooperate and ensure ecologically sustainable development and use of natural resources (GOK 2010, Art. 69 (2)). The Constitution, which is the supreme law of the country, has provisions to protect genetic resources and biological diversity (GOK 2010, Art. 69 (1) (e)). It expresses the citizens will on how their biodiversity should be governed. This constitutes the basis for enactment of domestic legislations, policies and institutional arrangements.

The Constitution of Kenya gives guidance on access and use of traditional knowledge, recognition and protection of their intellectual input including compensation. Its Chapter 2, Article 11 (1), (2) recognizes culture as a foundation of the nation, and it gives the State the responsibility to promote cultural expression through literature, science and, among others, intellectual property rights (IPRs). It further recognizes the role of science and indigenous technologies in the development of the nation. Article 11 (3) empowers parliament to enact legislation to:

a) ensure that communities receive compensation or royalties for the use of their cultures and cultural heritage, and
b) recognize and protect ownership of indigenous seeds and plant varieties, their genetic and diverse characteristics and their use by the communities of Kenya.

Article 69 (1), (2) of the Constitution focuses on the sustainable use of the environment and effective management of the natural resources. In particular Article 69 (1) (a) and (c)–(f) state that the State shall:

a) ensure sustainable exploitation, utilization, management and conservation of the environment and natural resources and ensure the equitable sharing of the accruing benefits;
b) protect and enhance intellectual property in, and indigenous knowledge of, biodiversity and genetic resources of the communities;
c) encourage public participation in the management, protection and conservation of the environment;
d) protect genetic resources and biological diversity; and
e) establish a system of environmental impact assessment, environmental audit and monitoring of the environment.

Legislative acts

Access to genetic resources and ATK is currently governed by various legislations and subsidiary legislations. The major ones are:

I   The Environmental Management and Coordination Act (EMCA) No.8 of 1999 and its subsidiary legislation, namely the Environmental Management and Coordination (Conservation of Biological Diversity and Resources, Access to Genetic Resources and Benefit Sharing) Regulations of 2006, hereafter referred to as ABS regulations. The EMCA of 1999 provides for an appropriate legal and institutional framework which establishes the National Environmental Management Authority (NEMA) with a statutory mandate to oversee the coordinated management of the environment. The ABS regulations set out a permit requirement for access to genetic resources, as well as a duty of permit holders to share benefits.

II The Wildlife Conservation and Management Act 2013 provides for management, protection, sustainable use and conservation of wildlife resources in the country. The Act is broad, referring to wildlife including animals, plants and microorganisms or parts thereof that do not qualify as agricultural plants or livestock under the Agriculture Act and are not listed in Annex 1 of ITPGRFA. The Act addresses aspects of *in situ* biodiversity. It mandates the Kenya Wildlife Service (KWS) through the cabinet secretary to develop regulations towards effective management of wildlife resources in the country. The Act empowers KWS to manage national parks and national reserves and, where possible, in collaboration with county governments. Before the ABS subsidiary legislation, the Wildlife Management Authority was responsible for granting access permits to the country's genetic resources, but currently KWS grants prior informed consent for access in protected areas and to wild genetic resources, while NEMA gives the access permit. The prior informed consent includes mutually agreed terms and material transfer agreement on the country's wild genetic resources. The Wildlife Act 2013 includes provisions on utilizing the country's wild biodiversity and ATK belonging to the communities. Article 22 states that the KWS is a joint collaborator for utilization of the wild genetic resources. There are provisions for the formation of the Community Wildlife Conservation Association for guided benefit flows and for optimizing holistic conservation efforts. The Act also gives guidance on collection and exports of wildlife specimen and the need to come up with guidelines. Based on previous experiences of biopiracy and poaching, the Act has imposed heavy fines and punishments in the event of noncompliance. In addition, KWS gives export/ import permits on wildlife specimens. KWS is the country's managing authority for CITES convention that regulates access to threatened and endangered wild fauna and flora. It issues all CITES-related permits.

III The Kenya Forest Act of 2005 provides for an appropriate legal and institutional framework which instituted Kenya Forest Service (KFS) with the statutory mandate to administer the establishment, development and sustainable management, including conservation and rational utilization of forest resources for the socioeconomic development of the country. KFS issues PIC for activities undertaken in gazetted forests.

IV The National Museums and Heritage Act No. 6 of 2006 provides for an appropriate legal and institutional framework establishing the National Museums of Kenya (NMK) with the statutory mandate to administer the management of past and present cultural and natural heritage of Kenya for purposes of enhancing knowledge, respect and sustainable utilization of these resources to the benefit of Kenya and the world. NMK includes, in addition to the directorates responsible for the implementation of this mandate, the Institute of Primate Research, which undertakes biomedical research using nonhuman primates and diverse pathogens. NMK issues permits for the collection and export of antiques and monuments. According to the ABS legislation, it is also a user through *ex situ* collections. It holds the national repository for biological specimens under its museum collection centre.

V Industrial Property Act, No. 3, of 2001 provides for an appropriate legal and institutional framework establishing the Kenya Industrial Property Institute (KIPI) with the statutory mandate to administer the promotion of inventive and innovative activities, the facilitation of the acquisition of technology through the grant and regulation of patents, utility models, technovations and industrial designs, as well as provision to the public of industrial property information for technological and economic development. In addition, this Act provides for the deposit of culture of microorganisms used in developing patentable inventions. KIPI is in charge of technology transfer licensing.

VI Science and Technology Act Cap 250, 1977, provides for an appropriate legal and institutional framework that instituted the National Council for Science and Technology (NCST) with the overall mandate of advising the government on the strategic role of science, technology and innovation in national development. Pursuant to one of the provisions of the Act, NCST recommended the establishment of the Kenya Agricultural Research Institute (KARI), Kenyan Medical Research Institute (KEMRI), Kenyan Marine and Fisheries Research Institute (KMFRI) and Kenyan Forestry Research Institute (KEFRI). The core mandates of all of these state agencies do have direct and indirect involvement in conservation and sustainable use of biological resources. In addition, NCST issues research authorization permits for research activities (most of which involve the use of Kenyan biological resources), especially research applications by non-Kenyan scientists.

VII The Seeds and Plant Varieties Act of 1972 (as amended in 2002 and also published in UPOV Gazette No. 94, 2002) and the Plant Protection Act Cap 324 and the accompanying Plant Protection (Importation of Plants, Plant Products and Regulated Articles) Rules 2009, and the Agriculture Act Cap 318 collectively provide the platform upon which the Kenya Plant Health Inspectorate Service (KEPHIS) was established through a Legal Notice No. 350 of 1996. The Plant Protection Act makes better provisions for the prevention of the introduction and spread of diseases destructive to plants. Similarly, the Seeds and Plant Varieties Act and Regulations confer power to regulate transactions in seeds, including provisions for the testing and certification of seeds; for the establishment of an index of names of plant varieties; for the imposition of restriction on the introduction of new varieties; control of the importation of seeds; to authorize measures to prevent injurious cross-pollination; and to provide for the grant of proprietary rights to persons breeding or discovering new varieties. KEPHIS issues phytosanitary permits for the export and import of plant materials.

Access and benefit-sharing regime: Conditions and procedure for access

ABS regulations

The ABS Regulations 2006 spell out the conditions and procedure for access to genetic resources and ATK which determine the architecture of the ABS regime in Kenya under Parts III, IV and partly V.

Scope of application of the regulations

The ABS regulations apply to access to genetic resources within the jurisdiction of Kenya. "Access" in the context of the ABS regulations means obtaining, possessing and using genetic resources, derived products and, where applicable, intangible components, for purposes of research, bioprospecting, conservation, industrial application or commercial use (sect. 2). These actions/activities will trigger the application of the regulations except in the following situations (sect. 3):

a) The exchange of genetic resources, their derivative products, or intangible components associated with them, carried out by members of any local Kenyan community amongst themselves and for their own consumption;
b) Access to genetic resources derived from plant breeders in accordance with the Seeds and Plant Varieties Act;
c) Human genetic resources; and
d) Approved research activities intended for educational purposes within recognized Kenyan academic and research institutions governed by relevant intellectual property laws.

However, the regulations will apply to entities falling under exemption (d) above if the biological material is to be taken as well as used abroad.

Application and processing of access permit

According to the ABS Regulations (sects 9–14), the processing of an access permit takes the following steps/procedure:

1   An applicant applies for an access permit from NEMA by filling a form set out in the ABS Regulations.
2   The application must be accompanied by evidence of PIC from resource providers for genetic resources or traditional knowledge being sought. The applicant must also seek PIC of and establish MAT with the relevant lead agency or agencies.[3] In the case of wildlife genetic resources and genetic resources in protected areas, PIC is issued by KWS and, where possible, jointly with recognized local community associations.
3   The application must also be accompanied by a research clearance from the National Council for Science and Technology, which was renamed National Commission for Science, Technology and Innovation (NACOSTI) in the Science, Innovation and Technology Act 2013. The NCST issues research clearance and authorization permits for research activities (most of which involve the use of Kenyan biological resources) before the start of research in Kenya. According to the National Council of Science and Technology Innovation Act 2012, the applicant must fulfil the following requirements before a permit can be granted:

a) Provide comprehensive CV of all applicants.
b) Submit projects proposal, including details of objectives, hypothesis, literature review, methodology and envisaged application of the research results.
c) Details of sponsor or institution providing financial or material support for the project.

---

3 According to sect. 2 EMCA, " 'lead agency' means any Government ministry, department, parastatal, state corporation or local authority, in which any law vests functions of control or management or any element of the environment or natural resources."

d) A copy of final reports/thesis must be submitted on completion duly endorsed by the affiliating institution.

e) Submit prior informed consent and material transfer agreements where necessary from lead agencies or providers.

f) Researcher's commitment to personally take responsibility for any loss or damage to materials or documents during the research.

g) Research association/affiliation with relevant Kenyan public research institutions, intended or finalized, must be shown on this application form. No research permit is issued until the affiliation is confirmed.

4 On receipt of the application, NEMA gives notice in the *Gazette* and in at least one newspaper with nationwide circulation for purposes of getting comments from any interested persons within a period of 21 days.

5 Once the 21 days have elapsed, the Authority arranges an ABS Technical Committee evaluation meeting to determine the application. The members of the committee are drawn from relevant lead agencies. The committee reviews the application and once satisfied that the activity will facilitate sustainable management and utilization of genetic resources, it approves the application and an access permit is issued.[4] However, sometimes the access permit is not granted if there are other reasonable grounds to deny it. The permit issued is valid for a period of one year and may be renewed for a further period of one year upon payment of the prescribed fee.

According to the ABS regulations it is the responsibility of NEMA to determine the application and communicate its decision in writing to the applicant within 60 days of receipt of an application for an access permit.

Terms and conditions of an access permit

The ABS Regulations give powers to NEMA to impose terms and conditions as it may deem necessary (sect. 15 (1)). In addition to such terms and conditions, the following conditions are implied in every access permit according to section 15 (2):

a) Duplicates and holotypes of all genetic resources collected shall be deposited with relevant lead agency.

b) Records of all intangible components of genetic material collected shall be deposited with NEMA.

c) Reasonable access to all genetic resources collected shall be guaranteed to all Kenyan citizens whether such genetic resources and intangible components are held locally or abroad.

---

4 The permit is usually denied if the applicant has not complied with the provisions of the law, and in the absence of PIC from the competent lead agency/agencies or any other relevant stakeholder, e.g. an indigenous community.

d)   All agreements entered into with respect to access of genetic resources shall be strictly for the purposes for which they are entered into.
e)   Quarterly reports shall be furnished to NEMA on the status of research, including all discoveries from research involving genetic resources and/or intangible components thereof.
f)   The holder of an access permit shall inform NEMA of all discoveries made during the exercise of the right of access granted under the access permit.
g)   The holder of the access permit shall provide the following reports: 1) A semi-annual status report on the environmental impacts of any ongoing collection of genetic resources or intangible components thereof; and 2) A final report on the environmental impacts of collection of genetic resources or intangible components thereof, in the event that the collection is of a duration of three months or less.
h)   The holder of an access permit shall abide by the laws of Kenya.

Although a permit issued upon satisfying all application requirements implies authorization for both commercial and non-commercial research, there are no inbuilt mechanisms for tracking the downstream utilization of the accessed material such that the possibility exists for its utilization for industrial applications. As a consequence, the procedure for application, processing and issuing of permits is intense, and that might cause frustrations to researchers due to resulting delays.

Management of information

Data exclusivity and inclusivity is crucial for both non-commercial and commercial research. Section 21 of the ABS Regulations provides an applicant with the option of requesting for certain information to be kept confidential upon the applicant's request.

Benefit sharing

Measures for benefit sharing in respect to both non-commercial and commercial research are found in section 20 of the ABS Regulations. The research activities have to be beneficial to the country and have to consider elements of IP and traditional knowledge as well as participation of the locals. The following are examples of benefits to be considered in negotiating for both non-commercial and commercial research:

A. Monetary benefits

a)   Access fees or fee per sample collected or acquired
b)   Up-front payments
c)   Milestone payments
d)   Payments of royalties

e) Licence fees in case genetic resources are to be utilized for commercial purposes
f) Fees to be paid to trust funds supporting conservation and sustainable use of biodiversity
g) Salaries and preferential terms where mutually agreed
h) Research funding
i) Joint ventures
j) Joint ownership of relevant intellectual property rights

B. Non-monetary benefits

a) Sharing of research and development results
b) Collaboration, co-operation and contribution in scientific research and development programmes, particularly biotechnological research activities
c) Participation in product development
d) Admittance to *ex situ* facilities of genetic resources and databases by participating institutions
e) Transfer to Kenya of knowledge and technology under fair and most favourable terms, including concessional and preferential terms where agreed, in particular, knowledge and technology that make use of genetic resources, including biotechnology, or that are relevant to the conservation and sustainable utilization of biological diversity
f) Strengthening capacities for technology transfer to Kenya
g) Institutional capacity building
h) Human and material resources to strengthen the capacities for the administration and enforcement of access regulations
i) Training related to genetic resources with the full participation of Kenya and where possible, in Kenya
j) Access to scientific information relevant to conservation and sustainable use of biological diversity, including biological inventories and taxonomic studies
k) Institutional and professional relationships that can arise from access and benefit-sharing agreements and subsequent collaborative activities
l) Joint ownership of relevant intellectual property rights

Offences and penalties

Contravention or failure to comply with any provision of the ABS Regulations shall constitute an offence and therefore, any persons convicted of an offence under the provisions of these regulations shall be liable to imprisonment for a term not exceeding 18 months, or to a fine not exceeding (approximately) USD 3990 (as at July 2014) or both. This will also be based on the nature of the offence according to the relevant legislation, for example the Wildlife Act 2013.

Current status of access and benefits-sharing regime and implementation – an appraisal

The Kenyan government does not have a comprehensive access and benefit-sharing regime in respect to the utilization of genetic resources and associated traditional knowledge resources. The only available legislation is the subsidiary legislation on ABS under EMCA 1999, which was enacted in 2006 and came into force in 2008. This subsidiary legislation was influenced by the Bonn guidelines and the CBD provisions. Since then many things have happened, including the enactment of the country's new Constitution of 2010, the adoption, ratification and entry into force of the Nagoya Protocol on access and benefit sharing. Therefore, review and enactment of a new ABS legislation has been proposed. However, the ABS subsidiary legislation 2006 still remains the basis of regulating access and ATK in the country. There are challenges experienced during the process of implementation of the country's ABS legislation. Some of the challenges noted include discrepancies in the legislation vis-à-vis the requirements of the NP and the new Constitution, lack of clarity and legal certainty, the bureaucratic nature of the access procedure and long durations of processing applications and issuing permits for ABS. There is hence a need for a one-stop shop (see below and also Boga, Ch. 12 in this volume). Other challenges include how to address aspects of noncompliance by entities that are not parties to the CBD and the NP, tracking, monitoring and creating a link between in situ–ex situ collections and research and development (R&D) value chain. Likewise, aspects of exclusivity and inclusivity in access of both genetic material and information management still remain a challenge. In addition, standards for the sharing of benefits, negotiations capacity and skills, biotrade in line with ABS, intercommunity connectivity and cross-boundary genetic resources and information flows are still a puzzle. Also, elements of sharing the results of R&D and benefits from commercial utilization of genetic resources and ATK still remain elusive.

Most of these benefits derived from genetic resources and ATK are controlled by IPRs. While some countries have already enacted measures linking the access regime with the intellectual property system, in Kenya there are proposals to introduce PIC as a measure of the process of granting intellectual property rights. The development and use of access permits as internationally recognized certificates of compliance will be useful as a mechanism for disclosure and downstream tracking. There is need to develop an effective ABS legislation that promotes R&D and collaborative partnerships and that attracts investments geared towards the promotion of conservation and livelihood improvement in the country.

Implementation and enforcement challenges under the access and benefit-sharing regime

Domestication of ABS rules

Domestication of access and benefit-sharing rules is highly complex, requiring the collaboration of experts in science, law and business. Many countries, like Kenya, lack the capacity to bring these experts together and thus face challenges in implementing the ABS provisions of the CBD. Even countries that have been able to create rules on ABS face challenges in maintaining the necessary institutions and in the monitoring and enforcing the application of the rules and any negotiated ABS agreements.

Downstream monitoring

The country providing access to genetic resources frequently faces difficulties in monitoring how the resources are used once they leave the country's jurisdiction and in enforcing compliance with ABS rules and negotiated terms (see also Kamau, Ch. 17 in this volume).

Differentiation of access procedure for commercial and non-commercial research

It is difficult to decide how to separate the procedure for commercial and non-commercial research, as the results of non-commercial research are often prone to misuse for commercial gains. A good example is the Lake Bogoria biopiracy case that began as non-commercial research and later commercialized results without consideration of benefit sharing. In previous experiences, general requirements waived for local researchers and students on split programmes to promote research have brought forth problems which have resulted in challenges in respect to access to genetic resources and ATK, third-party transfers, data management, tracking and reporting and compliance with the provisions of the Nagoya Protocol. This has been a source of abuse and a window for biopiracy.

Foreign researchers from countries where ABS regimes do not apply pose a challenge in regard to compliance and enforcement. The situation is made worse as most local institutions lack an administrative, policy and legislative framework on biodiversity ABS-related collaborative arrangements. Also, there are current concerns in respect to affiliation or collaborations with foreign institutions which operate oblivious of the existing national ABS focal points. Unclear legal arrangements lead to lawsuits on termination or conflict of agreements on patent applications or differences on safe deposits. The issues of ABS-based IP ownership, sharing of benefits and enforcement, aspects of specimen depository, compliance enforcement to monitoring and evaluation adversely affect conservation and the sustainable use of biological and genetic resources.

International treaties

Overlaps, contradictions and limited coherence in international treaties pose a challenge to the smooth implementation of the ABS regime. There are, for example, contradictions between sections of Articles 8(j) and 15 CBD which are reinforced by Article 9 ITPGRFA in terms of recognition of local communities, protection of their indigenous knowledge and ensuring that issues of access and equitable benefit sharing are addressed in bioprospecting and biotechnology initiatives. In addition, Article 12.3(b) of the ITPGRFA that provides for free access to certain genetic resources is in conflict with Article 15 CBD. Similarly, Article 9 ITPGRFA which provides for farmers' right to access and to save planting materials, contradicts the provisions of Article 27.3(b) of the WTO-TRIPS Agreement. On the other hand, the UPOV does not recognize the provisions of ABS under CBD and the provisions of farmers' rights under the ITPGRFA. CITES prohibits trade in endangered species while WTO lacks such provisions, yet it deals directly with trade. There is a contradiction between sections of Article 27.3(b) of the WTO-TRIPS Agreement and of Articles 8(j) and 15 CBD. Article 27.3(b) provides for patenting of plants, animals and microorganisms and does not recognize the rights of the local communities as providers and holders of indigenous knowledge on those biological resources, nor does it embrace any provisions on access to the resources and sharing of benefits accruing from their utilization. On the contrary, Article 8(j) recognizes the rights of the local communities in terms of their indigenous knowledge practices and innovations from biological resources while Article 15 provides for access to those resources and equitable benefit sharing of the profits made from their utilization.

Elimination of such contradictions in ABS-relevant international instruments would render great relief to national ABS implementation processes.

Uncoordinated policy framework

In order to provide clear and transparent decisions, competent national authorities, in accordance with the national administrative, legislative and policy measures, are responsible for setting up clear criteria and/or procedures towards establishing a coordinated policy framework and legal instruments in Kenya to ensure that biological resources are used safely, sustainably and ethically and benefits arising from the utilization of genetic resources are shared in a fair and equitable manner; adequate financial resources are provided for research; capacities are enhanced and biodiversity issues and values are mainstreamed to achieve cultural and socioeconomic development. A coordinated policy framework and legal instruments should at the same time contribute towards easing of the access procedure and enhancement of legal certainty, clarity and transparency as required by the Nagoya Protocol (Article 6.3 (a)).

These experiences and challenges establish a basis for making an informed decision on the review and development of appropriate ABS for the country that include both user and provider measures. Effective legislation will provide clarity, legal certainty and transparency, as well as provide a platform for the promotion of R&D that attracts investment of the country's biodiversity leveraging as a green economy driver of national agenda.

Current effort to streamline ABS permitting process

The current state of permit applications reveals a low trend in the number of applicants for both locals and foreigners. Since the entry into force of the subsidiary ABS law, there have been no applications for commercial research or commercial bioprospecting. However, spot checks in research institutions and universities reveal that quite a lot of research is being carried on locally and abroad based on the country's genetic resources. Further, random observations and discussions reveal a low level of awareness among various categories of stakeholders. Whereas most applicants would like to comply with the rules and procedures of access, they lack appropriate guidance. In addition, the ABS concept is new to most of the ABS permitting desk officers; some of the desk officers may not be quite knowledgeable in the laws governing ABS regimes.

In this regard there are various efforts to streamline and enhance ABS awareness among the key stakeholders through development of appropriate outreach and awareness materials. NEMA, with Global Environment Facility support, has developed various tools, among them, the ABS toolkit for awareness raising, established web portal linkages for various steps involved in ABS permitting, and also automated application procedures.

Recommendations from various consultative meetings and conferences have recommended a one-stop shop and harmonized institutional arrangements which can only be addressed through provision of the law. The Nagoya Protocol requires identification and establishment of a national focal point, competent authority responsible for granting PIC including for indigenous and local communities, national checkpoints and ABS-clearing house mechanisms, among others.

Already recommendations have been made to consider reviewing and amending the existing ABS legislation of 2006 and in addition to come up with a comprehensive national legislation. Linkage between *in situ* and *ex situ* collections including information use and beneficiation along the value chain remain a challenge. The Wildlife Management Authority is entering into collaborative arrangements with internationally recognized trusted specimen repositories with clear frameworks for PIC, MAT and MTA in order to promote R&D. This will guide researchers collecting wildlife specimens on where to deposit duplicate specimens as per the law.

The Kenyan government through NACOSTI is coming up with a policy to guide the establishment of repositories in compliance with national laws and EMCA. The Environment Management and Coordination Act of 1999 is also under the parliament's review to bring it into compliance with the Constitution and emerging issues at the national and global level. As already mentioned, there are also proposals to review the national IP laws to include PIC as a means of disclosure during intellectual property applications.

Recommendations and conclusion

I   Kenya should continue to take effective participation in regional and international meetings relevant to ABS.

II There is need to build capacity, which should include enhancing the ability of communities, private land owners, and state organs to, *inter alia*

- negotiate access and benefit-sharing agreements;
- analyze benefit-sharing agreements and understand the provisions they contain; and
- develop understanding of opportunities and risks associated with bioprospecting.

III Comprehensive sensitization exercise at different levels in relevant public institutions, research institutions, and within local communities is necessary. ABS system can only work in an environment of well-sensitized communities and policymakers.

IV Bilateral scientific cooperation should be enhanced in order to build strong institutions for technology transfer and uptake associated with biodiversity.

V Funding should be pegged on strong ABS project models.

VI Monitoring and tracking of all specimens under depositories and uses should be enhanced for effective enforcement and compliance.

VII For providers to ensure species survival, user countries need to develop ABS laws and be ABS compliant.

References

Environment Management and Coordination Act No. 8 of 1999, www.nema.go.ke

Environmental Management and Coordination (Conservation of Biological Diversity and Resources, Access to Genetic Resources and Benefit Sharing) Regulations, 2006, www.nema.go.ke

Government of Kenya (GOK) (2010). The Constitution of Kenya 2010, Nairobi, GOK Press, www.kenyalaw.org

Kenya Forest Act 2005, www.kenyalaw.org

Kenya Wildlife Service (2011) Strategy for Bio-prospecting within and outside Protected Areas

Nagoya Protocol on Access to genetic Resources and the Fair and Equitable Sharing of Benefits Arising from their Utilization to Convention on Biological Diversity, www.cbd.int.

National Council of Science and Technology Innovation Act 2012, www.kenyalaw.org

National Museums and Heritage Act No. 6 of 2006, www.kenyalaw.org

Science & Technology Act, Cap. 250 of 1977, www.kenyalaw.org

Science & Technology Act, Cap. 250 of 1979, www.ncst.go.ke

Wildlife Conservation and Management Act 2013, www.kenyalaw.org

7 Research on genetic resources and indigenous knowledge in the framework of the Ethiopian ABS law

Gemedo Dalle

Introduction

Ethiopia is a biodiversity-rich country known to be a centre of origin and diversity for many cultivated crop plants. It is a primary gene centre for field crops such as Niger seed (*Gastonia abyssinica*), teff (*Eragrostis tef*) and Ethiopian mustard (*Brassica carinata*) and a secondary gene centre for crops such as durum wheat (*Triticum durum*), barley (*Hordeum vulgare*) and sorghum (*Sorghum bicolor*). The diverse agroecological system of the country that extends from 120 meters below sea level to 4,620 meters above sea level contributes to the rich flora and fauna.

According to Article 40(3) of the Constitution of the Federal Democratic Republic of Ethiopia, natural resources are property of the state and peoples and are to be used for the common benefit of the people (Federal Negarit Gazeta 1995). To ensure implementation of this constitutional provision, different policies and related proclamations and also regulations have been put in place. Both the environmental and biodiversity policies of the country provide for the enactment of Access and Benefit Sharing (ABS) legislation and community rights. Furthermore, the biodiversity policy provides for the rights of community to share the benefit derived from genetic resources and associated traditional knowledge.

The Convention on Biological Diversity (CBD) has also recognized the sovereign rights of states over their natural resources in Article 15(1). It further states that the authority to determine access to genetic resources rests with the national governments and any access to these genetic resources is subject to national legislation (SCBD 2001).

ABS refers to the way in which genetic resources may be accessed, and how the benefits that result from their use are shared between the people or countries using the resources (users) and the people or countries that provide them (providers). The third objective of the CBD is "the fair and equitable sharing of the benefits arising out of the utilization of genetic resources, including by appropriate access to genetic resources and by appropriate transfer of relevant technologies, taking into account all rights over those resources and to technologies, and by appropriate funding". ABS is based on prior informed consent (PIC) granted by a provider to a user and negotiations between both parties to develop mutually agreed terms (MAT) to ensure the fair and equitable sharing of genetic resources and associated benefits (SCBD 2001).

The CBD does not define benefit sharing, but national laws related to access to genetic resources often stipulate the nature of benefits that are to be shared according to mutual agreement on the terms of access, following prior informed consent. Provided that they meet the requirements of relevant laws related to access and any earlier contractual commitments with respect to genetic resources, the parties to an individual agreement can be as imaginative and ingenious as they can in defining the benefits to be shared and mechanisms for doing so.

Benefits arising from the utilization of genetic resources can be direct, such as knowledge produced by research on genetic resources, or indirect, such as the incentive for conservation provided by profits arising from the commercialization of genetic resources. They can be either monetary benefits, such as collection fees, royalties and research grants, or non-monetary benefits of an environmental, social or economic nature. Non-monetary benefits might include research on host-country diseases; conservation projects; technology transfer of hardware, software and know-how; training in various disciplines of science, in information management, or in legal, administrative and management matters; joint research through participation in product development and joint ventures; institutional capacity building through developing partnerships to support groups such as communities, universities, botanic gardens, and small businesses; and the creation of employment opportunities.

After ratifying the CBD and the International Treaty on Plant Genetic Resources for Food and Agriculture (ITPGRFA), Ethiopia issued a proclamation on Access to Genetic Resources and Community Knowledge, and Community Rights and its regulation (Proclamation No. 482/2006 and Regulation No. 169/2009). In the proclamation, access was defined as the collection, acquisition, transfer or use of genetic resources and/or community knowledge. Furthermore, biological resource includes genetic resources, organisms or parts thereof, populations or any other biotic component of an ecosystem with actual or potential value for humanity. The legislations focus on PIC, MAT, Multilateral System of Access and how to implement relevant activities.

Access and benefit-sharing regime in Ethiopia

Ethiopia is one of the few countries that had an ABS legislation before the adoption of the Nagoya Protocol on ABS in 2010. The major driving force for the country to enact the proclamation on ABS was the urgent need to conserve and sustainably utilize the country's rich biodiversity; recognize the historical contribution the Ethiopian communities have made to the conservation, development and sustainable utilization of biological resources; recognize and protect the knowledge of the Ethiopian communities generated and accumulated with respect to the conservation and utilization of genetic resources; and promote the wider application of such knowledge with the approval and sharing of benefits with such communities, as well as involving them in the making of decisions concerning the use of genetic resources and community knowledge and the sharing of benefits derived from their utilization. Therefore, it was necessary to determine access to genetic resources and community knowledge by law and to provide for the rights of communities over genetic resources and community knowledge. As a result, in accordance with the country's constitutional provision, the Ethiopian government enacted Proclamation No. 482/2006.

The scope of the ABS Proclamation covers genetic resources found in both *in situ* and *ex situ* conditions and associated traditional community knowledge. However, the customary use and exchange of genetic resources and community knowledge by and among Ethiopian local communities and the sale of produce of biological resources for direct consumption are excluded from its scope.

Permit requirement and issuance of access permit

According to Article 12 (1) of the ABS regulation, access to genetic resources or community knowledge in Ethiopia is subject to a written access permit from the Competent National Authority (CNA), or the Ethiopian Biodiversity Institute (EBI), to which applications for such permits must be addressed. Any access is based on PIC and Material Transfer Agreement (MTA). Exporting genetic resources out of Ethiopia without a legal export permit obtained from the EBI is prohibited (Federal Negarit Gazeta 2006).

Upon giving prior informed consent, the Institute negotiates and concludes the access agreement for access to genetic resources. Where the access application involves access to community knowledge, the Institute negotiates and concludes the access agreement based on the PIC of the concerned local community to that effect.

Basic preconditions to access Ethiopian genetic resources and associated traditional knowledge

According to Article 12 of Proclamation No. 482/2006, the basic preconditions for access to Ethiopian genetic resources and associated traditional knowledge include the following:

- Access to genetic resources shall be subject to the prior informed consent of the Ethiopian Institute of Biodiversity.
- Access to community knowledge shall be subject to the prior informed consent of the concerned local community.
- The state and the concerned local community shall obtain a fair and equitable share of the benefits arising from the utilization of genetic resources and community knowledge accessed.
- An access applicant who is a foreigner shall present a letter from the competent authority of his national state or his domicile assuring that it shall uphold and enforce the access obligations of the applicant.
- In cases of access by foreigners, the collection of genetic resources and community knowledge shall be accompanied by the personnel of the

Ethiopian Institute of Biodiversity or the personnel of the relevant institution to be designated by the Institute.

- The research based on the genetic resources accessed shall be carried out in Ethiopia and with the participation of Ethiopian nationals designated by the Ethiopian Institute of Biodiversity, except where it is impossible.
- Where the research on the genetic resources accessed is permitted to be carried abroad, the institution sponsoring and/or hosting the research shall give a letter ensuring that access obligations attached thereto shall be observed.

If the above preconditions are fulfilled, any access seekers may be granted an access permit. However, according to Article 13 of the Proclamation, access to genetic resources and associated traditional knowledge may be denied where the access:

- requested is in relation to the genetic resource of an endangered species;
- may have adverse effects upon human health or the cultural values of the local community;
- may cause undesirable impact on the environment;
- may cause danger of loss of ecosystem; or
- is intended to use genetic resources for purposes contrary to the national laws of Ethiopia or the treaties to which Ethiopia is a party.

Community rights

According to the existing ABS regulation of Ethiopia (Federal Negarit Gazeta 2009), local communities have the following rights over their genetic resources and community knowledge: the right to regulate the access to their community knowledge, an inalienable right to use their genetic resources and community knowledge and the right to share from the benefit arising out of the utilization of their genetic resources and community knowledge.

Communities have the right to give prior informed consent for access to their community knowledge and also can demand the restriction or withdrawal of PIC given by the state where access becomes detrimental to their socioeconomic life or natural or cultural heritages.

The ownership of genetic resources is vested in the state and the Ethiopian people, whereas that of community knowledge is vested in the concerned local community. As a result, communities obtain 50 per cent of the monetary benefits received from the utilization of any genetic resource accessed from their area and 100 per cent of shared benefit arising from their associated traditional knowledge (Federal Negarit Gazeta 2009).

Penalty

Any person who accesses genetic resources or community knowledge without obtaining an access permit from the Institute, provides false information in the access application or in the course of subsequent monitoring of the access agreement, subsequently changes the purpose of access specified in the access agreement without obtaining a permit from the Ethiopian Institute of Biodiversity to the effect and explores genetic resources without obtaining an exploration permit from the Institute or provides false information in the application for an exploration permit shall be punished, depending on the gravity of the circumstance, with rigorous imprisonment of not less than three years and a fine of not less than 10,000 and not exceeding 30,000 Ethiopian birr (Federal Negarit Gazeta 2009).

Where the offence committed is in relation to genetic resources endemic to Ethiopia, the punishment shall be rigorous imprisonment of not less than five years and not exceeding 12 years and a fine ranging from 50,000 birr to 100,000 birr (Federal Negarit Gazeta, 2009).

Legal provisions for commercial and non-commercial researches in Ethiopia

According to Article 8(a) of the Nagoya Protocol on Access and Benefit Sharing (NP), contracting parties should create conditions to promote and encourage research which contributes to the conservation and sustainable use of biological diversity, particularly in developing countries, including through simplified measures on access for non-commercial research purposes, taking into account the need to address a change of intent for such research. The Ethiopian Access and Benefit Sharing Proclamation and its regulation has already provided for a clear and transparent legal system. First, it clearly differentiates between commercial and non-commercial research; second, it is simple; and third, it promotes facilitated access as long as the users are transparent and fulfil the identified minimal requirements.

Commercial access to genetic resources and benefit sharing

Access application has to be presented in accordance with the form specified in Annex I of the Regulation. The applicant should give detailed information on the following issues:

1   General information (name of applicant, address, qualifications, name of organization, registered address, establishment document and other details of the organization).
2   Detailed access information (financial details, technical particulars including specific taxa to be accessed, actual and potential uses of the genetic resources and their derivatives, specific locality from where the collection is intended to be undertaken, parts of the genetic resource to be accessed, quantity to be collected, and information on any community knowledge associated with the genetic resource).
3   Details of planned collection mission (identification of the provider of the genetic resource for which the access was sought, collection method to be used, expected date of start and completion of the collection mission, etc.).

4   Details of the proposed use of the genetic resource (the type of use to which the genetic resource will be put, the type and extent of the research as well as the expertise and equipment to be used, the expected research result and the estimated time of completion, the places where each element of the research and development program will take place, the manner and extent of participation of Ethiopian nationals in the research, national institutions that will participate in the research and also those in charge of monitoring the process, and the primary and probable subsequent destinations of the genetic resource).

5   Benefit-sharing information which includes details on the proposed mechanisms and arrangements for benefit sharing, the economic, social, technical, biotechnological, scientific, environmental or any other benefits that are intended or may be likely to accrue to the country or the concerned local communities, etc.

Non-commercial access to genetic resources and benefit sharing

Access application has to be presented in accordance with the form specified in Annex II of the Regulation. Required details related to general information (name of applicant institution and its address, establishment document of the applicant Institution) and technical information are more or less similar to those of commercial access. There is no request for detailed information on the financial issues or actual and potential uses of the genetic resources and its derivatives. Furthermore, under non-commercial research, there is no request for benefit-sharing arrangements, although non-monetary benefits are expected in the form of research publications and data generations. Access permit for non-commercial research is given in less than an hour, provided that the applicant submits all required documents. Furthermore, the access permit is granted free of any administrative fees. On the other hand, for commercial research, the duration for finalizing access permit depends on the readiness of both access seeker and provider and also on the time required to conclude the negotiations on benefit sharing.

Obligations for the utilization of genetic materials for non-commercial research

According to the Access to Genetic Resources and Community Knowledge, and Community Rights Regulation of Ethiopia (Regulation No. 169/2009), the researcher is permitted to utilize the material for scientific research purposes only. He cannot use the material for commercial purposes or obtain any intellectual property rights on the material. Besides, the researcher retains the material for the period of the research period only and has to return any remaining unused material to the EBI (the Provider) after the completion of the research. In addition, the researcher is not allowed to transfer the material to a third party without first notifying as well as securing explicit written agreement from the EBI. Any third party that obtains the material from the researcher in the absence of permission from the EBI shall not have any right whatsoever over the material and its components. The researcher is obliged to notify the Provider about the progress of his or her research through periodic research reports and also present to the Provider hard and electronic copies of the research results upon completion of the research work.

Practical challenges in implementing ABS

The demarcation between basic and commercial research is not always clear. Change of intent after accessing genetic material for non-commercial research could affect the effective implementation of ABS provisions. Furthermore, lack of transparency and legal certainty may cause mistrust. Limited capacity and lack of effective legal enforcement and follow-up mechanisms for the ABS agreement are the critical gaps identified which obstruct the proper implementation.

Conclusion

Ethiopia is one of the signatories to the Convention on Biological Diversity that requests contracting parties to create conditions to facilitate access to their genetic resources for environmentally sound uses. In line with Article 15 of the Convention, Ethiopia has put in place an ABS Proclamation and its regulation that differentiates between commercial and non-commercial research even before the adoption of the Nagoya Protocol. The ABS legislation in Ethiopia has clear provisions for accessing genetic materials for both commercial and non-commercial research. Access to genetic resources is subject to PIC and MAT. However, it has to be noted that access to Ethiopian genetic materials for non-commercial research is very much facilitated provided that access seekers submit all the required documents. Legal transparency and certainty as well as respect, transparency, cooperation and mutual trust are essential elements for effective and sustainable implementation of the ABS regime.

References

Federal Negarit Gazeta (1995) The Constitution of the Federal Democratic Republic of Ethiopia. Federal Negarit Gazeta First Year, No. 1.

Federal Negarit Gazeta (2006) Access to Genetic Resources and Community Knowledge, and Community Rights Proclamation No. 482/2006. Federal Negarit Gazeta 13th Year, No. 13.

Federal Negarit Gazeta (2009) Access to Genetic Resources and Community Knowledge, and Community Rights Regulation No. 169/2009. Federal Negarit Gazeta 15th Year, No. 67.

SCBD (Secretariat of Convention on Biological Diversity) (2001) *Handbook of the Convention on Biological Diversity*, Part 1, London: Earthscan.

8 Research on genetic resources in Latin America and the Caribbean (LAC)

Perspectives for facilitated access*

Mónica Ribadeneira Sarmiento

Introduction

This chapter consists of a general overview of the regional perspective on access to genetic resources and benefit sharing (ABS) and should not be considered a deep analysis covering all states in Latin America and the Caribbean (LAC).

LAC is more than a geographic area between Mexico and Argentina. It includes similar languages and common cultural standards as a result of the conquest processes of the Latin European empires Spain, Portugal and France. LAC has a wide variety of biodiversity resources as well as uncountable native populations and holders of associated traditional knowledge.

The study starts with some considerations regarding basic research in LAC. To show how different the national approaches to ABS and to facilitation of basic research are, two examples are analyzed in detail. One is the Andean Region and the other one is a country, Costa Rica. In both cases, general information is presented about the licensing process. Also, in each case, the question is answered as to whether access to genetic resources for scientific purposes is facilitated or not.

Finally, some recommendations are presented in order to achieve a region-wide implementation of facilitation mechanisms for scientific research. A group of them refer to national authorities and another to the research community.

* The author is grateful to the German Research Foundation, DFG, for the support to attend the International Workshop on ABS and the Nagoya Protocol – Research Cooperation and Facilitated Access, which was jointly organized by the Institute for International Law and European Law of the University of Göttingen and the Research Centre for European Environmental Law of the University of Bremen (Göttingen, Germany, January 2012). The author would also like to thank Mr. Jorge Cabrera Medaglia for the interview conducted with him and Ms. Martha Liliana Jimenez for her comments on the text regarding Costa Rica. Thanks also to Ms. Veronica Lemache and Ms. María Cristina Quiroga for their comments on the text regarding Andean countries. Finally, the author wants to thank Prof. Gerd Winter and Dr. Evanson Chege Kamau for their valuable comments given in order to improve this chapter.

Initial considerations about basic research in Latin America and the Caribbean

In the context of both commercial and non-commercial purposes, LAC countries may need to improve national scientific research (basic and applied) so as to benefit from their biodiversity wealth as much as possible. The role and importance of scientific research and higher education has been recognized in the constitutions of many LAC countries. For example, in Colombia, the constitution regards scientific and technological research as central elements of the State's public policy and stipulates that the State should strengthen scientific research at public and private universities and provide contributions for their development. The promotion of research, science and technology are declared as state duties.

The author states that there is a division between promoting research and the development of national legal regimes, as the former does not necessarily depend on legal instruments. Promoting basic research can be the result of administrative decisions, such as the provision of funds or the expansion of international cooperation lines, that do not rely on the existence and content of legal instruments.

It cannot be denied that legal frameworks, not only in LAC, but also worldwide, when in place but without acknowledging the intricacies of scientific research (see Kamau, Ch. 17 in this volume), have a negative impact on the promotion of research. This is particularly relevant, as:

a) generally, basic research is carried out through strategic alliances between researchers and countries of different levels of development and with different availability of researchable biodiversity. An example of studies on megadiverse mountain ecosystem in South Ecuador is analyzed in Bendix et al. (2010);

b) usually, legislation does not distinguish between the various stages of bioprospection, which are quite different and usually sequential. This means that a research project carrying out the most basic vegetation profiling as the first step towards identifying or collecting biological samples with potentially relevant genetic resources is subject to the same requirements as a full-blown bioprospection project already close to toxicity trials or chromatographic analysis; and

c) follow-up and monitoring mechanisms of bioprospection processes require technical specifications that legal instruments do not envisage, since these specifications develop and get updated much faster than the legal framework.

Two cases studies on facilitation of basic research in Latin America

In the region, standard references concerning the topic of ABS are Decision 391 of the Andean Community regarding Common Access Regime to Genetic Resources (1996) and the Costa Rican ABS regime.

It is fair to say that there is a notorious imbalance of ABS topics in Latin America and the Caribbean and also between countries at the subregional level. In Central America, for example, almost every analysis and national effort is based on the Costa Rican experience, despite the attempt a few decades ago to frame a "Regional Protocol for the Access to Genetic and Biochemical Resources and the Associated Traditional Knowledge".[1] Costa Rica is undoubtedly a world-renowned flagship case because of its experience with the Merck-INBIO contracting model of 1991, which tried out a concrete benefit-sharing system. Additionally, perhaps the most relevant strength of the Costa Rican case resides in the post-access follow-up actions that the national system has implemented.

The Andean subregion,[2] famous for its Andean Decision 391,[3] displays big differences between the national systems in Peru and Venezuela, as well as the efforts of Ecuador (see Cabrera Ormaza, Ch. 9 in this volume), compared to those made by Bolivia, the latter having degraded from a pioneer to a rather marginal state on this subject.[4]

Andean region

General information

The region became famous in the topic of genetic resources due to Andean Decision 391: Common Access Regime to Genetic Resources, a supranational decision that currently covers Colombia, Ecuador, Peru and Bolivia.[5]

---

1 The Central American Protocol for the Access to Genetic and Biochemical Resources and the Associated Traditional Knowledge was drafted between 1997 and 2001, and although no actual initiative was carried out, it pushed several countries to write their own national strategies on the subject. Available at: www.sur.iucn.org/ces/documentos/documentos/635.pdf.
2 Though the Andes is a continental mountain range that covers Argentina, Bolivia, Chile, Colombia, Ecuador, Peru, and Venezuela, "Andean countries" refers to the members of the Andean Community.
3 Andean Decision 391 (1996) Common Access Regime to Genetic Resources (Original in Spanish). Available at: www.wipo.int/wipolex/es/details.jsp?id=9446 (accessed 24 March 2015). The legal principles were completed by the Andean Resolutions: 414 (1996) Referential Model of Application to Access to Genetic Resources under Andean Decision 391, and 415 (1996) Referential Model of Access Contract under Andean Decision 391 (Both original ones in Spanish). Source: Gaceta Oficial Año XIII – Número 217, Lima 5 de Agosto de 1996.
4 Bolivia was the first Andean country to nationally transpose Decision 391 in 1997, one year after its adoption.
5 Venezuela, an original member of the Andean Community of Nations (CAN), began its separation from CAN in 2006 over its disagreement with the Free Trade Agreement (FTA) negotiation processes between Peru, Colombia, and the United States. The country's formal separation went into effect in April 2011. ABS mechanisms applied by Venezuela after its departure from CAN are still subject to legal review. Chile, also an original CAN member until 1976, has the status of "Associated Member" since 2006. Even with this status, it is not expected that Chile will apply the principles and processes of Andean Decision 391.

At the time Andean Decision 391 was adopted, five countries were members of the Andean Community,[6] and all of them had ratified the Convention on Biological Diversity (CBD). The main objective of Decision 391 was to develop a regional legal instrument to apply CBD and ABS principles.

Decision 391 was preceded by Andean Decision 345: Andean Common Regime on Protection of the Rights of Plant Breeders (1993). In Decision 345, there was a mandate to "approve a regional regime on access to biogenetic resources and to guarantee biosafety". The drafting and negotiation process of Decision 391 lasted from 1993 to 1996.

There are two main general characteristics of the Andean legal regime: (i) supranational character, and (ii) supremacy regarding national rules. As a result of the first principle, the Andean Decision should be applied directly and immediately; nevertheless, all laws need a national authority to apply them.

Decision 391 (or, the Decision) does not establish a national authority at state level. Therefore it is necessary for each Andean country to develop national rules according to their administrative legislation to designate the authority and procedures. In terms of national regulations, Andean Decision 391 has shown different paces of development – Bolivia approved a specific set of regulations in 1997 (Bolivia 1997), Peru in 2009 (Peru 2009), and Ecuador in 2011 (Ecuador 2011; see Cabrera Ormaza, Ch. 9 in this volume), whereas Colombia applies the Decision without any kind of additional national regulations (as Venezuela did when it was still a member of the Andean group).[7]

The Andean regime is a key and fundamental piece of international legislation on ABS that has also influenced various lines of thought, conceptual foci, laws and regulatory projects. The Decision was taken in 1996 when the state of the art on ABS was not too developed. As it was decided just four years after the CBD, the worldwide reflection on its third objective was at an early stage, therefore very few applied cases were analyzed and it was not an area of study for scholars or scientists.

Also, as a consequence of supranational character, Andean norms do not need to be ratified by Andean member countries. However, in accordance with general principles of administrative law,[8] internal regulatory frameworks must define: (i) scope, (ii) steps of the process, (iii) timelines and deadlines, (iv) requests, (v) internal registers, (vi) level and responsibility of national authorities and public officials, among others.

Andean Decision 391 defines genetic resources emphasizing their "real or potential use".[9] It also establishes access procedures, requirements for applications and the elements of the access contract.

---

6 The five countries were Bolivia, Colombia, Ecuador, Peru, and Venezuela.

7 As was explained above, Venezuela left the Andean Community in 2011.

8 Authors agree that some characteristics, among others, of administrative law are: (i) it governs the activities of administrative agencies of government; (ii) it can include rulemaking, adjudication, or enforcement of a specific regulatory agenda; (iii) it is a body of law which deals with the decision making of administrative units of government; (iv) decisions based on administrative law can be reviewed by administrative courts.

9 Andean Decision 391 defines genetic resources in Article 1 as all biological material that contains genetic information of value or of real or potential use.

It must be noted that though Decision 391 recognizes the associated traditional knowledge (TK), innovations and practices of indigenous and local communities (Article 7, Andean Decision 391),[10] further rules for the participation of these communities in ABS processes are still needed.

There is varying criticism regarding the Decision's text, mostly relating to the fact that many of its general regulations require clarification in order to be applicable. Regarding this issue, one should remember that Decision 391 sets principles that can guide the national regulations on ABS while respecting sovereignty rights. For example, the Decision leaves it up to national authorities to draft guidelines and procedures to facilitate its implementation (Article 5, Andean Decision 391). As it is considered a matter of national sovereignty, countries are also tasked with the design of technical, judicial and administrative manuals and protocols required to process applications, contracts, doubts and disputes, and to clarify negotiations about warranties, royalties and, more importantly, guarantees for community participation and protection of TK (known also as the "intangible associated component").

Access to genetic resources under Andean Decision 391

According to the Andean Decision, the process for accessing genetic resources has two stages: (i) presentation and evaluation of the application, and (ii) negotiation of the access contract. For the first stage, the Decision establishes a concrete procedure, while for the second, it proposes guidelines and general conditions in order to help the talks and negotiations between the authorities and the accessing parties. The procedure can be drawn as shown in Figure 8.1.

As said before, in 1996 there were very few examples of access processes done according to the CBD worldwide. In order to facilitate the accomplishment of the Decision, mainly to clarify requirements, the Andean countries approved a resolution which includes a model of an application (Andean Resolution 414, 1996).

Access to genetic resources for scientific research – facilitated or not?

Andean Decision 391 contains a number of provisions applicable to access to genetic resources, including:

a)   access to applications regarding genetic resources (Article 18);
b)   minimal conditions for access (Article 17);

---

10 In recognition of know-how, innovations and traditional practices, member countries – in keeping with the Decision and their complementary national legislation – recognize and value the rights and the authority of the native, Afro-American and local communities to decide about their know-how, innovations and traditional practices associated with genetic resources and their by-products.

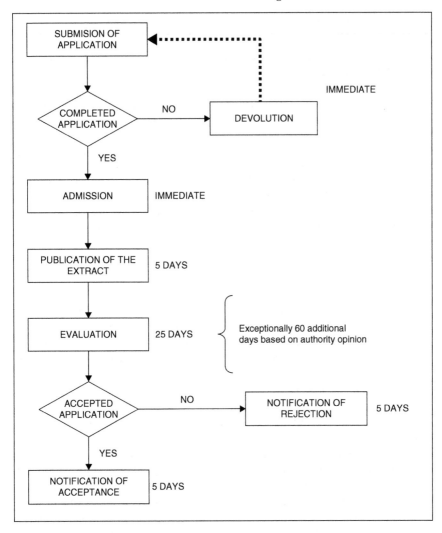

Figure 8.1 Procedure to access genetic resources under Andean Decision 391

Source: Estrella, J, Manosalvas, R, Mariaca, J, Ribadeneira Sarmiento, M (2005) Biodiversity and genetic resources: A guide for its use and access in Ecuador. Quito: EcoCiencia, INIAP, MAE y Abya Yala. (Original in Spanish)

c)   access contracts with the State and the owners of the biological resources and with the TK holders, also called "accessory contracts" (Articles 41 to 44);

d)   administrative procedures supervised by a competent national authority (Article 26 to 31);

e)   acknowledgement of ABS (Article 17); and

f)   the establishment of a national capacity-building process through the incorporation of scientific institutions (Article 17 b).

Table 8.1 Decision 391 Framework Contract

Andean Decision 391

Chapter III on the access contract

Article 36.- The Competent National Authority may enter into access contracts with universities, research centers or well-known researchers to support the execution of several projects, as provided for in this Decision and in keeping with the national legislation of each Member Country.

Article 37.- The *ex situ* conservation centers or other institutions that perform activities involving access to genetic resources or their by-products and, if appropriate, the associated intangible component, should enter into access contracts with the Competent National Authority, pursuant to this Decision.

That CNA may likewise sign access contracts with third parties in regard to genetic resources of which the Member Country is the country of origin and which have been deposited at those centers, bearing in mind the rights and interests referred to in Article 34.

Source: Unofficial translation from Spanish to English by the author of the chapter.

From the abovementioned provisions, other mechanisms and instruments, Andean Decision 391's most favourable element regarding basic research is a specific type of contract which aims at granting special treatment to research centres and academic institutions and promotes the subscription of access contracts with *ex situ* holders of genetic resources (Table 8.1), i.e. the so-called *contrato marco* (framework contract).

The framework contract was introduced in order to facilitate access to genetic resources for scientific purposes. It is important to mention that the framework contract does not consist of a mechanism of shifting the requirements, but an alternative to support basic researchers who might need access to more samples than originally imagined, due to the need of testing and cross information, for example. In case further physical access is needed, the framework contract can be used such that the researchers do not need to start a new access procedure again as further accesses are covered by the framework contract. When Decision 391 established this formula, the main group of researchers it had in mind were the researchers working on *ex situ* collections. It does not mean that other researchers cannot use this provision.

As Decision 391 does not establish a fixed deadline to make a framework contract, a deadline long enough to cover some accesses could be negotiated, for instance for a group of nonclassified varieties.

Since the beginning, the idea behind the framework contract was to make certain national authorities were approached by research institutions or universities in order to negotiate framework contracts, because this instrument also can help national authorities to monitor who, where and how long research on national genetic resources with basic purposes is being carried out.

Despite their advantages, these special contracts have enjoyed only limited development, mostly because such contracts need to be negotiated between the national authority and the university or research centre, and national/institutional and scientific/academic priorities rarely match during a negotiation process.

Regarding another important issue, the Andean Decision interestingly goes beyond and is more concrete than the Nagoya Protocol concerning transboundary resources; while the Nagoya Protocol urges countries to cooperate and collaborate, the Andean Decision defines a specific measure to do so. The mentioned measure established the duty for the country to report to the Secretary of the Andean Countries in the case that an agreed access contract includes transboundary resources. According to this formula, each Andean country should directly notify the other Andean countries and the Headquarters of the Andean Community of any applications, resolutions and authorizations, as well as cancellations and conclusions of any ABS contracts. This obligation includes bilateral or multilateral contracts or agreements and national regulations or judicial decisions.

The issue of transboundary resources is remarkable as the legal formula contradicts the ecological logic – by general rule, genetic resources do not respect national boundaries, while the CBD and the Protocol (Article 11 NP) consider the resources imply sovereignty rights. As is commonly known, biodiversity is spread in nature following ecologic rules, while national borders are a result of political and historical processes. From a scientific research point of view, transboundary resources create situations where different countries of origin for the same resource "compete" among themselves for the role of national counterparts for specific research projects. An ideal scenario would be if the level of judicial security offered by any of those countries would be the defining element that ends this competition. It is well known that these kinds of resources offer an opportunity for the establishment of regional negotiation formulae, regional agreements on participation, project execution and benefit sharing, as well as mechanisms for post-access control. All these measures would ensure legal certainty and also provide better conditions to plan research projects, which are mostly executed in cooperation between different research centres, universities or institutions. In many cases, they are granted by different donors and conditions. Almost all of the donors require clear and predetermined timelines before granting a research project, and during the execution, the fulfilment of announced steps is a condition of acceptance of the final reports.

As mentioned above, Andean Decision 391 includes a regional measure that, unfortunately, has not been applied to current signed contracts.

Through this provision, the Secretariat of Andean Countries serves as a common register and common exchange mechanism of information among the Andean countries; this could be also considered as a clearing-house mechanism regarding ABS contracts in the region.

As already said, it is an interesting mechanism to help the Andean countries to share information among themselves and to interested third parties. Until now, not even one of the signed ABS contracts has been officially communicated by any of the Andean countries to the other members.

Lastly, regarding the establishment of a national capacity-building process through the incorporation of scientific institutions and its particular relevance for scientific research, it is important to note that within the conditions of access requests and contracts, the Decision's text (Article 17) includes:

a) participation of national researchers (Article 17 a);
b) promoting research in the country of origin (Article 17 b);
c) the strengthening of mechanisms for knowledge and technology transfer (Article 17 c); and
d) the strengthening of national capacities (Article 17 e).

Still, access requests do not recognize particularities and limitations of basic research and hence access requirements might not consider the lack of required information, especially when certain information is not available and the search for it is the actual reason for the access request.

The presence of a national counterpart guarantees the building of national capacities in the resource's country of origin. However, in most countries, international cooperation is focused on major universities based on their installed capacity, which limits the participation of smaller academic centres.

Current processes

There are two ongoing processes to reform rules on ABS issues within the Andean subregion: one which is applicable to Decision 391 in order to bring it up to date with the Nagoya Protocol provisions and another one applicable to the Peruvian national rules.

During the sixth Meeting of the Andean Committee on Genetic Resources in Lima on 16 April 2013, Andean countries established a timeline to draft national proposals in order to modify the text of Decision 391 and update it according to the Nagoya Protocol. Some months later (in September 2013) while this process was still going on, the Andean Council of Ministries decided, as part of a restructuring process, to eliminate all committees not related to identified fields. As genetic resources were not mentioned, this might imply that the Andean Committee on Genetic Resources had disappeared (Andean Decision 792 2013). Currently, there is no clarity as to how the reform of Decision 391 will proceed. Until then, we will have to wait to see whether any changes will occur in regard to basic research.

Regarding Peruvian national rules on ABS, the draft of new national rules was opened for public comments and participation in August 2013.[11] As these are still in the form of an unfinished draft – and hence a nonofficial document – it is not possible to present its analysis in this chapter. It is also impossible to predict which changes will be applicable to basic researchers, and hence a need to wait.

11 The draft of the national rules on ABS is available online at www.minam.gob.pe/index. php?option=com_content&view=article&id=2625 (accessed 6 November 2014).

Costa Rica

General information

In Costa Rica, the CBD was included into the country's legal framework through Biodiversity Law No. 7416 (Costa Rica 1994a). The Biodiversity Law (and the CBD) does not include in their jurisdiction any human genetic material[12] or the exchange with commercial purpose between local indigenous communities of genetic resources or the traditional knowledge associated with genetic resources that result from their practices, traditions and customs.

The Costa Rican access regime is complemented by the country's "General Norms for the Access to Genetic and Biochemical Resources and Elements of Biodiversity and Protection of the Associated Knowledge" of 2003, and the "Regulations for Access to Genetic and Biochemical Resources and Elements of Biodiversity in *Ex-Situ* Conditions" of 2007.

Costa Rica's national ABS authority is the National Commission for the Management of Biodiversity, CONAGEBIO, which is structured as follows (Costa Rica 1994a, Article 15):

a) Decision Level: Plenary Commission attached to the Ministry of Environment, Energy and Telecommunications (MINAET), comprising 11 representatives: 6 from various other ministries, 4 belonging to civil society (environmentalists, farmers, native communities and businesspeople) and 1 representative of the public universities. This commission is presided over by MINAET.

b) Executive Level: Technical Office that processes, monitors and evaluates access permits.

As written before, the general rules were established in 2003, while the regulations applicable to *ex situ* conditions were settled in 2007. Though the first group of rules contain some prescriptions relevant to scientific research, the second ruling on *ex situ* conditions is without a doubt mainly devoted to research.

According to general rules from 2003, there are three types of access permits in Costa Rica (Costa Rica 1994a, Article 15 f), as shown in Table 8.2.

It appears evident that any switch from basic research to a different type of use requires a whole new authorization and permit processing. However, at the post-access phase when the results are published, it would seem possible that a new third party (neither the original researcher nor any stakeholder involved) could present an application to access the same resources identifying the application with a different type of research and for a different use. For instance, if the original

---

12 Regulated in Costa Rica by the General Health Law, Law No. 5395 (1973). Updated version published on Official Diary No. 8, January 13, 2004.

Table 8.2 Current types of ABS access permits in Costa Rica

Case / Permit Type	Basic research	Bioprospection	Commercial use
Objective	Research, examine, classify, or increase existing knowledge about genetic or biochemical elements of biodiversity	Systematic search, classification, and research	Interested party makes use of the genetic or biochemical resources and elements of biodiversity
Particularities	With no immediate interest in the commercialization of its results	For commercial purposes – from new sources – from chemical compounds – genes, proteins, microorganisms, and other products with actual or potential economic value that can be found in biodiversity	For commercial purposes Without necessarily being preceded by a basic research program or bioprospection as part of the request
Number of permits granted since 2004 to date[13]	207	34	0

Source: Author, based on JIMENEZ ML, Country Presentation. Inception Workshop – GEF UNEP UICN Regional Project: "Strengthening the Implementation of Access to Genetic Resources and Benefit-Sharing Regimen in Latin America and the Caribbean". Panama City, August 2011.

access was for "basic research", in a second access it could be possible to apply as "bioprospection" type.

Original rules from 2003 regarding the general processing were changed in 2007 in regard to genetic resources in *ex situ* conditions; therefore the procedure applicable to access to genetic resources in *ex situ* conditions in Costa Rica is as shown in Figure 8.2.

It must be taken into account that based on listed exceptions, this procedure is not applicable to: (i) genetic resources which involve traditional knowledge, (ii) genetic resources of domestic animals, and (iii) genetic resources under the scope of the Forest Law (Costa Rica, 2007, Article 2).

Access to genetic resources for scientific research – facilitated or not?

There are certain elements that make the Costa Rican biodiversity law special from a research point of view. The first is a statement saying that its law "does not

13 Updated to April 2012.

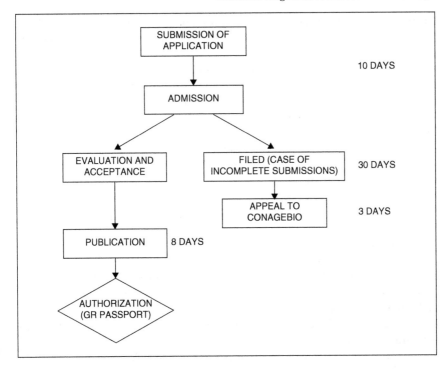

```
              ┌─────────────────────┐
              │  SUBMISSION OF      │
              │  APPLICATION        │
              └─────────────────────┘
                        │                        10 DAYS
                        ▼
              ┌─────────────────────┐
              │     ADMISSION       │
              └─────────────────────┘
              ╱                    ╲
             ▼                      ▼
┌──────────────────┐   ┌──────────────────────────┐
│ EVALUATION AND   │   │ FILED (CASE OF           │   30 DAYS
│ ACCEPTANCE       │   │ INCOMPLETE SUBMISSIONS)  │
└──────────────────┘   └──────────────────────────┘
         │                          │
         │                          ▼
         │             ┌──────────────────────┐
         │             │   APPEAL TO          │      3 DAYS
         │             │   CONAGEBIO          │
         │             └──────────────────────┘
         ▼
┌──────────────────┐
│  PUBLICATION     │  8 DAYS
└──────────────────┘
         │
         ▼
    ◇─────────────◇
    │ AUTHORIZATION │
    │ (GR PASSPORT) │
    ◇─────────────◇
```

Figure 8.2 General rules and procedure to access genetic resources in Costa Rica
Source: (*) Unofficial graphic made by the author of the chapter

affect the autonomy of the universities in matters pertaining to teaching and research in the field of biodiversity, unless such research is carried out with commercial purposes" (Costa Rica 1994a, Article 4). Prior to any analysis it is necessary to remember that in Costa Rica the autonomy of universities has strong social implications. The principle is established in the country's constitution and is granted only to public universities, unlike in other countries where no academic centres are completely autonomous.

Apart from the granted autonomy, the mentioned legal statement and a temporary provision[14] create what we call a "parasystem" of ABS permits. This parasystem owes its existence to the fact that public universities were granted the right one year after the issuing of the law to set up their own ABS regulatory framework. Only the University of Costa Rica made use of this opportunity. Research permits granted under the parasystem are not reviewed or registered by CONAGEBIO or

---

14 Temporary Provision: Public universities, in coordination with the National Council of Rectors, will set up in their internal regulations, in a period of one year after the coming into effect of this law, controls and rules applicable exclusively to the academic activities and research they carry out and that imply access to biodiversity with no commercial purpose. Universities that in the allotted time do not define those controls will remain subject to the ordinary jurisdiction established by this law.

any other authority unless access requires sampling in protected areas (in which case a sampling permit must be obtained from the National System of Conservation Areas, SINAC).

In 2006, CONAGEBIO sought the opinion of the country's attorney general concerning the legality of the parasystem. The attorney general stated that the University of Costa Rica was not required to request basic research permits from CONAGEBIO, thereby implying that the existence of the parasystem was in line with Costa Rica's legislation (Text of the General Attorney's opinion applicable to research done by University of Costa Rica, 2006).[15] His interpretation seems to show that the attorney general gives more favourable treatment to basic research done by the University of Costa Rica than the legal texts do. This ruling could be interpreted as discriminatory regarding basic research proposed or done by other national universities; up to now, this interpretation has not been claimed.

Our underlying hypothesis regarding the Costa Rican case is that facilitation of research does not imply absence of rules, but rather regulatory clarity and better compliance with deadlines. Costa Rican rules applicable to research permits on genetic resources do actually support scientific research. Experts consulted have said that processing of permits takes between two and four months, which seems reasonable though there is room for improvement. Exact times are difficult to determine since these depend on individual negotiations of the prior informed consent (PIC) contracts with the resource's stakeholders. A key element in establishing the processing time is the duration it takes for the applicant to gather the documentation required by the Technical Office.

Some opinions consider that this duration could be shorter. This chapter does not aim at comparing or criticising the duration of national processes, because a comparison of timelines depends on various elements which have not been included in this chapter.

According to one of the sources of information used in this chapter (Cabrera, interview 2011), the main opposition comes from foreign researchers who object to the legal requirement of having to appoint an in-country legal representative to be the spokesperson during the authorization process and the project execution as required by law (Costa Rica 1994b, Article 63 No. 5; Costa Rica 2003, Article 9.1 par. (b)).

15 The attorney general's opinion (C-240–2006) states that Biodiversity Law No. 7788 and Decree No. 31514-MINAE are only applicable to the University of Costa Rica in all that does NOT pertain to access to elements of biodiversity for research with non-commercial purposes. However, as far as the University's internal regulations are subsidiary norms, they still apply in regard to aspects of access and use of genetic resources that are not addressed by the national rules. The general attorney also established a caveat that in situations where basic research is to be conducted on biodiversity located in territories under private domain or when intellectual property rights are under consideration, the applicable law would be the Biodiversity Law. The complete text of the ruling of the general attorney is available online at http://webcache.googleusercontent.com/search?q=cache:eWW6XjL1_1MJ:www.vinv.ucr.ac.cr/girasol-ediciones/documgirasol/biodiversidad/DICTAMEN%2520C-240–2006.doc+&cd=1&hl=es-419&ct=clnk&gl=pe (accessed 11 November 2014) (available in Spanish).

Table 8.3 Competent authorities in matters of PIC in Costa Rica

Authority	Area
Director of Conservation Areas	Protected Natural Areas (belonging to the state)
Regional Councils	Access to border of public roads, rivers, lakes and wetlands
Private owners (ranches)	Access to land and private properties
Indigenous authorities	Law 7316 PIC can be (recommended) presented in native language Establishes protection of community intellectual property rights subject to the *sui generis* regime
National Fisheries Institute (INCOPESCA)	Access in coastal and marine areas outside of protected areas
Owners or representatives	Authorized *ex situ* collections

Source: Author, based on: Jimenez, ML. Country Presentation. Inception Workshop – GEF UNEP UICN Regional Project: "Strengthening the Implementation of Access to Genetic Resources and Benefit-Sharing Regimen in Latin America and the Caribbean". Panama City, August 2011.

Another operational difficulty that has recently developed and intensified is the need for a special procedure when PIC has to be granted by various stakeholders; this possibility was never considered in the law. Under Costa Rican law, the authorities from which PIC must be requested are listed in Table 8.3.

In practice, any project, including basic research projects, that requires access to genetic resources from the varying areas or sites will require as many PICs as the sampling sites imply, including from any provider involved.

Conclusions and recommendations for LAC region-wide implementation of facilitation mechanisms for scientific research

While most Latin American and Caribbean countries are signatories of the CBD, few have implemented national measures regarding ABS, as it can appreciate at List of Access and Benefit Sharing Competent Authorities[16] and List of National focal Points to the ABS Intergovernmental Committee on Nagoya Protocol.[17] This is changing and is expected to change even more after these nations adhere to the Nagoya Protocol.[18] Up to now, the countries that have ratified the Nagoya Protocol in LAC are, from a total of 19, Honduras, Mexico and Panama.[19]

16 Information updated to August 2013. Available online: www.cbd.int/doc/lists/nfp-abs-cna.pdf.
17 Information updated to August 2013. Available online: www.cbd.int/doc/lists/nfp-abs-icnp.pdf.
18 For deeper analysis, refer to Status of Signature and Ratification, Acceptance, Approval or Adhesion of the ABS Nagoya Protocol; Information updated to August 2013. Available online: www.cbd.int/abs/nagoya-protocol/signatories/default.shtml.
19 Information updated to August 2013. Available online at www.cbd.int/abs/nagoya-protocol/signatories/default.shtml.

The countries of the region, generally considered countries of origin or providers of genetic resources, face the dilemma of how to balance concerns regarding promoting basic research without eliminating or weakening prior and post-access controls and how to strengthen those controls without limiting research.

As has been mentioned throughout this chapter, countries in Latin America and the Caribbean need to strengthen scientific research and make use of their unique biodiversity to establish associations and cooperation with research institutions from other countries. The starting points are diverse depending on each country. Some countries do have legal instruments and national systems that allow them to grant permits for basic research, negotiate benefits and implement post-access monitoring, while others do not have any of these elements and experience. This situation could potentially foster South–South exchanges, with a focus on the development of basic research facilitation mechanisms. The fact that genetic resources are shared and have a transboundary characteristic provides an opportunity for future regional legislation to design and implement specific facilitation measures for basic research.

It is also expected that the development of national systems to regulate research on ABS will be done in a way that includes strategic visions that recognize the value of genetic resources for the economic development of LAC countries.

Recommended measures for national authorities

It is clear that basic researchers are faced with several challenges because of a lack of certainty regarding ABS issues for access to genetic resources resulting from unclear rules and differing approaches, scopes and results concerning basic and applied research. It is fair to say that the scientific community had made efforts to address those approaches and scopes over the years through networking, studies, meetings and workshops.[20]

Among them, the first directly implies the challenges caused by national authorities because the development and implementation of national ABS legislation and regulatory measures are completely in their hands. Even considering the national differences of legal systems, it is fair to say that in all cases, the duties of national authorities depend on and follow applicable and relevant laws.

National authorities are the main source of information; they can clarify and explain to basic researchers the legal framework and other situations in the

---

20 One example was the International Workshop on Access and Benefit-sharing in Non-Commercial Biodiversity Research, November 2008; as result of this workshop two submissions were presented to the ABS working group meetings during the Nagoya Protocol process, one to Technical Expert Meeting Concepts, Terms, Working Definitions and Sectoral Approaches relating to the International Regime on access and benefit-sharing (December 2008, Namibia). Available online: www. cbd.int/doc/meetings/abs/absgtle-01/information/absgtle-01-inf-02-en.doc) and a second one to the Technical and Legal Experts on Compliance in the Context of the International Regime on Access And Benefit-Sharing (January 2009, Japan). Available online: http://barcoding.si.edu/PDF/Tokyo%20AHTEG%20Submission%20-%20FINAL.pdf?lang=en.

countries and in the region. Among other situations, the author includes, as an example, political and local sensibilities regarding ABS issues (as in LAC there are uncountable traditional knowledge holders), and accessing genetic resources even with basic purposes and without traditional knowledge associated could be problematic.

National authorities of LAC countries should develop internal manuals in order to equip their officials with application tools. Such manuals must provide clarification for the officials regarding judicial, administrative and technical issues related to requests for access. There are situations that need to be handled in greater depth, e.g. when managing TK. Other cases require specialized knowledge, e.g. research on species not included in Annex I of the International Treaty on Plant Genetic Resources for Food and Agriculture (so-called FAO Treaty).

A key element to be clearly defined in order to ensure a certain level of confidentiality for the parties involved is which information should be maintained, e.g. databases, lists of researchers and public registers of applications, licenses, contracts and guarantees. The same applies concerning details of strategic elements of ABS contracts (including monitoring and evaluation) and procedures to deal with and execute guarantees in ABS, special licenses and contracts with scientific collections, museums, herbaria and zoos, among others.[21]

The Nagoya Protocol is quite specific regarding the principles that must be developed within national regulations in order to promote and facilitate basic research. In addition to these regulations, administrative measures must be implemented that clearly define different administrative scenarios, including the restructuring of government units and its responsible departments for effective management of the Protocol. These measures must become part of a strategy of institutional strengthening for the national authority and other institutions with secondary or ancillary competences, e.g. national offices of intellectual property.

National authorities must design and implement the necessary formats and instructions specific to each interest group related to scientific research. When only one format exists, it needs to acknowledge the limitations and particularities of each of these groups.

The existence of TK has the potential of turning topics such as ethnobotanical research into controversial issues. It is important that LAC countries define limits to the conceptual, social and geographic reach of the TK, the procedure around PIC and related disputes, as well as mechanisms that ensure the proper distribution of resulting benefits.

Recommended measures for researchers

Since the CBD, basic researchers demanded that national authorities and policy-makers enhance facilitation through a procedure that is as easy and quick as possible.[22]

---

21 For deeper analysis on contracts provisions, read Young (2009).
22 For deeper studies on effectiveness of ABS regimes, read Richerzhagen (2010).

It is necessary to strike a balance by acknowledging that, on the one hand, scientists need clear and predefined requests as much as they need to project how much time they need for doing the research, while, on the other hand, keeping in mind that researchers should not think that all the regulations are draconian measures and thus consider the licensing process and the authorizations as a waste of time.

It is undeniable that more effort should be made to implement the facilitation of research established in the Nagoya Protocol by national authorities. The scientific community must push for authorities to provide clear guidelines and materials that explain requirements and procedures to access resources located, for example, inside protected or disputed areas.

Although researchers are not expected to become legal experts, a basic familiarity with legal requirements of the CBD and Nagoya Protocol regulations would be highly beneficial.[23]

In that regard, a better situation would be if researchers increase their communication channels to national authorities, national focal points and other qualified resources such as national clearing-house mechanisms.

The author does not share a common opinion that all basic researchers are paramount to biopirates, but considers that the damages produced by misuse and misappropriations cause immeasurable detriment to the entire research community. So, all alternatives and changes to improve compliance should be utilized. In that regard, there are plenty of examples of serious research initiatives that strictly comply with the principles of the CBD and national regulations and fairly share the non-commercial benefits with the countries of origin. The author strongly supports the use of manuals, guidelines and codes of conduct that enhance the standards of behaviour of scientists and believes this group, as well as other users of genetic resources, mostly need legal certainty in the countries of origin where they work and the resources and partners are located (Ribadeneira Sarmiento 2014).

Being a basic researcher is not a guarantee in regard to respecting the law, therefore the author also believes that unaccepted and illegal behaviour from members of the research community (national or international) should be investigated, persecuted and punished by national authorities according to the law.[24] Efforts must be done by authorities to do so.

During previous research (Ribadeneira Sarmiento 2008), the author analyzed projects submitted for granting and learned that, as the compliance with the principles of the CBD and ABS rules was a binding request from the granting institution, the researchers adopted the recommendations given in order to include or develop benefits through a national partner, contact national authorities and check legal frameworks (Ribadeneira Sarmiento 2008). Therefore, the author would consider it a big step forward if national and international public granting of basic research institutions include binding rules regarding the CBD and ABS principles, as the German Research Foundation (DFG) (see Stoll,

---

23 For comprehensive analysis on legal elements of Nagoya Protocol, read Kamau, Fedder and Winter (2010).

24 For deeper analysis on irregular accesses and biopiracy cases, read Robinson (2010).

Ch. 18 in this volume) has done since 2008 (DFG 2008). This effort could be supported by including and making available in-house mechanisms for researchers, such as guidelines, a set of study cases, good and better practices and clearinghouse mechanisms.

References

Books, journal articles and grey literature

Bendix, J, Paladines, B, Ribadeneira Sarmiento, M, Romero, LM, Valarezo, C, Beck, E. (2010) "Benefit sharing by research, education and knowledge transfer – a success story of biodiversity research in southern Ecuador", in: Brooks, LA, Aricò, S (eds) *Tracking Key Trends in Biodiversity Science and Policy*. Based on the proceedings of UNESCO International Conference on Biodiversity Science and Policy, UNESCO.

Deutsche Forschungsgemeinschaft (DFG) (2008) Supplementary Instructions for funding proposals concerning research projects within the scope of the Convention on Biological Diversity (CBD), Available online at www.dfg.de/formulare/1_021e/1_021e.pdf (accessed 22 August 2013).

Estrella, J, Manosalvas, R, Mariaca, J, Ribadeneira Sarmiento, M (2005) *Biodiversity and genetic resources: A guide for its use and access in Ecuador*. Quito: EcoCiencia, INIAP, MAE and Abya Yala. (Original in Spanish).

Kamau, EC, Fedder, B, Winter, G (2010) "The Nagoya Protocol on access to genetic resources and benefit sharing: What is new and what are the implications for provider and user countries and the scientific community", *Law, Environment and Development Journal* 6(3), pp. 46–262, Available online at www.lead-journal.org/content/10246.pdf (accessed 22 August 2013).

Ribadeneira Sarmiento, M (2008) Guidelines of basic researchers, experiences made by DFG, Workshop Access and Benefit Sharing in Non-Commercial Biodiversity, November 2008, Bonn, Germany, Available online at http://absbonn.pbworks.com/w/page/1259729/FrontPage (accessed 22 August 2013).

Ribadeneira Sarmiento, M (2014, August) *The Nagoya Protocol on access to genetic resources and benefit sharing: Four challenges for its national implementation in LAC*. OPERA Magazine, Universidad Externado de Colombia. Number 15 (2014). (Original in Spanish). Available on http://revistas.uexternado.edu.co/index.php?journal=opera (accessed 24 March 2015)

Richerzhagen, C (2010) *Protecting biological diversity: The effectiveness of access and benefit-sharing regimes*, New York: Routledge.

Robinson, D (2010) *Confronting biopiracy: Challenges, cases and international debate*, London: Earthscan.

Young, T (ed.) (2009) *Contracting for ABS: The legal and scientific implications of bioprospecting contracts*. Gland, Switzerland: IUCN.

Legal instruments and legal proposals

Andean Decision 345 (1993) Common Regime on Protection of the Rights of Plant Breeders (Original in Spanish).

Andean Decision 391 (1996) Common Access Regime to Genetic Resources (Original in Spanish).

Andean Resolution 414 (1996) Referential Model of Application to Access to Genetic Resources under Andean Decision 391 (Original in Spanish).

Andean Resolution 415 (1996) Referential Model of Access Contract under Andean Decision 391 (Original in Spanish).

Andean Decision 792 (2013) Restructuration on the Andean Integration System (Original Spanish).

BOLIVIA (1997) "National regulation on common access regime to genetic resources within the framework of Andean Decision 391, National Decree No. 24676", *Official Diary*, June 21 1997 (Original in Spanish).

COSTA RICA (1994a) Biodiversity Law, Law No. 7416 June 30 1994.

COSTA RICA (1994b) Law No. 7788 June 30, 1994 (Original in Spanish: Ley 7788).

COSTA RICA (2003) "National rules for access to elements, genetic and biochemistry from the biodiversity and TK protection. Executive Order No. 31514-MINAE", *Official Diary*, No. 241 December 15 2003 (Original in Spanish).

COSTA RICA (2004) "Health general law, Law No. 5395", *Official Diary*, No. 8 January 13 2004.

COSTA RICA (2007) "National rules for access to elements, genetic and biochemistry from the biodiversity in ex situ conditions. Executive Order No. 33697", *Official Diary*, No. 74 April 18 2007 (Original in Spanish).

ECUADOR (2011) "National regulation on common access regime to genetic resources within the framework of Andean Decision 391", *Official Diary*, No. 553 October 11 2011 (Original in Spanish).

PERU (2009) Executive Order No. 003–2009-MINAM. "National regulation on common access regime to genetic resources within the framework of Andean Decision 391", *Official Diary*, No. 10508 February 7 2009 (Original in Spanish).

Internet available documents and information

COSTA RICA. Text of the General Attorney's opinion applicable to research done by University of Costa Rica. Available online at http://webcache.googleusercontent.com/search?q=cache:eWW6XjL1_1MJ:www.vinv.ucr.ac.cr/girasol-ediciones/documgirasol/biodiversidad/DICTAMEN%2520C-240–2006.doc+&cd=1&hl=es-419&ct=clnk&gl=pe: (accessed 11 November 2014) (available in Spanish).

List of Access and Benefit Sharing Competent Authorities; updated to 22 August 2013. Available online at www.cbd.int/doc/lists/nfp-abs-cna.pdf (accessed 22 August 2013).

List of National Focal Points to the Intergovernmental Committee on ABS Nagoya Protocol; updated to 22 August 2013. Available online at www.cbd.int/doc/lists/nfp-abs-icnp.pdf (accessed 22 August 2013).

Status of Signature and Ratification, Acceptance, Approval or Adhesion of the ABS Nagoya Protocol; updated to 22 August 2013. Available online at www.cbd.int/abs/nagoya-protocol/signatories/default.shtml (accessed 22 August 2013).

Submission from the international workshop on the topic of "Access and Benefit-sharing in Non-Commercial Biodiversity Research", Bonn, 17–19 November 2008 to Technical Expert Meeting Concepts, Terms, Working Definitions and Sectoral Approaches relating to the International Regime on access and benefit-sharing, Dec 2008, Namibia. Available online at www.cbd.int/doc/meetings/abs/absgtle-01/information/absgtle-01-inf-02-en.doc (accessed 22 August 2013).

Submission of views from an International Workshop on "Access and Benefit-sharing in Non-Commercial Biodiversity Research", Bonn, 17–19 November 2008 to the Technical and Legal Experts on Compliance in the Context of the International Regime on Access And Benefit-Sharing, January 2009, Japan. Available online at www.cbd.int/doc/?meeting=ABSGTLE-02 (accessed 24 March 2015).

9 Research on genetic resources in the framework of the Ecuadorian ABS law

Legal issues preventing the current system from being effective

Maria Victoria Cabrera Ormaza

Introduction

As a member of the Andean Community of Nations (CAN), Ecuador has been part of the CAN regime on genetic resources (GRs) since 1996 when it was established by Decision 391. Decision 391 is a communitarian norm for the protection and use of genetic resources and associated traditional knowledge (TK) within the CAN jurisdiction. Pursuant to articles 2 and 3 of the treaty creating the Court of Justice of the CAN, the Decision constitutes a binding and directly applicable norm for all CAN member states. As explained in more detail in another chapter (see Ribadeneira Sarmiento, Ch. 8 in this volume), the original purpose of Decision 391 was to help realize the Convention on Biological Diversity (CBD)'s third objective, namely the fair and equitable sharing of benefits arising from the utilization of GRs. Yet, Decision 391's strong emphasis on control seems to prevent rather than foster the attainment of this aim.

The Ecuadorian Constitution of 2008 contains specific provisions concerning GRs and TK. Inspired by the Andean norm, it reaffirms the ownership of the State over its GRs and the right of indigenous communities to preserve their traditional practices associated with the conservation of GRs. With the adoption of Executive Decree No. 905 in 2011, the Ecuadorian government attempted to improve the operationalization of Decision 391, though without major successful results until today (Lago Candeira & Silvestri 2014, 48).

This chapter provides an overview of the Ecuadorian ABS[1] law and outlines certain substantive and procedural problems that hinder its effective implementation. For this purpose, this chapter has been structured in three parts: Part I briefly explains the origins and foundations of the Ecuadorian ABS law in Decision 391. In doing so, it examines how the principles embodied in that communitarian

---

1 The abbreviation ABS refers to the set of rules governing access to genetic resources and associated traditional knowledge and the fair and equitable sharing of benefits arising from their utilization. Translations of the dispositions of the Ecuadorian and CAN laws are made by the author alone and for the exclusive purpose of this chapter. Shortcomings or inaccuracies in the translation shall be attributed to the author exclusively.

norm are reflected in the Ecuadorian Constitution of 2008 and Executive Decree No. 905. Part II identifies two normative problems of the existing ABS regime. The first relates to the broadly and unclearly defined sovereign rights of the State over its GRs. The second relates to the difficulties in addressing the question of GRs separately from that of TK, which means that any effort to facilitate research on GRs may fail if not accompanied by possible solutions for the protection of TK. Part III illustrates the access procedure established in 2011 and points out the complexities involved. In the conclusion, a summary of the findings will be provided along with some suggestions for reforms that may be needed to overcome the problems and hurdles of the existing regime.

Part I. Origins and foundations

The Ecuadorian ABS regulatory framework comprises basically three legal instruments: Decision 391, the Ecuadorian Constitution and Executive Decree No. 905. According to the principle of supremacy of the Constitution (Constitution, article 24), the constitutional provisions on GRs and traditional knowledge shall prevail, followed by Decision 391 and Executive Decree No. 905. In terms of procedures, the communitarian norm and the Executive Decree can be seen rather as mutually complementary. This chapter does not attempt to provide an extensive explanation of the content of Decision 391 as a regional model for ABS. It only focuses on certain aspects of Decision 391 which are relevant in the analysis of the ABS Ecuadorian law.

Decision 391 is founded on the principle of the sovereignty of the State over the GRs originating within its territorial jurisdiction (Decision 391, preamble and articles 5 and 6). It also recognizes the right of indigenous, Afro-American and local communities to decide on the use of their traditional knowledge, innovations and practices related to the GRs and their derivatives (Decision 391, article 7). In addition, the communitarian norm reflects the two core rules of the CBD in relation to ABS: The prior and informed consent (PIC) of the provider country constitutes a precondition for accessing GRs for both commercial and non-commercial research (Decision 391, article 5), and the benefits derived from any utilization of the GRs shall be fairly and equitably distributed between the provider and the user of such resources (Decision 391, article 2 a) on the basis of mutually agreed terms. The promotion of scientific and technological research also appears as one of the driving forces of the CAN instrument (Decision 391, article 2 d). This objective can be seen as related to the international obligation of States to endeavour to create conditions to facilitate access to their GRs for environmentally sound uses (CBD, article 15.2) Yet, the attainment of such an aim has proven difficult due to the apparently predominant restrictive approach of Decision 391 (Ruíz 2008, 140; Gómez Lee 2012, 50. See also Ribadeneira Sarmiento, Ch. 8 in this volume).

In line with Decision 391, the Ecuadorian Constitution of 2008 proclaims the sovereignty of the State over its GRs, which are regarded as public property (Constitution, article 400). It also acknowledges the right of indigenous communities to *maintain, protect and develop* their traditional practices associated with the con-servation of GRs (Constitution, article 57.12). Such rights are extended to other Afro-Ecuadorian and peasant communities (Constitution, articles 58 and 59).

PIC is embodied in article 1 of Executive Decree No. 905. In Ecuador, the authority to grant PIC rests with the Minister of the Environment, who acts as the competent national authority (Executive Decree No. 905, article 7). The Ecuadorian regulation reaffirms the commitment of the State to foster use of GRs by creating conditions that enable fair and equitable sharing of the benefits arising out of the use of GRs and their derivatives, and the transfer of the appropriate technology (Executive Decree No. 905, article 1.1, 1.3 and 1.4). In connection to this, the Decree specially promotes access and use of GRs for the purpose of developing scientific and technological capacities that help meet the basic needs of the population, to preserve biological diversity and to diversify the national production (Executive Decree No. 905, article 1.5).

Part II. Substantive problems

Undefined limits of the sovereign rights of the State over its GRs

The first problem of the current Ecuadorian ABS system is a conceptual one and relates to a broad and far-reaching understanding of the principle of sovereignty of the State over its GRs. In the context of Decision 391, the content of this principle can be read as implying two things: first, the ability of the State to decide on the terms and conditions upon which a person or institution can access GRs and their derivatives (Decision 391, article 5); and, second, the recognition of the absolute and perpetual ownership of the State over its GRs, including the deriva-tives (Decision 391, article 6). This second aspect was not explicitly mentioned in the CBD but can be found in the interpretation given by some scholars on the notion of State's sovereignty over GRs (see Aguilar 2003, 179; Winter 2009, 20). It is precisely in this element of the concept of sovereignty where difficulties arise, as explained below.

A closer look at the concept of GRs in the preamble of Decision 391 may help one to better understand what falls into the scope of this principle. "Genetic resources" are defined as "all biological materials that contain genetic information of real and potential value". This definition is repeated in article 6 of Executive Decree No. 905. It must be noted that the definition makes explicit reference to the "genetic information". Such a reference cannot be found in the CBD, in which GRs are simply defined as "genetic material of actual or potential value" (CBD, article 2). The incorporation of the term "genetic information" into Deci-sion 391's definition of GR raises doubts as to the extent to which the State, on the basis of that definition, could claim ownership and control over the informa-tional content of GRs that is explored and developed in the course of scientific research. This question becomes crucial if one considers that the economic value relates mostly to the discovered information (Stoll 2009, 9; Cabrera Medaglia &

Lopez Silva 2008, 41). Taken to the extreme, a broad interpretation of the principle of sovereignty in this case may assume that the State has absolute property rights over the discovered genetic content and, thereby, an unlimited ability to utilize and restrict the use of such information. Such an interpretation, however, would not necessarily take due account of the interests of the researchers, who may understandably claim for both moral and economic recognition of their findings.

Another problematic issue concerns the situation of derivatives of GRs. As mentioned earlier, in the light of Decision 391, the sovereign rights of the State over its GRs extends to the derivatives, which are defined as "the molecule or combination of natural molecules coming from the metabolism of living beings, including fractions of living or dead biological organisms" (Decision 391, preamble). The Constitution does not explicitly recognize the State's ownership of derivatives, but the Preamble of Executive Decree No. 905 does. Furthermore, it can be argued that, based on the direct applicability of Andean Communitarian law (Tremolada 2005, 155; Estrella, Manosalvas, Mariaca, & Ribadeneira Sarmiento 2005, 49), the silence of the Constitution with respect to the legal situation of derivatives may not prevent the State from attempting to assert its sovereignty rights over them. In such a case, a controversial question that remains unanswered is whether the derivatives that have been subsequently cultivated or bred by the user may also fall into the scope of sovereign rights of the provider country. Another question that needs to be addressed is whether the access to the derivatives is implied in the permission affecting the resources from which such derivatives come (Cabrera Medaglia & Lopez Silva 2008, 39–40). These uncertainties may eventually lead to conflicts among the affected parties (Tvedt & Young 2007, 74).

GRs and TK: two questions that seem to be inseparable

Both Decision 391 and the Executive Decree No. 905 contemplate the possibility that GRs include an inseparable intangible component, which consists of "any knowledge, innovation or individual or collective practice of real or potential value, associated with the GRs or their derivatives" (Decision 391, article 1; Executive Decree No. 905, article 6). In this case, Executive Decree No. 905 requires the PIC of the community that holds such knowledge (Executive Decree No. 905, articles 1.7 and 20). In an ABS transaction, the PIC of the holder of TK shall be materialized in the conclusion of an access and benefit-sharing agreement between the representative of the community concerned and the applicant (Executive Decree No. 905, article 34). According to the Decree, the applicant has the duty to submit a plan designed to obtain the PIC of the affected community and shall bear all the costs involved in the implementation of such plan (Executive Decree No. 905, article 20). Still, it is far from clear how the owners of the traditional knowledge are to be identified and how PIC of the community can operate effectively when there is still much uncertainty with regards to the representation of indigenous communities. These are questions that have often been pointed out in legal literature but to which no clear solutions have been provided (Wynberg & Laird 2009, 75; Duffield 2009, 65). One measure that has been recently put in place by the Government in its attempt to overcome this uncertainty is the registration of medical plants cultivated by indigenous communities. In 2014, it was announced that approximately 490 varieties of plants used in traditional medicine were registered by the Ecuadorian Institute of Intellectual Property (IEPI).[2] An evaluation of the efficacy of such policy measures is difficult to make at this stage and goes beyond the scope of this chapter.

Cognizant of the abovementioned problems relating to traditional knowledge, one could raise the question as to whether it would be possible, from a normative point of view, to address and discuss the question of GRs in isolation. To a certain extent, Executive Decree No, 905 attempts to do so by separating negotiations on GRs from that on traditional knowledge. However, such a distinction becomes blurred from a constitutional perspective, since traditional knowledge has been approached in very close connection with the use of biodiversity. For example, article 57.12 of the Constitution recognizes the collective right of indigenous communities to maintain and develop their traditional knowledge, including the GRs that contain biological and agricultural diversity. In a similar manner, article 57.8 confers upon indigenous communities the right to participate through the use of their ancestral knowledge in the use and conservation of biodiversity. Such constitutional provisions may suggest the existence of – what has been called – a "holistic approach" to traditional knowledge (McManis & Terán 2011, 142; Aguilar 2003, 177). Furthermore, it must be mentioned that, for Executive Decree No. 905, the determination of the existence of an intangible component associated with GRs seems to depend more heavily on the communities than on the competent authority. Articles 19 and 22 of the Decree, read together, seem to suggest that any community could claim the existence of associated TK in the course of any procedure for accessing GRs and, on this basis, attempt to assert their right to PIC. The foregoing suggests that any attempt to foster research on GRs in Ecuador may necessarily be accompanied by efforts to develop a legal system for the use and protection of the traditional knowledge and in consultation with the indigenous communities. The obligation to consult is required by the Indigenous and Tribal Peoples Convention ratified by Ecuador in 1998 and reaffirmed by article 57.17 of the Constitution. At this point one can recall the affirmation of some scholars that "obtaining the prior and informed consent of communities holding knowledge about biodiversity from the very outset of a project – and engaging them as active partners – is an absolutely fundamental principle of benefit sharing" (Wynberg & Chennells 2009, 118).

2 See Diario El Comercio, 20 March 2014, available online at www.elcomercio.com/actualidad/ ecuador/490-plantas-medicinales-de-comunidad.html.

Part III. Procedural aspects

Rules and procedures for accessing and using GRs

As mentioned earlier, Decision 391 established a standard procedure for accessing GRs which was further complemented by Executive Decree No. 905. As a caveat, it should be noted that even though the Ecuadorian environmental legislation contemplates the possibility to grant permissions for scientific research on the wild flora and fauna, such permissions do not entail the consent of the State to allow access to the genetic information of such species (Unified text of the Secondary Environmental Legislation of the Minister of the Environment (TULAS), Book IV, article 6). Such a consent can only be obtained according to the rules and procedures described below. Illegal access to and use of GRs without PIC of the competent authority has been punishable by the Ecuadorian criminal law since 2014 (Integral Organic Penal Code, article 248).

According to Executive Decree No. 905, use of GRs in *in situ* or *ex situ* conditions fall under the term "access", including derivatives and the related intangible components, for the purposes of research, bioprospection, conservation, industrial or any other commercial use (Executive Decree, article 6). It must be noted that bioprospecting has been defined by the Decree as the systematic exploration of GRs for commercial purposes (Executive Decree, article 6). The access procedure contained in the Executive Decree No. 905 includes a phase of revision of the application form and the required documentation and a phase of negotiation of the access agreement. It is the second phase where the rules for the distribution of the benefits derived from the use of GRs and the related traditional knowledge have to be discussed by the affected parties.

The procedure for accessing genetic resources begins with the submission of an access application to the Ministry of the Environment. Applicants are required to include in their applications indications concerning their professional and academic background; the purpose of the research project; the origin and geographical location of the GRs; the local university (so-called *Institución Nacional de Apoyo*) that will join the user in the course of research; and the communities whose knowledge is associated with the GRs (Executive Decree No. 905, article 15).

The application, once approved by the competent national authority, must be registered in the national record of access applications (Executive Decree No. 905, article 17). In addition, a notice informing of the approved application shall be published by the competent national authority in a newspaper with nationwide circulation, so as to allow affected parties the opportunity to object to the application (Executive Decree No. 905, article 18).

Subsequently, both the competent national authority and the applicant can enter into the negotiation of the access agreement. As mentioned earlier, the conditions on the use of associated traditional knowledge shall be conducted between the user and the community separately and stipulated in a separate agreement (Executive Decree No. 905, article 20). The Decree contains a list of basic issues that are subject to negotiation. These include, among others, the participation of nationals in the research activities, mechanisms for the distribution and payment of benefits, transfer of technology, transfer of biological material, monitoring mechanisms, reporting duties, follow-up mechanisms and disclosure of the outcome of the research (Executive Decree No. 905, article 26). With respect to benefit sharing, it must be mentioned that pursuant to article 26 of the Decree, the benefits that are to be distributed include economic, scientific, and technological ones. After the parties have agreed upon the conditions on access and use of GRs, the Ministry of the Environment has to issue the permission for accessing GRs in the form of a resolution that counts as evidence of the prior and informed consent (Executive Decree No. 905, article 46). Upon receipt of the permissions, users are required to provide liability guarantees whose amount may vary depending on the budget of the project (Executive Decree No. 905, article 31).

It is important to mention that under article 39 of Executive Decree No. 905, it is possible to conclude so-called *framework agreements* for the exclusive purpose of scientific research supported by local universities or research centres. The idea to allow for conclusion of such agreement stems from Decision 391 (see also Ribadeneira Sarmiento, Ch. 8 in this volume). Research on GRs under a framework agreement is not subject to the access procedure described above, but to the provision of detailed information concerning the research project and the methodology. Moreover users are required to assume the obligation to report to the authority on the findings of the research and the publications which have been done on the basis of such findings (Executive Decree No. 905, article 41). It must be mentioned that Executive Decree No. 905 does not offer a definition of "non-commercial research", but contains a nonexhaustive list of activities, which fall under the scope of a framework agreement. These include biological systematics, taxonomy, conservation, evolution, population biology, biogeography and phylogeography (Executive Decree No. 905, article 2.4). It is worth noting that, under this exceptional contract, users have the possibility to transfer GRs outside the country upon permission by the competent national authority provided that duplicates of the corresponding samples are deposited in the repositories authorized by such authority (Executive Decree No. 905, article 41.2).

Evaluation

One of the positive aspects of Executive Decree No. 905 is that it contains clear guidance in relation to the information that needs to be provided, as well as the steps to be followed from the submission of the access application until the conclusion of the access agreement. Considering that the national ABS regulation is primarily based on Decision 391, users can perfectly make use of the model application form designed by the CAN (Such models can be found under http://intranet.comunidadandina.org/documentos/Gacetas/gace217.pdf). Also, the participation of a local university in the whole process of access and use of GRs can be of great significance to ensure both the development of the capacities of nationals involved in research activities and a better monitoring over the use of the resources.

On the other hand, Executive Decree No. 905's procedure is weak in terms of time effectiveness and legal certainty. Time effectiveness can easily be affected by the fact that the applicant is requested to conclude a wide range of supplementary agreements with different stakeholders, including private owners of biological resources, local universities, holders of traditional knowledge and *ex situ* conservation centres, to mention only a few. Also, the high number of administrative agencies involved in the application revision process, from which expertise statements are demanded, make the whole procedure overly bureaucratic.

Another problem lies in the disparities between the State and the user when negotiating the terms of the access agreement. For example, Executive Decree No. 905 recognizes an apparently unlimited ability of the State to unilaterally suspend the access agreement in the case that it considers the use of GRs to entail a risk for such resources. Since the Decree does not provide clear indications as to what kind of risks may trigger the suspension of the agreement, the authority seems to be allowed a wide margin of discretion to decide on the matter. Put differently, the decision to restrict or suspend access to GRs that have been lawfully obtained seems to respond to political rather than to legal consideration. This may run counter to article 15.2 of the CBD which prevents States from imposing arbitrary restrictions to the use of GRs (Kamau & Winter 2009, 366). Furthermore, the Decree does not confer upon users any kind of rights or guarantees assuring that the conditions upon which permissions granted would not be simply altered at the will of the competent authority. The above suggests that the overall aim of Executive Decree No. 905 has been limited to emphasize the unlimited sovereign power of the State to regulate and control GRs, thus making promotion of scientific and commercial research on GRs a very difficult task under the existing ABS regime.

In addition, it must be mentioned that the Nagoya Protocol on Access and Benefit-Sharing of 2010, the ratification of which the Ecuadorian Government supports,[3] emphasizes the necessity to facilitate access. Article 8 (a) NP requires parties to "create conditions to promote and encourage research which contributes to the conservation and sustainable use of biological diversity, particularly in developing countries, including through simplified measures on access for non-commercial research purposes, taking into account the need to address a change of intent for such research". Concerning this issue, Decision 391 does not clearly envisage the possibility of change of intent on the basis of a framework access agreement. Moreover, under Executive Decree No. 905, a person or institution that has obtained permission for accessing GRs for non-commercial purpose on the basis of a framework access agreement is not allowed to modify its intent to a commercial one in the course of the research activity. Article 6 of Executive Decree No. 905 expressly prevents users from making commercial use of the

3 See public announcement posted on the official site of the Minister of the Environment on 29 July 2013, available online at www.ambiente.gob.ec/mae-apoya-la-ratificacion-del-ecuador-en-protocolo-de-nagoya/.

results of any research activity which was enabled through the conclusion of a framework access agreement.

Conclusions and suggestions

The aim of this chapter was to provide an overview of the Ecuadorian ABS legal framework and highlight the normative problems that may hinder its effective implementation. It was indicated that the Ecuadorian ABS regime comprises three legal instruments: Decision 391, a directly applicable communitarian law of the CAN, which dates back to 1996; the Ecuadorian Constitution of 2008; and Executive Decree No. 905, an administrative regulation aimed to help implementation of Decision 391. This chapter has also shown that despite the significant efforts to develop a comprehensive and explanatory framework for accessing GRs both at the communitarian and at the national level, from a legal point of view, the implementation of the existing rules continues to be problematic in Ecuador for different reasons.

First, it is uncertain as to what extent the State can exercise sovereignty powers over the informational content of GRs developed in the course of scientific research. The same holds true in the case of the derivatives resulting from subsequent breeding activities. In this regard, the author suggests that a reconsideration of the content and implications of the exercise of the sovereign rights of the State over the GRs is necessary both at the communitarian and national level. A narrower and more precise definition of the rights of the State over the GRs, both prior to and after the conclusion of ABS transactions, which takes the interests of users into consideration, is indispensable to create a climate of legal certainty.

A second problem relates to the absence of a set of norms for the protection and regulation of the use of traditional knowledge. It has been demonstrated that access to GRs simply cannot be approached in isolation. A solution for the problem of TK becomes crucial if one wants to ensure successful completion and further implementation of the access agreement. A legal solution can be developed on the basis of existing domestic norms on indigenous participation in other decision-making contexts, some of which have already been put in place in the last few years. This is the case of the regulation on consultation with indigenous communities concerning legislative measures (*Instructivo para la Aplicación de la Consulta Prelegislativa*) or the regulation on free, prior and informed consultation with indigenous communities concerning hydrocarbon exploitation activities (*Reglamento de Aplicación de los Mecanismos de Participación Social establecidos en la Ley de Gestión Ambiental*), both of them adopted 2012.

This chapter has also pointed out the shortcomings of the ABS procedures established in Executive Decree No. 905 which are basically twofold. The first shortcoming lies in the excessive number of institutions and actors involved, as well as in supplementary agreements that need to be concluded. In this regard it would be advisable to streamline the revision phase by, for example, reducing the number of regulatory agencies to two advisory bodies, a technical one and a legal one. A technical body may, for example, include academics and experts with wide knowledge on different kinds of biological resources, who could collaborate in the assessment of actual and potential risks involved in activities relating to GRs. A legal advisory body may include delegates of the intellectual property agency and indigenous representatives that could help in assessing compliance with the legal requirements. Another way to make the current access procedure more efficient is through what some legal scholars understand as "procedural integration". This means that a competent body shall coordinate the procedures and conditions of granting access to avoid any contradiction of requirements and a protracted waiting period (Kamau & Winter 2009, 371–373).

The second shortcoming lies in the evident disparities between the State and the user, both in terms of bargaining power and of recognized rights. This chapter calls for a revision of the existing regulations so as to fix such disparities, keeping in mind that, in light of the CBD, a power to regulate shall be read together with the obligation to facilitate. It must be noted that a more flexible legal framework aimed at fostering research on GRs may need to be accompanied by the further development and strengthening of monitoring mechanisms. In this regard, the CAN legal system could provide a legal and political basis for the development of common and more effective regulations (see Ribadeneira Sarmiento, Ch. 8 in this volume).

Finally, with respect to the question of change of intent, the Ecuadorian ABS law expressly excludes the possibility of change of intent (from non-commercial to commercial research) on the basis of a framework access agreement. A reform of Executive Decree No. 905 may therefore be necessary in order to enable change of intent through the use of the so-called "come-back clauses" (Kamau, Fedder, & Winter 2010, 256) that would open the possibility for renegotiation of the PIC and a discussion on the terms of benefit sharing. In such a case it would be fair for the State to demand certain guarantees from the users and to strengthen monitoring and reporting obligations.

References

Books and articles

Aguilar, G (2003) "Access to genetic resources and protection of traditional knowledge" in: Bellmann, C, Dutfield, G, Meléndez-Ortiz, R (eds) *Indigenous territories: Development perspectives on TRIPS, trade and sustainability*, London: Earthscan, pp. 175–183.

Cabrera Medaglia, J, López Silva, C (2008) "Efrentando los problemas de acceso mientras que se brinda certeza a los usarios", IUCN Serie de Política y Derecho Ambiental 67(1).

Dutfield, G (2009) "Protecting the rights of indigenous peoples: Can prior and informed consent help" in: Wynberg, R, Schroeder, D, Chennells, R (eds) *Indigenous peoples, consent and benefit-sharing: Lessons from the San-Hoodia case*, Springer, pp. 53–67.

Estrella, J, Manosalvas, R, Mariaca, J, Ribadeneira Sarmiento, M (2005) *Biodiversidad y recursos genéticos: Una guía para su uso y acceso en el Ecuador*, Abya Yala.

Kamau, EC, Fedder, B, Winter, G (2010) "The Nagoya Protocol on access to genetic resources and benefit sharing: What is new and what are the implications for provider and user countries and the scientific community", *Law, Environment and Development Journal* 6(3), pp. 248–262.

Kamau, EC, Winter, G (2009) "Streamlining access procedures and standards" in: Kamau, EC, Winter, G (eds) *Genetic resources, traditional knowledge and the law: Solutions for access and benefit sharing*, London: Earthscan, pp. 365–379.

Lago Candeira, A, Silvestri, L (2014) Acceso a recursos genéticos en América Latina y el El Caribe: Implementación del Protocolo de Nagoya a nivel nacional, in: Rios, M, Mora, A (eds), IUCN.

McManis, C, Terán, Y (2011) "Trends and scenarios in the legal protection of traditional knowledge" in: Wong, T, Dutfield, G (eds) *Intellectual property and human development: current trends and future scenarios*, Cambridge University Press, pp. 139–174.

Ruíz, M (2008) "Una lectura crítica de la Decisión 391 de la Comunidad Andina y su puesta en práctica en relación con el tratado internacional sobre los recursos fitogenéticos para la alimentación y la agricultura", *Recursos Naturales y Ambiente 53*, pp. 136–147.

Stoll, P-T (2009) "Access to GRs and benefit sharing – Underlying concepts and the idea of justice" in: Kamau, EC, Winter, G (eds) *Genetic resources, traditional knowledge and the law: Solutions for access and benefit sharing*, London: Earthscan, pp. 3–18.

Tremolada, E (2005) "Aplicación del derecho andino en Bolivia, Perú, Colombia y Venezuela frente a la experiencia Europea", *OASIS 11*, pp. 151–165.

Tvedt, MW, Young, T (2007) *Beyond access: Exploring implementation of the fair and equitable sharing commitment in the CBD*, Gland, Switzerland: IUCN.

Winter, G (2009) "Towards regional common pools of GRs – Improving the effectiveness and justice of ABS" in: Kamau, EC, Winter, G (eds) *Genetic resources, traditional knowledge and the law: Solutions for access and benefit sharing*, London: Earthscan, pp. 19–35.

Wynberg, R, Chennells, R (2009) "Green diamonds of the south: An overview of the San-Hoodia case" in: Wynberg, R, Schroeder, D, Chennells, R (eds) *Indigenous peoples, consent and benefit-sharing: Lessons from the San – Hoodia case*, Springer, pp. 89–124.

Wynberg, R, Laird, S (2009) "Bioprospecting, access and benefit sharing: Revisiting the 'grand bargain' " in: Wynberg, R, Schroeder, D, Chennells, R (eds) *Indigenous peoples, consent and benefit-sharing: Lessons from the San – Hoodia case*, Springer, pp. 69–86.

Legal documents

Convention on Biological Diversity, 1992.

Decision 391: Common Regime on Access to Genetic Resources (Decisión 391: Régimen Común sobre Acceso a los Recursos Genéticos), 1996.

Ecuadorian Constitution (Constitución de la República del Ecuador), 2008.

Executive Decree No. 905: National Regulation to the Common Regime on Access to Genetic Resources for the Application of the Decision 391 of the Andean Community of Nations (Decreto Ejecutivo núm. 905: Reglamento Nacional al Régimen Común sobre Acceso a los Recursos Genéticos en Aplicación a la Decisión 391 de la Comunidad Andina), 2011.

Integral Organic Penal Code (Codigo Orgánico Integral Penal), 2013.

Nagoya Protocol on Access to Genetic Resources and the Fair and Equitable Sharing of Benefits Arising from their Utilization to the Convention on Biological Diversity, 2010.

Treaty for the Creation of the Tribunal of Justice of the Andean Community of Nations (Tratado de Creación del Tribunal de Justicia de la Comunidad Andina), 1996.

Unified Text of the Secondary Environmental Legislation of the Minister of the Environment (Texto Unificado de Legislación Ambiental Secundaria del Ministerio de Ambiente), revised in 2012.

Part III

Experiences of research projects for non-commercial purposes with ABS

10 Experiences in international ecological/biological research

Erwin H. Beck

Introduction

This chapter reports on the experiences of German scientists working on biodiversity- and ABS-related projects in several tropical countries and of guest researchers from those countries at German universities. The nature of all the projects is basic, nonprofit-oriented research in the field and in the laboratory. Funding was provided almost exclusively by German research and capacity-building agencies such as the German Research Foundation (DFG), the Alexander von Humboldt Foundation, the German Academic Exchange Service (DAAD), the VW Foundation and Federal as well as State Ministries. The time period of the present overview extends from 1975 until recently, and two of the projects are still running. Working conditions, procedures of granting research permission, and obligations connected to the work will be reported on and capacity-building measures and their success emphasized, but scientific results will not be reported. With respect to confidentiality, names of counterparts, students and representatives of authorities will not be presented.

Nepal (1996–2010)

Field studies and laboratory work: The field studies aimed at the reconstruction of the paleoclimate and landscape history of the Annapurna region during the Holocene, i.e. the last 10,000 to 12,000 years. It was a collaborative study by geologists from Nepal and soil scientists and botanists from several German universities. Field work was performed during three expeditions at the Annapurna National Park, for which permission was granted from the Nepalese Royal Department of Mines and Geology and the Annapurna National Park Administration. During the entire fieldwork, the group was accompanied by scientists from Nepal and also by the military during the last expedition because of activities of the Maoists. The collection of plants and soil samples was permitted. Plant identification was performed with the assistance of the botany department of the Tribhuvan University in Kathmandu, Nepal, where a set of duplicate samples was deposited. The export of soil samples was only permitted in the context of a research stay of a Nepalese scientist in Bayreuth, Germany. Financing was provided by the German Academic Exchange Service and the VW Foundation.

The work was published in several articles with Nepalese co-authors. Unfortunately, the academic standard of the Nepalese geologist was not sufficient for admission to a doctoral study in Germany. This was decided by the German Central Office of International Education in Bonn. On the other hand, nonequivalence of academic degrees was not an obstacle for Nepalese doctoral students to work in a German institute if the PhD was awarded by a Nepalese university. A PhD study, "Genetic transformation of Nepalese spring wheat: Delaying aging of plants", was performed in the scope of a sandwich program, in which the German Academic Exchange Service paid for the stay in Germany. Since wheat is a plant species under the FAO treaty, export and import permission was not required. At the end of the laboratory work, the plant material was returned to Nepal. The candidate successfully completed the PhD program at the Tribhuvan University of Kathmandu. The thesis was published in an international journal with the student as lead author and the two supervisors (from Nepal and Germany) as co-authors.

Kenya (numerous projects since 1975)

Most of the projects were vegetation studies, studies on plant ecology and plant physiology, which were performed with colleagues from the University of Nairobi and later on from Maseno University (Maseno). Laboratory work was performed in Kenya as often as possible. Identification of plant species was done in cooperation with the botany department of the University of Nairobi and with the East African Herbarium in Nairobi, where duplicates of collected plant material were deposited. During many of the field trips to Mt. Kenya, Mt. Elgon, the Aberdare Mountains and the Shimba Hills, the researchers were accompanied by field assistants from the Kenya Wildlife Service and by colleagues from the collaborating Kenyan universities. Research for three German doctoral studies could be performed in the scope of these projects. Research permission was granted by the Office of the President, based on allowance from the former Ministry of Tourism and Wildlife and the headquarters of the respective national parks.

The procedures were sometimes time-consuming, but research clearance was always granted. The fees were moderate. Although not always free of logistical problems, the work was successful and documented in 24 international publications, to which the Kenyan cooperation partners have contributed as co-authors whenever possible.

On the basis of this cooperation, the author of this chapter was appointed external examiner of the botany department of the University of Nairobi for three consecutive years. He also worked as co-supervisor of five botanical PhD theses at Maseno University. In the past 37 years, during which the author had projects in Kenya, many political and administrative changes took place, and therefore detailed information will be presented here for only two projects from the last decade to which ABS regulations could have been applied.

The first project (2000–2005) was a doctoral study, "African traditional plant knowledge today: An ethnobotanical study of the Digo at the Kenya coast", performed by an MSc holder from the Digo tribe of the Kwale District. The work was supervised by a professor in linguistics and another in plant science, both from the University of Bayreuth. The aim of the work was to understand the views of the Digos on their plant world. To that end, linguistics is indispensable. The methods included interviews and participating observations, and the interview partners were farmers, healers, teachers, pupils/students, ordinary people, individuals and groups (Figure 10.1). Many of the interviews were done in the presence of the supervisors. Interview partners were friendly, open minded, self-confident, and mostly interested in the issues.

After three years of fieldwork (2000–2003), the student went to Germany for data analysis (2004) and his doctoral examination (2005). This was the first doctoral degree at a German university in the field of ethnobotany. The work was published as a book (Pakia Mohamed (2006), *African traditional plant knowledge today. An ethnobotanical study of the Digo at the Kenya coast.* Beiträge zur Afrika-Forschung Vol. 24, 217 et seq., Lit Publisher Berlin, ISBN 3–8258–9056–2).

The project was financed by the German Research Foundation in the scope of a collaborative research program on African studies. In spite of the delicate matter, a research permit was granted by the Office of the President ($100 per year) without major problems. Smaller problems arose with the German administration, as the student has two wives, which is not allowed in Germany. So he left his family in Kenya while doing his research in Germany.

The second type of projects concerns analysis of chemical constituents of plants used in Kenyan local medicine. These studies were done in a kind of sandwich

Figure 10.1 Interview with chiefs of Digo villages about farming methods and problems, knowledge about their crop plants and their opinion of modern agricultural techniques

Source: *Author*

program that was financed by a Kenyan University. The students brought their plant materials to Germany and analyzed interesting groups of so-called secondary compounds (like alkaloids) which might be effective in medical treatments. This type of capacity building in research, though still without practical use, is clearly on the borderline between basic and applied research. The students took all materials and data when returning after one year to their home university. During the stay in Germany, they were supervised by the author of this chapter, who kept the knowledge of these studies confidential and did not make any further use of it. Nevertheless, for the future, he would recommend the students to carry a document of research clearance or export permission.

Ecuador

Collaboration in ecosystem study

An outstanding comprehensive ecosystem study in a biodiversity hotspot has been performed for the last 17 years in South Ecuador and is a good example for capacity building. The main aims of the study are to gain a better scientific understanding of ecosystem processes, the biodiversity of the ecosystems, the mutual interactions of organisms and of organisms with their natural and man-made environments, and to examine the potential of different land-use strategies for sustainable use of tropical mountain ecosystems. Seventeen German, one Austrian and four Ecuadorian universities cooperate in this research program, which also collaborates with non-university institutions such as the Foundation Nature and Culture International (San Diego, Loja), several museums, the Smithsonian Institution, the national (Ministry of Environment) and local authorities of Ecuador and the involved provinces, and the European taxonomy program EDIT. The major scientific achievements of this cooperation comprise more than 400 publications in reviewed journals, three books, and a checklist of the species of the area. More than 30 per cent of these publications have Ecuadorian co-authors (Figure 10.2). In addition to this, 14 annual symposia, two international conferences, one international summer school, one international workshop and several teaching units in the collaborating Ecuadorian universities have taken place.

Capacity building within the scope of the research programme is considerable, as shown in Figure 10.3. One-third of the doctoral students are Ecuadorians and currently two of the Ecuadorian postdocs have their own projects in the programme. Several Ecuadorian junior scientists have already obtained their doctoral degrees from the German universities of their supervisors.

Ecuadorian universities are mainly concerned with teaching and, up to now, have not been permitted to award doctoral degrees. This situation will change in the near future, as several of the Ecuadorian universities have started their own research projects. The German research group was and still is instrumental in these endeavours. Twelve projects from Ecuadorian universities have been affiliated with the German programmes, which are primarily financed by the proposing universities.

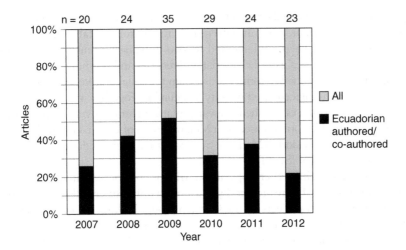

Figure 10.2 Number of articles (n) in peer-reviewed journals and percentage of Ecuadorian co-authored papers (black) from 2007 to 2012

Source: *The data warehouse of the research group "Ecuador" (www.tropicalmountainforest.org), Graphic: T. Lotz, Marburg. From Pohle P, López MF, Beck E, Bendix J (2013), The Role of Biodiversity Research for the Local Scientific Community. In: Ecosystem Services, Biodiversity and Environmental Change in a Tropical Mountain Ecosystem of South Ecuador (Bendix J, Beck, E, Bräuning A, Makeschin F, Mosandl R, Scheu S, Wilcke W, eds.) Ecol Studies Vol. 221: 411–428, DOI 10.1007/978–3–642–38137–9_29, Springer, Berlin Heidelberg.*

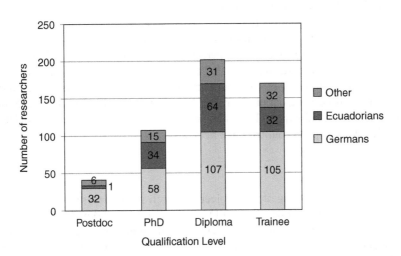

Figure 10.3 Researchers at different qualification levels working in the research programme

Source: *RU816-DW, www.TropicalMountainForest.org), Graphic by J. Bendix and co-workers; from Pohle et al. (2013).*

Seventeen years of collaboration have thoroughly changed the academic land-scape in South Ecuador, not only with respect to environmental sciences, where new curricula have been implemented by two universities, but also in several other related disciplines. Four Ecuadorian universities and two nongovernmental organizations have joined to form a consortium for collaborative research activi-ties, which is an unprecedented novelty in Ecuador. Together with the German group, this consortium established a research platform for biodiversity and ecosys-tem studies. This platform is based on a Memorandum of Understanding between the DFG and the Ecuadorian National Secretariat for Higher Education, Science and Technology (SENESCYT).

Because Ecuador, like other tropical countries, is confronted with serious envi-ronmental problems, future projects by Ecuadorian universities will be more appli-cation oriented than projects by the German group. Making use of the recently established DFG program for knowledge transfer projects, the German side could already implement projects in meteorology and forestry, in which methods and results from their investigations have been up-scaled for application in practice. Knowledge transfer projects require the involvement of nonacademic partners who contribute to the project with their own resources.

In contrast to the situation 17 years ago, when the research started, the German group has achieved sufficient credit by the local people, making participation in the knowledge transfer research projects possible. Means to build such kinds of trust are respecting Ecuadorian law and regulations for environmental research and activities; respectful contact with authorities; steady presence in the local and regional media; demonstration of activities for schools and the public; employ-ment of Ecuadorians as helpers in the field work and as casual workers; and, last but not least, personal connections, e.g. marriages between Germans and Ecuador-ians. A serious problem is language, as the common speech of Latin America is Spanish. Students, as well as a high percentage of the academic staff, hesitate or are not able to communicate in English, which is a severe obstacle for science. The situation is slowly improving but is not yet satisfactory. Environmental haz-ards such as fires getting out of control or diluvian rains coupled with the El Niño phenomenon and subsequent landslides are further, but locally confined, problems of fieldwork in tropical countries like Ecuador.

Research permits

Since the very beginning of the project, research permits were granted by the Ecuadorian Ministry of Environment (*Ministerio del Ambiente*) under strict condi-tions which ban any kind of bioprospecting. Conforming to the spirit of the CBD and, recently, of the Nagoya Protocol, access was permitted for non-commercial, academic research in a way that could be considered as facilitated procedure. PIC, MAT and MTA were covered by one application and one granting document. Material transfer of plants, animals, microorganisms, soil and water was permitted in quantities which had to be detailed and justified in the applications. In special cases, changes were possible. Initially, the application was for bundles of projects,

Table 10.1 Principles of the research permit for ecosystem and biodiversity studies of the German research team in South Ecuador (research permit from the Ecuadorian *Ministerio del Ambiente* 2012)

Allowed	Not allowed
Observation, collection (small numbers) and identification of organisms as specified in applications	• Use as material or parent material for commercial purposes • Any kind of bioprospection
Export for identification purposes as indicated in the applications	Use of organisms as genetic resources and for genetic experiments

Source: *Own illustration*

Table 10.2 Obligations imposed on the German research team and its Ecuadorian counterparts when conducting ecosystem and biodiversity research in South Ecuador

Obligations for	
Researcher	Local counterpart
Annual report, showing results and regulation consistent conduct	Appointment of an Ecuadorian scientist as technical, administrative and legal supervisor who should accompany the entire study and shall be co-author of the results and publications
Report with species lists and location of collection/observation with UTM coordinates	Acknowledgement (to the Ministry) of good conduct of the group and observance of all general and specific regulations; report of any irregularity
Deposit of duplicates of all samples with the counterparts as specified in the permit	Acknowledgement of the deposits and the timely presentation of the partial and final reports

Source: *Own illustration*

and applications and reports had to be submitted every three years. Now each project has to apply separately and the reports and applications are to be made annually. They have to be signed by the counterparts. Tables 10.1 and 10.2 present an overview of the major regulations and stipulations. There was a moderate increase of the fees for the research permits. For future biodiversity-related projects, a framework contract will be required in addition to the research permit.

Ethiopia

The author has had collaborative projects running since 1995, and the most current funding period by the German Research Foundation expired in 2012. Projects started with ecophysiological investigations of afroalpine plants in the Ethiopian uplands and were later extended to taxonomic questions. Research permits were applied for by the Ethiopian colleagues and were granted by the Ethiopian Wildlife Conservation Organisation (Ministry of Natural Resources Development and

Environmental Protection) and the headquarters of the visited national parks. The projects were consistently run in cooperation with scientists from Addis Ababa University, and were funded by the German VW Foundation, the German Academic Exchange Service, the Alexander von Humboldt Foundation and Addis Ababa University. Achievements were several Ethiopian MSc theses, one German doctoral thesis, and a three-year student exchange programme for joint academic studies. Two groups of German students joined fellow students in Addis Ababa and one group of Ethiopian students came to Germany. This period of collaboration resulted in six joint publications by German and Ethiopian authors in international journals. In spite of tough working conditions in the field, the projects were successful and stimulated further BSc and MSc theses under the supervision of the Ethiopian counterparts.

A collaborative project on a tropical montane forest ecosystem with a high share of exotic tree plantations was conducted in Central Ethiopia from 2003 to 2011 with seven German and two Ethiopian teams. The studied subjects were tree ecophysiology, soil structure, soil nutrients and hydrology, climate, biogeography, and management of the natural forest and the plantations. The projects were financed by the DFG and logistically supported by the biology department of Addis Ababa University, by the Ethiopian Agricultural Research Organization (EARO) and by the Sheshamene Forest Enterprise. With funding by DFG and Addis Ababa University, a research station was erected in the forest where several plots for special investigations were established. The academic output of the project included five German and five Ethiopian doctoral degrees, and several MSc theses by Ethiopian students. The results were published in 20 articles (more are still in development) in international peer-reviewed journals. Four binational symposia on the progress of the work were held in Ethiopia, and the results were presented at several international conferences in various countries.

The permit for this collaborative project was initially granted by the Sheshamene Province Administration in consultation with the Sheshamene Forest Enterprise. Recently the group applied for a research permit from the Institute of Biodiversity Conservation, Genetic Resources Transfer and Regulation Directorate (Biodiversity Institute, BDI). Research was permitted by the Ethiopian counterpart, Addis Ababa University, to which the responsibility for compliance with the Nagoya Protocol was allocated. In addition, national legal regulations are applicable, with drastic fines for noncompliance. In the initial phase of the project, export permission for samples was given by the Ministry of Agriculture and Rural Development. A prerequisite for export permission was that analysis of the samples was done by Ethiopian students in German laboratories. Three of these students received their doctoral degree from a German university. Other Ethiopian students came with their samples, for example stable isotope analysis, to Germany in the scope of a sandwich program. These students received or will receive their PhD degree from Addis Ababa University.

Close collaboration also prompted research stays of various duration for Ethiopian university staff members in Germany, e.g. in the form of scholarships by the Alexander von Humboldt Foundation.

Further experience includes the finding that field work is logistically much more difficult in Ethiopia than, e.g. in Ecuador. Without knowing the official languages of Amharic or Oromia, communication is almost impossible, and not all Ethiopians speak both languages. In spite of an enormous economic upswing, Ethiopia is still a developing country with severe overpopulation problems. Western researchers are confronted with an extremely wide range of social structures which are not easy to understand, especially in the countryside. While many features of daily life are still reflecting the impressive traditional Ethiopian culture, the organization and standard of the universities are comparable to European institutions and research is well entrenched in their management. Most of the projects in science are oriented towards application. Biodiversity is considered a precious commodity by most of Ethiopia's people.

Conclusions

The author has performed biodiversity-related research in developing countries, long before discussion about the CBD started. The focus of these "pre-CBD" studies was on the ecology and ecophysiology of plants and analysis of vegetation. One project was on defence mechanisms of certain tropical trees against herbivores, in which the toxic constituent of the leaves were chemically investigated.

After the entry into force of the CBD, the author's research projects addressed more applied questions, but the main fields of plant ecology and ecophysiology remained with one exception, the above-described project on traditional knowledge of plants in Kenya. None of the projects were ever done without a local counterpart, preferably from a university or a governmental authority. Whenever the counterparts scientifically contributed to the work, they co-authored the publications; when cooperation was only of a logistic nature, the counterparts were acknowledged in the papers.

For all projects performed in foreign countries, a research permit was applied for from the authorities in charge and was granted. Special attention was always paid to comply with the obligations of the research permits and the laws of the host country. Due to uncertainties with the handling of the ABS regulations, the permit-granting governmental authorities even very recently did not ask for a contract (PIC, MAT or MTA), considering a detailed research permit combined with an obligation for an annual progress report sufficient for giving research clearance. This kind of facilitated access to biological resources might have been fostered by the fact that the applications were mostly for a temporal extension of previous research permission, sometimes with a change of the research question. However, the clause that the planned project is basic, nonprofit-oriented research was always essential. In recent years, journals have requested the data of the research permits (number, data, and authority) upon submission of a manuscript for publication, and these were included in the acknowledgements. When applying for a research grant from the DFG, acceptance of the regulations of the "Guidelines for funding proposals concerning research projects within the scope of the CBD" had to be assured.

Albeit without contractual stipulation, capacity building was a major issue in the author's research projects. First, as a university scientist, his research generally relies on the work of students; second, scientific fieldwork in a foreign country usually requires more time than a university teacher has at his disposal. After having started the project, data collection is usually continued by students who have been introduced to the subject and have been trained in the handling of the equipment. Finally, performing as much of the research project as possible immediately in the host country is not only convenient with respect to material transfer regulations, but also provides the possibility of repetition of a measurement or experiment in due time and at reasonable costs. Internet facilities nowadays allow fast and detailed communication and supervision of the work. A considerable number of students from Kenya, Ethiopia, Nepal and Ecuador have received their doctoral degrees in the author's projects.

Striving for trust between the cooperating parties is the key for successful research, especially in projects which are not profit oriented. Wide gaps between the social status and literacy of the researchers from foreign countries and the local people are sometimes encountered in developing countries. Such gaps must be bridged by accepting each other as full partners in the projects, irrespective of the individual contributions. This holds true for the interactions with authorities, colleagues, students and ordinary people. Researchers from industrial countries should appreciate what they can learn – expectedly or adventitiously – from their counterparts.

11 Experiences in accessing biological resources for non-commercial research

Results of an informal survey in Switzerland

Susette Biber-Klemm and Sylvia I. Martinez

Introduction

The ABS program of the Swiss Academy of Sciences

The involvement of the Swiss Academy of Sciences (SCNAT) in Access and Benefit-Sharing issues correlates with its mission and its members. The SCNAT is a network of scientific disciplines and academic societies that focuses on science and policy and advocates ethics and responsibility in research.

Both the mandate to build a bridge between science and policy and the mission to advocate ethics and responsibility in research was a strong motivation for SCNAT to engage in work on ABS that was specifically directed at the needs of non-commercial academic research. Once the ABS principles were spelled out on a more concrete level in the Bonn Guidelines on Access and Benefit Sharing, we carried out a first survey in 2004 among researchers in Switzerland to inquire about their ABS-relevant projects and to assess the situation for researchers in Switzerland. The survey revealed two facts: 1) a multitude of research projects involve transboundary access to resources, and 2) the academic research community lacks knowledge of ABS issues (Biber-Klemm, Martinez, & Jacob 2010).

The ensuing ABS program of the Swiss Academy of Sciences aimed at raising awareness and building capacity within the Swiss research community while fostering the voluntary implementation of the Bonn Guidelines (Biber & Martinez 2009).

Rationale and goal of the survey

A negative perception of the ABS system by researchers was predominant at this time. Their comments ranged from "no problem" to "disastrous". Their complaints mainly concerned the additional formalities and the difficulties of access. There was a prevalent apprehension that in the near future, research with transboundary genetic resources would become impossible.

The presented and informal inquiry was carried out in 2009 to collect more detailed information about the experiences of researchers, in particular the problems they encountered and their causes. The objectives were to further develop the ABS program at the national level, to provide background information for the position of non-commercial research during the negotiations of the CBD's Nagoya Protocol, as well as to find ways and means to facilitate international research cooperation.

The survey

The personal, semi-structured interviews included a general section about the researchers, the main research questions of each project and the utilization of the accessed genetic resources. To clarify how the ABS procedures affect the research process, we asked researchers for contacted institutions, involved negotiation partners, conditions for access and established contracts. Researchers also answered questions on the benefits they shared. In addition, they were asked about their overall grade of satisfaction with the period of time for the ABS process, the involved costs and the outcome.

Results

Broad spectrum of access and utilization cases

The survey encompassed interviews with 10 researchers working in Switzerland who had carried out projects on 4 continents and in a total of 15 countries: (1) Africa: Burkina Faso, Ghana, Lesotho, Mali, South Africa, Tanzania, Zambia; (2) The Americas: Ecuador, Mexico, Panama, Paraguay, Peru; (3) Asia: China; and (4) Europe: Romania, Russia. This corresponds to 15 transnational "access situations" in 15 countries. In some of them several administrative levels were involved.

With regard to the research disciplines we found a large array of studies: systematics and taxonomy, biogeography and phylogeny, ethnobotany, botanical and zoological inventories (biodiversity monitoring), biocontrol of herbivores, plant pathology, agrisciences and geography. The type of accessed resources included samples of wild and cultivated plants, animals, microorganisms fungi, including DNA samples, and smoke (containing no genetic resources but access to traditional knowledge in context with ethnobotanical research).

The accessed material was used in various ways, such as for (1) species identification, (2) forwarding to taxonomic experts for species identification, (3) morphological studies, (4) chemical and genetic analyses, (5) conservation and storage in herbaria and zoological museums, (6) field experiments and (7) propagation of genetic resources for biocontrol studies.

From this follows that the survey encompassed a relatively broad range of access and utilization cases that can be seen as being representative for biodiversity research in general.

Scientists dissatisfied with procedures

In half of the cases, the principal investigator in Switzerland personally took care of the negotiations; in a great part of the remaining cases, doctoral students had to do this work. In most cases the permits were facilitated by the research partners in the provider country. However, researchers often had to contact several authorities for the different types of permits. Three projects had up to four different negotiation partners. With one exception, collaboration with international research centres expedited the procedure as the involved partners were informed about the national administrative process.

In two cases, the principal investigator did not understand the contracts since they were negotiated by the research partner in the providing country and the documents were issued in the national language.

It is interesting to note that all projects worked under research permits or collectors' licences but no project had an "official ABS contract", meaning a permit/contract under this heading and containing the crucial ABS elements that regulate, for instance, transfer of genetic resources to third persons, benefit sharing, or intellectual property rights.

The negotiation process proved to be rather time-consuming and expensive. As a general rule, scientists had to negotiate up to one year before having the necessary permits for their biodiversity research projects. Not all projects received export permits. The interview partners were of the opinion that in half of the provider countries the fees for access, collection and export permits are very expensive. In one of the cases, the high fees led to the abandonment of the research project. Some scientists also mentioned the rising costs for permits and the increased need to renew them due to cuts in permit duration by provider countries. The researchers experienced difficulties, such as that permits were only granted if the researcher was present in person, but there was no certainty that access would be granted and little consideration for the scientist's travel expenses; that in the absence of the head of office, no substitute had the authority to sign the permit; or that trips to the several heads of villages were necessary, but it was uncertain if the person would be present. Often, the ABS access point did not exist or the address was outdated and a competent person could not be found.

The grade of overall satisfaction with the negotiation process was rather low. Only one researcher was entirely satisfied. The majority criticized the procedures (time, personnel, and overall cost). Scientists were not satisfied with the negotiation process and considered it too time consuming and therefore not acceptable for further research.

All projects shared benefits

No project had a formal ABS agreement. Nevertheless, all projects shared benefits. In most cases they were non-monetary in nature. This included benefits such as research collaboration, co-publications, educational master and doctoral (PhD) student training, identification of species, identification of duplicate specimens deposited in collections of the provider country, species lists, information on research results to locals and administration. Nonetheless, academic benefit sharing also included monetary benefits, such as salaries, food and lodging for local technicians and assistants. Several master and doctoral (PhD) students of provider countries received full Swiss scholarships.

Conclusions and recommendations

The results allow conclusions regarding both users and providers of genetic resources, or – worded in CBD terms – regarding both the researchers seeking access to genetic resources and associated traditional knowledge and the national competent authorities of the countries providing the resources.

The findings of the survey confirm the results of earlier inquiries (Martinez & Biber-Klemm 2010): Difficulties for research can be caused by communication problems – such as finding information on access procedures and conditions and locating the agency and/or persons that need to be contacted – and the duration of the negotiations and costs involved (Prathapan et al. 2006; Jinnah & Jungcurt 2009; Nemogá Soto 2010). In Switzerland, publicly funded research projects usually run on a fixed budget and have a defined duration which typically amounts to three years for a doctoral thesis. This doesn't give much leeway for lengthy negotiations or flexibility regarding extra costs.

Yet, as a rule, scientists are used to applying for research permits, export permits, phytosanitary permits and so on. If ABS procedures come in addition to the abovementioned administrative steps – and moreover if they depend on multiple government agencies (e.g. the trade ministry in addition to the education and research ministry) – the situation becomes complex (Kamau & Winter 2009). The difficulties of scientists to find information on ABS procedures and competent agencies further impede compliance with these regulations.

The results of the survey have to be assessed against the background settings that characterize the situation of users, i.e. the researchers (in both user and provider countries) and the authorities that grant access.

From the inquiry – and other sources – it became evident that there is great mistrust by government authorities of scientific, non-commercial research. The fear to lend a hand to "biopiracy enterprises" seems to be omnipresent. One reason for this may be that scientific research, its goals, methods and products, are difficult to understand for nonscientists. In particular, the possibility that some research results might be further explored for research and development (R&D) in a commercial context, the obligation of academics to publish the research results and thereby to make them accessible for a wide public, and the difficulty for providers to monitor the downstream R&D contributes to the providers' anxiety. Confidence building between researchers of provider and user countries and between local research institutions and the government agencies responsible for granting permits is therefore crucial (Biber-Klemm et al. 2014). This includes transparency regarding the planned project and clear and generally understandable wording of written submissions.

Here, it has to be highlighted that despite the complete lack of formal ABS contracts, all projects were authorized by the host state authorities through some sort of permits. Moreover, all projects shared non-monetary benefits and some shared monetary benefits. This leads to the proposition that simple access procedures for non-commercial academic research should be based on the existing procedures, government structures, and an adapted research permit that clearly defines the ABS-relevant obligations (no commercialization, no intellectual property rights, benefits to be shared, reporting obligations) (Biber-Klemm et al. 2010), rather than establishing new procedures and drafting new documents.

These conclusions lead to practical recommendations for (1) non-commercial, academic research valid for scientists and science management in both user and provider countries, and (2) governmental agencies in the provider countries.

With regard to academic research, building provider countries' trust in academic research has been identified as a basic prerequisite. Therefore, engaging in long-term research collaborations between institutions of provider and user countries is meaningful and increases trust and credibility of research endeavours (Stöckli, Wiesmann, & Lys 2012). Provider country academic institutions can enhance research cooperation by offering support and legal advice. Their knowledge of governmental ABS agencies and good local networks can facilitate formalities and multilayered negotiations. In turn, the sharing of benefits is an expression of good scientific practice in research. Academia has a long-standing tradition of generating non-monetary and monetary benefits, such as the increase of knowledge relevant for the conservation and sustainable use of biological diversity, master and doctoral student training and funding, and technology transfer. Academia should raise the visibility of these benefit-sharing practices. Research funding agencies should recognize ABS transaction costs and costs generated by the sharing of non-monetary and monetary benefits as budgetary items in research projects.

All these components play a role in ABS negotiations. Therefore, the principal investigators should primarily be in charge. Handling the ABS formalities is difficult for (PhD) students and exceeds their administrative and financial skills.

If the research topic allows for geographical flexibility, it is suggested that scientists focus their research on countries with a clear and transparent ABS policy for academic research that includes reasonable ABS conditions and swift procedures.

From this it can be concluded that provider countries themselves can have a hand in fostering international cooperation in academic biodiversity research and the sharing of related benefits. Clear and conducive conditions regarding ABS enhance international cooperation and foster related transfer of capacities and technologies. An easy-to-locate national ABS contact point with corresponding competence (National Focal Point) is essential for researchers from abroad and for national individuals. Accurate national access and benefit-sharing conditions should be set up. The national ABS website should include all information about the necessary requirements and procedures and should be accessible via the ABS Clearing-House. It could be complemented by information on national research institutes to facilitate research collaborations. It is helpful to provide electronic forms of application. Stability of decisions over time, continuity within the administration, swift procedures and reasonable transaction fees foster ABS applications by researchers.

The suggestions presented address users and providers of genetic resources and are meant to serve as a discussion basis for the implementation of the simplified measures as described in Article 8(a) of the Nagoya Protocol, which aims at creating conditions to promote and encourage research that contributes to the conservation and sustainable use of biological diversity.

References

Biber, S, Martinez, SI (2009) *Access and benefit sharing – Good practice for academic research on genetic resources*, Bern: Swiss Academy of Sciences.

Biber-Klemm, S, Martinez, SI, Jacob, A (2010) *Access to genetic resources and sharing of benefits – ABS program 2003–2010 of the Swiss Academy of Sciences*, Bern: Swiss Academy of Sciences.

Biber-Klemm, S, Martinez, SI, Jacob, A, Jetvic, A (2010) *Sample ABS agreement for noncommercial research*, Bern: Swiss Academy of Sciences.

Biber-Klemm, S, Nemogá Soto, G, Payet-Lebourges, K, da Silva, M, Rodriguez, L, Prieur-Richard, A-H, . . . Warner Pineda, J (2014) *Access and benefit sharing in Latin America and the Caribbean – A science-policy dialogue for academic research*, Paris: Diversitas-International.

Jinnah, S, Jungcurt, S (2009) "Could access requirements stifle your research?", *Science* 323, pp. 464–465.

Kamau, EC, Winter, G (2009) "Streamlining access procedures and standards" in: Kamau, EC, Winter, G (eds) *Genetic resources, traditional knowledge and the law: Solutions for access and benefit sharing*, London: Earthscan.

Martinez, SI, Biber-Klemm, S (2010) "Scientists – Take action for access to biodiversity", *Current Opinion in Environmental Sustainability* 2, pp. 27–33.

Nemogá Soto, GR (2010) *La investigación sobre biodiversidad en Colombia : Propuesta de ajustes al régimen de acceso a recursos genéticos y productos derivados, y a la Decisión Andina 391 de 1996*, Bogotá: Universidad Nacional de Colombia.

Prathapan, KD, Rajan, PD, Narendran, TC, Viraktamath, CA, Subramanian, KA, Aravind, NA, Poorani, J (2006) "Biological Diversity Act, 2002: Shadow of permit-raj over research", *Current Science* 91, pp. 1006–1007.

Stöckli, B, Wiesmann, U, Lys, JA (2012) *A guide for transboundary research partnerships: 11 principles*, Bern: Swiss Commission for Research Partnerships with Developing Countries (KFPE), Swiss Academy of Sciences.

12 Local scientist's experience with bioscience research authorization process in Kenya

Need for facilitation

Hamadi Iddi Boga

Introduction

Kenya is rich in habitats and ecosystem types teeming with biological specimens of interest to researchers from all over the world. Over the years, Kenya has attracted researchers keen on studying Kenya's wildlife, soda lakes, microbes and plant biodiversity. The studies have generated knowledge critical for an understanding of species and ecosystems and for the management and conservation of plants and animals.

In the 1990s and even before that, access for researchers both local and international was not complicated. With good planning, one could secure a research and export permit for biological specimens within one month. The United Nations Convention on Biological Diversity (CBD) of 1992 reaffirmed the sovereignty of nations over their biodiversity (Article 15.1 CBD). Following that, Kenya enacted the Environment Management and Coordination Act (EMCA) 1999 (GOK, 1999) which domesticated the Convention on Biological Diversity, creating regulations for Access and Benefit Sharing for Genetic Resources. In 2006, the National Environment Management Authority (NEMA) published regulations for access to genetic resources in Kenya by researchers (GOK 2006). With these new guidelines, the time required to access biological materials for research increased and the procedure changed considerably. In this chapter, we map the processes and challenges faced by local and international researchers to access biological materials required for academic research and suggest solutions to improve access to genetic resources in Kenya and facilitate research.

Relevant institutions and mandates

Accessing genetic materials for research in Kenya requires the scientist to engage with various state agencies, all of which derive their mandate from legislation. From experience, the agencies that one might need to visit and get some form of authorization from for research include the National Commission for Science, Technology and Innovation (NACOSTI) formerly National Council for Science and Technology (NCST), the Kenya Wildlife Service (KWS), the National Museums of Kenya (NMK; for plant specimens and also endangered species in the

CITES list), Kenya Plant Health Inspectorate Service (KEPHIS), Department of Veterinary Services (DVS) for animal specimens, and the Department of Public Health and Sanitation for medical specimens. All the agencies base their mandates on relevant Acts of Parliament. How these agencies relate and/or coordinate the process of research authorization has never been clearly explained and has resulted in confusion among scientists and conflict among the agencies. Kamau and Winter (2009) present the access procedures in Kenya as complex, costly and time-consuming and in need of revision, a view shared by many researchers. Kamau (2009a, 2009b) further sees the existing legal framework as suffering from numerous shortcomings and unable to achieve the access and benefit-sharing (ABS) objectives of the Convention on Biological Diversity.

As the body whose primary role it is to advise government on research, science and technology, NACOSTI is the government agency where researchers would initially start engaging in the process to obtain a research permit. In the past, NACOSTI would issue the permit within one month after receiving the relevant documents and applicable fees and would refer one to the District Commissioner in the area where the research is to take place. NACOSTI is part of the Ministry of Education, Science and Technology. Before the Ministry of Education took over, the research permitting process had been in the hands of the office of the President, hence the requirement to report to the District Commissioner.

Access procedure and costs

Access procedure prior to the access and benefit-sharing regulations of 2006

Obtaining access to biological research samples was simpler prior to 2006, when the regulations on access to genetic resources in Kenya were enacted. What a researcher needed was basically a research permit from the Ministry of Education, Science and Technology through NCST. Where specimens were required from national parks or the wild, further authorization was sought from the Kenya Wildlife Service. The National Museums of Kenya were required to confirm that the specimens were not on the CITES list. This is captured in Figure 12.1. At the time, the concerns of biopiracy and demands for benefit sharing from biological wealth were not very strongly etched in the consciousness of Kenyan authorities.

The research authorization process would proceed as such whether the researcher was local or foreign when the samples were to be exported.

Access procedure after the access and benefit-sharing regulations of 2006

With the enactment of the 2006 Regulations on access and benefit sharing, the process has gotten somewhat complicated, equally for foreign researchers and Kenyan researchers and students working in foreign laboratories. According to

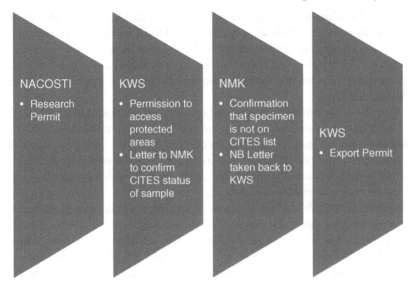

Figure 12.1 Research authorization process for access to and export of termite specimens between 1996 and 2005

Source: *Own illustration*

the Regulations, Legal Notice No. 160 Section 9 (1), "any person who intends to access genetic resources in Kenya shall apply to the Authority for an access permit in the form set out in the First Schedule, and such application shall be accompanied by the fees prescribed in the Second Schedule to these Regulations and (2) the application shall be accompanied by evidence of Prior Informed Consent from interested persons and relevant lead agencies, and a research clearance certificate from the National Council for Science and Technology".

These regulations added an extra bureaucratic step and brought in NEMA as a major player in the research permitting process for genetic resources. That NEMA would control the authorization process was further re-enforced by section 148 of the EMCA 1999, which states that "any written law, in force immediately before the coming into force of this Act, relating to the management of the environment shall have effect subject to modifications as may be necessary to give effect to this Act, and where the provisions of any such law conflict with any provisions of this Act, the provisions of this Act shall prevail". With this legislation, NEMA firmly became the gatekeeper to the genetic resources in Kenya. It is not clear, however, what added value this extra step brought into the whole process.

The regulations make a distinction between a local researcher working fully in Kenya and a foreign researcher coming to access biological specimens for research abroad. Section 3 (d) of the Regulations exempts "approved research activities intended for educational purposes within recognized Kenyan academic and research institutions, which are governed by relevant intellectual property laws from these regulations" but sometimes, local researchers are also referred to NEMA for clearance or access permits even when working locally. This arises from suspicion that local scientists abet the unregulated movement of biological materials outside Kenya.

With the enforcement of the regulations for access to genetic resources, the process of accessing research materials for local and foreign researchers was structured as shown in Figure 12.2, which specifically applies for biological specimens of any nature, but especially those collected from protected areas. Interestingly, at the exit points, the customs officials appear not to know which permits to refer to when releasing material for export.

In practice, NEMA would also require the researcher to contact the host community to get prior informed consent (PIC) from them, especially around sensitive ecosystems such as the Soda Lakes of Kenya. This would include holding a meeting with communities and their chiefs and explaining to them the research and its benefit. In my experience, most host communities are interested in immediate benefits aimed at solving their pressing needs, which a researcher or postgraduate student may not be in a position to fulfil. Those engaged in basic science research especially find it cumbersome to explain and justify complicated science to the ordinary communities.

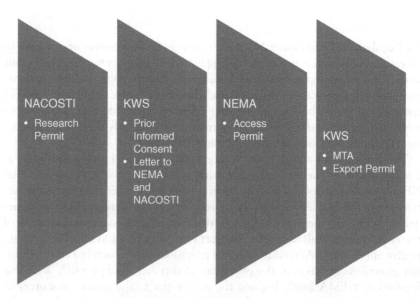

Figure 12.2 The process of securing a permit for accessing genetic resources under the 2006 regulations. Depending on the samples, researchers may be asked to get a letter from NMK, DVS, KEPHIS, Kenya Medical Research Institute (KEMRI) and such other lead agencies as may be deemed necessary.

Source: Own illustration

From experience, the process of getting all the necessary documents can take a minimum of six months. According to Kamau (2014), some local scientists have even waited longer than a year, with others giving up entirely. The NACOSTI and KWS permits/authorization can be concluded in about one month; the application at NEMA takes the longest because it requires publication in the *Kenya Gazette* and the national newspapers and consultation with the community to get a PIC. For foreign researchers, it might mean travelling to Kenya and incurring expenses even before getting guarantees to access research materials.

This very long process has frustrated many researchers. Local researchers working at local institutions are at times directed to NEMA, even when the regulations on access and benefit sharing clearly do not apply to them when doing research locally. Indeed, there had been talk that even local researchers should be subjected to the same access and benefit-sharing regulations as their foreign counterparts. This view was driven by the unfortunate perception that local researchers serve as agents of foreign researchers in accessing research samples. Considering the lack of resources for research and the frustration that local researchers experience in their effort to establish research in the country's institutions, such rules serve as a major disincentive for participation in research by local scientists.

Realigning to the Constitution of Kenya 2010

Recent legislation created to respond to the Constitution of Kenya 2010 has continued to perpetuate the contradiction outlined previously, despite sustained protests from researchers. This is evident in the Wildlife Management and Conservation Act (GOK 2013a) and the Science, Technology and Innovation Act (GOK 2013b), both of which should have taken into consideration concerns raised over the years about the cumbersome research authorization process.

Despite the many discussions that have gone forth regarding research authorization, the competition between agencies continues, as evident in the Wildlife Management and Conservation Act 2013 which established the Wildlife Research and Training Institute (WRTI). According to section 59 (i) of that Act, "a person shall not undertake research on the wildlife sector unless that person has a research permit granted by the Institute to carry out the research." Indeed, on the issue of bioprospecting, the same Act in addition gives powers to the Cabinet Secretary to grant permits for bioprospecting in section 22 (1) where it says, "No person may, without a permit from the Cabinet Secretary on the advice of the Service – (a) engage in bio-prospecting involving any wildlife resources; or (b) export from Kenya any wildlife resources for the purpose of bio-prospecting or **any other kind of research** and (2) any person desirous of undertaking bio-prospecting involving any wildlife resources may apply to the Authority for a permit in a prescribed format and on payment of prescribed fees." The same Act seems to place authorization for research in the wildlife sector in two agencies, and one wonders how the two will relate or coordinate.

Section 22 of the Wildlife Management and Conservation Act 2013, if interpreted liberally, could mean access to any wildlife resources inside or outside the protected areas is now the jurisdiction of Kenya Wildlife Authority. How the interaction with NEMA and NACOSTI will happen will have to await the application of this new law. Whereas in the past the Deputy Director in charge of research at the Kenya Wildlife Service could issue the research authorization letters and Material Transfer Agreements (MTAs), in the future it looks like researchers will have to seek this from the Cabinet Secretary, thereby adding another layer to the bureaucracy.

The Science, Technology and Innovation Act in its part states in section 12 (1) that "subject to the provisions of any other law, a person shall not undertake scientific research in Kenya without obtaining a licence under this Act" but in subsection (2) exempts a person conducting scientific research under a university or a research institution programme from the licensing requirements in subsection 1. In section 12 subsection 3, it further goes on to state, however, that "Any person undertaking or intending to undertake research in science and technology in the country, or who accesses, handles, or transfers any material or technology or moves it within, from or into the country, shall apply to the Commission for the grant of a licence in accordance with this Act." This seems to further suggest that import and export license for research materials of any nature will have to be sought from the Commission, further intensifying competition with KEPHIS and KWS or its successor.

Thus, access to genetic materials in Kenya for research will continue to be a challenge as competition between agencies continues unabated. The need to facilitate scientists to grow and deepen their research does not permeate the spirit of all these laws, where more emphasis is placed in controlling and monitoring their activities.

In general, the research authorization regime which has been in existence is cumbersome and discourages researchers; this has been noted by others (Kamau & Winter 2009; Kamau 2009a; Kamau 2009b). New legislation which attempts to align with the Constitution of Kenya 2010 seem to be carrying on the bottle-necks of the past. Yet research is necessary for better understanding of Kenya's biodiversity and ecosystems, and this knowledge is necessary for the conservation and sustainable utilization of biodiversity. A balance between regulation and facilitation of research is therefore very critical for the future, as also recommended by others (Kamau & Winter 2009; Kamau 2009a; Kamau 2009b).

In discussions involving diverse stakeholders while developing the proposed Bioscience Bill, it was recommended that a one-stop shop should be established at NACOSTI to facilitate research authorization. This one-stop shop would be a committee bringing all the agencies engaged in any form of research permitting to the same table to hasten the decision-making process. The government of Kenya under President Uhuru Kenyatta has been trying to cut down bureaucracy and is challenging state agencies to make it easy to do business in Kenya. Academic research also needs a one-stop shop and an easier way to do business. The Kenyan version of the proposed one-stop shop was a consensus position, in which the competing agencies would sit in a joint committee at NACOSTI, referred to as the Biosciences and Biosecurity Research Authorization Committee (BBRAC).

This would eliminate the "run around" that researchers go through under the current procedures and would enable all the agencies to participate and be aware of what is taking place. Although this approach does not amount to a full integration of the procedure as recommended by Kamau and Winter (2009, 371–373), attempts to have one agency take the mandate seem unlikely to succeed unless there is intervention from the highest authority. This is because most of the agencies are at the same operational level in government. Likewise, although a reading of the law seems to suggest that NEMA should play the role of the lead agency (LA) to coordinate the others,[1] in Kenya this role is more suited for NACOSTI as the government agency charged with advising on and coordinating research and innovation. Likewise, the structures and culture at NACOSTI are more suited for this role, and this is widely accepted by researchers and most stakeholders. Should NACOSTI take responsibility of the one-stop shop, existing laws will have to be revised and harmonized to give its mandate a legal basis, as well as eradicate researchers' uncertainty of a possible future legal interpretation to their detriment.

Costs of accessing genetic resources

Apart from the cumbersome process of accessing research samples outlined above, the costs of research permits can be a challenge, especially for local researchers and students. At NACOSTI, locals who apply for permits pay KES 5,000 (NSCT 2009), while at NEMA the cost is KES 20,000 for individuals and KES 50,000 for institutions (NEMA 2006). At KWS the research authorization fee is KES 1,000, 5,000 and 10,000 for undergraduate, masters and doctoral students respectively (KWS (undated)). The cost is obviously higher for foreign researchers. In a situation where most student research projects are not funded, requiring the student or their supervisor to part with anywhere between KES 5,000 and 30,000 is adding to the cost of the projects and the cost of doing research. Part of the struggle between various agencies to have a role in the research authorization process also stems from the desire to raise some money from the exercise, hence the reluctance to let go, leading to duplication and overlap.

Differentiation of commercial and non-commercial research

In the discussions and debates that have gone forth, one has the impression that there is always suspicion that all research is geared towards commercial exploitation. Even simple basic research projects are scrutinized and handled as if they

1 Article 53 (1) EMCA states that: "The Authority shall, in consultation with the relevant lead agencies, issue guidelines and prescribe measures for the sustainable management and utilisation of genetic resources of Kenya for the benefit of the people of Kenya." Kamau and Winter (2009) also see NEMA as better suited to undertake this role based on an interpretation of the ABS provisions of the Legal Notice 160.

were commercial research projects. Whereas most research done by universities is basic research and publicly funded, most commercial research is, on the other hand, done by bioprospecting companies and industries. Further, it should be possible to distinguish academic research from commercial research by looking at (i) the mandate of the institution from which a researcher is coming, (ii) the proposal submitted for evaluation and (iii) the curriculum vitae of the lead researchers. Thus, an objective criterion should be developed for approving research permits, which should involve peers from the relevant disciplines as assessors. In addition, the composition of the committee approving permits should avoid persons who may have a conflict of interest. Where potential for commercialization exists or is recognizable, the institution and researcher should be advised on intellectual property rights. A different criterion should be used for giving research permits to bioprospecting firms and industry, where the fees charged could be higher and the authorization process more rigorous. In addition, companies should be made to partner with small, local biotechnology firms and be required to mentor and support them to establish small laboratory units for technology transfer.

Handling microorganisms differently

Reading the NEMA guidelines (NEMA 2006), one gets the impression that they were designed for plant and animal scientists. The requirement for depositing voucher specimens, providing the name of the organisms, etc., assumes that all organisms have been identified and named. The process of naming a new plant, insect or bacterium might take several months and may even lead to the award of a PhD. This issue actually gets complicated when dealing with microorganisms. Their requirement to deposit sediment, water and soil samples as voucher specimens makes little sense, as the samples have to be frozen, which kills the microorganisms. Soil samples stored in a freezer deteriorate so fast that hardly any quality DNA can be retrieved from it after a year of storage.

Microbes are fundamentally different from animals and plants. Whereas plant and animal specimens can actually be endemic to a region, it is unlikely that microorganisms can be confined to a unique region. Due to their small size and abundance, microbes can be transported over long distances across land masses and water bodies and are able to establish themselves across the globe (Finlay & Esteban 2001). Essentially, this means that similar habitats across different continents harbour the same groups or types of microorganisms. For example, *Bacillus thuringiensis*, first isolated in soil in Germany, has been isolated from all soil types across the world, while *Penicillium notatum*, first isolated on a contaminated agar plate in Scotland, can be recovered in any environment in other parts of the world. It is therefore challenging when researchers are required to talk to indigenous communities when accessing microbial samples from whatever habitat. One would ask whether the microbes in soil or a water sample belong to an indigenous community. Should we treat microbes the same way we treat plant specimens? Whereas this might make sense for traditional fermentation technologies, it is difficult to imagine in the case of environmental microbial samples.

Thus, rules meant for plant and animal specimens should not just be copied for microorganisms. Lead agencies should work with researchers when designing some of the requirements so that these can be aligned to the disciplines.

Confidence-building measures

The suspicion that scientists are "stealing" samples that eventually will be commercialized is a burden that local and international researchers will carry collectively for a while. On their part, researchers must take immediate steps to understand and fulfil existing requirements so as to build confidence with the responsible agencies. Conscious efforts should be made to include local researchers, recruit MSc and PhD students and build local capacity. Researchers should also regularly share their findings in workshops and conferences and also through publications with the participation of relevant agencies. Information and knowledge should, where applicable, be used to provide solutions to local challenges. A common complaint has been that even those who get access permits rarely bother to submit progress reports or reports of their findings. Even as lobbying and negotiations for a simpler research authorization regime go on, scientists should make a conscious effort to cooperate with the responsible agencies and also help the capacity-building efforts for those organizations and for local research. Scientists should also establish partnerships with local communities where necessary.

Recommendations

Following the above observations, certain recommendations come to mind:

i Kenyan researchers working with local institutions should not be required to have a permit to access research resources locally. In most cases, these researchers work for institutions such as universities and research institutes which derive their research mandates from their acts or legal notices. They should, however, be required to deposit their proposals and findings with NACOSTI and other relevant agencies for documentation and information purposes.

ii Local researchers working with foreign collaborators should be required to get a permit from NACOSTI and should deposit a collaboration agreement between the said institutions which addresses issues of material transfer and intellectual property rights. However, they should not be required to get an access permit since by law, local research institutions were made to conduct research and they can only do so through their researchers.

iii Students should not be charged research fees. As locals, they should not be required to have access permits even if they will use the samples abroad. It is obvious that these students are engaged in academic research for the award of higher degrees which are needed to develop the country. However, institutions from where the students originate should have an MTA with the host institution in the foreign country. This should be presented to NACOSTI during the application process.

iv Foreign researchers must apply through a local collaborating institution for a research permit and must enclose a collaboration agreement and an MTA. The proposal must show strong elements of capacity building and technology transfer. NACOSTI should, where necessary, link foreign researchers to local institutions.

v The waiting period for a research permit should not exceed 2 weeks for local researchers and not more than 30 days for international researchers. In this case, NACOSTI should provide the one-stop shop for research clearance. Where NACOSTI requires the opinion of other agencies on a particular application, they should seek this directly from those agencies or include them in the decision-making process at NACOSTI.

vi Where a local researcher is applying and will collaborate with an international researcher for part of the work, their inherent right to access research materials should not change. They should be allowed to access research materials as they would if they were doing the research locally, however an MTA should be executed which should capture intellectual property rights and recognize Kenya's sovereignty over the biological resources.

vii The PIC should only be obtained if foreign researchers want to access research materials and are the lead scientists in a project, with local researchers only playing a supporting role. For access to protected areas under KWS or Kenya Forestry Service or on private land, the PIC can be obtained from the respective bodies/persons, as had been the case previously.

viii Academic research is geared towards generating new knowledge. Hence, researchers should be able to design and implement their experiment as they desire as long as they are not violating any ethical requirements.

ix For microorganisms, the process of depositing isolates, clones, plasmids or DNA (not soil or water samples) should be done even when isolation is done abroad. Isolation of microorganisms is not an easy affair and at times takes months, if not years.

x The relevant agencies should facilitate the establishment of the proposed Microbial Culture Collection Centre to facilitate the depositing of duplicate specimens of microorganisms. Efforts to this end being undertaken by Kenya Wildlife Service and the Jomo Kenyatta University of Agriculture and Technology with sponsorship of UNEP-GEF funding should be continued and supported.

xi Researchers on their part should robustly engage with lead agencies, share their findings locally and make deliberate effort to build local capacity in science and research.

Conclusion

Any research done about Kenya and on Kenyan resources can only be good for the country. Kenya's ability to exploit and benefit from its resources can only be realized if scientists are able to fully study and understand the resources and their potential. A casual scan through the proposals submitted to NACOSTI every year shows a serious deficit of research capability. This has resulted from years of research inactivity in Kenyan academic and research institutions due to lack of funding and equipment. Most of the research that was and is being done in these institutions is funded and driven by donors and foreign research organizations. Recent investment by NACOSTI, Lake Victoria Research Initiative (VicRes) of the Inter-Universities Council of East Africa, Regional Universities Forum for Capacity Building in Agriculture (RUFORUM) and other organizations have seen increased research activities. The complex research authorization process can only erode the gains so far made. Thus, NACOSTI and other agencies should promote research by reducing any barriers that may discourage researchers and find ways to foster increased international collaboration in research. As per its mandate, NACOSTI should promote more investment in research to facilitate research-driven decision making and policy making.

According to Article 6.3 of the Nagoya Protocol (NP), "each Party requiring prior informed consent shall take the necessary legislative, administrative or policy measures, as appropriate, to: (a) Provide for legal certainty, clarity and transparency of their domestic access and benefit-sharing legislation or regulatory requirements; (b) Provide for fair and non-arbitrary rules and procedures on accessing genetic resources; (c) Provide information on how to apply for prior informed consent (d) Provide for a clear and transparent written decision by a competent national authority, in a cost-effective manner and within a reasonable period of time; . . ." (UNEP 2011). From the experience of many researchers, the Kenyan framework falls short of the Nagoya Protocol in spirit due to the challenges outlined previously.

The fear of "loss of biological wealth" as experienced with the Genencor case on Kenyan soda lakes microorganisms (Heuer (undated)) is real, but the gains made from years of international research on the lakes are very significant and should not be overlooked. The information gathered over the years is key to any conservation and ecosystem management efforts, and the potential for further application still exists. As Kenya struggles to ensure compliance with the laid-down regulations and existing laws by researchers, the country should also develop mechanisms for supporting researchers and promoting research. By so doing, it would be responding to the dictates of the Constitution of Kenya 2010 (GOK, 2010), which recognize the role of science and indigenous technologies in the development of the nation and promote the intellectual property rights of the people of Kenya. Section 33 subsection 1b specifically promotes "academic freedom and freedom of scientific research".

In developing or revising guidelines, Kenya should also pay special attention to international treaties and agreements as required by the constitution. Article 2 number (5) states that "The general rules of international law shall form part of the law of Kenya," and number (6), "Any treaty or convention ratified by Kenya shall form part of the law of Kenya under this Constitution." The letter and spirit of the CBD and the Nagoya Protocol should be embraced. The thrust of the treaties is to facilitate research and not to impede it, even as states seek to protect, conserve and benefit from their biological materials (Article 15.2 CBD; Articles 6.3, 8 (a) NP).

There is so much more to be learned in Africa! Scientific research is the only tool Africa has to learn about its resources and to benefit from them. Knowledge about Kenya's biological resources can come from local as well as international researchers. The value in science and technology is not only in the monetary gains, but it is also in its power to change and improve the human condition, which Africa needs.

References

Finlay, BJ, Esteban, GF (2001) "Ubiquitous microbes and ecosystem function", *Limnetica* 20(1), pp. 31–43.

GOK (1999) The Environment Management and Co-ordination Act.

GOK (2006) The Environmental Management and Coordination (Conservation of Biological Diversity and Resources, Access to Genetic Resources and Benefit Sharing) Regulations 2006. Legal Notice No. 160.

GOK (2010) The Constitution of Kenya 2010.

GOK (2013a) The Wildlife Management and Conservation Act of 2013.

GOK (2013b) The Science, Technology and Innovation Act of 2013.

Kamau, EC (2009a) "Sovereignty over genetic resources: Right to regulate access in a balance. The case of Kenya", *Revista Internacional de Direito e Cidadania*, 3, pp. 73–88.

Kamau, EC (2009b) "Facilitating or restraining access to genetic resources? Procedural dimensions in Kenya", *Law, Environment and Development Journal* 5(2), pp. 154–166.

Kamau, EC (2014) "Valorisation of genetic resources, benefit sharing and conservation of biological diversity: What role for the ABS regime?" in: Dilling, O, Markus, T (eds), *Ex Rerum Natura Ius? – Sachzwang und Problemwahrnehmung im Umweltrecht*, Baden-Baden: Nomos, pp. 143–173.

Kamau, EC, Winter, G (2009) "Streamlining access procedures and standards" in: Kamau, EC, Winter, G (eds), *Genetic resources, traditional knowledge and the law: Solutions for access and benefit sharing*, London: Earthscan, pp. 365–379.

KWS (undated) Guidelines for conducting research in protected areas, Available online at www.kws.org/export/sites/kws/parks/education/research_forms/GUIDELINES_FOR_CONDUCT_OF_RESEARCH_IN_PROTECTED_AREAS.doc (accessed 5 November 2014).

NEMA (2006) Procedure for accessing genetic resources under the EMCA (Conservation of Biological Diversity and Resources, Access to Genetic Resources and Benefit Sharing) Regulations 2006, Available online at file:///C:/Users/Evanson/Downloads/Information%20on%20procedures%20on%20Accessing%20Genetic%20Resources.pdf (accessed 5 November 2014).

NSCT (November 2009) Procedures and guidelines for research authorization in Kenya, Available online at www.healthresearchweb.org/files/ResearchClearanceGuideline.pdf (accessed 5 November 2014).

Sarah Heuer (undated) The lake Bogoria extremophile. A case study, www.public.iastate.edu/~ethics/LakeBogoria.pdf (accessed 11 July 2014).

UNEP (2011) Nagoya Protocol on Access to Genetic Resources and the Fair and Equitable Sharing of Benefits Arising from their Utilization to the Convention of Biological Diversity.

13 Researcher's experiences in ecosystem research

A case study of Indonesia

Wolfram Lorenz and Aiyen Tjoa

Introduction

The Collaborative Research Centre CRC 552, "Stability of Rainforest Margins in Indonesia", is a long-term, large-scale, comprehensive interdisciplinary research collaboration between the Georg-August-University of Göttingen (with participation of the University of Kassel) and partners in Indonesia, consisting of the Bogor Agricultural University (IPB) and the Tadulako University in Palu. It aimed to study the interactions between socioeconomic development, rainforest conversion, and biodiversity in Indonesia. The overall research objective over three funding periods was to assess and analyze different factors and processes that contribute to the stability of rainforest margins.

Funded by the German Research Foundation (DFG), more than 100 scientists worked in international teams between July 2000 and June 2009 in 15 scientific projects (belonging to four project groups) in the vicinity of the Lore Lindu National Park in Central Sulawesi (Figure 13.1). The park is part of a UNESCO Biosphere Reserve, encompassing more than 60 villages with heterogenic structure and compositions of locals and migrants. The region is characterized by mountain and sub-mountain habitats. Road access started to develop in the late 1970s, and many parts of the region were difficult to reach until recent years. In this small region, four different local languages are spoken. Historically, rice dominated the agricultural landscape, which has been largely replaced by cash crops such as coffee and cacao within the last two decades.

All research activities were guided by a Joint Management Board, supported by coordination offices in Göttingen, a coordination office at the partner University in Bogor (near Jakarta, the capital of Indonesia) and a coordination office at the partner university in the project region in Central Sulawesi.

The University in Bogor is one of the most important and well-known universities in Indonesia, providing strong links and networks to the Indonesian government. At the beginning of our collaboration, our partner university in Palu had a less-developed and rather poor infrastructure. Accordingly, only a few lecturers at that university held at least a PhD degree, and even less had international experience. IPB, with its well-established scientific and political networks, played an important role in implementing the research activities in our study area, even

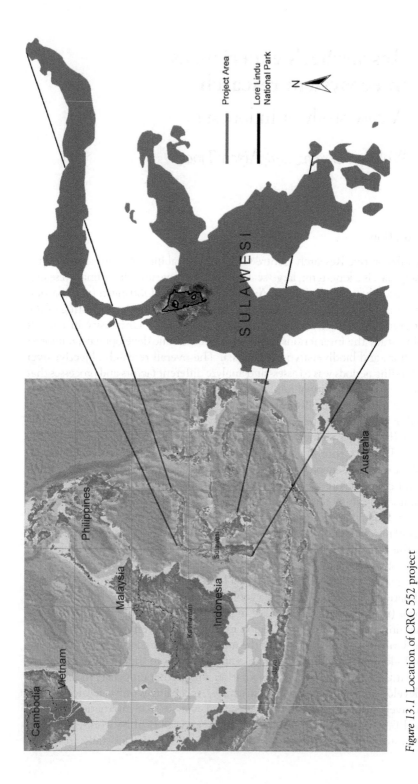

Figure 13.1 Location of CRC 552 project

Source: CRC 552: *"Stability of Rainforest Margins in Indonesia"* (STORMA); *based on Microsoft Encarta, Redmond, WA: Microsoft Corporation, 2001.*

though it is 2,000 km away from Central Sulawesi. The collaboration with IPB also had a major impact on the academic development of the Tadulako University in Palu.

Legal basis of the project

CRC 552 was established much earlier than the adoption of the Nagoya Protocol in October 2010. The DFG guidelines concerning biological research had not been published at that time either. Nevertheless, the Joint Project Management of CRC 552 developed several pioneering legal documents for Indonesia in relation with its research activities. In general, the collaboration in the field of higher education between Germany and Indonesia was regulated by "The Agreement between the Government of the Republic of Indonesia and the Government of the Federal Republic of Germany regarding Technical Cooperation" of 9 April 1984. To support the development of the Collaborative Research Centre in Indonesia, the DFG initiated the "Agreement on Scientific Cooperation between the 'Deutsche Forschungsgemeinschaft' (DFG) and the 'Directorate General for Higher Education' " (DGHE) of the Department for National Education of Indonesia, as well as the Joint Guidelines for the Implementation of this agreement, which was signed on 21 November 2000 in Bonn, Germany.

Based on the general agreements mentioned above, the collaboration of the CRC 552 was developed on the basis of the following legal documents:

a) Memorandum of Arrangement (MoA)
b) Agreement on Intellectual Property Rights (IPR)
c) Protocol of Data Exchange (PDE)
d) Material Transfer Agreement (MTA)

Memorandum of arrangement

The MoA defines regulated aspects of the project implementation, including contribution, duties and rights of the collaborating parties. The MoA was approved by the Indonesian State Secretary, providing CRC 552 with the strongest possible status for its work in Indonesia. The MoA contained a general IPR provision by the Indonesian government, which was further developed by a joint task force group of CRC 552. This development of the IPR included specific documents, such as the PDE and MTA. All documents also covered legal issues of the jointly developed data management system (see Stietenroth, Nieschulze & Arend 2005).

The agreement on intellectual property rights

The general IPR provision of the MoA was later replaced by a specific IPR agreement, which was developed by the joint task force group of CRC 552. The innovation of this agreement was the waiver of all possible economic benefits resulting from the utilization of research results by the German party. In other words, the Indonesian partners were granted the right to utilize all results of the joint basic research collaboration. Though the project was not expected to result in any utilization, the point was important for building trust.

The protocol of data exchange

This document provided a framework for the use, exchange, and storage of data created by the project members. In this context, the rights of Indonesia associated to natural resources, as well as rights of project members regarding their scientific efforts and results, were fully respected and formally acknowledged. At the end of the research collaboration, the database was transferred to servers of the Indonesian Institute of Science (LIPI).

The material transfer agreement

In the early years of CRC 552, clear procedures for transfer of materials between Indonesian and German partners were uncommon in the existing science community in Indonesia. Therefore, the Material Transfer Agreement of CRC 552 has attracted Indonesian authorities interested in the development of international research cooperation. Further, the MTA was used as a blueprint for the development of similar documents in other projects on higher education cooperation in Indonesia.

Getting access to the research location – Indonesian permit procedures

Institutional mandates

All research by foreigners in Indonesia is subject to extensive and complex regulations, which are widely seen as highly restrictive by the foreign research community. For individual research activities, it is almost impossible to follow all regulations and fulfil all requirements without serious loss of time (see Jordan 2005).

In Indonesia, international research cooperation is the responsibility of the central government. But until late 1990s, the legal situation was ambiguous: Different governmental institutions issued research permits and also universities were granted the right to collaborate directly with partners abroad. This situation caused confusion, particularly about responsibilities regarding the research procedure. Thus, in its early years, our project also used instruments provided by higher education institutions in Indonesia to manage visas, residence permits and research permits for research colleagues from Germany, bypassing LIPI, which was actually in charge of all research permit matters for foreigners since 1993 when the presidential decision 100/1993 (KEPRES) came into force. With this legal step, the Indonesian government provided a legal basis for foreign research activities in Indonesia and an instrument to increase the benefit for national development.

In fact, LIPI became the sole research permit-issuing institution just years after this presidential decision. LIPI professionalized its performance and service for scientists and developed an efficient and transparent online application system in 2005.

In 2007, law no. 41/2006 came into force. The authority to issue research permits was moved to the Ministry of Research and Technology (MENRISTEK).

There, the Foreign Research Permit (FRP) team of MENRISTEK coordinated the permit process, which involved up to 30 governmental institutions (the number of reviewers/departments depending on the research theme). All involved institutions have a veto power, which frequently leads to the rejection or postponement of research permits, often due to lack of involvement of relevant local partners or because of security concerns.

Permit procedures and requirements for foreign scientists

However, research permit procedures and requirements for foreign scientists introduced by KEPRES 100/1993 have, in general, not been changed since then, although some minor adjustments have been made. The research permits can only be issued for individuals, not for groups, institutions or similar entities. This had an implication on project planning, because any research stay required an individual time-consuming application process as described below.

Prior to entry into Indonesia

The basic procedure consists of pre- and post-arrival procedures. Before entering Indonesia, the following documents are required for submission to the permit-issuing institution:[1]

1 A formal letter of request
2 Copies of the research proposal
3 Copies of the abstract of the research proposal
4 Copies of the curriculum vitae (CV)
5 Letters of recommendation from supervisor and employer
6 Letters of support from Indonesian counterparts or partner institution, if applicable an MoU and an MTA
7 A letter guaranteeing sufficient funds
8 Health certificate from legally practicing medical doctor stating that the researcher is physically and mentally capable to conduct the research
9 Copies of the researcher's passport
10 Close-up photographs (4 × 6 cm) with red background
11 A recommendation letter from a related Indonesian representative (Indonesian Embassy or Consulate General) abroad

1 The text in the list has been shortened by the author. For the complete current version see http://international.ristek.go.id/onlineService/detail/view/1-procedure-foreign-research-permit (accessed 3 November 2014).

12. A list of research equipment that will be brought to Indonesia, along with a brief technical specification mentioning the estimated value for each piece of equipment in use
13. If the researcher plans to bring his/her spouse and children, he/she must also submit a copy of marriage certificate, etc.

On average, the application process lasted about 2–3 months before the approval and visa to enter Indonesia were ready. For a better understanding of the procedure, the following part provides some comments.

Doing research in Indonesia is only possible if an appropriate Indonesian partner is involved. Point 6 of the list above shows the requirement conditioning authorization on the existence of a local partner. The permit-issuing institution, however, has the right to reject a partner and/or to suggest another person. It happened several times in our project that our researchers were requested to include an additional partner, e.g. persons from local governmental institutions. The reason for that might have been to foster capacity building and benefit sharing.

Local partners have many responsibilities. Besides providing technical support and guidance for the foreign researcher, the partners are responsible for any samples to be exported. They and their institution have to act as the provider on behalf of the Republic of Indonesia.

Fulfilling point 11, to get the recommendation from an Indonesian representative abroad is a time-consuming procedure by itself, depending on the procedure laid down. In our case, we had a collaboration agreement approved at the governmental level – which made such additional recommendation unnecessary.

Point 12 could lead to misunderstanding: Submitting a list of research equipment that will be brought to Indonesia does not automatically mean that the intended import will be free of tax and customs fees. To get such an import tax and custom exemption, specific regulations apply that involve various institutions and a lot of paperwork. Dealing with such issues can take up to three months.

Our project was registered by the Indonesian government as a foreign aid organization – similar to the German Agency for International Cooperation (GIZ). With this status, we were granted tax exemption by the Indonesian Ministry of Finance. Import administration of our research equipment was handled with great support by the GIZ office in Jakarta.

Getting a research permit is one thing, but further permits and administrative work may be required. Permits involving working with biological material and taking and sending samples are subject to separate regulations. Unfortunately, sample collection and export is not granted automatically by MENRISTEK. But even if a researcher does not intend to take samples, the approval of a research permit is not sufficient to start the field activities, because further post-arrival procedures need to be fulfilled.

Post-arrival procedures

When a research permit has been approved and the immigration office has sent the visa authorization to the Indonesian representative abroad, the researcher has to apply for the research visa. After arrival in Indonesia and a visit at MENRISTEK's Foreign Research Permit Office, the researcher has to make some reports to further institutions like the Police Headquarters and the Ministry of Home Affairs in Jakarta, but also to the regional police office and office of National Unity and Community Protection (KESBANGPOL).

The report process works like a chain: The researcher reports his or her arrival, research plans and permit to the institution and in return each institution will issue response letters for the next institution in the chain, all the way down to village level where the researcher intends to conduct the field research. Due to this kind of permit-letter chain, the time needed to get all letters issued to fulfil all requirements in order to start the field research can sum up to another two months. Someone could expect that such a permit-letter chain would work automatically from institution to institution, but this is not the case – the partner's institution is in charge of the process. A further challenge is that sending letters to governmental institutions in general does not work by postal service; communication between a remote university in Central Sulawesi and governmental offices in the capital of Jakarta is complicated and most offices involved in the research permit process are not really prepared to receive foreign visitors. Without the support of the partner institutions and a service office like the central coordination unit of our research project, a researcher would get lost or lose too much of the scarce and valuable time for what the researcher actually applied for – research.

Benefit-sharing measures

Benefit sharing with collaborating institutions

As already mentioned, one goal of the research permit procedures in Indonesia is it to make sure that the partner institutions benefit from the research collaboration. Benefit sharing in non-commercial basic research collaboration should mainly be in the form of joint publications, capacity building and knowledge transfer. But how can this be achieved when the local partner institutions and the collaborators have insufficient language skills and lack functioning laboratory facilities or even access to scientific literature? It was clear right from the beginning that significant investments would be necessary.

Institutional benefit sharing was agreed on centrally in the technical cooperation agreement (MoA). At the subproject level we developed Counterpart Agreements (CPA) containing individual benefit-sharing measures. Key points were task sharing for joint publications and capacity-building measures such as scientific work visits at the University of Göttingen and participation in scientific conferences.

Benefit sharing by involving partners in joint publications is not always possible the way the partners would like. Guidelines for good scientific practice require an appropriate scientific intellectual contribution to publications for co-authorship, but due to inadequate scientific background of partners, lack of language skills, lack of access to scientific journals or other reasons, their contributions were often not sufficient. Leading authors sometimes were in a dilemma of choosing between good scientific practice and good relations with disappointed collaborators.

Our project involved soil chemical analyses as well as taxonomic identification of biological material or material containing genetic resources. We initiated the development of a laboratory for sample preparation and chemical analyses and provided the basic equipment and instruments – including a 25 kV independent uninterrupted power supply unit to make the laboratory independent from the unstable power grid. Established in 2001, the laboratory at Tadulako University is certified today and provides service for its scientists and students as well for external requests.

CRC 552 also initiated and supported the development of a botanical reference collection and respective capacity building. Basic equipment was funded and staff was trained. Training was done in the field, systematic theoretical courses at the Indonesian Institute of Science, a master course at the partner university in Bogor, and practical trainings at the herbarium and the botanical garden of the University of Göttingen. With financial support from the Indonesian government, the partners from Tadulako University in Palu could further develop the reference collection and built a two-story herbarium located on the campus in Palu. Today this herbarium is registered as Herbarium Celebense (CEB) and known as the best and most complete, steadily growing reference collection for Sulawesi.

Interestingly, capacity building took place not only between Indonesian and German parties, but also between the local Indonesian partners. Lecturers from Tadulako University in Palu participated in PhD programs at IPB Bogor. Often scientists of CRC 552 supervised the PhD training and respective field research were conducted and financed in the framework of CRC 552. Our project was in the lucky position to have funds available to support field research in a number of complementary research topics developed by our partners.

Getting to the field was a big logistical challenge. Motorbikes and 4-wheel drive (4WD) cars with drivers were financed and managed by CRC 552. This was another big investment. Also, the maintenance of the vehicles was cost intensive, due to the difficult terrain and off-road conditions in the field. Unfortunately, financial support from the Indonesian partner universities for the maintenance could not be realized due to conflicting administrative systems of the parties. However, today the remaining vehicle park is fully under the responsibility of the Indonesian partner institution. The remaining part of the vehicle park is still functioning and used for research collaborations of Tadulako University.

Benefit sharing with farmers and villages

For the success of our research project it was seen as very important to get the general acceptance of the planned activities. For the development of good and trustworthy relations with the communities in the territories, we conducted our activities and organized public events to inform about and discuss our planned research there (Figure 13.2). Such public events were repeated from time to time to keep the villages up to date about our activities. Besides this, we discussed benefit-sharing measures for the village with village heads and village representatives to avoid the perception that only some selected farmers would get benefits from us and others

Figure 13.2 Public awareness meeting with villagers
Source: *Photograph by author*

excluded. Such central measures were e.g. books, toys for a local elementary school, support for community sport facilities or construction material for the maintenance of central public buildings in the communities.

Major research activities of CRC 552 took place in small cocoa plantations owned by local farmers. For each research plot we made agreements with its own-ers. To make these agreements as transparent as possible and to avoid mispercep-tions by villagers, the justification of the plot-selection process, the planned research activities and goals, as well as details of the agreements and justification of compensation payments were discussed in public under the presence of local authorities such as village heads and representatives of the village government.

The agreements guaranteed for the researchers access to the plots for the time needed and the activities planned. In return, the farmers received compensation in the form of cash, as well as in non-monetary form, e.g. reports of research results. Of course it would have made no sense to hand over to them copies of scientific publications resulting from the research on their plots. Instead, we com-piled some basic facts about each individual plantation, like soil composition and the health condition of the cacao trees on the plots. We combined this with research results and developed individual recommendations on how to improve the management of the cacao plantation. Again, such feedback, rounded off with general results and recommendations, were given in public events at village level, to give others the chance to benefit from our research. In addition, we cooperated with local extension service institutions from the governmental as well as the nongovernmental sector and organized cacao management trainings. These trainings were open to the public as well.

A big challenge was the construction of a climate research tower inside the Lore Lindu National Park. We needed to make sure that the forest around the tower would not be disturbed. Even though the tower was located inside the park, local people used the area for hunting and to collect raisins from trees. Needless to say, the results of carbon flux measurements at the tower in the forest would be not regarded as an appropriate benefit for them. Finally, with the personal support of the governor and the regional and local government, a community agreement was developed. To make its content public, a big inauguration ceremony with lots of cultural activities for the communities nearby was organized when the tower was ready for use (Figures 13.3 and 13.4).

For this ceremony, the governor of Central Sulawesi came to the location, accompanied by several representatives of departments in charge of rural development. In his public speech to the villagers living in the area, the governor disseminated all important information necessary to make the people understand the importance of not disturbing the measurement equipment of the climate research tower and keeping the surrounding forest untouched.

Figure 13.3 Inauguration ceremony of climate tower at Besoa Valley, Lore Lindu National Park

Source: *Photograph by author*

Figure 13.4 Inauguration ceremony of climate tower at Besoa Valley, Lore Lindu National Park

Impressively, the event and the governor's speech had a long-lasting effect on the well-being of the tower such that until today the tower and the surrounding forest are in very good condition.

But not all local communities are so well organized and structured to make long-lasting public agreements possible. The big challenge is: Which is the right and legitimate local community institution to address? Traditional communities often lack in legitimacy and they tend to compete with governmental structures. In our research region in Central Sulawesi the situation was heterogenic. Besides the communities described above with strong cultural bonds and strong links to the government, we had to face community representatives who were less respectful to government regulations. Acting in line with official governmental regulations, we once ran into a conflicting situation with such a local customary group.

Conclusion

Classical benefit-sharing measures in the framework of non-commercial basic research collaboration, like joint publications and scientific capacity building, are not sufficient to meet the real needs in collaborations where partners and stakeholders are so different, such as in our example. Additional efforts are necessary, going far beyond typical research collaboration.

A major instrument to grant access to research locations and research material by foreign researchers in Indonesia is the Research Permit Regulation. This regulation tries to secure the interests of Indonesia to protect its biodiversity and to generate benefits – which is a very positive intention. However, the complicated and time-consuming procedures are discouraging to researchers, particularly to those who do not have such strong and experienced partners as we had.

It would be of great assistance for all partners, and it would encourage more scientists to come to Indonesia, if researchers could be provided with easily understandable and simplified time-saving procedures – ideally through a one-door-service/one-stop shop (clearing house). Research collaborations and research could be much more efficient, effective and beneficial – particularly for Indonesia.

References

Foreign Research Permit Procedures, http://international.ristek.go.id/ (accessed 2 June 2014).

Jordan, R (2005) "Forschungsbedingungen in Südostasien. Zum fehlenden Diskurs über die rechtlichen Bedingungen in ausländischer Forschungsvorhaben", *Pacific News*, 23.

Stietenroth, D, Nieschulze, J, Arend, K (2005) "Rechtliche Aspekte und Umsetzung des Datenmanagement in internationalen interdisziplinären Forschungsprojekten. Erfahrungen aus dem DFG-Sonderforschungsbereich 552 Stability of Rainforest Margins", *Zeitschrift für Agrarinformatik* 3(05), pp. 64–76.

Part IV

Good practice and legislative options

14 *Ex situ* collections of plants and how they adjust to ABS conditions*

Susette Biber-Klemm, Kate Davis, Laurent Gautier, Michael Kiehn, and Sylvia I. Martinez

Starting points

Non-commercial academic biodiversity research is an important factor in the scenario on Access and Benefit Sharing (ABS): Research on genetic resources (GR) is to a substantial degree carried out by academia; its results are essential for the conservation and sustainable use of biological diversity. It generates non-monetary benefits that have the potential to contribute to the development of the provider states. This research also provides a vital basis for potential commercial uses that generate monetary benefits (Biber-Klemm et al. 2014; Kamau and Winter, Ch. 1 in this volume).

Ex situ collections of biological material have an essential function in academic research on biological diversity. However, as repositories and hubs for genetic information in the service of biodiversity research, their mode of operation regarding the transfer of the resources is diametrically opposite to the bilateral contractual system introduced by the CBD and the related interests of the providers of genetic resources.

This chapter describes challenges of collections of genetic resources triggered by this dilemma and discusses solutions found in response. Thereby it focuses on the role of *ex situ* collections for academic[1] non-commercial research.

Ex situ collections

For biodiversity science, public *ex situ* collections[2] are important instruments. They contain specimens collected across time and space (Thomson 2003) and thus form huge libraries of scientific data serving as a basis for additional analytical

---

* The authors wish to thank China Williams, Conventions and Policy Section, Royal Botanic Gardens, Kew for updated information on specimen flows and ABS implementation at Kew.

1 The NP speaks of "non-commercial research". "Academic" is used here in the sense of "related to an institution of higher learning . . . a scholarly institution" (Oxford Dictionary) to more clearly define the scope of the text. Moreover, academic research has to follow specific standards and integrated control mechanisms that are important in the context of ABS (Martinez & Biber-Klemm 2010).

2 In contrast to collections held by commercial enterprises that are generally not accessible for outside research.

studies. Current knowledge relies on specimens collected between the 16th century and yesterday that are held in repositories spread around the entire globe.

Ex situ collections are very diverse: They are held by a great variety of institutions and include, for instance, culture collections, cell banks, germplasm collections, stock centres, herbaria, museum collections, zoos and botanic gardens. The institutions differ in types of resources held as well as in size, structure, legal status and available capacities.

Ex situ collections may comprise diverse GR (dead, living, or abstract information) that have been accessed at various times (before or after entry into force of the Convention on Biological Diversity (CBD); or the Nagoya Protocol (NP)). Material stored *ex situ* may either originate from collections carried out *in situ* or be obtained from other *ex situ* facilities through acquisition, donation or exchange.

The common denominator of all collections is that they are an essential infrastructure for non-commercial, academic research (OECD 2001): *Ex situ* collections are in charge of hosting reference material for science and education. According to scholarly standards, collected material, data and analyses have to be submitted to appropriate repositories and databases and propagated and/or stored for longer periods of time and beyond the completion of related research projects (ed. Salathé 2008). This guarantees the credibility of published research results and enables peer scientists to interpret, reproduce, and validate the obtained results (ed. European Science Foundation 2000). This practice is rooted in the requisites for advancing scientific knowledge, the basic principle being to make results and data publicly available for others to build upon. This essentially also entails the exchange of resources within a peer network (Martinez & Biber-Klemm 2010; Biber-Klemm, Davis, Gautier, & Martinez 2014). For instance, taxonomy relies on strong and close networking between specialized scientists and an incessant exchange of specimens for examination, identification and classification, in order to test and expand on former findings with new methods. For these reasons, material stored in a botanical or zoological institute can potentially be sent to any other interested institution as an exchange, purchase, gift for identification, or loan. Well-established systems are in place in different fields of science to regulate and facilitate these kinds of exchanges.

ABS relevance

In sum, with regard to the ABS system, the following characteristics of academic research and *ex situ* collections are essential: *ex situ* collections serve non-commercial scientific biodiversity research that relies on free access to the stored resources and on strong and close networking and exchange of resources between scientists throughout repositories. It generates information that is – to a great part – in the public interest (among others for conservation and sustainable use of biological diversity) and publicly accessible.

In turn, the ultimate goal of the ABS system is to generate monetary or nonmonetary benefits that are generated through utilization of the resources accessed and accrue to the provider of the resources, with the aim of contributing to the conservation and sustainable use of biological diversity. This provider–user relation regarding the benefit sharing is based on a bilateral contract.

However, the access–benefit scenario is frequently characterized by an important divide in time and space. Moreover, the linear process from access to final product – as originally envisaged by the creators of the CBD – hardly ever takes place. The chain from access to product may involve a series of intermediaries, research in some cases being one of them.[3] This makes the tracking of the resources and the monitoring of the implementation of the bilateral contract extremely difficult for the providers.

In our view, this problem is rooted in the ABS system itself. It seems that at the time of its inception, the idea was based on a linear model of bioprospecting.[4] Yet in practice the ABS processes prove to be complex indeed. For the provider countries, the problem of controlling the movements of informational values through the innovation and value chain in industrialized countries, and the reluctance of "user countries" to introduce effective control and compliance measures, led to an increased anxiety of the providers that they might miss out on the sharing of benefits resulting from commercial use (Biber-Klemm, Martinez, & Jacob 2010, 15–17; Biber-Klemm 2008). With regard to academic research, the providers' concern is that a resource or information accessed for non-commercial, academic research willingly or unwillingly crosses over to commercial use (change of intent), outside of the sphere of control of the providers (Biber-Klemm et al. 2014). These concerns may be expressed in strong claims for stringent control and compliance measures (Richerzagen and Müller-Holm 2005).

The concern of academic research is that these fears will have a large impact on research practices in various regards: They are bound to create bureaucratic hurdles that hamper access in the providing states (Kamau 2014; CBD 2008; Biber-Klemm et al. 2014; Kamau, Ch. 17 in this volume; Biber-Klemm and Martinez, Ch. 11 in this volume). This can lead to a practical stop of projects with a high relevance for research and conservation. In particular, as regards special knowledge in biodiversity-rich regions, the number of researchers with special knowledge can be expected to drop drastically. Further, keeping track of all movements of the resources within the research community is complex. Requests for comprehensive recording therefore are bound to cause heavy administrative burdens that are difficult to shoulder for academia and the collections.

The basic dilemma consists of the conflicting interests of easy access to the resources and their free exchange versus securing the share of benefits through tight control measures. As regards *ex situ* collections, this is fostered by the

---

3 See EU Regulation No 511/2014 of the European Parliament and of the Council of 16 April 2014 on compliance measures for users from the Nagoya Protocol on Access to Genetic Resources and the Fair and Equitable Sharing of Benefits Arising from their Utilization in the Union (EU L No 511/2014), Recital 27 and 28: "The collection of genetic resources in the wild is mostly undertaken for non-commercial purposes by academic, university and non-commercial researchers or collectors . . ." and "Collections are major suppliers of genetic resources and traditional knowledge associated with genetic resources utilized in the Union . . .".

4 Compare the early examples, in particular the InBio Merck case, in Cabrera Medaglia 2004.

academic practice of transparency and open access and their function as a scientific hub, which makes tracking difficult. The problem is amplified by the divergences regarding the time and scope of the NP (Biber-Klemm et al. 2014) and the ensuing apprehension that access to *ex situ* resources is replacing bioprospecting *in situ* (Meyenberg & von Weizsäcker 2010).

The hope is that the entry into force and the implementation of the NP – in particular the implementation of the compliance mechanisms – will succeed in building trust and alleviating pressure from non-commercial research and *ex situ* collections.

The question here is what the collections have undertaken in the meantime to resolve the dilemma and to answer the challenges described, and whether and how this contributes to the achievement of the CBD's ultimate goals.

Answers to the challenges

Overview

After the adoption of the CBD, public *ex situ* collections became aware of their potential problems with regard to the CBD's ABS principles. A series of instruments and systems were created as an answer to the challenges and to find a solution to ease access and at the same time secure benefit sharing.

One solution enshrined in an international agreement is the system on facilitated access to collections of certain plant genetic resources of the International Treaty on Plant Genetic Resources for Food and Agriculture (ITPGRFA) with its decoupled benefit-sharing system. Its rationale is the vital need of free access and global exchange of GR for breeding new varieties (Kamau & Winter 2013; Biber-Klemm et al. 2014).

Other instruments were created in a bottom-up process that was initiated by the concerned collections (culture collections; botanic gardens and *ex situ* collections in general). There are, on the one hand, sectoral voluntary codes of conduct, principles and best practices, for instance:

- the sectoral approach of MOSAICC, the Micro-Organisms Sustainable use and Access regulation International Code of Conduct, which provides a tool to support the implementation of the CBD;
- the TRIPS Agreement and the Budapest Treaty (Deposit of Micro-organisms for the Purposes of Patent Procedures) for microbial collections;
- the framework approach of the Principles on ABS[5] ("the Principles"), which offers core principles for endorsement by botanical institutions (botanic gardens and herbaria) for use in the development of individual institutional policies; and

---

5 The Principles on Access to Genetic Resources and Benefit Sharing, www.bgci.org/resources/ abs_principles (accessed 5 November 2014).

- the newest, a broader approach by the Consortium of European Taxonomic Facilities (CETAF), which offers a package of model documents, a code of conduct and a best practice, "in order to provide guidance on means to successfully implement the NP" that are directed at all taxonomic collections and non-commercial biological research institutions – zoological as well as botanical ones – that wish to implement their principles and content.

On the other hand there are instruments that propose a more binding answer for defined sectors, *in concreto* the botanical gardens: the International Plant Exchange Network (IPEN) which offers a code of conduct, standard documentation and registration as a member of a closed network. IPEN and the abovementioned Principles on Access to Genetic Resources and Benefit Sharing are discussed in more detail below, using the Royal Botanic Gardens, Kew, as an example of an institution that uses the Principles as its policy framework.

The EU Regulation for the implementation of the NP on compliance measures for users[6] is a recent public instrument that gives the *ex situ* collections a prominent role in the R&D chain. Based on the assessment that "collections are major suppliers of genetic resources and traditional knowledge associated with genetic resources in the Union" (recital (28)), it features a voluntary certification of collections: Against the backdrop of the due diligence obligation of all users, the regulation defines criteria for the management of *ex situ* collections. If the criteria are met, the collection can request a certification by registration in the Union's "Register of collections". Users sourcing their material in registered collections are considered to have fulfilled their due diligence obligation. The system is meant to ease the obligations of users (recital (28)). The question (that will be assessed at a later stage) is, whether it also contributes to enhancing transparency of the movement of GR, thus building trust of the providers.

With the exception of the ITPGRFA which has an institutionalized system, the ultimate rationale of all instruments is to facilitate access to the resources (*in situ*, and/or, in cases of legally restricted exchange, of *ex situ* resources), by 1) trust-building measures such as enhancing transparency on utilization and movement of the resources and defining a point when they are considered to have transited to commercial research; and 2) securing the sharing of benefits while at the same time minimizing the bureaucracy for the exchange of material.

Case studies

In the following, the question is approached by presenting and analyzing two different systems in more detail: the IPEN system and the Principles framework as implemented by the Royal Botanic Gardens, Kew. The ITPGRFA will not be discussed further. The two case studies will be presented and, with a focus on the

6 Above, fn 3.

above-identified "hot" issues, the following questions will be broached: facilitating access and exchange for research; the handling of pre- and post-CBD/NP accessions; and measures at the interface of non-commercial research and for commercial ends to assure the sharing of benefits (with a specific focus on the inner-academic transition from (basic) research to research and development (Biber-Klemm et al. 2014)). In this context, the following are considered ABS-relevant stages in the "collection life cycle" of a resource: 1) acquisition, in particular as regards verification of the legitimacy of the specimens; 2) curation and maintenance as regards the data management as well as practices for access for research and loans; and 3) ultimately, permanent transfer to third parties as regards the transfer of conditions of use and the control of their implementation.

The International Plant Exchange Network

The International Plant Exchange Network is a system for CBD-compliant non-commercial exchange between botanic gardens. It was originally developed by the *Verband Botanischer Gärten* (an association of gardens in German-speaking countries) and has been taken over by the European Consortium of Botanic Gardens.

IPEN is a network open only to botanical gardens[7] covering the exchange of living plant material (including derived living material such as parts of plants and diaspores[8]). The network aims at implementing the ABS principles and creating a climate of confidence between the countries providing the GR – frequently countries of the South – and the gardens. Its ultimate goal is securing access to material in provider states and transfer of material in accordance with the ABS regulations of the CBD and the NP in a way that is transparent for provider countries and also facilities exchange by minimizing bureaucracy for the needed documentation between the members (Godt 2013; Gröger 2007).

Participating gardens have to adhere to a common policy, setting out their responsibilities for acquisition, maintenance and supply of living plant material and associated benefit sharing. A core obligation is the commitment to non-commercial use only.[9] The system, however, also defines procedures for material "leaving" the system as a pathway for commercial uses.

In order to create transparency, build trust and control the movement of the material, IPEN features the following instruments: 1) the common policy defined in a Code of Conduct (CoC); 2) a documentation and coding system that enables the tracking of resources and their derivatives within the network; 3) a uniform Material Transfer Agreement (MTA) for material leaving the

---

7 Botanic gardens are institutions holding documented collections of living plants for the purposes of scientific research, conservation, display and education (Wyse Jackson, BGCI 1999). Code of Conduct, footnote 1.

8 See "IPEN Code of Conduct for botanic gardens governing the acquisition, maintenance and supply of living plant material", www.botgart.uni-bonn.de/ipen/criteria.html#box3, footnote 2.

9 Criteria for IPEN membership at www.botgart.uni-bonn.de/ipen/criteria.html#box3 (accessed 28 October 2014).

system for non-commercial use; and 4) a procedure for material leaving the system for commercial use.

Material entering IPEN has to be "cleared" by the supplying garden for compliance with the domestic ABS rules of the provider. The network members will decline acceptance of plant material from organizations and individuals if they are not sure about them acting in good faith and being committed to the CBD. This checkpoint function (Godt 2013, 251) is obligatory for both material sourced *in situ* and material received from third parties.

The accession then has to be documented and assigned an IPEN number. The documentation must record all relevant information such as taxonomic data, source of material, existing permits and certificates, and terms and conditions made by the country of origin (CoC, Annex 4).[10] This documentation rests with the garden that acquires the accession and supplies it to the system (supplying garden). The IPEN number encodes 1) the country of origin; 2) whether or not there are restrictions on use and transfer; 3) the acronym of the supplying garden; and 4) the supplying garden's accession number for the specimen. This number must follow the material and all its descendants through all exchanges within IPEN. It guarantees that ABS rules have been observed and allows the receiving IPEN members to go back to the detailed documentation kept by the first garden if necessary. In effect, it is a unique identifier that ensures the traceability of material for the provider states (Godt 2013). Within the IPEN, no additional formalities are needed for exchange and supply.

Transfer to third parties outside the network depends on the intended use of the material. For non-commercial use, a standard MTA is sufficient; it transfers all conditions agreed to by the supplying garden to the third party and defines standard obligations of the recipients, such as documentation of the material in their own data system; non-commercial use only; sharing of benefits; supply to other users under the same conditions; and documentation of the transfer (CoC, Annex 6). All connected information is transferred with the material.

In case of any use not covered by the original MAT, including intended commercialization – be it by a user outside or within IPEN – a new PIC of the country of origin needs to be acquired. In case of a third party requiring access, evidence of the PIC needs to be submitted to the responsible garden prior to the transfer of the material and a new MAT must be negotiated with the country of origin. This procedure is facilitated by the IPEN system, which allows an immediate tracking of the provider country and the original conditions under which the material was received.

IPEN provides an internal system of control of compliance by its members. The Task Force of IPEN contacts gardens in cases of potential infractions of the IPEN regulations. It also provides training and answers questions regarding the implementation of IPEN (especially in the context of documentation or material transfer). In addition, IPEN membership is subject to renewal after a period of time, and

---

10 Yet, it is recommended not to enter material that has been acquired under conditions that hamper easy exchange (Code of Conduct, above, fn 8).

practical compliance with the Code of Conduct (as exemplified by the implementation of IPEN) is one prerequisite for the renewal of membership. Member gardens are very much aware of this.

In sum, the system of IPEN assures a smooth exchange of resources between the members of the network. At present, 172 gardens are registered (9 April 2015), which is about 10 per cent of the approximate 1,800 botanical gardens worldwide. All except nine (from Argentina, Israel, New Zealand and the United States) are situated in Europe.[11] Two-thirds of these are university collections (Godt 2013, 251). So there is (still) a strong focus on the European tradition and network. However, it is interesting to note that since the discourse on the NP and its implications started, there has been a significant increase in requests for information on IPEN by botanical gardens, and membership has increased by more than 10 per cent since the end of 2012 (150 members at that time), with indications of a tendency to more global coverage (members from the United States and from New Zealand). Considering the fact that gardens, up to now, are not obliged to use an NP-compatible documentation system, this tendency clearly indicates the botanic gardens community's awareness of the need to cope with ABS issues in general.

There are, however, several reasons for gardens not to access the network. First, gardens in many countries do not seem to benefit from joining IPEN, because they primarily work on a national scale or because the national legal framework does not allow sending out seeds without additional permits or restrictions.

A second reason for gardens not to become IPEN members might be that the Code of Conduct strongly recommends that the gardens treat all plant material "as if" acquired under the CBD (CoC 1.3). This means that the entire collection would have to be scanned for material suitable for IPEN and then recorded according to its standard. Moreover, the system indirectly requires two different data sets – IPEN material and non-IPEN material – so the system requires an elaborate system for data management.

Another point discussed in literature is the issue of change of intent/commercialization of resources held by the gardens. In IPEN, even if the transition to commercial use is provided for in the system (see above), in practice very little or no transfer to third parties occurs (Godt 2013, 252). This might be, in part, due to the material stored. Yet, according to Kamau and Winter (2009, 29), another concern of the gardens is that provider states would then refrain from providing material. This observation adds an additional facet to the basic dilemma between the interests of non-commercial research in easy access and transfer and of the providers in the tracking of the resources throughout the research and value chain. The voluntary "non-commercial commitment" by botanical gardens as an answer to the concerns of the providers might lead to the exclusion of the potential to generate benefits through commercial use – one of the core rationales of the ABS system as originally designed and one of the core interests of the providers.

---

11 See www.bgci.org/resources/ipen/ (accessed 9 April 2015).

Another observation in literature refers to potential loopholes regarding transition into the commercial-oriented research, in particular in the academic system (Godt 2013, 253). In modern universities, the non-commercial/commercial divide in the research and value chain is not always clear cut. This is in part due to the fact that at present, direct bioprospection *in situ* or *ex situ* by companies takes place, only to a small extent. Industrial companies are rather licensing in from or forming partnerships with [small companies and universities] that generate interesting leads in their natural products discovery research (CBD 2008). It is therefore possible that academic research that as a rule generates mainly non-monetary benefits, in some cases leads to monetary benefits such as licence fees in cases of patented results that are licensed out. The question in this context is how university IPEN member gardens transfer material to their colleagues in the natural science institutes such as botany and pharmacology. In principle, these institutes are clearly "non-IPEN"; transfers would need to be handled accordingly. In practice, however, a risk exists that they are treated as belonging to the network. In such cases the link to the garden and the original provider might easily get lost in the further downstream research and value chain.

Negotiation and adoption of the NP have triggered a set of activities within IPEN in order to fully adapt it to the provisions of the NP. So, its Task Force is actually carefully redrafting the Code of Conduct. Being aware of the above debate, the Task Force will take up the issues of commercialization and possible loopholes in more detail (Kiehn 2015, 318f.).

Further, in order to provide legal security and transparency regarding their pre- and post-NP holdings, at the initiative of the IPEN Task Force, botanic gardens in a number of countries deposited copies of their holdings on 12 October 2014 (the date of entry into force of the NP) at different places (notaries, ABS Focal points, other governmental bodies) (Kiehn 2014).

IPEN will continue to support botanical gardens in their compliance with the NP obligations. It will further interact with and provide information to relevant ABS stakeholders in provider and user states, aiming at reaching regulations and frameworks that will enable botanic gardens to carry out their research and conservation activities in an effective and "ABS-friendly" way in compliance with the NP regulations.

The principles on access to genetic resources and their implementation by the Royal Botanic Gardens, Kew

In contrast to the above example that has an institutional character, the Principles on Access to Genetic Resources and Benefit-Sharing ("the Principles") offer a procedural approach that is based on an internationally tested framework (Latorre García, Williams, ten Kate & Cheyne 2001). This approach allows for 1) adaptation to the specifics of the particular institution and its types of resources and uses; 2) coverage of the entire "research chain" including potential commercialization; and 3) responding to changing situations. The Principles have been developed within the global botanic gardens' network, Botanic Gardens

Conservation International (BGCI), and endorsed by a globally diverse range of gardens.[12]

The Principles[13] provide a one-page framework that covers acquisition, maintenance, use and supply of GR; use of written agreements; and benefit sharing. They require gardens to develop and communicate an institutional policy indicating how they will implement the Principles. Further, since gardens may be involved in some commercial activities, the Principles require that they prepare a transparent policy on the commercialization (including plant sales) of GR and their derivatives acquired before and since the CBD entered into force.

The following describes the implementation of the Principles in The Royal Botanic Gardens, Kew ("Kew"). Kew uses the Principles as the framework for its current ABS policy.[14] Kew is also a CETAF member with policy and documentation in line with the new CETAF measures.

Kew's many-layered institutional response to the one-page Principles is a reflection of the complexity of Kew's ABS needs for its diverse collections, research programmes and international collaborations. However, some of the elements of Kew's detailed ABS strategy might serve as building blocks for smaller and/or less diverse collections.

Kew Gardens

The Royal Botanic Gardens, Kew is a botanical garden and charitable trust in the United Kingdom with the mission of inspiring and delivering science-based plant conservation worldwide, thus enhancing the quality of life. Kew receives a portion of its funding from the UK government to fulfil its statutory obligations under the UK's National Heritage Act (1984), which include requirements to carry out research on plant science and disseminate results and to keep the collections as national reference collections, secure and available for study.[15]

Kew has significant exposure to ABS issues, as it acquires, holds, uses and exchanges living and preserved genetic resources from around the world, collected pre- and post-CBD. Kew's collections are large, varied and held in several different science departments: among them, the Herbarium contains around 7.5 million dried, pressed specimens; the living plant collection contains around 70,000 specimens of 30,000 taxa; the Millennium Seed Bank contains around 2 billion live, frozen seeds from over 10 per cent of the world's flora; and Kew's DNA bank contains over 42,000 samples of plant genomic DNA.

Specimens are studied by Kew staff and Kew's many scientific visitors and may be loaned or transferred to partners and colleagues in the scientific and conservation communities, if their terms of acquisition allow. Kew acquires genetic resources *in situ* by undertaking field work with partners in countries of origin. It

12 www.kew.org/conservation/endorsements.html (accessed 28 October 2014).
13 www.bgci.org/resources/abs_principles/ (accessed 28 October 2014).
14 www.kew.org/sites/default/files/ABSPolicy.pdf (accessed 28 October 2014).
15 www.kew.org/about-kew/our-work/statutory-obligations/index.htm (accessed 28 October 2014).

also receives materials donated or exchanged with Kew by other botanical institutions and individuals. Kew's size, complexity, history and increasingly limited staff resources present major challenges for ABS implementation. Kew's practical approach has been to conduct an initial audit of its CBD-relevant collections and activities to establish an appropriate policy, then to use a mix of centralized bodies and processes (committee to examine fieldwork proposals, agreements signed at a high level), dispersed departmental resources and procedures (collection managers, departmental databases), and a centre for CBD advice, expertise and training, the CBD Unit (currently with 1.5 full-time staff positions). It has adapted preexisting structures and uses standard terms and documents where possible. Material that might have a greater risk of misuse (DNA, tissue samples, live plants and seeds) and scientifically invaluable type/historic herbarium specimens are prioritized for detailed per-specimen documentation and monitoring.

Kew receives a significant amount of material from *in situ* sources outside the UK (Kew staff typically participate in about 60 collecting trips per year). In this international work, it now (post-CBD) largely focuses on longer-term partnerships with in-country institutions. The partnerships are formalized using written agreements that clearly set out the terms of the collaboration, including terms of use of material at Kew and benefit sharing. Agreements are negotiated mutually with partners; Kew has developed model agreements, but any agreement developed by the country of origin will be used as well. Agreements vary in complexity depending on the nature of the partnership and resources: the Millennium Seed Bank's agreements for live germplasm generally have a government agency as one of the signatories and explicitly include that body's PIC for specified uses (Cheyne 2004), while partnerships concerning less-sensitive dead herbarium material may be covered by simpler Memoranda of Collaboration, in addition to any permits or other PICs required by the countries in question. On Kew's side, the agreements are co-developed by the CBD Unit, checked by Kew's lawyer, and signed by the director or his deputy, so that all agreements are centrally registered and benefit-sharing expectations can be met. Agreements typically identify persons responsible for the project/partnership and may contain a schedule for reporting and/or clauses that will survive a project's end date, so these terms must be passed forward in the event of staff changes. At the time of writing, Kew is a partner to over 60 access and benefit-sharing agreements and memoranda of understanding/collaboration in approximately 40 countries.

All overseas fieldwork by Kew staff and associates must first be approved by Kew's Overseas Fieldwork Committee (OFC). The committee – originally an interdepartmental body to dispense funding for fieldwork – has been transformed into a centralized peer-review and awareness-raising process. It is a core element of Kew's practical ABS implementation. Kew staff will not receive funds or travel insurance without OFC approval, which entails showing that they are working with partners, requesting PIC from appropriate sources and planning MAT including benefit sharing. Kew staff travelling with other institutions' expeditions are expected to ensure that PIC has been obtained for their participation and for any transfer of GRs to Kew. After travel, copies of permits are deposited with the CBD

Unit and obligations are noted. Any terms that are stricter than Kew's standard terms (below) are noted as necessary in departmental database fields and/or labels by collections management staff.

Kew receives much of its material from other *ex situ* sources. Huge specimen flows in the herbarium make it difficult and costly to handle widely varying terms of use, so standard terms are used (e.g. for non-commercialization), and providers are asked to agree to those terms before herbarium material is accepted by Kew (Davis, Middlemiss, Paton, & Tenner 2004). Terms of use are kept with the material, using labels and/or departmental database fields. Certain additional restrictions required by the provider country (e.g. no transfer to third parties) can be noted on labels/in databases, but if material comes with other restrictions that would overly restrict access and research at Kew or require PIC/reporting for all uses, it usually must be declined. Kew also declines material from organizations and individuals if it is not sure that those parties are acting in good faith and have fulfilled the letter and the spirit of the CBD, CITES and national laws.[16]

Kew's various departments utilize different documentation systems to manage and monitor acquisitions, curation, loans, exchanges and research needs. Higher-risk specimens (living plants, seed batches, DNA samples) are individually accessioned and, where applicable, exchanged under their own identifiers, while lower-risk herbarium material is generally accessioned and exchanged on a batch basis. However, major projects to digitize (database/barcode/image) specimens are gradually populating Kew's herbarium database, enabling per-specimen documentation of the movement of type and historic specimens and, crucially, online access to greater numbers of specimens for study by the global scientific community.

Visitors to Kew's collections must abide by the conditions laid down.[17] It is forbidden to remove specimens or part of specimens from the collection without written permission, even to remove them from the herbarium on a temporary basis. Each visitor is assigned a responsible staff member.

Loans and supply of herbarium material and living specimens are all under a strict non-commercialization condition. As in the acquisition of resources, Kew commits itself to only supply genetic resources to third parties if it is satisfied that they are acting in good faith and are committed to the letter and spirit of the CBD.

Herbarium material is loaned under standard "Conditions Governing Loans from the Herbarium", a document that must be signed by the head or collections manager of the recipient institution and the researcher. Loan recipients are permitted to dissect small portions of non-type material but normally may not remove parts for studies in palynology, anatomy or phytochemistry and must not extract DNA. Removal of portions and DNA extractions are only carried out by Kew staff, and such material is transferred to recipients after they have signed a Material Supply Agreement (MSA).

---

16 Policy, above fn 14, 1.2.
17 www.kew.org/collections/herb_conditions.html (accessed 28 October 2014).

Live plants and seeds are transferred using MSAs. Kew's MSAs require, among other conditions, that the material is not used for commercial purposes and that benefits are shared in accordance with the CBD. The recipient is to maintain retrievable records linking the material to the MSA terms and must contact Kew to request prior permission from Kew or, where appropriate, from the provider of the material to Kew for any activities not covered by the MSA. The conditions of the MSA need to be transmitted, in particular the conditions of non-commercial use only, and Kew has to be notified of such transfers. A somewhat simpler MSA is used when duplicate herbarium specimens are donated to other herbaria; it does not require those institutions to notify Kew or keep retrievable records of the MSA, though it still requires prior permission from Kew or the original provider for activities not covered by the MSA. MSA records are kept by each collection manager, so transfers can be tracked.

As to potential commercialization, Kew's policy is not to conduct commercial activity on collections without prior informed consent and mutual agreement of any terms for benefit sharing. A small number of Kew sustainable use projects are conceived with the aim of discovering and developing marketable products; these projects are governed by agreements with countries of origin setting out specific MAT. Kew also offers authentication services, verifying the identity of genetic resources provided for analysis by a range of commodity and user groups but not accessioned into Kew's collections.

To implement its policy across the institution, Kew relies on having CBD-aware researchers in the field and collection manager "gatekeepers" in each department to monitor GR input and output, as well as on staff awareness at all levels, from senior managers to garden visitor guides. The CBD Unit has developed CBD training modules (Williams, Davis, Cheyne & Ali 2012) and runs staff training courses. An intranet staff guide has been developed to help the staff understand the ABS context and to steer them through Kew's varied procedures.

In varied and complex institutions like Kew, ABS is a cross-cutting issue that cannot be answered by an institutional solution and largely standardized procedures alone. The IPEN approach, covering only living material, therefore, would not be a practical option. The Principles framework offers a broad and flexible solution: Kew's ABS policy covers acquisition, curation, loans, and supply of various material such as living resources, herbarium samples, DNA samples and seeds, curated by different departments.

Accordingly, Kew's transfer agreements are adapted to the ABS risks represented in the transferred material (i.e. more stringent conditions for live material than for herbarium specimens) in contrast to IPEN, which differentiates the role of the recipient (within the network, outside of the network, commercial use).

Kew's policy explicitly includes the possibility that some of its scientific research, in particular the sustainable use projects, might lead to a marketable product. However, these are governed by agreements specifically negotiated with the countries of origin. In other cases of commercialization,[18] PIC and benefit

---

18 For Kew's definition of commercialization see Policy, above fn 14, 4.1.

sharing are obligatory if post-CBD material is involved. If pre-CBD material leads to a marketable product, benefits are to be shared "as far as possible". Another safeguard against illegitimate appropriation is the clearly declared policy to only acquire GR from sources that are reliable and trustworthy as regards their commitment to ABS principles "in letter and spirit". The same is true for recipients of Kew's resources (ABS policy, 1.2 and 2.4).

Kew's (unstated) goal in developing its ABS policy, procedures and tools has been to ensure that it can build and keep partners' and governments' trust and continue to be a global leader in plant science and conservation. Though its procedures and terms are sometimes perceived as being cumbersome and costly, its early commitment to ABS action and its leadership in the development of best practices and capacity building have gained global recognition. Kew has thus been able to develop valuable conservation partnerships in many countries where it is otherwise increasingly difficult to work, to keep pace with the development of the NP, and to meet the requirements for registered collections set out in the new EU regulation on compliance.

In the sense of the "building blocks" mentioned at the beginning of this section, three steps stand out for their contribution to ABS progress and problem solving at Kew: (1) doing a "CBD audit" – establishing precisely what Kew holds and does – to build a realistic policy on the Principles framework; (2) raising staff awareness across the institution, via involvement and training; and, importantly, (3) establishing a centre for ABS knowledge and advice, a CBD Unit, working with a cross-departmental group of scientists and horticulturalists.

Comparison and assessment: answers to the dilemma

One of the main points in the access–control dilemma is the fear of the providers to forego the sharing of (monetary) benefits resulting from R&D of their resources. The two examples of botanical gardens strongly focus on building trust *vis-à-vis* the providers through instruments and/or mechanisms promoting transparency and permitting (some) control, including control of a transition into the commercial field.

The standards established to this end aim at resolving the access–control dilemma by defining obligations of users (and providers) within the system and in the case of the resources leaving the system/institutions. They contain provisions regarding the utilization of the resources (non-commercialization) and the sharing of non-monetary benefits; they define responsibilities of participating entities; and they include mechanisms aimed at covering (or preventing) a possible change of intent.

They take up the above-identified "critical" points: proving legal access to the material to be integrated in the collection/system; transfer of data between users within the system; defining the utilization within the system (as a rule encompassing research and education and excluding commercialization); and measures in case of resources leaving the system (non-commercialization, commercialization with PIC, commercialization and benefit sharing). They establish responsibilities of the participating institutions/stakeholders to assure that these conditions are met. For instance IPEN's Code of Conduct gives the garden hosting the resources the responsibility to assure the PIC of the providers when a resource is accessed for commercial R&D. Kew disposes of institutional and procedural means to this end (CBD Unit; Overseas Fieldwork Committee). These standards are transferred to other users through MTAs.

This leads to the first weak point of the systems: the conditions regarding the utilization of the resources, including the conditions regarding a possible commercial use, are laid down in and transferred to other users via the MTAs. Material Transfer Agreements are bilateral contracts between the providing collection and the receiving collection/user.

In bilateral contracts, control of compliance with the set conditions is *a priori* based on this contractual relationship only and therefore the responsibility of the providing collection.

To control the fulfilment of these contracts – that is the MTAs – in particular as regards non-commercialization, outreaches the capacity of the collections. (This is comparable to the position of the providers in the country of origin in regard to their capacity to track the use of GR that is based on the – bilateral – MAT.)

Some awareness of the problem surfaces and some measures are made transparent in both policies (for instance transfer to trustworthy partners only, network-internal control in IPEN). But these measures are hardly sufficient. According to Godt (2013, 252), members therefore would, in addition, depend on other means to secure compliance, for instance by "blaming and shaming" in cases of biopiracy.

The second point that needs to be discussed is the so-called "change of intent" – i.e. the transition from basic research to R&D with a commercial outlook. This change of intent has been demonized (by the providers of the resources) to an extent that the collections refrain from taking up this option, fearing the mistrust of the providers. Yet the generation and sharing of monetary benefits is at the core of the ABS system: its rationale is to provide a means to share the costs as well as the benefits of biodiversity conservation between developed and developing countries and therefore it is in the interest of the providers (Biber-Klemm 2014).

Both examples illustrate the importance for the collections of the implementation of compliance measures by the State. The EU and Switzerland have both introduced a general obligation of due diligence. Its implementation (including the existence of PIC and MAT) is – formally – controlled at the moment of the market admission of the product resulting from the utilization of the resource. Substantive control is only effectuated in cases of alleged potential breach of PIC and MAT. It will have to be assessed in practice to what extent this system is apt to build the trust of the providers in a way that is essential for the good functioning of the collections in their contribution to essential biodiversity science.[19] It is evident that, in this context, the political disagreement on the temporal scope of

---

19 For a critical assessment see Kamau and Winter (2013) and Biber-Klemm et al. (2014).

the NP/the definition of "access" creates insecurity and mistrust that first and foremost affect the collections. It is to be hoped that within the framework of the NP and its implementation solutions to these problems can be developed (Biber-Klemm et al. 2014).

In this context, the question asked above ought to be assessed on the basis of to what extent the EU system of certification of collections as "Union trusted collections" also contributes to building trust with the providers and safeguarding their interests.[20] As mentioned earlier, the mechanism is primarily meant to help the users – i.e. natural or legal persons who utilize genetic resources (Art. 3 (4)) – to conduct research and development in the chain of custody to comply with their obligations (recital 28). If users undertake access through a registered collection, they are considered to have exercised due diligence as far as *seeking* information is concerned. This results in a reversal of the burden of proof (in favour of the user but on the shoulder of the collections) regarding the fulfilment of the due diligence obligation.

The regulation on registration of collections (or parts of collections) establishes criteria to be fulfilled. The criteria are selected in order to ensure that collections apply measures to assure that samples are provided to third persons with documentation providing evidence of legal access, and to ensure the establishment of MAT (recital (28)). They consist of *standardized procedures* for exchanging samples and related information between collections or in supplying them to third persons; to supply the resources to third persons only with *documentation of legitimate access*; to *keep records* of all samples supplied to third persons; where possible establish unique identifiers for samples supplied; and use appropriate *tracking and monitoring tools* for exchanging samples between collections (Article 5).

These criteria can be read as qualification of the basic due diligence obligations that are to be applied by all collections as users of the resources (the general obligation consisting of "seeking, keeping and transferring to the subsequent user" either an internationally recognized certificate of compliance or a defined set of information[21]). The qualification primarily consists in the establishment of systems and instruments to allow the tracking and monitoring of the movements of the samples "in order to ascertain the legitimacy of the utilized resources and the sharing of benefits". The requirement of documentation of legitimate access can be read as a service to the users (including collections) that otherwise would have to assure it themselves (Article 4.5).

This bundle of measures corresponds, in fact to a large extent, to the trust-building measures of the two systems described above and so – even if primarily favouring the user accessing resources through collections – may also contribute to the transparency of the movement of the resources at least within the network of collections. However, it is not clear to what extent the information generated

---

20 Regulation (EU) No 511/2014, above fn 3, Article 5.
21 Date and place of access; description of the resources, the source from which the resources were directly obtained *as well as subsequent users* . . .; the presence or absence of rights and obligations; access permits and MATs (Regulation (EU) No 511/2014, above fn 3, Article 4.3(b)).

by monitoring the flow of resources through the R&D chain would be accessible for the providers. In any case, the substantive control of the correspondence of the utilization of the resources within the original PIC and MAT will further be based on the bilateral provider–user relation as evoked above, secured by a chain of subsequent MTAs (see also Kamau & Winter 2013; Biber-Klemm 2014).

However, at present the system is not yet operational. From the viewpoint of research, the question as to possible negative repercussions on collections that are not in a situation to answer to the set criteria and to build up the required systems needs to be followed. The risk remains that for such collections participation in the access and exchange network could become more difficult.

References

Biber-Klemm, S (2008) "Access to genetic resources and the fair and equitable sharing of the benefits resulting from their use – the challenges of a new concept", *Elni Review* 1, pp. 12–18.

Biber-Klemm, S (2014) "Gedanken zu Sorgfaltspflicht und Vorteilsausgleich gemäss Schweizer Gesetzgebung zur Umsetzung des Nagoya Protokolls" [French: "Réflexions sur le devoir de diligence et le partage des avantages selon la législation de mise en oeuvre du Protocole de Nagoya"] in: Durabilitas, S (ed.) "Durabilitas" 2014: *Die biotechnische Nutzung genetischer Ressourcen und ihre Regulierung. Ein integrierender Ansatz* [French: *L'utilisation des ressources génétiques en biotechnologie et son cadre réglementaire. Pour une approche integrative*], pp. 58–62, www.sanudurabilitas.ch/publikationen.

Biber-Klemm, S, Davis, K, Gautier, L, Martinez, SI (2014) "Governance options for ex-situ collections in academic research" in: Oberthür, S, Rosendal, KG (eds) *Global governance of genetic resources access and benefit sharing after the Nagoya Protocol*, New York and London: Routledge, pp. 214–230.

Biber-Klemm, S, Martinez, SI, Jacob, A (2010) Access to genetic resources and sharing of benefits – ABS program 2003–2010, Swiss Academy of Sciences, Bern, Switzerland, Available online at http://abs.scnat.ch/downloads/documents/ABS_Report2003–2010_SCNAT_web.pdf (accessed 27 October 2014).

Biber-Klemm, S, Nemogá Soto, G, Payet-Lebourges, K, da Silva, M, Rodriguez, L, Prieur-Richard, A-H, . . . Warner Pineda, J (2014) *Access and Benefit sharing in Latin America and the Caribbean – A science-policy dialogue for academic research*, Paris: Diversitas-International, www.diversitas-international.org/resources/outreach/abs-docs/ABS-Brochure_ENG.pdf (accessed 27 October 2014).

Cabrera Medaglia, J (2004) "Bioprospecting partnerships in practice: A decade of experiences at INBio in Costa Rica", *IP Strategy Today* 11, pp. 28–40. Available online at www.biopirateria.org/otrosdocs/04-b-%20IP%20Strategy.pdf (accessed 27 October 2014).

Cheyne, P (2004) "Access and benefit-sharing agreements: Bridging the gap between scientific partnerships and the Convention on Biological Diversity" in: Smith, RD, Dickie, JB, Linington, SH, Pritchard, HW, Probert, RJ (eds) *Seed conservation: Turning science into practice*, United Kingdom: Royal Botanic Gardens, Kew.

Davis, K, Middlemiss, P, Paton, A, Tenner, C (2004) "The Royal Botanic Gardens, Kew: Herbarium and Millennium Seed Bank", Case study contribution to Tobin, B, Cunningham, D, Watanbe, K (eds) *The feasibility, practicality and cost of a certificate of origin system for genetic resources: Preliminary results of comparative analysis of tracking material in biological resource centres and of for a certification scheme*. Report prepared as background information for WG-ABS-3 (UNEP/CBD/WG-ABS/3/INF/5), UNU-IAS, www.cbd.int/doc/meetings/abs/abswg-03/information/abswg-03-inf-05-en.pdf (accessed 27 October 2014).

European Science Foundation (ed.) (2000) Good scientific practice in research and scholarship, European Science Foundation Policy Briefing, Strasbourg, France, www.esf.org/fileadmin/Public_documents/Publications/ESPB10.pdf (accessed 27 October 2014).

Godt, C (2013) "Networks of ex situ collections of genetic resources" in: Kamau, EC, Winter, G (eds) *Common pools of genetic resources. Equity and innovation in international biodiversity law*, New York and London: Routledge, pp. 246–266.

Gröger, A (2007) "Botanic Gardens and the International Plant Exchange Network (IPEN) – A brief statement" in: Feit, U, Wolff, F (eds) *European regional meeting on an international recognized certificate of origin/source/legal provenance*, Bonn: BfN, pp. 121–123.

Kamau, EC (2014) "Valorisation of genetic resources, benefit sharing and conservation of biological diversity: What role for the ABS regime?" in: Dilling, O, Markus, T (eds) *Ex Rerum Natura Ius? – Sachzwang und Problemwahrnehmung im Umweltrecht*, Baden-Baden: Nomos, pp. 143–173.

Kamau, EC, Winter, G (2013) "An introduction to the international ABS regime and a comment on its transposition by the EU", *Law, Environment and Development Journal* 9(2), pp. 108–126.

Kamau, EC, Winter, G (eds) (2009) *Genetic resources, traditional knowledge and the law: Solutions for access and benefit sharing*, London: Earthscan.

Kamau, EC, Winter, G (eds) (2013) *Common pools of genetic resources. Equity and innovation in international biodiversity law*, New York and London: Routledge.

Kiehn, M (2014) (in press) The International Plant Exchange Network (IPEN) – a Botanical Gardens' strategy to comply with the Access and Benefit Sharing regulations of the Convention on Biodiversity. Proceedings of the 13th IABG Conference, Guangzhou, China, November 13–15, 2012.

Kiehn, M (2015) "The International Plant Exchange Network and the Nagoya Protocol of the Convention on Biodiversity" in: Krigas, N et al. (eds) European botanic gardens in a changing world: insights into Eurogard VI, Thessaloniki: Balkan Botanic Garden of Kroussia (Hellenic Agriculture Organization-Demeter), pp. 377–384.

Latorre García, F, Williams, C, ten Kate, K, Cheyne, Ph (2001) Results of the pilot project for botanic gardens: Principles on access to genetic resources and benefit sharing, common policy guidelines to assist with their implementation and explanatory material, The board of trustees, Royal Botanic Gardens, Kew, United Kingdom, www.bgci.org/files/ABS/Principles_on_ABS.pdf (accessed 25 October 2014).

Martinez, SI, Biber-Klemm, S (2010) "Scientists – Take action for access to biodiversity", *Current Opinion in Environmental Sustainability* 2, pp. 27–33.

Meienberg, F, von Weizsäcker, C (2010) "Will we share the biggest part of the benefits?", Third World Resurgence No. 242/243 (October–November), pp. 16–25, www.twnside.org.sg/title2/resurgence/2010/242-243/cover02.htm (accessed 27 October 2014).

OECD (2001) Biological Resource Centres: Underpinning the Future of Life Sciences and Biotechnology Science and Technology series, Organization for Economic Cooperation and Development, Paris.

Richerzhagen, C, Holm-Müller, K (2005) "The effectiveness of access and benefit sharing in Costa Rica: Implications for national and international regimes", *Ecological Economics* 53, pp. 445–460.

Salathé, M (ed.) (2008) *Integrity in scientific research – Principles and procedures*, Bern: Swiss Academies of Arts and Sciences.

Thomson, KS (2003) *Treasures on earth: Museums, collections, and paradoxes*, London: Faber and Faber.

Williams, C, Davis, K, Cheyne, P, Ali, N (2012) "The CBD for botanists: A guide to the Convention on Biological Diversity for people working with botanical collections", Version 4 on Biodiversity Conventions for Botanists (CD-ROM), Royal Botanic Gardens, Kew, United Kingdom. Version 2 available online at www.kew.org/data/cbdbotanists.html (accessed 27 October 2014).

15 *Ex situ* collections of microbes and how they adjust to ABS conditions

Dagmar Fritze and André Oumard

Introduction

Microbiological resources and their derivatives are the essential raw material for the advancement of human health, food security, biotechnology, and research and development in all life sciences. Besides being used in basic research and e.g. as models for genetic and metabolic studies, microorganisms have an endless array of capabilities ranging from the degradation of compounds to the synthesis of secondary metabolites. Applications for countless processes and experiments can be listed (see Figure 15.1). Microorganisms can provide basic material for the development of compounds for products in health care and for bioremediation, biocontrol, food, drink, toiletries and numerous other areas.

Besides these applied aspects from the utilitarian point of view, the immense role that microorganisms play in the environment cannot be valued highly enough. Nutrient cycles in nature would not function without microbes at the basis of the transformation chain and, ultimately, the fertility of soil, the climate and our life depend on them.

To be able to study microorganisms in depth, they need to be isolated from their natural habitat and, to subsequently make these pure strains accessible for future studies, they are typically deposited and conserved in culture collections. Here, they form the living archival basis for our knowledge on microbial diversity. The complexity of legitimate collection, distribution and use of living biological material demands the coordination and sharing of activities.

Biological Resource Centres (BRCs) that preserve microbial resources *ex situ* and distribute these for science, industrial development and education are key contributors to the Convention of Biological Diversity's (CBD) main objectives of conservation of global biological diversity and its sustainable use (Smith, Fritze, Thompson, & Stackebrandt 2013). In that respect, BRCs facilitate the identification of and access to resources, as well as to the associated information in specific public databases.

These activities are accompanied by the strong impact of regulations, legislation and policies. This is especially true for the field of Access and Benefit Sharing (ABS) and particularly in combination with Intellectual Property Right (IPR) rules. The design of standardized conditions for the deposit/acquisition of living

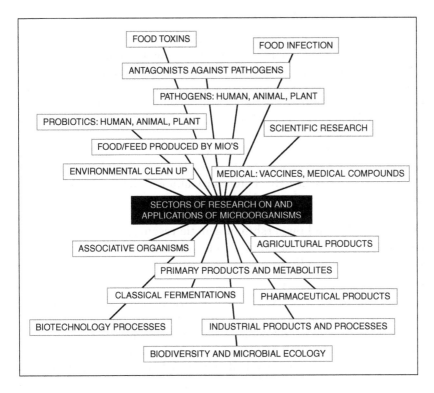

Figure 15.1 Sectors of research on and application for microorganisms

Source: www.mirri.org

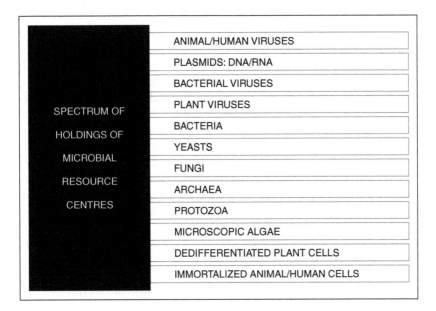

Figure 15.2 Spectrum of holdings of microbial resource centres

Source: www.mirri.org

microbiological material, as well as for its handling and supply, will be the basis of a confidence-building system to facilitate access and exchange.

Activities of microbial collections in this area go towards finding common approaches for BRCs. These build in particular upon general expertise gained from the valuable OECD initiative on BRCs which resulted in best practice guidelines for BRCs (OECD 2007). They also build upon specific expertise gained in past projects, such as MOSAICC, which provided guidance on procedures and documents for issues like Prior Informed Consent (PIC) and Material Transfer Agreement (MTA), on approaches like the Microbial Research Commons, and on practical approaches like the European Culture Collections' Organisation (ECCO) Core MTA for the supply of cultures.

Sovereign rights and ownership of genetic resources from the point of view of microbiology and microbial service culture collections

Whereas Article 15.1 CBD grants sovereign rights to states over their natural resources, the decision of ownership of genetic resources remains subject to national law. In the microbiological area and in particular regarding *ex situ* service collections of microbiological material, this has given rise to varied discussions. Once a sample has been taken from nature (from any environment) and subsequently a microbial culture isolated therefrom, who of the long chain of value-adding stakeholders might lay claim to it in one way or another: Is it the isolator; the depositor; any other involved researcher having studied it; the collection(s) authenticating, preserving and maintaining it and adding data to it; or the user(s) having received it and performed additional studies on it?

A sample may be a piece of soil or dung, a spoonful of sand, a few millilitres of lake water or the like. Such a sample may contain millions of microbial cells of possibly thousands of species – most of which we still do not know. Typically, only a few of these will be isolated from the sample matrix depending on the methods applied and the intent of the researcher and will be propagated as pure cultures.

Subcultures of a given organism may thus be simultaneously in many hands and places. In addition to the natural site where an organism had been isolated and where this organism persists and is not depleted by the sampling, it may exist at the same time in many collections and research laboratories in multiple countries worldwide. The issue of "multiple ownership" of microbial cultures has been raised. However, it is the view of most collections that, once a culture has been isolated from nature, no one person or entity can "own" a microbial culture. Rather, a microbial culture obtained by recipients can be used by them subject to certain restrictions while they have to assume full responsibility when working with this material. Most collections see themselves as custodians with a mandate to receive the microbial resource, grow, authenticate, maintain and preserve it for distribution and add data through research.

The Nagoya Protocol from the point of view of microbiology and microbial service culture collections

The Nagoya Protocol on Access to Genetic Resources and the Fair and Equitable Sharing of Benefits Arising from their Utilization to the Convention on Biological Diversity is intended as an international regime on access to genetic resources and benefit sharing with the aim of adopting an instrument/instruments to effectively implement the provisions of the benefit-sharing articles of the Convention on Biological Diversity (see Kamau, Ch. 2 in this volume). From the point of view of microbiology and microbial collections, the following articles of the NP are among the most relevant:

- Article 2 which makes it clear that *any* activity carried out with the respective biological material is covered by these regulations.
- Article 8 (a) which requires each country, when developing and implementing its ABS legislation or regulatory requirement, to create conditions *to promote and encourage research* which contributes to the conservation and sustainable use of biological diversity.
- Article 11 which refers to the situation where the *same genetic resources* are found *in situ within the territory of more than one Party*. In this regard the following question is in particular relevant: What would constitute "same" material in microbiology? Is it the same species, or the same strain? The more advanced the identification methodologies are in microbiology, the more variations can be seen within microbial species, between strains and even between subcultures of a given strain. What would be an appropriate cut-off point for the decision to be "the same"?
- Article 16 which recognizes the *development, update and use of voluntary codes of conduct, guidelines* and *best practices* and/or standards in relation to access and benefit sharing. The microbial service collections, organized in the WFCC (World Federation for Culture Collections) and in Europe in the ECCO, have a long tradition of discussing and agreeing on voluntary harmonized rules, procedures and processes. While some of these have been developed in direct response to the CBD, most of the more general ones are usually from pre-CBD times but would also serve the aims of the CBD and its NP.
- The Annex which lists the types of monetary and non-monetary benefits that may arise out of the utilization of genetic resources and which may be shared. From the length of the two lists (the list for non-monetary benefits is twice as long as the one for monetary benefits) it can be concluded that participation in research, as well as institutional and human capacity building is given high priority. This is in particular relevant for microbiology where the greater part of work in research and development needs to serve basic science on which then – only in a later step – commercial exploitation could be based, which would eventually lead to potential monetary benefit.

In principle, the NP seeks to cover two main requirements: First, signatory countries shall provide a clear national framework of regulations so that legal certainty/predictability of legal decisions is provided to all who intend to access biodiversity in that country. Second, signatory countries shall lay down regulations to the fact that they recognize the legal regulations in other signatory countries set up in connection with the NP. The NP does not require countries to implement restrictions for regulating access to their genetic resources, and it is up to them to decide whether they require or waive PIC.

The need to support and facilitate international/ global cooperation

The innovative development of the biotechnology industry and its application to the agriculture, health, chemical or energy industries depends upon society's ability to harness the potential of biodiversity and what it has to offer: improving health, boosting productivity of agricultural and industrial processes, and enhancing environmental sustainability.

The EU initiative for a knowledge-based bioeconomy considers the transformation of knowledge from the life sciences into new, sustainable, ecologically efficient and competitive products as an enormous challenge. The OECD Report, *The Bioeconomy to 2030: Designing a policy agenda* (OECD 2009), emphasizes that the biological sciences are adding significant value to a multitude of products and services (see Figure 15.3). The expectation is that by 2030 the products of white

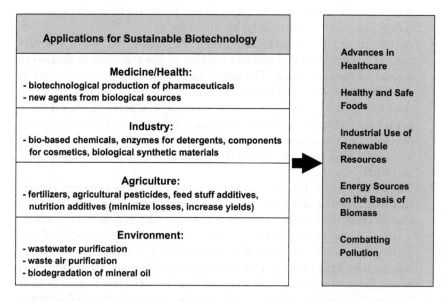

Figure 15.3 Applications of biological systems

Source: Adapted from "Final Report on the GBRCN Demonstration Project" (ISBN 978-3-00-038121-8)

biotechnology and bioenergy will constitute around a third of the industrial production.

Against this background, a growing scientific and economic demand is being witnessed for increased cooperative research and joint development that is based on living biological material. The necessary consequence following this demand is the need for increasing global exchange of and access to living biological material. However, exchange and application of living biological material underlies a series of regulations therefore, to enable the necessary access, especially on a global scale, coordinated or harmonized processes or in certain cases even standardized processes and generally simplified procedures would be highly supportive.

Such processes would be needed in particular in the areas of

- **biosafety** (import, export, transport; who is entitled to work with which material)
- **biosecurity** (regulated access to certain material and data)
- **legitimacy** (meeting e.g. the requirements of CBD)
- **quality** of material and data (comparability under quality management aspects)
- **stability, purity, authenticity, performance** of the material (comparability under scientific and systematic aspects)

In turn, such coordinated processes would favourably enhance the accessibility of material and data and boost innovations and development.

Unfortunately, a counterproductive development seems to be taking place regarding national implementation of the NP. In some instances the approaches taken seem to attempt to ensure "watertight" and "all-inclusive" national regulations, which researchers consider as strangling rather than supporting their research efforts. So far, ABS-relevant legislation seems to be unclear in many countries or does not yet exist. Where it is being developed, competencies and procedures are often not clear or overwhelmingly complicated (see for example Kamau 2009). Reportedly, it is often difficult for applicants to find out which authority to address for which question and for which permit, or which permit would be needed for which action and in which sequence. Even among themselves, authorities sometimes seem to be uncertain about who is responsible for certain matters, which results in extremely strenuous situations bearing high administrative burdens. Additionally, this situation seems to be especially difficult for microbiological researchers, as microbial resources and the related types of work seem not to easily fit into the systems that are being developed, which usually have plants and animals as their focus.

A danger that emerges through the establishment of very high hurdles is the fragmentation of research and restraint or even discontinuation of cooperation because researchers cannot afford to "waste their time" with unnecessary bureaucratic paperwork. Researchers in microbiology have indeed expressed their views that they would rather go sampling and isolating new organisms from their own local environments and study them alone than to have to face months of paperwork distracting them from research. A scientifically and socially unacceptable consequence could be the duplication or multiplication of the same research being done in parallel in several places in the world by scientists not knowing of each other's work. Individual countries' development would be hampered, respectively, their researchers left alone and behind from scientific progress. Research money would be wasted and knowledge lost. Similarly, it is to be expected that the deposit of genetic resources in service collections for open access would cease and, in consequence, follow-up research and biotechnological developments and applications would be severely impaired.

Some examples for related recent regulative, legally binding and voluntary approaches

Recently, one of the first countries to set up a comprehensive national ABS framework, Brazil, revised its legislation and put in place facilitated regulations for scientific research (information presented by representatives of the Brazilian Ministry of Environment at an EU meeting on ABS issues with Brazilian government representatives, Brussels 5/3/2012). Brazil's own researchers had been too heavily and negatively impacted by the original regulative framework, so that a revision was felt necessary. It has been reported that one main change concerns the lengthy originally up-front administrative work that has now been shifted as much and as far as possible towards the end of the whole process, to a point where a potential benefit might become visible (see also Pittaluga Niederauer and da Silva, Ch. 5 in this volume).

Another recent and encouraging first step was taken by the Kenyan government after several years of struggle towards workable solutions for microbiology. What happened? A Kenyan PhD student, supported by a grant from the German Academic Exchange Service (DAAD), had isolated from certain Kenyan environments microorganisms which he proved to be hitherto unknown species and wanted to publish these results. As outlined further down in this chapter, the internationally agreed regime for the validation of a new microbial species requires the deposit of cultures of the type strain for that species in two public service collections in two different countries. However, Kenyan authorities obviously had great difficulties with that requirement and had been very reluctant to approve such deposits.

The scientific work itself, the isolating from the environment and the studying of the strains in the laboratories of the DSMZ had been covered by a specific Memorandum of Agreement between the institutions involved, JKUAT and DSMZ, and the Kenyan competent authority, the Kenyan Wildlife Service (KWS). This agreement did not yet include the issue of eventual deposit of the strains in a collection outside Kenyan territory; this was to be dealt with separately. The problem arising out of this delay for the researcher was that he could not fulfil the requirement of deposit and could not publish his research. But without publications a researcher cannot enter into scientific dialogue with the research community and cannot hope for a career.

Finally (the researcher accomplished his PhD a few years ago), the approval was issued by the KWS that the Kenyan researcher had obtained PIC and was granted authorization to deposit the said type strains in the open collection of the DSMZ. The approval requests that each of the strains be assigned a certain KWS designation in addition to the strain designation assigned by the researcher and the designation assigned by the collection, so that the country of origin can have their own system of documentation. This is a fair request which can be easily granted. The deposits are now being processed at DSMZ and, finally, the door is open for publishing the descriptions of the new species. This encouraging approval certainly needs to be seen also against the background of the spirit of the ECCO-MTA for the supply of cultures (see further down) which has been adopted by DSMZ, as well as against DSMZ's long-standing high standards of documentation and handling procedures in laboratory, administration and information technology and its acknowledged reputation. It could be expected and is to be hoped that on the basis of this process and experience, future collaborations around the topics of research, especially in systematics and taxonomy, including the deposit of microbial cultures, would be eased and accelerated, and, for all sides involved, the administrative burdens considerably lowered.

The ECCO Core Material Transfer Agreement for the Supply of Cultures to the User had been agreed among ECCO collections acknowledging that a level of uniformity of actions of collections with regard to the various regulative requirements was desirable. The topics to be covered in such a document were agreed to be points of core relevance to which all collections need to develop a position. This document was also meant to demonstrate that all important issues with regard to the availability and use of the biological material would be handled in the same way by the many different collections in Europe, and that necessary individual variations in handling by an individual culture collection would concern only minor aspects.

The following main points are covered in 11 sentences in the MTA:

Safety and security: This has been formulated with regards to the recipients of samples: their entitlement to receive samples, their being informed on potential risks associated with samples, and their responsibilities when handling the received samples.

Traceability of samples of biological material: This is deemed central under consideration of the requirements of the CBD and is also important for safeguarding individual collections.

Quality of microbiological material: This has been considered with respect to protection of the scientific user community and to make the collections responsible, but to confine this responsibility to certain limits.

Fair and equitable benefit sharing: Several items have been formulated with regard to the rights of the country of origin according to the CBD, the rights of other institutions entitled to be involved and to exempt research from restrictions. Of relevance here in particular is the requirement not to pass on the biological material to third parties and, in case of commercial intent, that the country of origin should be contacted.

Intellectual property rights: The main point here is to inform recipients that they have no rights to the received material other than working with it.

In summary, this Core MTA for the supply of microbial cultures to third parties was formulated to form the minimum common denominator for service culture collections, taking into account the responsibilities imposed by legislation, while not imposing restrictions on research and facilitating exchange between the collections.

In the EU, work is being done to develop and implement a Union-wide ABS framework. Emphasis is obviously being laid on the side of implementing regulations to prevent the illegal acquiring of genetic resources by EU residents. It is intended to leave the decision on implementing access restrictions or not to the resources that belong to them to the discretion of the individual Member States. As an example, Germany is laying down in its national legislation that it will not pose restrictions on the access to its genetic resources. Regarding *ex situ* collections on EU territory, it has been suggested to define and designate "Union Trusted Collections" which would constitute an important link in the chain of biological resources' movements. Best practices developed should play an important role.

The EU Commission has recently published the final version of the EU Regulation: Regulation No. 511/2014 of the European Parliament and of the Council of 16 April 2014 on compliance measures for users from the Nagoya Protocol on Access to Genetic Resources and the Fair and Equitable Sharing of Benefits Arising from their Utilization in the Union. It entered into force on 9 June 2014, and is applicable from the date on which the Nagoya Protocol entered into force for the European Union, namely on 12 October 2014. Some Articles, however (Art. 4: Obligations of users; Art. 7: Monitoring user compliance; and Art. 9: Checks on user compliance), where details need to be laid down and implemented, will apply one year after the date of entry into force of the Nagoya Protocol for the Union, hence on 12 October 2015.

This regulation applies directly in all EU member states without need for transposing measures. It encourages but does not yet cover agreements with non-EU countries or regions to facilitate mutual access to respective resources. The proposal strongly follows the "due diligence" and "user compliance" principles, which shift most of the responsibility towards the end of the chain of activities.

Article 4 *Obligations of users* outlines that all users would need to seek, keep and transfer to subsequent users certain information relevant for access and benefit sharing. While most points of this article seem to be realistic and sensible, it is the seemingly high requirement in bureaucratic paperwork described, e.g. in sentences 3 and 5, that worries the scientific community. Depending on what is envisioned, this might exceed the legal and administrative potential and rights of an individual scientist or their institution. It urgently needs to be clarified what exactly is expected to be done by the individual scientist. The delayed application of Art. 4, as indicated above, will hopefully provide the time to resolve outstanding questions.

In Article 7 the foreseen monitoring measures for user compliance are described, differentiating between scientific and the industrial users. Respective recipients of public research funding are expected to declare that they will exercise due diligence in accordance with Article 4. For the case of commercialization, it is outlined that users should declare that they exercised due diligence in accord with Article 4 either on the occasion of request of market approval or at the time of commercialization of a product.

The foreseen system of "Register of Collections" (Article 5) is expected to substantially lower the risk that illegally acquired genetic resources are used in the Union. Such registered collections would apply measures to only supply samples of genetic resources to third parties with documentation providing evidence of legal acquisition and the establishment of mutually agreed terms, where required. In principle, the system of ABS-related Union Trusted Collections would perfectly match the spirit of the OECD Best Practice Guidelines (BPG) and fill an important gap therein. However, like with Article 4, it urgently needs to be clarified what exactly would be expected from collections to implement as compliance measures. While it should be expected that most requirements of Article 5 can be easily met by microbial collections that have implemented the ECCO Core MTA and are implementing the BPG resulting from the OECD BRC initiative, sentence 3 (b) is alarming to the collections. Depending on the interpretation of the wording, the requirements could substantially exceed the legal and administrative abilities and rights of the collections. A forum for discussions on this EU regulation from the microbiological side will be provided by the EU-funded project Microbial Resource Research Infrastructure (MIRRI), which is presented further below.

Concerning third countries setting up regulations for access to their genetic resources that allow monitoring and tracking, it could be suggested that those countries chose to allow deposit of their microbial resources to collections that are e.g.

- registered with WFCC/WDCM (World Data Centre for Microorganisms)
- are implementing the OECD BPG
- have implemented the ECCO MTA (or a similar declaration for non-EU collections) and
- are registered as Register of Collections (or a similar system in non-EU regions).

Respective statements could be included in their regulations. The combination of these (binding regulation, voluntary codes of conduct/best practices and registries) would not only guarantee a transparent and trustworthy system for exchange of genetic resources, but could also be a perfect basis for developing umbrella solutions for future scientific cooperation, which would help to avoid most of the time-consuming and burdensome individual bilateral agreements.

Why does microbiology need a different/facilitated approach?

Many articles of the NP refer to providers and users of genetic resources. While it is understood that any country can be both, this is in particular true with respect to microbial resources, which do not allow a clear-cut differentiation of providers and users of microbial genetic resources. While it is stated for zoology and botany that their "hotspots" lie in the southern developing countries, the breadth of existing biodiversity may be more balanced in microbiology. For example it could be expected that in the northern countries, despite their less broad zoological and botanical diversity (and related microflora), a specialized diversity of microorganisms can be found, adapted to the industrial activities and their pollutants. Additionally, being the much younger discipline and by nature of its objects of study, microbiology has had, from the beginning, a strong emphasis on international cooperation. The majority of microbial resources in EU-located collections originate from the northern hemisphere. As an example, about 60 per cent of the holdings of the DSMZ come from Europe and North America, about 27 per cent from Asia and about 6 per cent from Africa. The holdings of microbial collections show where in the world the collections had cooperation. These holdings depict in particular the general development of the discipline of microbiology in the world.

Regarding the term "user", microbial collections hold that – in their core activities as collections – they do not operate as "users". They are rather brokers between providers (who could, as said before, be all countries or individual researchers as isolators, descriptors and depositors of microbial diversity) and users (who could again be all countries or individual researchers in research and development as recipients of microbial diversity). It would be the responsibility of collections to clearly differentiate between these core activities as collection on one hand and research activities of staff members, including *in situ* sampling, on the other hand. The latter activities would of course fall under the "user" provisions and under the regulation of the country where the sampling shall take place.

In contrast to botany and zoology, it is estimated that only less than 1 per cent or even 0.1 per cent of all microbial diversity is known today. Thus most of the research done in microbiology must serve basic science: increasing knowledge, inventorying, understanding complex ecosystems, revealing metabolic and katabolic abilities, etc. Any ecosystem still harbours a plethora of unknown microorganisms.

Microorganisms are not geographically confined. Similar habitats in different places in the world may harbour the same microorganisms. There have been studies showing that the same organism could be isolated from samples taken from Denmark, England and Germany. Another study identified the same organisms in samples taken from such distant sites as the Antarctic, the Arctic, and the West African deep sea trench. Microorganisms are easily transported across boundaries and continents by wind, water, dust and animals. Humans carry them on their skin, shoes and clothes. Photographs taken from satellites e.g. reveal the large dust clouds that cross continents and oceans because of storms. Myriads of microorganisms are carried along by those dust particles (see Figure 15.4). Hence microbial diversity can only be exploited for the benefit of mankind through cooperative international/global research efforts.

In this context, the issue of commercial versus non-commercial use of microbiological material needs further definition. Where does non-commercial end and commercial start? In principle, any result out of basic microbiological research and any data can one day be picked up and proven useful for commercial use. To this

Figure 15.4 Dust clouds crossing the Atlantic Ocean

Source: Photographs taken from www.spiegel.de/wissenschaft/natur; origin NASA. See on each picture on the left the coastline of South America, on the right side the West African coastline and the dust clouds crossing the Atlantic Ocean (Staub = dust)

end, a recent suggestion could be helpful, in that the fact of publication or non-publication of research results could be used as a criterion for differentiation (see von Kries and Winter, Ch. 3 in this volume).

Why do researchers deposit their strains with a Microbial Service Culture Collection? Four main reasons to deposit

The deposit of type strains

Following the concept of Valid Description of Species and Validation of Names as described in the International Code of Nomenclature of Bacteria (Lapage et al.1992), which lays down rules for the description of a bacterial species, it is required to designate and deposit the type strain of the species and to publish the new name in the International Journal of Systematic and Evolutionary Microbiology (IJSEM), previously International Journal of Systematic Bacteriology (IJSB), or in its Validation Lists.

Most important in this context is Rule 30 which demands: ". . . a viable culture of the type strain of a given species *must be deposited with two public service culture collections*, located in two different countries, from which subcultures would be readily available."

Every year more than 700 new species are described in bacteriology and their type strains deposited.

The deposit of strains for patent purposes according to the Budapest Treaty (WIPO 1989)

To be able to rework especially biotechnological inventions which involve living biological material, it might be *required by patent law to deposit* this biological material in a recognized International Depositary Authority (IDA), so that this material becomes available to authorized third parties without undue restrictions. Most of the larger microbial service collections have acquired the status of IDA vis-à-vis the World Intellectual Property Organization (WIPO). The Budapest Treaty regulates in detail the obligations and rights of patent offices, patent holders, depositaries and third parties with respect to the microbiological material and related data (Fritze & Weihs 2001).

Scientifically and biotechnologically/biomedically interesting microorganisms

For researchers who study and publish scientifically interesting features of microorganisms, e.g. metabolic pathways, life in extreme environments, microecosystems, end products, degradation abilities, etc., it is in most cases not mandatory to deposit. The same is true for researchers who study and publish new features of particular microorganisms for biotechnological or biomedical applications, such as enzymes for degrading, converting and building up substances, or other compounds such as dextranes or glycosides. Both types of deposit are made regularly on the free decision of researchers, triggered by their own interest or the interest of their institutions in contributing to the furthering of research in life sciences. However, a recent study showed that of all the microorganisms mentioned in publications, only a minor fraction of less than 0.9 per cent (Stackebrandt 2010) is actually deposited in service collections. This may be partially due simply to the ignorance of the authors, but certainly also partially due to the lack of capability of collections to cope with the sheer quantity of biological material. This urgently calls for a concerted action of the research funding agencies together with the collections and their users, which will be addressed in the EU project MIRRI. Today, already more and more scientific journals encourage authors to deposit the biological material under study in service culture collections for safeguarding continuity in scientific progress. Whoever does research and publishes is using previously published information and know-how and thus should accept the responsibility to share their findings in their function of a link in the knowledge chain.

All these deposits are made (or should be made) for one reason: published data can only be verified if the biological material they pertain to is available for comparison and further study (see Figure 15.5). The furthering of research can only be realized if new research can be built upon existing results and the related tools: trustworthy data and authentic biological material.

This is also the main reason why researchers work with organisms obtained from *ex situ* service culture collections. Without this supportive service, scientists would constantly have to conduct the skilled and expensive processes of isolation, characterization and identification of organisms again at the start of each new study.

To demonstrate the extent of exchange and supply of microbial living material worldwide and the measures taken voluntarily by microbial resource centres, a few

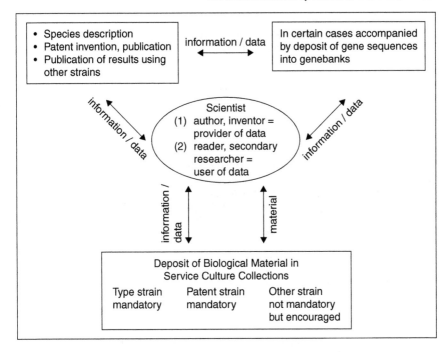

Figure 15.5 Published data can only be verified if the biological material they pertain to is available for comparison and further study

Source: Own illustration

figures and facts are given below on the deposit and supply of living microbiological material using the example of the DSMZ.

The DSMZ stock of cultures amounted in 2013 to over 23,000 cultures available from the open catalogue. Additionally, over 8,000 cultures had been deposited for patent or safe deposit purposes.

On average, DSMZ receives about 800–1,000 strains for deposit annually (as a service collection, DSMZ usually receives these cultures without requesting them). The cultures come from researchers all over the world from about 70 different countries. DSMZ also supplies approximately 21,000 samples of living microbiological materials to authorized third parties annually. About half of these cultures go to researchers and institutions in about 70 countries worldwide. Overall, in the collections affiliated with the World Federation for Culture Collections, supply and exchange of microbiological material amount to more than 500,000 samples annually. Imagine the amount of work that would pile up if for each and every action bilateral agreements would have to be worked out.

DSMZ has, for various reasons, like all major service culture collections, given itself standard procedures and processes for administering curatorial work. While

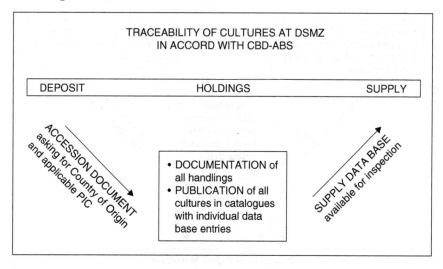

Figure 15.6 Traceability of cultures at DSMZ
Source: Own illustration

most of these had been in place long before the CBD, they all serve in principle the aims of CBD ABS of transparency and traceability (see Figure 15.6). The ones of direct importance to CBD ABS are

- registration with the WDCM
- request for information on country of origin on accession form (since 1993, no acceptance without this information)
- request for information on PIC on accession form
- assignation of an individual accession number to each biological material
- individual data entries for each biological material, showing the complete history that is available for this material
- catalogues of holdings are published and regularly updated
- information on the CBD and the resulting responsibilities for depositors and recipients is provided
- implementation of the ECCO-agreed Core MTA for the supply of cultures (requesting from the recipient "no passing on to third parties" and "if commercial use – contact country of origin") besides own terms and conditions of supply

These in-house regulations result from work in the WFCC and ECCO, as well as from the valuable work in the OECD BRC initiative and match the requirements formulated for collections in the recent EU proposal on an ABS regulation. As stated before, this should be the standard that countries of origin should expect from a microbial depositary/culture collection to consider deposit of their microbiological resources with it. A microbial collection in the EU, having implemented the ECCO Core MTA and following the OECD Best Practice Guidelines, should be considered a trustworthy institution to deposit genetic resources. In this context, the suggestion in the EU ABS Regulation to set up a central European Register of Collections is additionally helpful.

MIRRI – The pan-European Microbial Resource Research Infrastructure

The EU-funded pan-European Microbial Resource Research Infrastructure has amongst its goals a harmonized approach to ABS. Its Preparatory Phase project has the intention of building the basis for the construction and operation of a pan-European distributed infrastructure dedicated to microbial resources. MIRRI will support European research and development by providing microbiological services, facilitating the deposit of, preservation of, and access to high-quality samples of viable microorganisms, their derivatives and associated data. It will add value to the microbial resources and services needed for research and thus accelerate the discovery process. To make this possible in a coordinated and comparable way, the partners will implement the OECD Best Practice Guidelines for microbial BRCs.

MIRRI will build upon the achievements reached by ECCO and national networks of microbial culture collections and on regional initiatives such as the European Consortium of Microbial Resources Centres (EMbaRC) and the Common Access to Biological Resources and Information (CABRI). In particular, it will strongly rely on and further develop the profound expertise gained in the Global Biological Resource Centre Network (GBRCN) initiative. MIRRI will provide transnational and open access to

- living authentic microbial resources and associated data,
- microbiological services,
- expertise and knowledge, and
- training.

Regarding CBD and ABS issues, MIRRI will take into consideration previous activities of the culture collection community for a binding framework for BRCs. Among these are e.g. the WFCC database system *World Data Centre for Microorganisms (WDCM)*. Members are registered through a unique acronym and numerical identifier and are urged to catalogue their microbiological resources allowing tracking of microbiological items. The MOSAICC project *Micro-organism Sustainable Use and Access Regulation International Code of Conduct* has dealt with ABS issues on Material Transfer Agreements and Prior Informed Consent. This has resulted in an ECCO-agreed Core MTA for the supply of cultures.

Valuable background details are provided by two WFCC publications: the 1996 WFCC *Access to ex situ Microbial Genetic Resources within the Framework to the Convention on Biological Diversity – Background Document to the UNEP/CBD/ COP/3/Inf. 19 Information Document*, and the 2007 WFCC Paper to COP9.

MIRRI's goals are to support developments towards a favourable environment for research and application in the European area. With this in mind, the partners to MIRRI together with renowned experts in the field will tackle coordinated approaches to ABS in microbiology and participate in respective regulatory discussions. An opportunity can be seen, e.g. in the harmonization of national legislation under the finalized EU-wide framework. Additionally, EU cooperation with non-EU regions/countries with respect to standardization and harmonization of regulations would greatly support joint research.

Potential schemas for approach to ABS in microbiology should take into consideration the main three steps in working with microbial biodiversity (see Figure 15.7):

1   collecting samples *in situ* and isolating organisms from collected material;
2   depositing organisms in *ex situ* collection where the organism is subcultured, purified, authenticated, characterized, preserved, catalogued, and supplied; and
3   using the organism in research and development.

These three steps might be regulated individually and differently. Activities carried out under step one would underlie national regulations where the sampling is taking place, while it could be hoped that in the future more and more general agreements would replace the individual, bilateral, and repetitive agreements. For step two, it should be attempted to develop a global overarching regime, a common framework to clearly describe the rights, duties and obligations of service

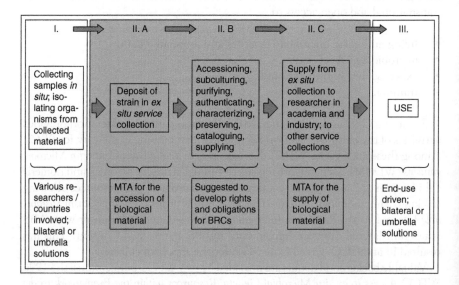

Figure 15.7 Suggested approaches for ABS in microbiology and *ex situ* BRCs
Source: Own illustration

culture collections/BRCs, thus making one-to-one agreements unnecessary. Step three would then embrace the pragmatic approach of end-use-driven and user compliance regulations, like e.g. suggested in the EU Regulation for an ABS regime.

Summary

The CBD ABS regulations will be implemented on the individual, national level. As a consequence (and examples already exist), a multitude of national legislations and national competent authorities are to be expected; a multitude that might adversely impact research and development. Being strongly shaped from and for zoological and botanical issues, the expected regulations might (unnecessarily!) adversely impact science and development, especially in microbiology and on microbial *ex situ* collections. It has to be reiterated that "user" and "provider" cannot be easily differentiated in microbiology. Essentially, any researcher from any country, who is going to collect e.g. soil samples in their own or another country and will be isolating microorganisms and doing research on them, is a user. Any researcher from any country who receives a culture from a culture collection is a user. However, huge up-front costs might emerge on all sides, if for any sampling, isolation, deposit or exchange of biological material detailed agreements would have to be formulated, which try to foresee any potential use and theoretical benefit without knowing whether any economic success can be expected of it. To avoid negative impacts, common approaches are needed wherever possible as well as education of all parties involved: governing bodies, academia and industry. Tailored solutions for compliance and for facilitating access should be designed for microbiology and its *ex situ* collections, which are tools promoted by CBD Art. 9 and which have a special role in the process that ensures resources are available for the enhancement of science. There is a clear demand for networking approaches delivered by regional, interregional and global collaboration.

References

Books, chapters, papers

Fritze, D, Weihs, V (2001) "Deposition of biological material for patent protection in biotechnology. Mini-Review", *Applied Microbiology and Biotechnology* 57, pp. 443–450.

Kamau, EC (2009) "Facilitating or restraining access to genetic resources? Procedural dimensions in Kenya", *Law, Environment and Development Journal* 5(2), pp. 152–166, www.lead-journal.org/2009-2.htm.

Lapage, SP, Sneath, PHA, Lessel, EF, Skerman VBD, Seeliger, HPR, Clark, WA (eds) (1992) *International code of nomenclature of bacteria: Bacteriological code, 1990 revision*, Washington DC: American Society for Microbiology Press.

OECD (2007) OECD best practice guidelines for biological resource centers, www.oecd.org/science/biotechnologypolicies/38777417.pdf.

OECD (2009) Long-term technological & societal challenges: The bioeconomy to 2030: designing a policy agenda, www.oecd.org/futures/bioeconomy/2030.

Smith, D, Fritze, D, Thompson, F, Stackebrandt, E (2013) "Public service collections and biological resource centres of microorganisms" in: Rosenberg, E, DeLong, EF, Lory, S, Stackebrandt, E, Thompson, F (eds) *The Prokaryotes*, 4th Ed – Vol *Prokaryotic Biology and Symbiotic Associations*, Berlin Heidelberg: Springer-Verlag, doi:10.1007/978-3-642-30194-0_14.

Stackebrandt, E (2010) "Diversification and focusing: Strategies of microbial culture collections", *Trends in Microbiology* 18, pp. 283–287.

WFCC (1996) Access to *ex situ* microbial genetic resources within the framework to the Convention on Biological Diversity – Background document to the UNEP/CBD/COP/3/Inf. 19 Information Document, www.wfcc.info/index.php/wfcc_library/publication/.

WFCC (2007) Paper to COP9 in UNEP/CBD/WG-ABS/6/INF/3 13 December 2007 Compilation, Canada, UNEP/CBD, 68–70.

Legal documents

EU Regulation No 511/2014 of the European Parliament and of the Council of 16 April 2014 on compliance measures for users from the Nagoya Protocol on Access to Genetic Resources and the Fair and Equitable Sharing of Benefits Arising from their Utilization in the Union, http://eur-lex.europa.eu/legal-content/EN/ALL/?uri=CELEX:32014R0511.

WIPO (1989) Budapest Treaty on the International Recognition of the Deposit of Microorganisms for the Purposes of Patent Procedure (done at Budapest on April 28, 1977 and amended on September 26, 1980) (ISBN 92–805–0744–3), www.wipo.int/treaties/en/registration/budapest/.

Websites

CABRI Common Access to Biological Resources and Information (www.cabri.org).

ECCO European Culture Collections' Organisation (www.eccosite.org).

GBRCN Global Biological Resource Centre Network (www.gbrcn.org).

Microbial Research Commons (www.nap.edu/catalog.php?record_id=13245).

MIRRI Microbial Resource Research Infrastructure (www.mirri.org).

MOSAICC Micro-Organisms Sustainable use and Access regulation International Code of Conduct (http://bccm.belspo.be/projects/mosaicc/).

OECD Organisation for Economic Co-operation and Development (www.oecd.org).

WDCM World Data Centre for Microorganisms (www.wdcm.org).

WFCC World Federation for Culture Collections (www.wfcc.info).

16 Biodiversity knowledge commons and sharing of research results with providers in East Africa*

Fabian Haas

Introduction

The Convention on Biological Diversity (CBD) entered into force in 1993 with the aim to protect nature, ensure sustainable use of natural or living resources and ensure that the access and benefits arising from the sustainable use are shared in a fair and equitable way between the "providers" and "users" of biodiversity. In order to enable this fair and equitable exchange, the countries' sovereign rights over the biodiversity inside their borders were reaffirmed. Lengthy and complex negotiations followed (e.g. Bonn Guidelines CBD Decision VI/24, CBOL 2008) to come to an understanding on how to do this exchange, which benefits may arise and how the proceeds may be shared.

As much as the terms "fair and equitable" are difficult to define (de Jonge 2011; Rojahn 2010), reality is complex and a wide range of providers meet a wide range of users resulting in a huge range of possible uses, which may or may not change over time. Therefore, Rojahn's (2010) question of whether it is "fair share or biopiracy" clearly has an element of time scale and indeed cannot be answered easily. It should be pointed out that provider and user roles in one exchange of material can be reversed in another exchange and are by no means fixed or permanent. This is regularly the case, for example, in biological control, where organisms from the home country of a pest or invasive alien species combat this pest in its new environment, providing an environmentally safe method to mitigate the effects of the pest. Invasive alien species are a global problem against which no country can claim immunity. So, today's providers in biocontrol are often tomorrow's users of organisms. Problems created by the ABS regime have been discussed already (Cock et al. 2009, 2010; Steiner, Djoghlaf & Gabriel 2008a,b; Kamau & Winter 2009).

In contrast to the assumed user and provider relationship of a market economy under ABS (e.g. IUCN 2012), which is involved most typically when actual biological resources are transferred such as in biocontrol, I would like to examine

* Dr. Scott Miller, Smithsonian Institution, Washington, DC, US, allowed me to use his extensive knowledge on the global institutions, and I am very grateful for this. I would also like to thank the editors, Dr. Evanson C. Kamau and Prof. Gerd Winter, for helpful feedback and their patience during the writing of this chapter as well as their input in this publication; Dr. Tom Moritz, Los Angeles, CA,US, for advice and discussions; and the members of the TAXACOM Mailing List for detailed information on the commercialization of biodiversity data.

the sharing of information on specimens in a "commons approach" to ownership and licenses. I will focus on Kenya and eastern Africa, since at the time of writing Internet connectivity improved by connecting these countries to the glass fibre deep sea cables in 2009/2010 and I could participate in many meetings held by relevant organizations (e.g. GBIF) to bring countries into the biodiversity network, have them actively participate and build up their own infrastructure. For example, Tanzania developed its own GBIF portal, and Kenya signed on as a full member in GBIF. The biodiversity network has used the commons approach; the most well-known examples of which are Creative Commons (CC) with regards to intellectual property rights and open source license with regards to software. CC licensing allows the use of items, but prevents commercial appropriation of items covered, while encouraging their use and return to the community under similar conditions. This ensures free access and encourages developments of public goods that can be continued to be shared.

Open Source and CC are certainly the most popular form of these licenses, but the idea of a commons approach to data sharing was advocated in biodiversity research and became known as "Biodiversity Commons" (Moritz 2002). While the term was largely overlooked, the commons approach was seminal in promoting several international organizations that make biodiversity-related data freely available to all and encourage their use. The tremendous success of the data sharing demonstrates how important the free exchange of data is and the synergies that arise from the combination of such sources. In the following, I would like to examine the structure, contents and ways of data sharing of the most important initiatives. Their origins lie in the belief that we need biodiversity data everywhere, not only in an ABS perspective and not only in the developing world. Open exchange of information is the way forward to promote human and environmental well-being.

Global institutions in the Biodiversity Commons

The Global Biodiversity Information Facility (GBIF)

GBIF[1] was founded in 2001 and has its headquarters in Copenhagen, Denmark, with a staff of about 30 persons employed permanently. There are several types of memberships. Voting Members (38) are countries that pay a membership fee to GBIF and include Kenya, Tanzania, and Uganda in the east African region. Another 19 countries are Associate Countries without voting rights. Participants (46) are intergovernmental organizations or nongovernmental organizations, such as *icipe* (International Centre for Insect Physiology and Ecology), which may provide data and have influence on GBIF's discussions but neither pay fees nor have voting rights. The membership fee is based on the national GDP and often contributed by research ministries.

Although the origin of GBIF lies outside the CBD, it is obvious that GBIF serves to fulfil Operational Objective 3 of the GTI (Global Taxonomy Initiative)

---

1 www.gbif.org, accessed 14 October 2014.

Decision VI/8: "Facilitate an improved and effective infrastructure/system for access to taxonomic information; with priority on ensuring countries of origin gain access to information concerning elements of their biodiversity".

Its mission "is to make the world's biodiversity data freely and universally available via the Internet. As a megascience initiative, GBIF aims to provide an essential global informatics infrastructure for biodiversity research and applications worldwide."[2] Currently, GBIF makes about 416 million occurrence records available through its data portal page.[3]

As the mission states, GBIF is concerned with biodiversity data and not with physical specimens. The specimens remain in the custody of the present owner (often public museums), and it is only the data connected to the physical specimens that are made accessible. Typically these data consist of taxonomic hierarchy, the identification of the organism, when and where it has been found and by whom; this information is called "occurrence record" for a species.

The portal is accessed via a standard web browser. When a query is done, e.g. for the striped earwig *Labidura riparia*, the central services of GBIF connects to all linked databases, searches and returns all entries matching this term – after accepting a data-sharing agreement. In this example, 287 occurrences are found, contributed by 15 data providers across the world.

The data quality, i.e. accuracy of species name and geographic location of its occurrence, has been discussed (Robertson 2008) and is a major challenge for the organization. An even bigger problem for the developing world is the unequal distribution of data collection (Yesson, Brewer, Sutton, Caithness & Pahwa 2007; Boakes, McGowan, Fuller, Chang-qing & Clark 2010). Despite world-famous expeditions, e.g. the American Museum Expedition to the Congo in 1909–1915[4] and activities of colonial powers, such as the Royal Museum for Central Africa, Tervueren,[5] or the National Museums of Kenya, which has its roots in 1910 when settlers and naturalists needed a place for their collections,[6] the sampling density in developing Africa is much lower than that in North America and Europe. Accurate data for e.g. a climate change model are scarcer and often nonexistent in the quality needed.

The data-sharing information[7] is provided by GBIF after a query for a species has been sent, but before the result of the first query in the session is returned. So, the data-sharing information appears in each new session. It does not refer to a specific CC license. It states, however, that GBIF does not hold any intellectual property rights on the contents and makes the data publisher responsible for the permission to publish the data via the GBIF network. The data publisher is not necessarily the data owner, so the former needs the permission for publication from the latter. Each

2 www.gbif.org, accessed 11 September 2014.
3 http://data.gbif.org, accessed 11 September 2014.
4 http://diglib1.amnh.org, accessed 11 September 2014.
5 www.africamuseum.be, accessed 11 September 2014.
6 www.museums.or.ke/content/view/7/50/, accessed 11 September 2014.
7 http://data.gbif.org/tutorial/datasharingagreement, accessed 11 September 2014.

dataset is supposed to have information available on its ownership. According to the MoU Paragraph 8 Point 7, legality of data collection lies on the side of the data publisher, that any data collected are consistent with any "applicable laws, regulations and any relevant requirements for prior informed consent".

This statement covers a wide variety of laws and regulations. Following the workflow of a museum collection, the first permit is for entering the area (a visa, an agreement with a local community) where the specimens might be found. The second permit covers the specific taxon that may be collected on site, e.g. you are allowed to collect insects or spiders but not birds or mammals. Contrary to common belief, all European countries require a collection permit to collect e.g. insects, feathers or plants, even outside protected areas. Then there is the export permit (even for non-CITES species), with an agreement on where the specimens and type of material are deposited in the long term. In the spirit of ABS, more and more agreements include paragraphs on what you are allowed to do with specimens and how any result, e.g. publication, is shared with scientists in the country of origin (see Kamau, Ch. 17 in this volume).

Once identified and furnished with a collection label (i.e. the basic information of where and when a specimen has been found), the data are entered into a database which is typically used by the departments' scientists for documentation and further research. It is a current trend supported by donors that these data are made available online, either as a separate website that allows online search, or via GBIF, Barcode of Life and others. Thus, the data enter the Internet with all the possible ways to copy and to use. Data from several sources (holding the specimens and/or the data) are often combined to answer a range of questions, such as on climate change or creating new datasets.

Not all of the above-described permits are needed in every case, e.g. if you collect in your residential country or on private land. However, it is clear that if formal negotiations are needed at each step, scientific research is hardly possible with the increasing pressure on time and results. A commons approach is definitely favourable 1) for access to and use of the specimens, and 2) for the use of data. While the latter is available via different Creative Commons license models, Open Source, and good scientific practice, the former is not yet under an "ABS Commons" model. Despite several treaties such as the International Treaty on Plant Genetic Resources for Food and Agriculture (ITPGRFA), often colloquially called the Plant Treaty of the FAO, and contributions of Oldham (2009) on an explicit "ABS Commons", this idea did not create a wider discussion in the CBD and ABS circles. A "Global Multilateral Benefit-Sharing Mechanism", as one suggestion on how such an ABS Commons could be structured, was presented by the African Group to the Nagoya Protocol negotiations in an informal non-paper format (see Greiber & Feit 2011, 32). However, it did not generate much interest, as inferred from the short list of Internet search engine results. So, the commons approach here refers only to data and not to ABS as such, which I think is unfortunate.

As a matter of good scientific practice, the use of GBIF data (they are free for download) needs to be documented in the form of a citation. In the example given by GBIF, the data publisher is in the centre, not GBIF: "Biodiversity occurrence data published by: Field Museum of Natural History, Museum of Vertebrate Zoology, University of Washington Burke Museum, and University of Turku (Accessed through GBIF Data Portal, data.gbif.org, 2007–02–22)". The GBits Science Supplement (GBIF 2012), an addition to GBIF's newsletter, gives only an incomplete glimpse on the number of publications and topics that use biodiversity data from GBIF. There is, however, no mechanism provided by GBIF to enforce the legitimacy of specimen or data collection or the appropriate citation of the source of the data. This is left to the social control in the scientific community and by editors.

GBIF uses a wide, decentralized network of databases to store the biodiversity data, i.e. the databases are typically located at the data publisher's institution/server. The distributed network used by GBIF is more challenging on the IT side, enforcing the data formats and consistency of programming and interoperability, as well as quality control. However, a decentralized network has the clear advantage in that contributors have a much stronger sense of ownership and control over the data. The contributor is free to remove the database at will, which, according to Juan Bello (former Senior Programme Officer for Nodes, pers. comm.), has never happened, and updates are carried out more regularly if the database remains under close control. Based on personal experience as a GTI Focal Point in Germany, this approach makes potential contributors much more eager to submit their data into a larger network, since it avoids the impression that someone else has control over "your" data.

Contributors also provide valuable data on endangered species to GBIF. There is a twofold danger to that. First, the GBIF data might be used for poaching in the wild (rhinoceros, some antelopes) or illegal collection of high-priced species such as marine turtles or butterflies. Second, the specimens might be stolen from the collections. To encourage potential data publishers to join GBIF, it provides policies and recommendations on how to include endangered or rare species. However, this is an issue for only a minority of species (less than 5 per cent).

In any event, the actual specimens remain with their owners and receive an individual number to connect dataset with specimen. This is pertinent, as mistakes may occur on all levels, from simple typos to misidentification. So, questions of ownership, including ABS-related issues, need to be discussed with the owner of the specimen and not with GBIF. GBIF does not have access to physical specimens but to information only.

In eastern Africa, Tanzania has developed a national portal accessing the whole wealth of GBIF, but selecting only those data and species that lie within its borders,[8] and informing the general public as well as tourists on Tanzania's biodiversity. Tanzania produced a printed version of a national checklist based on these data (Gideon, Nyinondi & Oyema 2012). All data available for Kenya come free of charge from non-Kenyan institutions and allow for research and planning within Kenya.

8 www.tanbif.or.tz, accessed 11 September 2014.

The Encyclopedia of Life (EoL)

EoL[9] was launched in 2007 and its secretariat is in the Smithsonian Institution, Washington, DC. EoL is centred on the concept of a "webpage for every species".[10] The idea of collating all available information on one biological species has been discussed before EoL, also in GBIF, FishBase[11] and BirdLife Data Zone,[12] but was finally started with support of the MacArthur and Sloan Foundations (both US). At the time of writing, EoL holds 1.33 million "pages with content" and a total of 4.29 million pages,[13] with an estimated 5–10 million biological organisms existing today. The information accessible through their webpages is based on "content partners" (245), which hold databases on a group of animals or plants and allow EoL to access this information through its website. Amongst the content partners are GBIF, BHL, CBOL, iBOL/Boldsystems, NCBI, and many other data providers.

This connectivity to other databases makes EoL a data portal or web portal: "A **web portal** is a web site that brings information from diverse sources in a unified way. Usually, each information source gets its dedicated area on the page for displaying information (a portlet); often, the user can configure which ones to display."[14] It can be considered a one-stop shop that provides one with all available information, e.g. behavioural, morphological, taxonomical, physiological, distributional, conservational, and molecular, on one page in a structured way. The amount of information varies with the organism, virtually none for some (e.g. an oriental earwig *Allodahlia*) to overwhelming for others (e.g. the lion *Panthera leo*).

In addition to this strong portal functionality, EoL provides a platform in "EoL Communities" and "EoL Curators" to involve specialists and citizen scientists in revising and adding information, such as to confirm the identifications of the photos submitted, to single species' pages. These structures provide new and original content to the EoL webpages.

Each piece of content in the portal has a link/reference to the data source and copyright (often Creative Commons license) as requested by the content provider. If one wants to reuse this piece of information, permission from the original right holder is required. EoL does not provide permissions but leaves that to the contents' providers. No special or dedicated tracing, enforcing or penalizing mechanisms are in place.

EoL is accessed through a standard web browser, and simple registration on the web pages allows involvement in Communities and Curators groups. EoL members may leave comments and may create virtual collections and contents, but there is no exclusive information to them. All information is available to the general public. EoL's own software is under the open source model and is freely

---

9   www.eol.org.
10   www.eol.org, accessed 11 September 2014.
11   www.fishbase.org.
12   www.birdlife.org/datazone/home.
13   http://eol.org/statistics, accessed 11 September 2014.
14   http://en.wikipedia.org/wiki/Web_portal, accessed 11 September 2014.

available from specified websites. EoL, in contrast to GBIF, is very focused on the species, so national faunas and floras are not easily assembled; the information on the occurrences of a species is more secondary here than in GBIF.

The usefulness of EoL for a certain region, such as East Africa and Kenya, which has been my working area for more than six years, depends on whether one's research is focused on a single species and how much information is already available from other webpages. Often researchers, being rather specific in their interest, prefer to use the source database instead of the portal. EoL, however, allows access to all kinds of information through a single portal instead of accessing many databases separately. This clearly saves searching time, and one may find additional and useful information even if not having thought of requesting it.

The Biodiversity Heritage Library (BHL)

BHL[15] was founded in 2005 and launched in 2007 with primary funding from the MacArthur Foundation. In addition, EoL projects and several other North American foundations have contributed directly to the project. It has a staff of about 10–20 persons and 15 institutional members, mostly US and UK academies of science and libraries, and the secretariat is in the Smithsonian Institution, Washington, DC. There are additional partners for BHL-Europe, BHL-Australia and BHL-China.

BHL's mission and structure ". . . is a consortium of natural history and botanical libraries that cooperate to digitize and make accessible the legacy literature of biodiversity held in their collections and to make that literature available for open access and responsible use as a part of a global 'biodiversity commons'. The BHL consortium works with the international taxonomic community, rights holders, and other interested parties to ensure that this biodiversity heritage is made available to a global audience through open access principles. In partnership with the Internet Archive and through local digitization efforts, the BHL has digitized millions of pages of taxonomic literature, representing tens of thousands of titles and over 100,000 volumes."[16]

Legacy literature, colloquially speaking "old literature", is often at the core of biodiversity work, since it contains the still important first descriptions of species and stretches back to the mid-1800s, when today's biological/taxonomic system of organisms was developed. Such books and journals are rare and thus often not included in the interlibrary loan and are practically not accessible, in particular to the developing world. The BHL made it a priority to digitize these publications and provide access through a website. It offers access to approximately 44.65 million pages of 86,723 titles and allows download of these pages or complete volumes.[17]

---

15 www.biodiversitylibrary.org.
16 http://biodivlib.wikispaces.com/About, accessed 11 September 2014.
17 http://biodiversitylibrary.org/, accessed 11 September 2014.

BHL is directly concerned with material that is traditionally under strong copyright regulations. In order to avoid extensive negotiations with the copyright holders, the project started with publications that are already in the public domain in the United States due to expiration of their copyrights. These are publications dated before 1923. If material is newer than that, then the copyright holder either gave permission or the material is free for use for other reasons already. Permissions were given by a number of publishing houses for their journals and so publication up to present can be found on this website. Again, this takes place under a Creative Commons License (CC BY-NC-SA 3.0). The publications ". . . in the BHL are free to access, download, reuse and repurpose under the principles of open access and open data".[18] It is pointed out on the same page that the data are reused, e.g. by EoL, Tropicas, and BioStor,[19] promoting the network idea.

The data and information that is created by BHL (BHL metadata) can be used under the Creative Commons CC0 1.0 Universal (CC0 1.0) Public Domain Dedication license. BHL encourages people to "Go ahead, take our metadata and do something creative with it! If you do repurpose BHL metadata please share your story with us."[20]

A subproject of the BHL is BHL-China, which focuses on literature related to the territory of China and uses the Chinese language and symbols (BHL apparently includes publications only using the Latin alphabet). BHL-China currently focuses on botanical literature and holds approximately 1.8 million pages in 9,070 volumes.[21]

Another subproject of the BHL that was initiated in 2009 is BHL-Europe, which, rather than digitizing, supports interoperability of legal and technical aspects and also focuses on legacy literature. The project portal, EUROPEANA,[22] provides multilingual access to the data and combines the biodiversity literature with culture collections. Taxonomy and biodiversity research are international endeavours, and Europe and North America are part of the same scientific culture. So, there is a great amount of overlap in the library catalogues. Similar projects include Gallica[23] and AnimalBase,[24] with partly different scopes and approaches.

BHL uses a centralized database to store the downloadable files, while the physical book remains with the contributing library. A centralized database is easier to maintain and back up and allows more complicated indexing and search functions than does a distributed model. Since books and publications are not considered unique or acquired with great personal effort, unlike specimens of organisms, providing a copy of a book poses no psychological problem, which is sometimes encountered in specimen (information) database.

18 http://biodivlib.wikispaces.com/Collection+Development+Policy, accessed 11 September 2014.
19 http://biostor.org/, accessed 11 September 2014.
20 http://biodivlib.wikispaces.com/Data+Exports, accessed 11 September 2014.
21 www.bhl-china.org/cms/, accessed 11 September 2014.
22 www.europeana.eu/portal, accessed 11 September 2014.
23 http://gallica.bnf.fr/, accessed 11 September 2014.
24 http://animalbase.org/, accessed 11 September 2014.

Like the two previous global organizations GBIF and EoL, BHL does not provide enforcing, tracing, or penalizing mechanisms, but relies on the mechanisms in copyright laws.

Before BHL, many books and publications based on research in the developing world never found their way to the countries of origin of the specimen. In particular, the old and rare taxonomic legacy literature is now freely available, only limited by the bandwidth of the Internet connection, which has been greatly improved since East Africa was connected to the glass fibre deep sea cables in 2009/2010. In case of copyright protected or current literature, many publishers of taxonomic journals decided to make their journals available through BHL. They may be partially or completely free using different license models. It cannot be denied that access to current literature can be expensive and limited; however, in a somewhat exaggerated statement, one could say that information scarcity has changed to information overflow. The developing world and eastern Africa are largely benefiting from open access to the legacy and other biodiversity literature provided by northern countries, which allows for research and planning.

The International Barcode of Life Projects (iBOL)

iBOL[25] is headquartered in Guelph, Canada, and is sponsored by a wide range of institutions and donors (about 35[26] from around the world) and promotes the use of DNA barcoding for specimen identification. The basic concept of DNA barcoding is to use one gene that is present in all species and specimens and to use the same standardized methods to sequence this gene. There are a number of requirements on such a gene, such as being simple to isolate and sufficiently variable to contain enough information to discriminate between species. Some genes are virtually identical in all organisms, while others are very different between individuals of a species. Thus, they may be used to reconstruct deep phylogeny, i.e. relationships of groups like Arthropods (lobsters, spiders, insects) and Molluscs (octopus, mussels, snails) or Chordates (fish) in case of conserved genes or, for forensic questions, to look for an individual human being in case of highly variable genes. Research has shown that indeed there is no single gene that would be usable for all organisms (plants, animals, and fungi). Rather, each major group of an organism requires a different gene or combination of genes: mitochondrial cytochrome c oxidase subunit 1 gene (COI) for animals, the internal transcribed spacer region (ITS) for fungi, and two genes for plants, the ribulose-bisphosphate carboxylase and maturase K genes (rbcL & matK). Each of these is in a different location in the genome and serves very different functions in the organisms, but they are variable enough to allow species identification. A detailed description of the workflow and concept is given by Hanner and Gregory (2007) and Floyd, Lima, deWaard, Humble and Hanner (2010).

25 www.ibol.org.
26 http://ibol.org/about-us/sponsors/, accessed 11 September 2014.

At the time of writing this chapter, more than 2.89 million specimens and 192,480 named species are accessible in the database.[27]

The merits of this approach are evident. Since DNA is identical in all parts of an organism, incomplete samples, such as hairs, dung, pieces of muscle tissue (bush meat), insect eggs, or larvae, can be used for identification. This is not the case with classical taxonomy, where identification is often restricted to adults and to one sex. In many circumstances this is not helpful, e.g. at quarantine control of fruits when larvae are detected but the identification key is based on adult flies. This may lead to the unjustified rejection of whole consignments and huge economic losses. Huge exporters of cut flowers, vegetables, and fruits, such as Kenya, have a keen interest in avoiding rejection and can make use of this technology.

The reference library is built through the submission of sequences from already identified and thoroughly documented specimens. iBOL requires photos, GPS coordinates, and identification, as well as a catalogue number to locate the voucher specimens in the partner institution's collection. As DNA sequencing is destructive, typically a specimen is subsampled, i.e. a leg is taken from an insect and sequenced while the remaining specimen is preserved in the collection as a voucher (reference) specimen. As mistakes can happen on all levels, whether in identification, data collection, or sequencing, the voucher specimen is kept as a control for the results.

The actual sequencing can be done in-house in a museum or at a university, but low commercial rates for DNA sequencing made this unattractive. Running and servicing the necessary equipment is costly, and more and more commercial companies provide this service. The specimen samples are destroyed after sequencing and the resulting sequence is returned by email.

This approach to identification has become possible through the collapsing costs of DNA sequencing, and led Miller to conclude, "Barcoding is emerging as a cost-effective standard for rapid species identification" in a renaissance of taxonomy (Miller, 2007). According to the National Human Genome Research Institute,[28] the cost of sequencing a strand of 1 million base pairs (i.e. a megabase) was approximately 5,300 USD in 2001, passed the 1,000 USD mark in October 2004, and was below 1 USD in July 2009 and arrived at approximately 0.10 USD in July 2011. In April 2014 the cost was estimated to be 0.05 USD per megabase. The cost for sequencing one genome decreased from 95 million USD in 2001 to about 4,500 USD. The market for DNA sequencing was estimated at 3 billion USD in 2012 and is expected to more than double to 6.6 billion USD in 2016. China is now the world leader in genome sequencing capacity.[29] It should be emphasized that the 3 billion USD is the value of the sequencing service and not of any product or information that may be generated through the sequencing itself.

---

27 www.ibol.org/resources/barcode-library/, accessed 11 September 2014.

28 www.genome.gov/sequencingcosts/, accessed 11 September 2014.

29 www.darkdaily.com/why-china-is-now-the-world-leader-in-genome-sequencing-capacity-062810#axzz3DO2HiE5C of 28 June 2010, accessed 11 September 2014.

The huge amount of data generated through this sequencing rush made the term "megascience" obsolete; rather, the founding of an open-access journal *GigaScience*[30] became necessary, and its aim is, put simply but boldly, ". . . to revolutionize data dissemination, organization, understanding, and use". Since 2010, there is a new platform called "BioSharing",[31] which is dedicated to working at the global level to implement data sharing policies. This enormous dynamic is driven by life science companies, i.e. diagnostics, medical, and pharmaceutical research and not by biodiversity research. However, biodiversity research on a global level clearly benefits from this development through lower costs, accessibility of services, and IT tools to analyze data. The huge market value of sequencing services ensures the future development and maintenance of the infrastructure, unlike in biodiversity research, where projects may collapse after the end of funding.

iBOL's database system[32] is highly centralized, being essentially one database housed at the University of Guelph, Canada. The centralization allows extensive data cleaning, processing, analyzing tools, and front end to be included. According to Ratnasingham and Hebert (2007), 65,000 lines of code are involved in analyzing data and providing a front end through a standard web browser. However, once released by the researcher, essential specimen data and the sequence are migrated to sister genomic repositories (DNA Data Bank of Japan (DDBJ), European Molecular Biology Laboratory (EMBL), NCBI), providing safety copies against data loss and expanded access. iBOL's own data portal[33] provides access to the general public, including the submission of its own sequences into an identification form. If present in the reference library, this will return the most likely identification. After free registration, more options to work with the data become available, such as tree construction and a variety of analytical steps.

Data quality lies with the project participant, and since accurate identification is at the heart of biological science (and thus reliability of these data for e.g. climate change models), the accuracy is discussed in several publications (Bridge, Roberts, Brian, Spooner & Panchal 2003; Nilsson, Ryberg, Kristiansson, Abarenkov & Larsson 2006; Kvist, Oceguera-Figueroa, Siddall & Erséus 2010) pointing to a significant percentage of problematic cases. iBOL reacted to the criticism and implemented high standards of documentation, including a required voucher specimen, to be stored in the contributor's collection for further reference. In the first 18 months after submission, contributors have exclusive access to their own submitted data. This is useful and makes scientists much more eager to participate, as personal careers and publications depend on these data. An immediate release to the public would obviously rather hinder than promote the project. After this period of time, the data are released and become publicly available.

---

30 www.gigasciencejournal.com, accessed 11 September 2014.
31 www.biosharing.org, accessed 11 September 2014.
32 www.boldsystems.org, accessed 11 September 2014.
33 www.boldsystems.org.

Data-sharing policies were widely discussed in the scientific and donor communities and are now in place. They are aligned with the data release policies of large-scale collaborations in genetics, such as the National Human Genome Research Institute, Genome Canada, the Gordon and Betty Moore Foundation in the United States, and the Wellcome Trust in the United Kingdom. Again, the data are freely shared: "iBOL members consider all barcode data within BOLD a community resource to be shared publicly according to the terms and conditions outlined in this policy. There is no Intellectual Property associated with these data."[34] Photos are under CC license as chosen by the copyright holder. No particular mechanism is provided by iBOL to enforce, track, or penalize their data-sharing provisions. Unlike other institutions related to sequences,[35] iBOL does not provide or store samples (with the exception of voucher specimens for sequences they themselves contributed).

CBOL (Consortium for the Barcode of Life[36]) is a partner organization of iBOL; its secretariat is in the Smithsonian Institution, Washington, DC. The consortium has 120 member organizations in 45 nations and supports the barcoding effort through conferences, workshops, and public relations activities/outreach. However, it does not generate or house any sequence data. They are stored in iBOL/ Boldsystems, and so CBOL is not discussed any further here.

The falling prices and the availability of commercial sequencing services made this technology a viable option even in the developing world. In Nairobi alone, there are two sequencing machines available. Currently, this is most interesting for research topics in biology and medicine, but its use in forensics and other nonscientific applications, such as customs, is increasing. A publicly available reference library, as provided by Boldsystems, is therefore useful even in the context of a developing country. Currently, KenBOL[37] adds sequences of medically and agriculturally important species to the database, but still many African species are not in Boldsystems yet. However, sequencing programmes in other regions of the world help Africa by providing information on potential invasive alien species (IAS) from these regions (Darling & Blum 2007; Floyd et al. 2010[38]), and many species occur not only in Africa but in adjacent regions too.

Important in the light of ABS is that these genes have been known for a long time, e.g. COI was first sequenced around the mid-1980s and is thus well understood, yet there is no product that would make use of this information. It is highly improbable that with the new information made public through DNA barcoding, no commercial product has been realized and no patent has been granted on any of the barcoding genes.

---

34 http://ibol.org/resources/data-release-policy/, accessed 11 September 2014.
35 www.dnabank-network.org, www.dsmz.de or www.ggbn.org, accessed 11 September 2014.
36 www.barcodeoflife.org.
37 www.ibol.org/kenya/, accessed 11 September 2014.
38 Also www.qbol.wur.nl/UK/about-qbol/, accessed 11 September 2014.

Assessment and context

The objective of the described international organizations is information sharing with regards to biological organisms, i.e. the actual specimen and information associated with it. The organizations build on the research activities of the last 250 years and most of this kind of research is basic research.

A typical example for basic, nonapplied research is the distribution and phenology of species, such as the sanderling. It is a fairly small bird found in wetlands and seashores around the world and occurs in Kenya only for a certain period of the year. In itself, this appears fairly insignificant. It is only in combination with other data and observations, such as the nesting areas of this species, that we can answer highly relevant and urgent questions, such as biodiversity loss in a country, the state of wetlands, and how to protect biodiversity hotspots and detect the effects of climate change by range shift in species. Availability of such (digitized) data is a great step forward, especially for the developing world where such data were not available or scarce until a few years ago.

The text of the CBD tends to assume that biodiversity-rich and technology-poor countries are developing nations in the South that are providers of genetic and biological resources to biodiversity-poor and technology-rich and developed countries in the North. While this might have been true in the 1980s when the CBD was negotiated, the current transformation of Brazil, Mexico, India, and China, amongst others, into industrialized nations, successfully challenging classical industrial Western countries in the field of science and technology, demonstrates that this division is by no means carved in stone. These countries now have significant biotechnological capacities: China has the biggest sequencing capacities worldwide, India is the third biggest producer of pharmaceuticals using expired patents, and in Nairobi alone there are two sequencers for DNA. These countries have capabilities to develop pharmaceuticals and other products from their own biodiversity within their borders. Obviously on the level of a country, provider and user can be the same. In the 1980s and 1990s, biotechnology was seen as the new "green gold rush" while now it is biofuels, and it can be argued that the economic hopes for biotechnology were disappointed (or, in the first place, exaggerated). However, we do recognize the changing roles of provider and user in biotechnology as well as in other fields of research, e.g. in the field of biological control (Cock et al. 2009, 2010).

The focus of access and benefit sharing lies in a bilateral user and provider relationship, basically similar to a producer–customer relationship in a market economy. Accordingly, contracts and agreements need to be negotiated between the two. The Nagoya Protocol (CBD, 2012, UNEP/CBD/X/1[39]) tries to provide a framework for these negotiations; however, they remain difficult since there is a huge range of possible providers met by an equally huge diversity of users and uses. In the end, every access and use needs to be negotiated separately by the partners. This may be time-consuming for a variety of reasons, such as divergence of

39 www.cbd.int/abs/, accessed 11 September 2014.

expected benefits on user and provider side, timelines of product development, existing (or nonexisting) legal framework, level of information, and competence on user and provider side on each other's objective and subjective situation.

The discussed organizations form a part of the biodiversity commons (Moritz 2002) that prefer to pool and combine data for free access (but not the actual specimens or, in the case of BHL, books). They are not involved in any form of commercial activity. They use a commons approach to distribute and make their information available for free to anybody, provided the source of this information is acknowledged. This is in clear contrast to a commercial and privatized model, where companies hold their own large physical and information collections, and another example of the "open source revolution" described by Hope (2008).

Putting biodiversity data in a pool

Despite being initiated and financially supported by the (so-called) North, the global organizations are open to contributions and provide direct benefits to developing countries. GBIF and iBOL are open networks of contributors. Membership provides the opportunity to access direct support from them or donors, requiring cooperation with them. GBIF allows only persons from member countries and institutions to participate in training workshops on data management or georeferencing, and to facilitate programmes where European nodes provide mentoring for new African nodes, such as that of Kenya. Tanzania could receive financial support through the Expert Center for Taxonomic Identification to build up its own data structure and portal, which is now used to produce national flora and fauna (Gideon et al. 2012). The cooperation with iBOL made the International Development Research Centre (IDRC) funding for the Kenyan Barcode of Life (KenBOL) possible. Besides generating DNA barcodes of African species for availability to other African countries, KenBOL involves training and networking opportunities which would not be possible without the global organizations.

The global organizations also provide a technical platform or infrastructure in which national biodiversity data can be hosted by other countries. In a concrete example, *icipe*'s contributions to GBIF (*icipe* is an institutional member) were hosted in the Zoologisches Forschungsmuseum Alexander Koenig (ZFMK) Bonn, since the infrastructure was not there at *icipe*. IT infrastructure has greatly improved and so the data are now hosted by *icipe* itself, but using software that is freely available from GBIF (IPT Toolkit v2). The same applies to iBOL and its database system Boldsystems: none of the eastern African countries would have the resources to provide this kind of hosting and distributing of DNA barcode data or could pursue the development of new analytical tools and web interfaces. If there were such capacity, it would probably be criticized by donors as a duplicate effort. Hosting by a partnering institution is a strong benefit because it is much more than putting a few megabytes on other people's servers. It includes back up, structuring, and data control, availability to queries, and adding information from e.g. taxonomical or geographical catalogues.

Great care is taken by the organizations to emphazise that they do not own the data that are accessible through their portals. Rather they host the data, providing a platform or framework to share the information. Ownership remains with the author, collector, or institution that decides by itself to share data in the network. The openness of data sharing may invite illegal (i.e. not compliant with data-sharing agreements or CC license models) copying and use of the data. This problem is as old as authorship exists. However, the act of copying has become easier than ever by computers and the Internet. With regards to images, visible and invisible watermarks are used. However, there is no foolproof system to prevent completely the unauthorized use of images. Watermarks are not an option for texts, which may simply be retyped and authorship claimed.

Since most data provided by the global organizations are text based, rather than image based, the appropriate use of data and reference to source is extremely difficult to control. GBIF, for example, has no reliable list of publications that are using data provided by the GBIF portal. Authors may or may not acknowledge use and do not consistently return to GBIF if a contribution is published. While this might just be negligence, active illegal use is even harder to trace, and it is these difficulties that prevent the global organizations from enforcing any tracing or penalizing mechanisms against illegal use.

The user (scientific) community has the responsibility to find these cases of illegal use. This could be done on various levels, for example journal editors may have a role to play. They already insist on collection permits or repository numbers to be included in the manuscript. Some research and science donors already insist that applicants need to make an ABS agreement with the hosting countries/institutions in order to receive funds. So the access to specimens is to some extent controlled in scientific research, and this could be extended on clear statements on the source of biodiversity data. As much as computers help in copying, they also help find cases of illegal behaviour, as in the case of the former federal minister of defence of Germany, who had to resign after a group of activists could prove that large parts of his PhD thesis from other texts were unreferenced. They used library and Google searches to find sentences and paragraphs.[40] Other politicians had to resign or return their PhD titles as well.

Globally unique identifiers (GUIDs) and digital object identifiers (DOIs) respond to the need for stable reference to a data source or an object. They provide mechanisms on how to trace an article, for example, on the Internet where links and web addresses are constantly changing. However, they do not provide any protection against illegal use of the source material. There is no absolute protection against fraudulent and criminal efforts.

None of the organizations is in a position to actually control the provenance of a specimen or a printed material. A book might be stolen or otherwise not legally acquired by a library or person, and a specimen collected without a collection permit. While the former is probably not relevant to the actual copyrights

---

40 https://de.wikipedia.org/wiki/Plagiatsaff%C3%A4re_Guttenberg, accessed 11 September 2014.

involved, the latter matters in the light of ABS where provenance is a key issue. None of the organizations described can possibly assess the legality of collecting with the millions of specimens involved but must rely on the truthfulness of the contributors. Under ABS and other legislation, resident scientists need collection permits to do research inside their own countries. Consequently, this issue not only applies to foreign institutions. While, for example, Germany and the United States do not have ABS regulations, they do require collection permits. In most cases, records with (legally but not geographically) doubtful provenance will not be found in these organizations, but will remain unpublished and will not become available for research.

Biodiversity informatics is not bioinformatics or genomics

Parry (2004) notes in his book titled *Trading the Genome* that collecting efforts and information technology have generated a new situation in which information rather than specimens is actually transferred. This is in itself nothing new, but has been taking place in many sectors, and similar trends can be seen in music and photography where information is sent rather than existing as physical objects like CDs or prints. The described institutions are a part of this trend of transmitting information instead of physical objects.

There are concerns that a specimen actually becomes less and less important once its genome, i.e. all DNA in an organism, is known and then made available through databases (see discussion on iBOL above). Since this information can be turned again into molecules and then introduced into bacteria or mice to produce a gene product, the concerns are genuine. However, the organizations discussed above do provide information that has long been published (BHL, EoL) or exists as occurrence data (GBIF) or sequences of well-researched genes (iBOL). Biodiversity informatics analyzes this information and occurrence data and may deliver important clues on, for example, climate change and niche modelling. Bioinformatics and genomics, however, deal with huge amounts of sequence data, mostly DNA sequences, to find new genes with possible applications in science and medicine and to better understand genes and gene regulation.

But has only the amount of data increased or has a new quality been generated by all these data? With digitization came also the option to interconnect data sources: geographic data, such as an atlas and rainfall/temperature, with the distribution of species and information on their physiology such as water needs. These previously atomized and inaccessible data are now being used to predict climate change, possible corridors of invasive alien species, and even unsuitable sites for growing genetically modified (GM) crops. Clearly, the quality of biodiversity data and their use is at a whole new level.

Conclusion

All of the above-described platforms and portals make basic biological and taxonomic information available to the developing world at no charge. They thus fulfil the requirement of the CBD regarding the repatriation of information and help to fulfil the countries' obligations on biodiversity reporting under the CBD. Whereas a few years ago, developing countries lamented the shortage of information about their own biodiversity, today the problem is rather of information overflow. In East Africa, the improved connectivity to the Internet since 2009/2010 greatly encouraged the use of the information provided by these organizations.

None of the discussed organizations are supported by a donor traditionally active in the developing world. Most of the donors focus on science and projects in North America or Europe, and the motives of making publications or DNA sequences available are clearly domestic. The Internet is the technology to share this information and thus the data become available to all.

The key decisions were to a) digitize collections and b) use a commons approach and actively encourage countries, institutions, and even individuals to make use of the data. The developing world is clearly benefitting from the free sharing of biodiversity information and the biodiversity commons approach.

There is a clear advantage of free (but referenced) sharing of data on the components of biodiversity, i.e. the organisms. The data proved extremely useful for all kind of activities from large-scale climate change modelling to small-scale management of protected areas or city planning. Any stricter regulation on data sharing would exclude large groups of users in developed and developing countries alike and deprive them of information they badly need for fact-based decision making. The range of websites and portals portrayed here make information available that was not accessible for the better part of the developing world but has very often been published in various ways, usually in print publications. So in the perspective of new patents and products, the information was already in the public domain and prevents commercial appropriation. It is unlikely that any product is developed with information from these databases but, if so, it cannot be patented and is free to be copied by developing countries. All of the organizations introduced here refer to the holder of the copyrights for a given record. The information can therefore be traced to its origin and cross-checked for legality on all levels. For the kind of information presented by these websites, stricter regulation would create more disadvantages than advantages, especially for biodiversity-rich areas.

Publications as well as specimen data which were not accessible a mere 10 years ago are now available. Further, initiatives such as iBOL provide new data, which may not be focused on the developing world. However, many species have wide ranges and either occur in the developing world naturally or because they are invasive alien species. These data become directly available through the freely accessible websites and IT infrastructure provided by the global organizations. The portals of the global organizations provide simple and reliable access to a number of data sources and ensure that the IT infrastructure is maintained and free of charge for most users.

It is highly unlikely that new products will be developed on the data provided in the biodiversity commons enterprise.

While noncompliance to data sharing and license agreements cannot be completely prevented, the benefits of sharing the data do clearly outweigh possible damages. GUIDs and DOIs provide technical help in tracing the data source more reliably than before.

References

Boakes, EH, McGowan, PJK, Fuller, RA, Chang-qing, D, Clark, NE (2010) "Distorted views of biodiversity: Spatial and temporal bias in species occurrence data", *PLOS Biology* 8(6), e1000385, doi:10.1371/journal.pbio.1000385.

Bridge, PD, Roberts, PJ, Brian, M, Spooner, BM, Panchal, G (2003) "On the unreliability of published DNA sequences", *New Phytologist* 160, pp. 43–48, doi:10.1046/j.1469-8137.2003.00861.x.

CBD (2012) The Nagoya Protocol, UNEP/CBD/X/1, www.cbd.int/decision/cop/?id=12267 (accessed 16 October 2012).

CBOL (2008) Report of a workshop on access and benefit sharing in non-commercial biodiversity research, http://barcoding.si.edu/PDF/BonnABSWorkshopReport-FINAL.pdf.

Cock, MJW, van Lenteren, JC, Brodeur, J, Barratt, BIP, Bigler, F, Bolckmans, K, Cônsoli, FL, Haas, F, Mason, PG, Parra, JR (2009) The use and exchange of biological control agents for food and agriculture. Background Study Paper no. 47, FAO Rome.

Cock, MJW, van Lenteren, JC, Brodeur, J, Barratt, BIP, Bigler, F, Bolckmans, K, Cônsoli, FL, Haas, F, Mason, PG, Parra, JR (2010) "Do new access and benefit sharing procedures under the Convention on Biological Diversity threaten the future of Biological Control?", *Biocontrol* 55, pp. 199–218, doi:10.1007/s10526-009-9234-9.

Darling, J, Blum, MJ (2007) "DNA-based methods for monitoring invasive species: A review and prospectus", *Biological Invasions* 9, pp. 751–765, doi:10.1007/s10530-006-9079-4.

de Jonge, B (2011) "What is fair and equitable benefit-sharing", *Journal of Agricultural and Environmental Ethics* 24, pp. 127–146, doi:10.1007/s10806-010-9249-3.

Floyd, R, Lima, J, deWaard, J, Humble, L, Hanner, R (2010) "Common goals: Policy implications of DNA barcoding as a protocol for identification of arthropod pests", *Biological Invasions*, doi:10.1007/s10530-010-9709-8.

GBIF (2012) GBits Science No. 4 August-September 2012, www.gbif.org/page/2996.

Gideon, H, Nyinondi, P, Oyema, G (eds) (2012) *Checklist of Tanzanian species (version 1, 2012)*, Dar es Salaam, Tanzania: Tanzania Commission for Science and Technology.

Greiber, T, Feit, U (2011) "Access and benefit sharing in relation to marine genetic resources from areas beyond national jurisdiction – a possible way forward", *BfN Skript* 301; BfN, ISBN 978-3-89624-036-1, available online at www.bfn.de/0502_skriptliste.html.

Hanner, RH, Gregory, TR (2007) "Genomic diversity research and the role of biorepositories", *Cell Preservation Technology* 5(2), doi:10.1089/cpt.2007.9993.

Hope, J (2008) BioBazaar: *The open source revolution and biotechnology*, Cambridge, MA: Harvard University Press.

Kamau, EC, Winter, G (2009) "Streamlining access procedures and standards", in: Kamau, EC, Winter, G (eds) *Genetic resources, traditional knowledge and the law: Solutions for access and benefit sharing*, London: Earthscan, pp. 366–379.

Kvist, S, Oceguera-Figueroa, A, Siddall, ME, Erséus, C (2010) "Barcoding, types and the Hirudo files: Using information content to critically evaluate the identity of DNA barcodes", *Mitochondrial DNA* 21(6), pp. 198–205.

Miller, S (2007) "DNA barcoding and the renaissance of taxonomy", *Proceedings of the National Academy of Sciences* 104(12), pp. 4775–4776.

Moritz, T (2002) "Building the biodiversity commons", *D-Lib Magazine* 8(6).

Nilsson, RH, Ryberg, M, Kristiansson, E, Abarenkov, K, Larsson, K-H (2006) "Taxonomic reliability of DNA sequences in public sequence databases: A fungal perspective", *PLoS ONE* 1(1), e59, doi:10.1371/journal.pone.0000059.

Oldham, P (2009) "An access and benefit-sharing commons? The role of commons/open source licenses in the international regime on access to genetic resources and benefit sharing", UNEP/CBD/WG-ABS/8/INF/3, Available online at www.cbd.int.

Parry, B (2004) *Trading the genome: investigating the commodification of bio-information*, Columbia University Press.

Ratnasingham, S, Hebert, PDN (2007) "BOLD: The Barcode of Life Data System" *Molecular Ecology Notes* 7(3), pp. 355–364, doi:10.1111/j.1471–8286.2006.01678.x

Robertson, DR (2008) "Global biogeographical data bases on marine fishes: Caveat emptor", *Diversity and Distributions* 14, pp. 891–892.

Rojahn, J (2010) *Fair shares or biopiracy? Developing ethical criteria for the fair and equitable sharing of benefits from crop genetic resources*, PhD Dissertation (Tübingen, Germany: Eberhard Karls Universität Tübingen).

Steiner, A, Djoghlaf, A, Gabriel, S (2008a) "Reversing the loss of biodiversity", *Gulfnews* 23 May 2008, http://gulfnews.com/opinions/columnists/reversing-the-loss-of-biodiversity-1.106572.

Steiner, A, Djoghlaf, A, Gabriel, S (2008b) The last extinction? *Guardian*, 26 May 2008, www.guardian.co.uk/commentisfree/2008/may/26/thelastextinction.

Yesson, C, Brewer, PW, Sutton, T, Caithness, N, Pahwa, JS (2007) "How global is the Global Biodiversity Information Facility?", *PLoS ONE* 2(11), e1124, doi:10.1371/journal.pone.0001124.

17 Model agreements on ABS for non-commercial research and development

Evanson Chege Kamau

Background information

This chapter has its background in preceding research projects, consultancy work, and interviews conducted with various scientists[1] by the author together with Professor Gerd Winter. These activities were undertaken with the financial support of the German Research Foundation (DFG). Particularly inspiring were the findings of a project with the theme, "Law and Practice in Access to Genetic Resources and Benefit-Sharing with the Example of Kenya, Brazil and Germany," that was conducted between 2006 and 2009. The project aimed to analyze the legal frameworks and the actual practices in two exemplary provider countries, Kenya and Brazil – both of which are megadiverse – and one exemplary user country, Germany. Paying attention to specific aspects of ABS, namely, the proportion or extent of administrative impediments on research and development (R&D) activities, the possibility of securing benefits from utilized genetic resources, and the linking of access and compensation systems of resource states with the rules of user states, the goal was to develop suggestions for improvement of existing regimes.

The main findings[2] showed how complex it was to regulate access and benefit sharing (ABS) due to flaws in provider measures and lack of compliance measures in user countries. The relevant findings for this chapter are:

- Many provider measures pose overly bureaucratic hurdles which are designed to restrict commercial research but unintentionally impede basic research.
- Scarcely is any differentiation made in ABS legislation between access requirements for basic research and commercial research.
- Many provider measures use vague legal language.
- Many provider regimes suffer from legislative gaps and inconsistencies.
- Major gaps remain with respect to the interface between ABS legal frameworks and intellectual property rights.

---

1 Scientists participating in the interviews had projects in Bolivia, Central Africa, Kenya, Brazil, South Africa, Namibia, Indonesia, China, Peru, Chile, Argentina, Ecuador, Colombia, and Mexico. The projects were financed by German Research Foundation (DFG), German Academic Exchange Service (DAAD), and German Federal Ministry of Education and Research (BMBF).
2 All research findings of the project are published in book format in Kamau and Winter (2009).

- Prior consultation and capacity building are very decisive to a successful access process.
- Public law measures must be complemented by precise agreements in order to ensure fair and equitable benefit sharing.
- A claim for benefit sharing can be raised in a user country on the basis of a contract or tort.
- Most user countries have done little to implement the obligation in Art. 15.7 CBD.

Two solutions were proposed to counteract these shortcomings: a radical turn towards common pool solutions and improvement of the current bilateral exchange between providers and users through better agreements. The first option was explored in an extensive project on common pools of genetic resources and was concluded in 2013.[3] The second option involved the design of a model access agreement (MAA) mainly for scientists funded by the DFG, but easily usable by other scientists.[4] This chapter focuses on the latter idea.

The predicament of researchers and providers in ABS

Basic research

Importance of basic research

Basic research, which is non-commercial by nature, plays a critical role in conservation and sustainable use of biological diversity and the appreciation of the value of the diversity of genetic resources (Greiber et al. 2012, 17). Its activities in this regard are diverse, ranging from the collection of genetic resources to their identification, evaluation, characterisation, documentation, and storage in *ex situ* facilities (also Biber-Klemm, Davis, Gautier & Martinez 2014, 213) for different purposes, including scientific and educational (Biber-Klemm et al. 2014, 213). These activities are also crucial in saving vanishing diversity as well as restoring ecosystems that have been degraded as a result of *inter alia* human activity and climate change impacts[5] (see further Biber-Klemm et al., Ch. 14 in this volume).

Research helps to unveil alternatives and new sources to meet human needs and avoid reliance on a limited supply, which might, in turn, deplete species or exert undue pressure on ecosystems. It is said, for example, that although human beings rely on 150–200 plant species for food – with three of them contributing up to 60 percent of calories and proteins that humans obtain from plants – science has it that there are 10,000–12,000 known edible plant species (FAO, 2011). Nonetheless, research also shows that existing knowledge of biological diversity

---

3 The results were published in book format in Kamau and Winter (2013).
4 The MAA is currently under review to update it to new realities and the Nagoya Protocol.
5 E.g. the Royal Botanic Gardens Kew Millennium Seed Bank Project, see www.kew.org/science-conservation/save-seed-prosper/millennium-seed-bank/about-the-msb/index.htm (accessed 28 October 2014).

is still insignificant, bearing in mind all available biodiversity wealth (Shimmield 2013, 8; Pittaluga Niederauer and da Silva, Ch. 5 in this volume). Of the significant microorganism diversity of the world's oceans, for example, scientists have managed to thoroughly study only 2 percent (Shimmield 2013, 8). In making new discoveries of available *in situ* biodiversity wealth, scientific research tries to understand its sensitivity to human interference and develop procedures that can prevent damage. In expanding knowledge on biological diversity therefore, scientific research makes a substantial contribution in revealing the *existence*, the *use*, and the *nature* of such wealth. Such revelations and relevant technology and skills are often made freely as well as easily available and accessible to a wider group of researchers, which is a great benefit to society.

Challenges faced by researchers in ABS

The problem of ABS in relation to non-commercial biodiversity research and providers of biological/genetic resources[6] is centred on the dilemma between control over such resources and their accessibility (Biber-Klemm et al. 2014, 214). Unlike the period prior to 1992, when the Convention on Biological Diversity (CBD) was adopted, access to biological/genetic resources has been subjected to the authorization of states since its adoption, based on their sovereign rights over natural resources. Such authorization entails a variety of procedures, mainly the requirement of prior informed consent and the establishment of mutually agreed terms. Over the years following the adoption of the CBD, these conditions have applied equally for all forms of research based on biological diversity: pure scientific (academic, basic), applied, and commercial.[7]

The shift from formerly free to controlled access has seen research that relies on genetic resources and associated traditional knowledge (ATK) being subjected to extremely restrictive conditions. Due to past cases of misuse and misappropriation, the perception by providers that access results to huge benefits and the lack of compliance measures in user countries, most access and benefit-sharing requirements of provider countries are extensive and at times too prohibitive. As an obvious consequence, the access procedures are *inter alia* too bureaucratic and complex, long, not transparent, and expensive. Such challenges give rise to legal uncertainty and high transaction costs, among other setbacks (see e.g. Kamau & Winter 2009; Kamau 2009; Kamau 2014).

Substantive and administrative/procedural flaws of national ABS measures are regarded as readily hindering non-commercial research in particular (Greiber et al. 2012, 117; see Biber-Klemm et al., Ch. 14 and Fritze and Oumard, Ch. 15 in this volume). Some of the reasons supporting this argument are based on:

1   The conventional source of funds for basic research. Basic research essentially relies on public funds, which are usually inadequate and often hard to get

---

6   Some ABS regimes take a broad approach of regulating access to biological resources.

7   These are referred to in two groups in this chapter: non-commercial (academic, basic) and commercial (applied, commercial) biodiversity research. The focus though is on the former.

(Laird 2013), whereas most academic (student) research projects in some countries attract no funding (see Boga, Ch. 12 in this volume).

2   Research timelines. Basic research often works under strict timelines. The funds for research projects normally cover a fixed period of time within which the research must be carried out and concluded, including the publication of results. The danger presented by ABS measures comes *inter alia* with the delay in obtaining research and access and/or export permits in a timely manner, thus risking the loss of the funding opportunity or failing to complete the research on time.

3   Aim/purpose of basic research. Basic research does not aim at monetary gain and hence cannot bear high transaction costs. In extreme cases involving a heavy monetary burden for administrative costs and monetary benefit-sharing demands, the research might fail to take off, especially if alternative or cheaper sources of genetic resources are unavailable. In addition, as basic research aims to increase knowledge as well as seek (new) solutions to existing challenges, it strives to bring knowledge into the public domain so that it is accessible to and usable by anyone. Prohibition against publishing results as soon as the research is concluded thus exposes basic research to the risk of undesired prior entry of research results into the public domain – i.e. before they are published, or similar research results being published out of a different research project thus rendering the entire undertaking meaningless. An absolute prohibition on the other hand would totally deny the character, purpose, or essence of basic research (see also Fritze and Oumard, Ch. 15 in this volume).

Striving for facilitation

The concerns of the international research community *vis-à-vis* the abovementioned difficulties were among the discussion items in the negotiations leading to the adoption of the international regime of access and benefit sharing, the Nagoya Protocol. Concerned about restrictions that readily hinder non-commercial research (Greiber et al. 2012, 117), the international scientific community lobbied for facilitated access, i.e. a simpler and faster procedure initially referred to as "fast track" (Kamau Fedder & Winter 2010, 256).

Based on the work of a non-commercial research sector workshop in 2008 in Bonn, Germany,[8] a working group elaborated definitions characterizing commercial and non-commercial research (see Table 17.1). The results of the workshop were fed into the negotiations and were critical to the final achievements of the sector.[9]

8 See http://absbonn.pbworks.com/w/page/1259729/FrontPage (accessed 24 September 2014).
9 See CBD GTLE information document 1/INF/2, Concepts, Terms, Working Definitions and Sectoral Approaches Relating to the International Regime on Access and Benefit Sharing, UN Doc. UNEP/CBD/ABS/GTLE/1/INF/2 (2008) at 5 and CBD WG-ABS official document 7/2, Report of the Meeting of the Group of Legal and Technical Experts on Concepts, Terms, Working Definitions and Sectoral Approaches, UN Doc. UNEP/CBD/WG-ABS/7/2 (2008), Paragraphs 13 and 43–44.

Table 17.1 Characteristics differentiating commercial and non-commercial research

	Commercial research	*Non-commercial research*
Public availability	Often restricts access	Produces public domain results which are publicly available
Intentions	Generates market products	Purely non-commercial
Beneficiary	Primarily benefits users	Results benefit providers, conservation, ecosystem analysis, and characterization of organisms
Types of benefits	Generates long-term, monetary benefits	Generates near-term, non-monetary benefits

Source: Author, *based on UN Docs. UNEP/CBD/ABS/GTLE/1/INF/2 (2008) at 5 and UNEP/CBD/ WG-ABS/7/2 (2008), paras 13 and 43–44*

It has been argued that it would be hard to make a clear differentiation between the two types of research,[10] especially one that can assist in defining varying access procedures for non-commercial and commercial research purposes. The reasons quoted are as follows:

- Both the private sector and research institutions (for example universities) can be involved in commercial as well as non-commercial research.
- Similar research methods and processes are generally used in commercial as well as non-commercial research.
- Both types of research usually require access to the same biological materials and genetic resources.
- Both types of research can be beneficial for conservation and the sustainable use of biological diversity.
- Often research takes place under a public–private partnership.
- Often initial research for commercial purposes is conducted in public laboratories and institutions.

It is essential to concretely add that often research is a continuous process that transits from non-commercial to commercial dimensions,[11] a fact that is subsumed in some of the reasons mentioned above. All factors taken together, the differentiation suggested in Table 17.1 is still considered as not being able to draw a convincingly clear dividing line between the two types of research and such a task is thought of as still being almost unachievable. That, however, cannot be the end

10 Ibid. and UNEP, "Report of a Workshop on Access and Benefit-Sharing in Non-Commercial Biodiversity Research" (9 March 2009) UNEP/CBD/WG-ABS/7/INF/6, 5.

11 According to Winter (2013), for example, results of basic research especially in genomics and microbial research are suitable for patenting. See "Common pools of genetic resources and related traditional and modern knowledge. An overview" in: Kamau and Winter (eds), *Common pools of genetic resources. Equity and innovation in international biodiversity law*, London: Routledge 2013, 3–25, p. 22.

of the search of a better way for deciding the criteria upon which some types of research could be facilitated. This is especially true owing to the binding nature of the Nagoya Protocol, which foresees such an obligation under its Article 8.[12]

There could be different ways of defining when research shall be considered as non-commercial. Even the approach used in Table 17.1 seems to be a basis for a functional criterion of delimitation. It suggests that any research aiming to enrich the public domain is non-commercial, whereas if it aims at the privatization of material and knowledge then it is commercial (Kamau & Winter, 2013).[13] In other words, "basic" research whose substance is taxonomy can nevertheless be commercial, if the result (such as a gene) is patented (Kamau & Winter, 2013).[14] On the other hand, "applied" research whose substance is, for example, the development of a marketable product can be non-commercial if the result is made publicly available (Kamau & Winter, 2013).[15] But even with such a distinction, the complementary importance of a "come-back clause" in case of a change of intent is evidently colossal. The focus of this chapter does not permit us to further explore how such differentiation can best be done, but an in-depth discussion on this has been undertaken by von Kries and Winter in Chapter 3 of this volume.

Provider concerns

The concerns of the provider can be grouped under a number of issues which include R&D value chain, downstream tracking and monitoring, third-party transfer, change of intent, territoriality principle, execution of contractual rights, access to justice, and capacity to utilize public domain knowledge.

Value chain

The R&D chain is usually a long and elaborate process that can take many years due to *inter alia* the way the material changes hands, the related knowledge being shared and exchanged, and the complexity of technology used. After being taken from their *in situ* conditions, the collected sample of a genetic resource may become accessible to multiple users through transfer to third parties or exchange by scientists with peers or access from *ex situ* collections. Through the R&D process, it also continuously changes its nature partly because the process might involve combining a number of genetic resources of different origins and makeup. In addition, technology has made it possible to grow organisms in laboratory conditions, construct their genetic makeup through genomics, use sophisticated computer models to test biological models, drugs, and medical interventions (*in-silico* testing), etc. All this often takes place outside the territory where the

---

12 The Nagoya Protocol is an international binding legal instrument in force since the 12 October 2014.
13 For a detailed discussion see von Kries and Winter Chapter 3 in this volume.
14 See also ibid.
15 Ibid.

physical access to the sample took place, and it is therefore barely possible for the provider to establish what happens with the material and to follow up many years after it has left the country. This would only be possible through effective downstream tracking and monitoring and the development of provider technical skills and capacity. Better still would be the involvement of providers in R&D in a joint venture kind of relationship.

Downstream tracking and monitoring, third party transfer, change of intent

"Third party transfer" is used to describe the handing over or sharing of the material (received from the provider) by its contractual recipient to/with a noncontractual party whereas "change of intent" is normally used to describe a change of use from the agreed non-commercial to commercial use. Both occur in the downstream process of R&D and, therefore, can only be discerned through downstream tracking and monitoring. It thus makes more sense to group the three together.

Tracking and monitoring can be described as a mechanism of establishing and maintaining the link between access and utilization of a genetic resource as well as the conditions of access and adherence thereto, including outside the geographical or jurisdictional area of the physical access of the genetic resource. The two terms are closely related, but "tracking" has more to do with following the movement of genetic resources (and their derived products) along the R&D chain. Thus tracking may imply identifying what institutions are actually doing research on collected genetic resources while monitoring may imply verifying if research by those institutions is permitted in the light of obligations assumed in the original (or subsequent) ABS contracts and national laws under which R&D are undertaken in terms of the uses being made of these resources, the products made from them and the initial intent (Ruiz Muller & Lapeña 2007, 111). Hence both tracking and monitoring are supportive to compliance and enforcement as they help to establish violations and identify relevant actors.

The challenges related to downstream tracking and monitoring are manifold, *inter alia*:

- The process might entail unbearable costs for a provider.
- Possible lack of transparency by the user. Often providers depend on reporting by the user according to the intervals agreed upon and have no possibility of verifying the accuracy of such reports themselves.
- Most providers are unlikely to have the technical capacity and skills necessary to comprehend some of the processes in the R&D chain as well as establish their outcome. For example, it will be hard to determine whether the final product contains a proportion of the genetic resource accessed at all (Kamau 2014, 157) and, if it does, what the fair and equitable benefit from that proportion would be considering the costs of R&D or when the benefits to be shared would arise.
- A provider is unlikely to discern when a violation or abuse has taken place. Apart from the challenges discussed above, *viz.* lack of capacity and skills

and distant location of the R&D process, many times the recipient of the material is an individual researcher whose activities cannot be followed easily if the ABS agreement did not contain any details of a hosting institution. But even if a violation or abuse is established, the territoriality principle of international law (discussed below) will bar any action by the provider in a foreign jurisdiction.

Territoriality principle, execution of contractual rights

The territoriality (or territorial) principle of international law holds that States have jurisdiction over conduct that occurs within their territorial borders (Brownie 2003, 299ff.). Accordingly, this principle denies a provider country the right to exercise jurisdiction in a user country. Thus, the execution of the contractual rights of the provider as well as penalizing violation/abuse by the user can only be done by the courts of the user country.

Access to justice

The concept of access to justice is underpinned by several issues. Greiber et al. (2012, 187ff.) try to show how it should be understood in the ABS context by looking at its usage in a number of international instruments, *viz.* 1998 Aarhus Convention on Access to Information, Public Participation in Decision-Making and Access to Justice in Environmental Matters; 2002 New Delhi Declaration of Principles of International Law relating to Sustainable Development (adopted by the International Law Association); and 2010 Guidelines for the development of national legislation on access to information, public participation, and access to justice in environmental matters (adopted by the United Nations Environmental Programme (UNEP)). The underlying rights under the concept of access to justice, which the NP will hopefully achieve, can be summarized as follows:

- the right of access to a court of law or other independent and impartial body to challenge the substantive and procedural legality of any decision,
- the right of access to affordable or free legal procedures/non-prohibitive costs of litigation,
- the right of access to expeditious procedures,
- the right of review of decisions made without adequate public participation, and
- the right of nondiscriminatory access to judicial procedures as well as information on the court's decision for persons not domiciled in the jurisdiction of the court.

Capacity to utilize public domain knowledge

Whereas it is true that non-commercial research which aims at bringing research results into the public domain for use by anyone benefits society in general, many provider countries might not regard this as incentive enough to grant facilitation.

This is because most of them do not possess the capacity that would be necessary in order to make use of such public domain knowledge independently. Likewise, once the research results are in the public domain they can be utilized for commercial purposes without the provider reaping any benefit. For the provider, some of the vital incentives should include assistance in building capacity for utilization of such knowledge through involvement in research (and development) as well as in development of watertight contracts as a baseline for facilitation.

In spite of the right of the provider to couple the use of genetic resources and traditional knowledge with certain conditions, e.g. benefit sharing, all of the above-mentioned challenges can easily preempt that right. A thorough exploration of some of the potential tools of regulating ABS could make a big difference.

ABS agreements: A suitable solution?

We imagine that well-designed access and benefit-sharing agreements should provide fair equitable solutions to most of the challenges mentioned above. A fair solution would be one that takes care of both providers' and users' concerns. In the following, we look at the common elements of an ABS agreement, the concerns they aim to resolve, and points to consider while developing an ABS agreement. The focus is on non-commercial research.

What is an ABS agreement?

An access and benefit-sharing (ABS) agreement is a contract between the provider and recipient/user of genetic resources and/or associated traditional knowledge which defines and governs their rights and obligations, the terms and conditions mutually agreed by them on the use of the accessed material and/or knowledge, and the sharing of benefits. In ABS, such an agreement is commonly referred to as a material transfer agreement (MTA) and is binding upon execution/ signing by the parties. The question as to whether this makes them easily executable in practice/law is a different issue which this chapter does not deal with.[16]

There are different types of ABS agreements. The WIPO Intergovernmental Committee on Intellectual Property and Genetic Resources, Traditional Knowledge and Folklore document WIPO/GRTKF/IC/7/9 identifies five types of ABS agreements:[17] letters of intent or heads of agreement;[18] confidentiality or

---

16 On issues to take caution of while framing as well as entering into a contractual agreement on ABS in order to ease legal execution of rights/obligations in user countries' courts see Godt (2009) "Enforcement of benefit sharing duties in user countries' courts" in: Kamau and Winter (eds), and Hiroji Isozaki (2009) "Enforcement of ABS agreements in user States" in: Kamau and Winter (eds).

17 WIPO/GRTKF/IC/7/9 (30 July 2004), GENETIC RESOURCES: DRAFT INTELLECTUAL PROPERTY GUIDELINES FOR ACCESS AND EQUITABLE BENEFIT-SHARING, Available online at www.wipo.int/edocs/mdocs/tk/en/wipo_grtkf_ic_7/wipo_grtkf_ic_7_9.pdf (accessed 18 September 2014).

18 Recording preliminary agreement on the overall framework of a proposed collaboration, including any commercial arrangements that may apply, and ensuring that the future negotiations on the details of a contract or license have a solid basis of understanding.

nondisclosure agreements;[19] material transfer agreements;[20] licensing agreements;[21] and research agreements or research and development agreements.[22] In reality though, most ABS agreements combine the elements of the various types in one agreement, depending on the nature of the activity to be undertaken. This is obvious in most ABS model agreements that are available. The basic elements to be included in the agreement and the content will often be determined by varying factors, including applicable law, the genetic resources to be accessed, who the provider and the user of the genetic resources are, and the relationship they intend to enter into.[23]

Table 17.2 condenses the basic or common contents of the main body[24] of an ABS agreement, issues they aim to address and who between the provider and the user (recipient/researcher) receives the **greatest relief**. As already mentioned, the final contents of the particular agreement will depend on prevailing circumstances and hence must be viewed in the context of the individual case.

Points to consider when drafting an ABS agreement

Available ABS agreements vary in structure and in content. This might be influenced *inter alia* by the nature of the relationship between the parties, the purpose of the agreement, and the distinct characteristics of the sector aiming to undertake access. It is therefore the parties' business to decide what is important for them and what they wish to include in the agreement. Of course it pays to seek

19 Requiring the recipient of information to keep it confidential, such as information concerning source of genetic resources, associated TK, or know-how, which may be used in gaining access to genetic resources for evaluation purposes, in developing a research collaboration, or as a condition of employment; such agreements frequently limit the purposes for which such information can be used – depending on the circumstances, this may include limiting its use to evaluation, research, or non-commercial purposes or limiting it to certain agreed purposes.

20 Common tools in commercial and academic research partnerships involving the transfer of biological materials, such as germplasm, microorganisms, and cell cultures; these are used for exchange of materials in various contexts – exchanges between research institutions, setting conditions for access to public germplasm collections or seed banks, and access by a researcher to *in situ* genetic resources, where the agreement will be between the research institution and the access provider. In most MTAs, a provider agrees to give identified physical material to a recipient, and the recipient agrees to restrict the uses that may be made of that material, and often of any improvements or derivatives.

21 Agreements setting out certain permitted use of materials or rights that the provider is entitled to grant, such as agreements to license the use of genetic resources as research tools or to license the use of associated TK or other IP rights.

22 Agreements that define various inputs to research and development, including financial, material (including genetic resources), and intellectual contributions; specify various responsibilities in relation to the conduct of research and development of new products or processes; and set out how the monetary and non-monetary benefits from this research and development should be managed and shared.

23 See also SECO (Switzerland) (2007), ABS Management Tool. Best Practice Standard and Handbook for Implementing Genetic Resource Access and Benefit-sharing Activities. Available online at www.iisd.org/pdf/2007/abs_mt.pdf (accessed 18 September 2014).

24 Initial parts of an agreement *viz.* parties, preambles, definitions, and other recitals are not included.

Table 17.2 Basic contents of model ABS agreements, issues they aim to address and beneficiary

Provisions	Questions that provisions aim to address, i.a.	Concerns/issues addressed, i.a.	Relief mainly for: Provider (P) / User (U)
Definitions	- Understanding of what meaning parties give to terms	- Ambiguity - Uncertainty	P/U
Access & export of materials	- Which permits/consents are required - Who is responsible to obtain which permits/consents - Which genetic resources and passport data the recipient is permitted to access - Unforeseeable situations *vis-à-vis* access, e.g. need to access species not known at the time of signing of the contract - Depositing of samples - Where the material may be transferred - Storage of materials – how & where? - Collaboration with local institutions in the use of materials - Sharing of materials with peers - Administrative fee & other charges - Who bears the costs for access and transfer of specimens/samples	- Ambiguity - Uncertainty - (Non)transparency - Time loss - Transactional costs	P/U
Use of materials	- Allowed uses - Allowed research - Change of purpose/intent (non-commercial to commercial) - What happens to the specimens accessed after premature or final conclusion of research	- Ambiguity - Uncertainty - (Non)transparency - Time loss	P
Third-party transfer	- Whether recipient is allowed to transfer materials to third parties - Under what conditions may materials be transferred to third parties - To whom is the recipient permitted to transfer the materials - For what purposes is the recipient permitted to transfer the materials to third parties	- Ambiguity - Uncertainty - (Non)transparency - Downstream monitoring/tracking	P

Reporting & sharing of information	- Records to be maintained - How often (written) reports have to be made or submitted to the provider - Content of the report - Provision of progress results of research to provider - Assistance to provider in assessment and/or interpretation of data & samples - Diligence in dealing with advance research results - Duration within which the final results should be sent to the provider after the conclusion of research - Copies of final results of research to be furnished by researcher to provider - The format in which the provider should receive the research results - Guard against premature disclosure of final research results	- Ambiguity - Uncertainty - (Non)transparency - Downstream monitoring/tracking - Capacity of provider to use research results - Benefit-sharing	P
Publications	- Co-authorship - Acknowledgement of provider, local scientists - Swift publication of results - Where the researcher may publish the results of research - Copies of publication to be given to the provider by researcher - Format of publications to be given to the provider by researcher	- Uncertainty - (Non)transparency - Downstream monitoring/tracking - Equity	P/U
Dissemination of knowledge	- Fate of public domain knowledge - Management of data - Responsibility/liability of recipient - Responsibility of databases - Limit of provider's rights	- Uncertainty - (Non)transparency - Ambiguity - Downstream monitoring/tracking - Equity	P
Sharing of benefits	- Types of (non-monetary or monetary) benefits to be shared, including co-authorship of results	- Ambiguity - Uncertainty - Equity	P

(Continued)

Table 17.2 (Continued)

Provisions	Questions that provisions aim to address, i.a.	Concerns/issues addressed, i.a.	Relief mainly for: Provider (P) / User (U)
Conservation & sustainable use of biodiversity	- Prior & regular environmental impact assessment - Consequences of anticipated or established damage to environment, e.g. discontinuation of collection & removal - Measures to be undertaken in case of damage to environment, e.g. remedy & mitigation - Who bears the costs for such measures	- Environmental - Sharing the burden of conservation & sustainable use of biodiversity - Equity	P/U
Confidentiality	- Restriction of access to materials, results & reports - Reciprocal confidentiality of confidential information, including results prior to publication - Non-violation of confidentiality clause in specific circumstances - Duration of confidentiality requirements	- Uncertainty - Downstream monitoring/tracking	P/U
Liability & indemnity	- Reciprocal indemnification of parties	- Uncertainty	P/U
Termination of agreement	- Who may terminate the agreement - When, why & how the agreement may be terminated - Rights & obligations surviving expiration or termination of agreement - Fate of recipient's rights upon termination of the agreement, e.g. non-assignment of such rights to any person	- Ambiguity - Uncertainty - (Non)transparency	P/U
Dispute resolution	- Procedure of initiation of dispute resolution - Dispute resolution mechanisms - Effect of decisions, e.g. reached through arbitration	- Ambiguity - Uncertainty	P/U
General provisions	- Duration of agreement - Renewal of agreement - Serving of notices - Effect of unenforceability of some provisions or parts thereof on the agreement - Effect of unforeseeable circumstances or events/force majeure - Matters not stipulated in the agreement or regarding its interpretation or execution - Applicable law	- Ambiguity - Uncertainty - (Non)transparency	P/U

the advice and assistance of an expert, especially a competent contract lawyer with good knowledge of underlying ABS issues.

Table 17.2 gives an outline of some of the questions and concerns (columns 2 and 3) that the provisions of the main body of an ABS agreement (column 1) aim to address. This section does not aim to reproduce them but to point at issues that parties ought to give serious thought to when contemplating or including the relevant provisions or entering into an agreement. The considerations proposed will attempt to reflect the ABS concerns mentioned above as well as offer balanced recommendations as far as possible, taking into account the provider and user perspectives. The proposed issues to consider or proposed contents of provisions **must not form individual clauses**; where possible and if dealing with the same issue several clauses could be combined into one clause.

The discussion follows the common full-fledged structure of an ABS contract containing nonsubstantive (sections A, B, C, D, F, and G) as well as substantive provisions (section E). Often references of the Micro B3 model agreement found in Chapter 20 of this book will be used for illustration and will be highlighted in bold for easy identification. We advise readers to refer to the agreement for overview and legal background of corresponding articles and to keep Table 17.2 of this chapter in mind while reading sections D and E. The Micro B3 agreement may also be referred to for possible clauses but we would like to point to the fact that **not all of them may apply to generic situations** because they are tailored to the Micro B3 project. The Micro B3 agreement nonetheless tries as much as possible to produce a template also for situations that are beyond the Micro B3 project. The structure of the Micro B3 agreement (hereinafter MicroB3 MA) slightly differs from the one used here, but the two can be considered as being concomitant.

A. Title

The title is intended to provide a summary description of the purpose and/or scope of the agreement. Like other descriptive components, e.g. the preamble, the title will seldom affect the operative provisions except where the operative provisions are unclear or ambiguous and the title provides a clear statement of the intended context or meaning.

B. Parties

This section contains the names and contacts of the parties to the agreement. In many ABS agreements and in the following, the parties are referred to as "provider" and "recipient." Each party needs to establish the status of the other party for different reasons, *inter alia*:

- The user has to be sure that the provider's representative or the representative of an indigenous and local community – if the community has established rights to grant access to genetic resources or if access involves ATK – is the legally mandated entity in order to avoid future snags in the R&D process, including accusations of biopiracy or failure to proceed with R&D due to a declaration of noncompliance with the ABS domestic legislation or regulatory requirements of the provider by the user institutions in accordance with Articles 15 and 16 of the Nagoya Protocol.

• The provider has to be sure that the recipient is attached to an institution in the user country and as far as possible demand that the latter only enters into the agreement as a representative of the institution and not in an individual capacity. The provider has no chances of tracing the whereabouts of an individual once he/she leaves the provider country. It is recommended that the recipient shall present proof from the institution hosting the research confirming that the recipient is attached to that institution, that the research shall take place in that institution, and that the institution bears the responsibilities and liabilities foreseen in the agreement.

C. Preamble

A preamble (at times referred to as recitals) can be described as a statement of facts or assumptions upon which a *contract* is based. It introduces what the parties have agreed to in the substantive part of the agreement. It puts the agreement into context. It describes the goals of the agreement. On the other hand, it does not contain any promises. It does not contain any restrictions or commitments and possesses no independent vitality as a source of rights or obligations and that is perhaps the reason it has been called "a pious hope clause."[25] It could be removed entirely without disrupting the specific terms of the agreement. However, the preamble can be a very useful tool of construing and interpreting ambiguous language of the substantive provisions of the agreement.

A preamble forms an integral part of the contract if included; it is not mandatory though to include one in every agreement. The approach of the parties to this effect may be determined by the parties' decision or influenced by the importance given to preambles by the relevant jurisprudence. In many jurisdictions, preambles are no longer used in statutes, especially because they can inadvertently influence the subsequent interpretation of the statute, whereas some jurisdictions give special significance to them (see Winter, Ch. 19 in this volume). Indeed, certain judgments attribute considerable importance to the interpretive assistance that the preamble can render in litigation.[26]

---

25 *Sherbrooke Community Centre v. Service Employees International Union*, 2002 SKQB 101 (CanLII) [[2002] 7 WWR 145; 216 Sask R 169]. Available at http://canlii.ca/t/5j2p (accessed 1 October 2014).

26 See for instance *Allen v. Renfrew (Corp. of the County)*, 2004 CanLII 13978 (ON SC) [69 OR (3d) 742; [2004] OJ No 1231 (QL); 117 CRR (2d) 280]. Available online at http://canlii.ca/t/1gsbr (accessed 1 October 2014).

The following are some of the issues the parties should consider in regard to the preamble:

- The meaning given to preambles in the jurisdiction of the parties, especially of the state where the contract will be executed.
- Avoid (extreme) ambiguity which could complicate the interpretation of the substantive provisions of the contract.
- Reflect on the language and aim of the substantive provisions of the contract while choosing the language of the preamble.
- Consider whether it is necessary or not to include a preamble.
- If included, the preamble should avoid general statements but rather concretely formulate the underlying concerns and motivations, identify the issues addressed in and the actual need for an agreement, as well as explain the reasons for its main provisions.

D. Definitions

Definitions are provisions explaining the meaning of specific terms used in the agreement. They help to provide clarity and legal certainty on the meaning attributed to such terms which may differ from those in ordinary, scientific, or technical use. They also facilitate the drafting of substantive provisions of the agreement. Legal definitions are specific to a particular legal text and are intended solely to facilitate the interpretation of the terms used in the given agreement (Greiber et al. 2012, 62).

Parties are normally at liberty to give or attach a meaning to a term different or slightly deviating from that given to similar terms in other agreements. They may even replace or customize terms with long-established meaning and usage according to their needs and/or planned research activities, as well as choose between a narrow(er) or broad(er) interpretation (see also Biber-Klemm, Martinez, Jacob & Jevtic 2010, 11). In an area such as ABS, which involves interaction of varying regulators and researchers and which also has a system that operates at a global level, e.g. the Clearing-House Mechanism of the CBD, giving new meanings to terms that have found consent internationally can be counterproductive causing instead ambiguity and uncertainty. Except for terms that have not been defined yet, or which are activity specific (e.g. **"Ocean Sampling Days"** in the Micro B3 model agreement), we advise that agreements adopt the terminology of the relevant international instruments, e.g. the Convention on Biological Diversity, the Nagoya Protocol, the International Treaty on Plant Genetic Resources for Food and Agriculture, and World Intellectual Property Organization, and their usage.

The main terms used in ABS and their definitions have been listed in Winter, Chapter 19 in this volume. Winter also proposes more clarification and concretization to some of the terms already defined, as well as new definitions for vital undefined terms. Von Kries et al. (Ch. 20 in this volume) likewise expound on the term "utilization," specifying what utilization for proprietary or public domain purposes shall denote. These definitions will not be reproduced in this chapter, so reference should be made to Chapters 19 and 20.

E. Terms and conditions

I. Access and export of materials

The preconditions for lawful (physical) access/collection and transfer of genetic material by a potential user are spelled out here. Usually, they are the obtainment of the relevant consents (commonly referred to as prior informed consent, abbreviated PIC) and permits, but depending on the law and practice of the provider country, more authorizations might be required additionally. Also, the genetic materials for which access is permitted are listed, but often as an annex to the agreement. Likewise, it is determined where the user is allowed to use the material or to undertake R&D, with whom the material as well as research information related thereto can be shared or exchanged, and whether or not a specimen should be deposited with a local institution. Accruing costs and to whom they accrue and in which amounts are also determined.

According to prevailing practices of provider countries, ABS procedures vary considerably. Therefore, it is absolutely important that the person interested in accessing genetic material familiarizes him- or herself in advance with the access requirements of the individual provider. Below are some of the things to pay attention to (it is helpful to concretize such details as much as possible in the agreement):

- How many consents are necessary for a single access and who between the provider and the recipient or a local partner obtains which consents.
- Whether a single permit suffices for both access and export or separate permits are required and if these are issued by the same or separate authorities/institutions.
- The provider will often require the applicant to give a precise description of the specimens to be accessed and utilized and amounts *ex ante*. As this might not always be possible, it is advisable for the applicant to seek for the inclusion of a clause allowing for *ex post* submission of such information. The reasonable timeline to do that should be mutually agreed with the provider (see **MicroB3 MA, Art. 3.2**).
- Research work often involves collaboration between work groups or peers. This inevitably demands exchange of specimens and relevant information. In such circumstances, it is crucial that a clause is inserted indicating with whom the recipient is permitted to share or exchange the material and related information and to which or in which facilities such material can be transferred or shall be used, respectively (see **MicroB3 MA, Art. 3.3**).
- If such exchange and transfer is acceptable, then the issue of collaborators could be solved based on the following classification:

    - Collaborators who are parties to a collaboration agreement and therefore have a special status *vis-à-vis* the ABS agreement as *quasi* parties. Such parties may be excluded from the category of third parties by insertion of a clause in this regard that likewise declares them bound by the contractual obligations (see **MicroB3 MA, Art. 3 f) and i)**).

- Collaborators who qualify as third parties. This category of collaborators is discussed under section III below.

- Consider whether an environmental impact assessment study for the foreseen research is necessary.
- Ensure that an agreement is reached in advance as to who bears the costs for access and transfer of the material, or how they are shared.
- Geographical areas from where collection is allowed.

II. Use of materials

Provisions on use define the uses that the recipient is allowed to make of the material and the form of research permitted on it. They also aim to counter any breach of the terms and conditions of use by disallowing a change of research that was initially declared as non-commercial to commercial (usually referred to as "change of intent") without the prior consent of the provider. In addition, whichever the form of research, they forbid the use of the material for environmentally unsustainable or any other illegal or unethical way. Likewise, they address the aftermath of either the completion of the allowed research or its discontinuation *vis-à-vis* the material.

There are some considerations here that are important, *inter alia*:

- The parties should decide whether to include a "come-back" clause obliging the recipient to seek new consent from the provider and to renegotiate the terms of the agreement prior to using any material that was meant to be used in non-commercial research for commercial purposes. It is upon the parties to agree whether the come-back clause will take effect once a commercial potential is detected or when the recipient changes the intent. It is advised that the latter option is used (see e.g. **MicroB3 MA, Art. 4.4**) unless the recipient's intent changes midway, because fresh negotiations during research can interfere with its progress or even stop it depending on the provider's demands. Such a clause could protect the provider from violation by the user and loss of likely benefits. It could also protect the user from any accusations by the provider if a commercial potential is discovered.
- A recipient of material for non-commercial research should decide early whether commercial research would be a possible way to go if a commercial potential is anticipated in the process of researching (see **MicroB3 MA, Art. 4.3, 4.4**). If that is indicated from the onset and put down in the agreement, it may ease things when new terms are later renegotiated and also help to create transparency as well as build trust.
- If the provider also wishes to utilize the results of hitherto non-commercial research and any information thereto for proprietary purposes after the

conclusion or advance discontinuation of the research, a clause should be inserted to this effect obliging the provider to renegotiate with the recipient for adaptation or termination of the agreement (see **MicroB3 MA, Art. 4.5**).

- Parties should decide forthwith what should happen to the material after the conclusion or discontinuation of research, e.g. if it should be destroyed, sent back to the provider, or donated for further research.

III. Third-party transfer

In this section, it is determined whether the recipient is allowed or not to transfer the material, its derivatives, or information related thereto to third parties. If this is permitted, the terms and conditions of such transfer are spelled out here:

- Third parties can be grouped into two: peers or any other researcher interested in the material and/or information thereto. Consequently, the provisions here can be tailored according to applicable circumstances.
- As noted earlier, researchers often collaborate widely and may even have groups or specific individuals with whom they share equipment, materials, and related information. For this group, a clause may be included allowing for sharing, exchange, and transfer.
- It is advisable that peers and their affiliations are listed in the agreement (or permit).
- However, the provider should also be protected by a viral clause obliging the recipient to ensure that such collaborators are bound by the same contractual terms and conditions (see **MicroB3 MA, Art. 5**; Winter, Ch. 19 in this volume).
- If the recipient cannot ensure nonviolation by peers by viral clause either due to prevailing circumstances or their unwillingness to adopt the relevant obligations, then the prior informed consent of the provider should be sought before any transfer takes place.[27] The provider should be free to decide whether the terms would need renegotiation.
- In regard to other third parties, a "come-back" clause should be included to oblige the recipient to seek the provider's consent prior to any unregulated exchange or transfer and to renegotiate the terms and conditions of the initial agreement.[28]
- It should be decided whether third-party transfer would permit uses that are not agreed upon in the initial agreement.

27 See also the practice of some *ex situ* collections of plants (IPEN, Kew Gardens) in Biber-Klemm et al., Ch. 14 in this volume, and *ex situ* collections of microbes (DSMZ, ECCO) in Fritze and Oumard, Ch. 15 in this volume.
28 It would be unrealistic to expect the recipient to monitor and track the downstream movement of the material from a transaction costs and logistics point of view.

IV. *Reporting and sharing of information*

This section determines which records should be kept, how research progress should be documented, and which reports should thereto be shared with the provider. Both providers and users would have concerns concerning how reporting and sharing of information is handled.

- The provider may be uncertain concerning a possible change of intent, use of material for disallowed uses, third-party transfer, use of public domain results for commercial purposes, loss of control, or loss of benefits. To the provider, provisions under this section are hence an important tool for downstream monitoring and tracking, ensuring transparency, etc.
- To protect the provider some clauses may be included to oblige the recipient to

  - Report at intervals agreed upon by the parties.
  - Report on the handling, storage, and physical movement of the material and related passport data.
  - Report on the parties with whom the material and passport data are shared/exchanged.
  - Report on the progress of the approved research; where ATK is involved, this may include reporting on any steps towards obtaining intellectual property protection, product marketing, etc. (see **MicroB3 MA, Art. 8.3**).
  - Report on any anticipated activities in the ensuing phase until the next reporting.
  - Furnish the provider with the final results of the research.
  - Assist the provider in assessing and interpreting the results (see **MicroB3 MA, Art. 9.1**).

- The user's concerns are normally centred on the risk of premature disclosure of research information, the extreme monitoring and tracking burden during the research and after its conclusion, and the publication of the final research results. To the provider, provisions under this section are hence an important tool for ensuring legal certainty and moderate transaction costs, *inter alia*.
- To protect the user some clauses may be included to oblige the provider

  - To keep all preliminary results and any confidential information secret until the completion of the project and the publication of the final results.
  - To limit reporting to reasonable and manageable intervals.
  - To limit reports to reasonable and manageable content.

- It is also important for parties to agree

  - How the reports shall be submitted. The process of sending the reports can present some disclosure risks and can also be costly, so the procedure

284 Evanson Chege Kamau

has to be well thought out. If the foreign recipient has a local collaborating partner, it could be agreed that the local partner will take the
responsibility of reporting. Also the use of electronic submission procedure with protective functions instead of hard copies could be an
option.

- How the final results shall be submitted. Again, the options chosen for
  report submission could be used.

V. Publications

The provisions on publication regulate *inter alia* the manner in which the results
of research are disseminated following the conclusion of the project and the right
of the provider *vis-à-vis* the publication.

- The provider may want to

  - Ensure that future users of the material or information thereto are aware
    of its origin.
  - Share in the ownership of the results.
  - Use the results for proprietary purposes.
  - Benefit from further use of the material or information thereto.

- To address the provider's wishes some clauses may be inserted

  - Requiring the recipient to indicate the origin of the genetic resources
    and/or ATK and to acknowledge the provider in the publication (see
    MicroB3 MA, Art. 7.1).
  - Requiring the recipient to acknowledge the role of local scientists or
    to co-author the publication with them (see **MicroB3 MA, Art. 7.2**).
  - Requiring the recipient to include a statement in the publication asking
    further users of the results to acknowledge the provider and to seek the
    provider's consent for proprietary use (see **MicroB3 MA, Art. 6.3**).
  - Requiring the recipient to furnish the provider with a copy or copies
    of the publication (see **MicroB3 MA, Art. 9.4**).
  - To buy some time to enable the provider to explore the possibility of
    protecting commercially viable information.
  - Obliging the recipient to maintain secrecy after the expiry of the agree-
    ment for any confidential information.

- The recipient may want to

  - Prevent the provider from hindering the publication of results or pub-
    lishing and disseminating with an outlet of own choice.
  - Prevent the possibility of similar results (from unrelated project(s))
    being published before his/her own.
  - Prevent undesired disclosure of the results prior to publication.
  - Prevent co-authorship with local scientists if their contribution in the
    research was not considerable.

- Avoid excessive monitoring and tracking burden.
- Contain transaction costs.

- To address the recipient's concerns some clauses may be inserted

  - Declaring forthwith that the research results will be placed in the public domain following the conclusion of the project (see **MicroB3 MA, Art. 6.2**).
  - Setting the maximum duration between the conclusion of the project and the publication of results and their dissemination.
  - Obliging the provider to maintain secrecy until the results have been published.
  - Conditioning acknowledgement of local scientists to reasonable contribution in the research.
  - Conditioning co-authorship of local scientists to substantive contribution of local scientists in the research.
  - Determining the end of the recipient's responsibility *vis-à-vis* further use of published research results.
  - Obliging the provider to maintain secrecy after the expiry of the agreement for any confidential information.
  - Determining the format of furnishing results/publication and, if in hard copy, the number of copies.

VI. *Dissemination of knowledge*

This section aims to regulate how knowledge placed in databases after the conclusion of research should be managed and how access should be regulated. Mainly addressed here are two issues: 1) the concern of the provider that after facilitating access for non-commercial purposes, results with a commercial potential can be used commercially and proprietary rights established over knowledge without any gain accruing to the provider, and 2) the concern of the provider that for allowed commercial use, the ability of the provider to track and monitor the downstream R&D activities is as good as nonexistent. So the provider's wish would be to allot some responsibility, and maybe to a certain extent liability, to the recipient, as well as have the recipient pass on some responsibilities to databases, in regard to tracking of such knowledge down the value chain. The consequent challenge of such an approach is the colossal burden it would exert on the recipient and databases in terms of transaction costs, logistics, etc. Indeed, such a burden would be unbearable to most researchers, collections (see also Biber-Klemm et al., Ch. 14 in this volume), and databases. As von Kries et al. (Ch. 20 in this volume) note, as a practice, databases usually ask users to agree with a disclaimer which frees them (databases) from any liability *vis-à-vis* the right holder.[29]

---

29 Like von Kries et al. (Ch. 20 in this volume), we are of the opinion that such disclaimers need to be reconsidered in relation to the rights of the provider, albeit this will require more discussion and a longer learning process that cannot be predetermined by strict clauses currently.

So to what extent can the provider oblige the recipient? We think that the only reasonable clauses would be

- if no commercial research is allowed, one that requires the recipient to place a condition when depositing information in the database requiring the database to pass on the requirement of seeking the provider's consent to the user prior to using such information for proprietary purposes (see e.g. **MicroB3 MA, Art. 6.3**), and
- if commercial research is allowed, one that obliges the recipient to make reasonable efforts to ensure that benefits arising from utilization are shared with the provider, including by requiring that the database pass on such obligation to users/subsequent recipients.

VII. Sharing of benefits

This section determines *inter alia* the forms of benefits that shall be shared and when they shall be shared or what shall trigger their sharing. The resulting provisions and agreed benefits may be influenced by the parties' interests or their intentions. Therefore, the parties should consider

- Whether the provider is interested in building own capacity and acquiring own skills.
- Whether a joint venture kind of relationship is possible (see **MicroB3 MA, Art. 10**).
- Whether the recipient is certain that the intent to restrict the research to non-commercial research will not change.
- Whether the anticipated results can have a commercial potential.
- Whether the recipient would be willing to give input in areas which are either not directly related to the approved research or not at all related.

Depending on these and other considerations, the spectrum of possible benefits can stretch from such non-monetary benefits as expert capacity building, technology transfer, collaboration in research, co-authorship of results, and research funding for local scientists or institutions, education, and training in local institutions of learning to monetary benefits (including intellectual property). The choice of benefits can be made from the list of the Bonn Guidelines which is annexed to the Nagoya Protocol. The list is, however, not exhaustive and parties can think of other possible benefits.

A clause we recommend for inclusion – and the only one proposed because we consider its function to be closely related to other provisions, e.g. on use – is one that will either oblige the recipient to share monetary and/or intellectual property benefits if the intent changes, or a come-back clause requiring the terms for benefit sharing to be renegotiated once the intent changes from non-commercial to commercial or once monetary benefits arise (see **MicroB3 MA, Art. 11**).

VIII. *Conservation & sustainable use of biodiversity*

In this section, it is determined *inter alia* which responsibilities the parties bear *vis-à-vis* the environment prior to, during, and after the physical access. The provisions here usually aim to

- Hinder detrimental environmental consequences of access.
- Lay down the consequences of undue behaviour.
- Share the burden of conservation.
- Encourage sustainability.
- Determine who bears the costs for remedy and mitigation.

Clauses could be inserted to

- Oblige the recipient to undertake environmental impact assessment at agreed intervals.
- Oblige the recipient to observe the principles of international environmental law.
- Oblige the recipient to undertake measures to mitigate negative environmental effects.
- Require the recipient to cease collecting and removing specimens if any detrimental effect is detected after access has begun.
- Oblige the recipient to undertake measures to restore the ecosystem to its initial status.
- Oblige the recipient to bear the costs for remedial activities for damages caused to the environment.
- Require the recipient to assist the provider in applying the results of approved research for conservation activities in ecosystems whence the recipient undertook access.

IX. *Confidentiality*

Provisions in this section aim to mollify the risk of disclosure of confidential information by either party, including information not related to the approved research and/or accessed material without the prior (written) consent of the other party, and to regulate the duration of such confidentiality. Clauses may be inserted to

- Forbid the disclosure of unpublished research results to third parties.
- Forbid the disclosure of confidential information owned by either party to third parties. The provider may even forbid disclosure of confidential information to the recipient's peers if such information is sensitive, especially if it is not related and has no impact to the approved research.
- Indemnify either party for disclosure of information regarded as confidential if the law requires that such information be disclosed.
- Fix the date when the obligation for confidentiality shall expire.

- Regulate whether some of the obligations for confidentiality will survive the expiration of the agreement.

X. *Liability & indemnity*

Here the parties insert provisions to *inter alia* define their onus for breach of their obligations under the agreement and to protect one another from responsibility from any acts of the other party resulting in damage, loss, injury, etc. Clauses may be inserted to

- Indemnify the provider against any liability and damage, loss, or injury arising out of the recipient's taking, using, and/or disposing of the materials.
- Indemnify the provider for blame resulting from the recipient's unauthorized use of the material, e.g. unethical use.
- Indemnify the recipient for any loss that occurs as a result of the provider's acts or omission.
- Define concrete penalties, including monetary, for breach.
- Define how colossal the benefit to be shared by the recipient would be if research that was initially approved as non-commercial is commercialized without the prior informed consent of the provider (see **MicroB3 MA, Art. 11.5**).

XI. *Termination of agreement*

Termination provisions define how the contract may come to an end: by either expiring naturally or through premature termination by either party. They also determine what happens to the parties' rights. Clauses may be inserted to

- Determine the right of parties to terminate the agreement (see **MicroB3 MA, Art. 16.1**).
- Fix the date of expiration of the agreement or the duration after which it expires.
- Determine events and circumstances the occurrence of which the agreement shall terminate (see **MicroB3 MA, Art. 16.2**).
- Determine the procedure for terminating the agreement (see **MicroB3 MA, Art. 16.3**).
- Determine the rights surviving termination and their fate.
- Determine any obligations that may survive termination, e.g. the obligation of the recipient not to assign any rights under the agreement to any person upon the termination of the agreement (see **MicroB3 MA, Art. 16.4**).

XII. *Dispute resolution*

This section establishes the manner by which disputes between the parties shall be settled and the mechanisms that shall be applied. Clauses may be inserted to establish

- The right of parties to seek dispute resolution upon the impression that the other party is in breach of the agreement (see **MicroB3 MA, Art. 15.2**).
- The procedure of instituting dispute resolution, e.g. through issue of notices (see **MicroB3 MA, Art. 15.2**).
- The procedure of issuing notices.
- The mechanisms of dispute resolution, e.g. negotiation in good faith, independent and impartial third-party mediation, or arbitration (see **MicroB3 MA, Art. 15.3**).
- How mediators and arbitrators shall be selected, e.g. by mutual agreement between the parties.
- The procedure of choice and change of dispute resolution mechanisms, e.g. starting with the least judicially binding in hierarchy and less costly and only changing to the next if it fails.
- The right of the mediator or the arbitrator to independently determine the procedure of mediation or arbitration, respectively.
- The finality and binding character of the mediator's or arbitrator's decision.

XIII. General provisions

This section is often used for *varia* and at times even *trivia*, or a mishmash of the two. These are general issues that do not fall under any of the other sections and which are either auxiliary information or inconsequential oddities. The clauses may be inserted to

- Regulate how long the agreement will last if that is not determined under termination provisions (see **MicroB3 MA, Art. 13**).
- Establish whether the agreement is renewable. If yes, whether the renewal shall take place automatically or by an agreement of the parties.
- Establish whether the renewal, if this applies, shall be for the same duration as the initial one.
- Determine the procedure for terminating, renewing, or amending the agreement, e.g. through a written statement signed by both parties.
- Determine the procedures and format of serving all manner of notices.
- Determine what happens if some provisions or parts thereof are unenforceable or become invalid, e.g. whether they shall be modified or expunged.
- Establish the fate of the rest of the agreement upon modification or expunction of some provisions or parts thereof, e.g. declare that the enforceability and validity of the rest of the agreement shall not be affected.
- Determine whether the agreement constitutes the entire rights and obligations of the parties or whether additional rights and obligations shall be derived from other agreements and/or laws and if yes, which ones (see **MicroB3 MA, Art. 12**).
- Determine how the parties shall deal with any matters and/or clarifications that have not been agreed upon in the agreement regarding its interpretation and execution, e.g. in good faith.

- Establish the consequences of unforeseeable circumstances, e.g. *force majeure*, on the agreement and the rights and obligations of parties, e.g. whether the rights and obligations of the parties shall be postponed pending the cessation of such circumstances, whether the agreement shall resume its full force upon their cessation, whether the parties shall be held liable for damages, loss, or injury that occurs during the duration of such circumstances, etc.
- Establish the moment the agreement will enter into force upon its execution by the parties (see "signatures" below).
- Determine the state law and regulations in accordance with which the agreement shall be construed and governed (see **MicroB3 MA, Art. 14.1**).
- Determine the court jurisdiction subject to which disputes shall be settled (see **MicroB3 MA, Art. 14.2**).

F. Signatures

This section contains the names and signatures of the parties to the agreement – and by choice their witnesses – and the date of its signing. The act of appending signatures on the agreement constitutes the evidence that the parties have agreed to bind themselves by the terms of the agreement and that the agreement is therewith executed.

G. Annex/Appendix

The Annex contains documents or lists related to the agreement. The parties can append e.g. the list of species and samples allowed for access/collection and copies of relevant laws and regulations.

How a model ABS agreement can be used

A model access agreement (MAA) can be used as a *vade mecum*, a blueprint, or a fallback text.

Vade mecum

Due to its cross-cutting nature, the complexity of the legal character of the elements it regulates, and the *quasi* partial development of the legal structures necessary to form a comprehensive regulatory system, ABS is an arduous subject. There is a plethora of legal texts and literature explaining how ABS functions. National ABS laws vary in their substantive and procedural character. In addition, funding organizations have ABS guidelines[30] which researchers have to abide by in order

---

30 E.g. DFG guidelines: Research Funding Regulations of the German Research Foundation within the scope of the CBD, www.abs.bfn.de/fileadmin/ABS/documents/guidelines.pdf; Swiss Academy of Sciences: Access and benefit sharing. Good practice for academic research on genetic resources, http://abs.scnat.ch/; Common policy guidelines for (participating) botanic gardens, Cartagena, November 2000, http://bogard.isu.ru/cbd/cpg99_e.htm.

to secure funding. Understanding all these materials and laws and the complexity of the subject matter they deal with is taxing even for a lawyer; for a scientist/ researcher it is an overwhelming task. A well-developed MAA especially with annotations, e.g. the Micro B3 (see Ch. 20 of this volume) and the Swiss Academy of Sciences model agreements, can act as a *vade mecum* or kind of pocket reference containing the most vital information for an ABS procedure. This can help to raise legal certainty because it would

- Simplify observation by the researcher of often complex ABS requirements.
- Give guidance where no national tools are available.
- Give guidance where the law and institutions of a provider state are under-developed and the right procedure is obscure.
- Offer bargaining support where the law of the provider state is overambitious and elaborate and thus likely to catapult transaction costs.
- Give orientation where the model agreement of the provider focus on commercial activities and is not applicable to or easily convertible for non-commercial research.
- Offer legal security where sudden changes in law that retroactively affect existing research activities are likely to occur.

Blueprint

A model access agreement can also be used as a blueprint or a basis upon which an agreement presented by the provider for signature can be assessed. It would help the researcher to compare the terms of the provider's agreement before making a decision whether to sign it, negotiate certain terms, or come to a new agreement.

Fallback text

A model access agreement can be used in case of inertia. A state of inertia can either be a result of the researcher's impossibility or inability to negotiate a specific agreement on his/her own terms or if the process of negotiation seems to have hit a snag. In such circumstances, the researcher can present the MAA as a possible text for the agreement – with the possibility of fine-tuning it to the parties' interests.

Conclusion

Both researchers and providers have genuine concerns regarding constraints that arise from implementing and complying with ABS obligations. Based on their pragmatic nature and requirement of less implementation effort, ABS agreements are useful tools for counteracting such constraints and operationalizing the Nagoya Protocol. If well designed, they can *inter alia* raise legal certainty, improve transparency, and lower transaction costs and thus serve as an incentive for research and development on genetic resources and ATK.

References

Biber-Klemm, S, Davis, K, Gautier, L, Martinez, SI (2014) "Governance options for ex-situ collections in academic research" in: Oberthür, S, Rosendal, GK (eds) *Global governance of genetic resources*, London: Routledge, pp. 213–230.

Biber-Klemm, S, Martinez, SI, Jacob, A, Jevtic, A (2010) *Agreement on access and benefit sharing for non-commercial research*, Bern: Swiss Academy of Sciences, Available online at www.bfn.de/fileadmin/ABS/documents/6C33Ed01__2_.pdf (accessed 1 October 2014).

Brownie, I (2003) *Principles of public international law*, 6th edition, New York: Oxford University Press.

FAO (2011) Introduction to the International Treaty on Plant Genetic Resources for Food and Agriculture, Rome. Available online at www.planttreaty.org/sites/default/files/edm1_full_en.pdf (accessed 21 March 2014).

Godt, C (2009) "Enforcement of benefit sharing duties in user countries' courts" in: Kamau, EC, Winter, G (eds), *Genetic resources, traditional knowledge, and the law. Solutions for access and benefit sharing* (pp. 419–438). London: Earthscan.

Greiber, T, Peña Moreno, S, Åhrén, M, Nieto Carrasco, J, Kamau, EC, Cabrera Medaglia, J, Oliva, MJ, Perron-Welch, F, in cooperation with Ali, N, Williams, C (2012) *An explanatory guide to the Nagoya Protocol on access and benefit-sharing*, Gland, Switzerland: IUCN.

Isozaki, H (2009) "Enforcement of ABS agreements in user States" in: Kamau, EC, Winter, G (eds), *Genetic resources, traditional knowledge, and the law. Solutions for access and benefit sharing* (pp. 439–454). London: Earthscan.

Kamau, EC (2009) "Facilitating or restraining access to genetic resources? Procedural dimensions in Kenya", 5(2) *Law, Environment and Development Journal*, pp. 152–166, Available online at www.lead-journal.org/2009-2.htm.

Kamau, EC (2014) "Valorisation of genetic resources, benefit-sharing and conservation of biological diversity: What role for the ABS regime?" in: Dilling, O, Markus, T (eds) *Ex Rerum Natura Ius? – Sachzwang und Problemwahrnehmung im Umweltrecht*, Baden Baden: Nomos, pp. 143–173.

Kamau, EC, Fedder, B, Winter, G (2010) "The Nagoya Protocol on access to genetic resources and benefit sharing: What is new and what are the implications for provider and user countries and the scientific community?", *Law, Environment and Development Journal* 6(3), pp. 246–262, Available online at www.lead-journal.org/current_issue.htm.

Kamau, EC, Winter, G (2009) *Genetic resources, traditional knowledge, and the law. Solutions for access and benefit sharing*, London: Earthscan.

Kamau, EC, Winter, G (2013), "An introduction to the international ABS regime and a comment on its transposition by the EU", *Law Environment and Development Journal* 9(2), pp. 167–126.

Laird, SA (2013) "Bioscience at a crossroads: Access and benefit sharing in a time of scientific, technological and industry change: The pharmaceutical industry, SCBD", Available at www.cbd.int/abs/policy-brief/default.shtml/ (accessed 24 September 2014).

Ruiz Muller, M, Lapeña, I (eds.) (2007) *A moving target: Genetic resources and options for tracking and monitoring their international flows*, Gland, Switzerland: IUCN.

SECO (Switzerland) (2007) "ABS management tool. Best practice standard and handbook for implementing genetic resource access and benefit-sharing activities, IISD", Available online at www.iisd.org/pdf/2007/abs_mt.pdf (accessed 6 November 2014).

Shimmield, G (2013) Extent and types of research, uses and applications, IUCN Information Papers for the Intersessional Workshop on Marine Genetic Resources 2–3 May 2013, pp. 7–14. Available online at www.un.org/depts/los/biodiversityworking group/documents/IUCN%20Information%20Papers%20for%20BBNJ%20Inter sessional%20Workshop%20on%20MGR.pdf (accessed 13 October 2014).

Winter, G (2013) "Common pools of genetic resources and related traditional and modern knowledge. An overview" in: Kamau, EC, and Winter, G (eds) *Common pools of genetic resources. Equity and innovation in international biodiversity law*, London: Routledge, pp. 3–25.

18 Guidelines for ABS and their potential to implement the Nagoya Protocol

Peter-Tobias Stoll

Introduction

Guidelines, codes of conduct, and similar instruments have played a considerable role throughout the long-lasting efforts to put the CBD's provisions on access to genetic resources and associated traditional knowledge and the sharing of benefits (ABS) into practice. For the purposes of this chapter, such guidelines or codes of conduct can be understood as guiding documents of certain stakeholders in ABS. They describe and prescribe the conduct of such stakeholders in ABS matters and are elaborated in a process which makes such a document representative of a certain group of stakeholders have legitimacy and the ability to impose certain normative effects on its members.

As will be seen, a closer look reveals that a number of such guidelines exist which vary widely regarding types of stakeholders, purpose, and content. Furthermore, such guidelines and codes of conduct apparently have different functions and employ different means.

The adoption of the Nagoya Protocol is a welcome occasion to review these guidelines and codes of conduct and to explore their potential for the further implementation of the ABS provisions of the CBD as well as the Nagoya Protocol.

Guidelines and codes of conduct appear well suited in this regard, as they may determine the conduct of certain groups of stakeholders in ABS and communicate this to others. They may thus be used to define the position of a group and to signal to other stakeholders what they may expect and how ABS transactions may be initiated and undertaken with the members of the relevant group. Potentially, these guidelines and codes of conduct could be an effective means to guide ABS transactions, because they are not necessarily dependent on a particular jurisdiction and are thus not confined to its limitations. Also, they could at least have a persuasive effect on the members.

In order to assess the real impact and the future potential of such guidelines, some of them shall be briefly examined to assess their potential in the context of the Nagoya Protocol and its implementation.

An assessment of existing guidelines and similar instruments

An assessment of existing guidelines can be based on the collection published by the CBD secretariat on its website. This collection can be assumed to be quite comprehensive and accurate.[1] The following discussion takes into account guidelines listed on that website which can be considered as being particularly representative for certain fields of activity.[2]

The Society for Economic Botany's (SEB) Guidelines of Professional Ethics

The assessment starts with the *Guidelines of Professional Ethics* of the Society for Economic Botany (SEB Guidelines). The society was founded in 1959 for the purpose of "fostering research and education on the past, present, and future uses of plants by people."[3] The SEB Guidelines were adopted in 1995 and revised in 2006, with some additions in 2008.[4] The document aims at ". . . reflect[ing] the vision of the Society and provides a framework for decision-making and conduct for ethnobiological research and related activities. The goals are to facilitate ethical conduct and equitable relationships, and foster a commitment to meaningful collaboration and reciprocal responsibility by all parties."[5]

The guidelines highlight that members of the Society have a duty to the public and that they will "strive to use their knowledge, skills and training to enhance the well-being of human kind."[6] The SEB Guidelines clearly point out that "members of the society . . . have responsibility to those studied,"[7] "those studied" meaning the individuals or groups which have been the subject of research. In this regard, the SEB Guidelines envisage that the objectives and possible consequences of research done by the members of the society will be clearly and honestly communicated to all with whom the members work. It is explicitly clarified: "If the research has a commercial objective, researchers will make that explicit to those studied and will disclose what the commercial result might reasonably be expected to be."[8] Further obligations in this regard include that members "will comply with all rules and limitations that local people, their communities or their institutions play on the research."[9] Also, the SEB Guidelines envisage that reports or materials

---

1 See webpage "Existing instruments, guidelines, codes of conduct and tools addressing ABS," www. cbd.int/abs/instruments/.
2 Some of the instruments listed on the website have been left aside, as they were mainly government-driven or related to the specific sector of agriculture, which is governed by other instruments, including the International Treaty on Plant Genetic Resources for Food and Agriculture.
3 See www.econbot.org/.
4 www.econbot.org/pdf/SEB_professional_ethics.pdf.
5 Guidelines, introductory sentence.
6 See No. 1.A of the SEB Guidelines.
7 No. 2. of the SEB Guidelines.
8 2.A of the SEB Guidelines.
9 2.B of the SEB Guidelines. The SEB Guidelines also envisage that members "will not 'trick' people into revealing 'secret' information" (2.B).

resulting from research will be offered and that compensation will be paid where a commercial benefit can be reasonably expected to arise from the material and information provided by those people. People can reasonably expect to have a commercial payoff when they provide material or information.[10] The SEB Guidelines also envisage that "members of the society . . . have responsibilities to host governments and other host institutions."[11] More specifically, the SEB Guidelines state that members "will comply honestly and completely with all regulations requesting disclosure of project objectives, sponsorship and methods, as well as supply reports and specimens to perform specified services (e.g., seminars and training)."[12] Furthermore, it is stated that the members of the Society "will assist their collaborators in enhancing the physical and human resources of the institutions."[13]

The SEB Guidelines furthermore stipulate that members have professional responsibilities. In this regard, it is envisaged that they "maintain a level of integrity and professional behaviour in the field so as not to jeopardize future research by others."[14] This statement is important, because it clarifies one of the purposes of the SEB Guidelines, namely to set a standard of professional behaviour in order to build confidence.

Although having been adopted in the summer of 1995, the SEB Guidelines do not explicitly refer to the Convention on Biological Diversity of 1992. Also, they do not specifically refer to its provision on access and benefit sharing. Their main focus is on people, who are characterized as local rather than indigenous.[15]

The Code of Ethics of the International Society of Ethnobiology (ISE)

Another example of guidelines adopted by a professional society is the Code of Ethics of the International Society of Ethnobiology (ISE Code of Ethics).[16] The ISE was founded in July 1988 during the First International Congress of Ethnobiology which took place in Belém, Brazil, and adopted the Declaration of Belém.[17] This document has been very influential in regard to international discourse concerning the conservation and use of biological diversity and cultural diversity and in view of the rights of indigenous peoples. The Declaration of Belém highlights the disappearance of tropical forests and other fragile ecosystems and the extinction of many species, as well as the disruption and the destruction of indigenous cultures around the world. The declaration further emphasizes that people are

---

10 2.E of the SEB Guidelines reads: "When materials or information obtained from those people can reasonably be expected to have a commercial payoff, they will arrange with employers for equitable economic compensation for those who have provided the information and/or plants and will do all in their power to ensure that compensation is paid."

11 3. of the SEB Guidelines.

12 3.A of the SEB Guidelines.

13 3.C of the SEB Guidelines.

14 4.A of the SEB Guidelines.

15 Indeed, the word "indigenous peoples" does not appear in the text.

16 http://ethnobiology.net/.

17 http://ethnobiology.net/docs/DeclarationofBelem.pdf.

dependent on such forests, ecosystems, species, and indigenous cultures, and, like-wise, that native people have been stewards of 99 percent of the world's genetic resources. The Declaration of Belém also points to the "inextricable link between cultural and biological diversity." In addition, the declaration calls for action concerning development aid and the participation of indigenous specialists in all sorts of programmes. Furthermore, the declaration calls for the recognition and guarantee of inalienable human rights and calls for procedures to be developed "to compensate native peoples for the utilization of their knowledge and their biological resources." A number of further issues concern educational programmes, medical programmes, the sharing of results of ethnobiologists' work with the peoples at hand, and the exchange of information.

The ISE is a recognized professional society with a whole range of activities. The vision statement of the organization highlights the complex relationships which exist within and between human societies and the environment. The society endeavours to promote a harmonious existence between humankind and the biosphere for the benefit of future generations. A further fundamental element of the society is the recognition of indigenous peoples and their rights.

A key achievement of the society is the ISE Code of Ethics, which was initiated in 1996 and completed in 2006, with the current edition containing additions from 2008.[18] The entire ISE Code of Ethics is built on the Declaration of Belém[19] and driven by the concept of "mindfulness," "which invokes an obligation to be fully aware of one's knowing and unknowing, doing and undoing, action and inaction."[20] Furthermore, it highlights that cultural and biological structures and processes are closely interrelated.[21] The ISE Code of Ethics aims at facilitating the establishment of "ethical and equitable relationships." It highlights the esteem "to recognize, support and prioritize the efforts of Indigenous peoples, traditional societies and local communities to undertake and own their research, collections, images, recordings, databases and publications. This Code of Ethics is intended to enfranchise Indigenous peoples, traditional societies and local communities conducting research within their own society, for their own use."[22] The Code contains a number of principles[23] and practical

---

18 International Society of Ethnobiology (2006). International Society of Ethnobiology Code of Ethics, adopted at the 10th International Congress of Ethnobiology, Chiang Rai, Thailand, 8 November 2006, with addition of an Executive Summary and Glossary of Terms, adopted at the 11th International Congress of Ethnobiology, Cusco, Peru, 26 June 2008, http://ethnobiology.net/docs/ISE%20COE_Eng_rev_24Nov08.pdf.

19 See ISE Code of Ethics, 2.

20 ISE Code of Ethics, Preamble, para. 1.

21 "The ISE recognises that culture and language are intrinsically connected to land and territory, and cultural and linguistic diversity are inextricably linked to biological diversity," ISE Code of Ethics, 4.

22 ISE Code of Ethics, 4.

23 The Code mentions the following ones: "Prior Rights and Responsibilities; Self-Determination; Inalienability; Traditional Guardianship; Active Participation; Full Disclosure; Educated Prior Informed Consent; Confidentiality; Respect; Active Protection; Precaution; Reciprocity, Mutual Benefit and Equitable Sharing; Supporting Indigenous Research; The Dynamic Interactive Cycle; Remedial Action; Acknowledgement and Due Credit; Diligence," ISE Code of Ethics, 5–8.

guidelines.[24] These address ethnobotanical research and primarily aim at fully taking into account the rights and expectations of indigenous peoples affected by or included in such research activities. The practical guidelines address an "educated prior informed consent" (para. 2), full disclosure (para. 3), good faith (para. 5), mutually agreed terms and conditions (para. 6), respect for moratoriums by communities and countries (para. 8), educational uses of research materials (para. 9), the handling of project materials (para. 10), research practices which are potentially harmful (para. 11), and an endeavour for the cross-cultural nature of research (para. 12). The practical guidelines further more state, that "[a]ny intellectual property ownership claim or application related to the knowledge or associated resources from the collaboration research should not work against the cultural integrity or livelihood of communities involved."[25]

While the ISE Code of Ethics does not contain any explicit reference to the CBD and its key terms and mechanisms, it certainly reflects some of the Convention's main principles. This is especially true in view of the full participation of indigenous peoples in research activity and the principle of mutual benefit and equitable sharing of benefits resulting from such research. As the ISE Code of Ethics primarily addresses the question of how to respect and involve indigenous peoples, little has been said about the authority of States to dispose genetic resources and the rights of States to determine access to such resources.

In 2006, the ISE initiated the elaboration of a tool kit, the ISE Ethic Tool Kit, which will include, *inter alia*, template agreements and educational and training materials.[26]

Ethical and professional responsibilities – The Society for Applied Anthropology (SfAA)

The CBD website further refers to a text on ethical and professional responsibilities which has been adopted by the Society for Applied Anthropology.[27] The SfAA Statement of Ethics is basically concerned with anthropology and its application for practical purposes.[28] In this context, the referenced document on ethical and professional responsibilities spells out a number of obligations in view of the peoples studied and the communities ultimately affected by research. They mainly include a duty to disclose research goals, methods, and sponsorship and call for participation. In sum, these obligations are not explicitly and specifically related to the issue of access and benefit sharing.

24 Ibid, 8–12.
25 Ibid, 10.
26 See http://ethnobiology.net/code-of-ethics/ethics-toolkit/ and http://ethicstoolkit.net.
27 www.sfaa.net/about/ethics/.
28 See the information on the "mission, vision, values, and goals" of the SfAA provided at www.sfaa. net/about/governance/mission/.

The guidelines of the Biotechnology Industry Organization (BIO)

Two further documents must be mentioned which have been developed by the private sector. One was authored by BIO. According to its own statement, BIO is the world's largest industry organization in the field.[29] BIO has adopted "Guidelines for BIO Members Engaging in Bioprospecting" (BIO Guidelines).[30] The document, which is drafted in a very legal and technical manner, contains a number of very precise and specific actions that the members of the association should undertake when bioprospecting. BIO Guidelines foresee that, prior to bioprospecting activities, the focal point of the relevant country be contacted[31] and prior informed consent be obtained.[32] Furthermore, BIO Guidelines contain a description of possible forms of benefit sharing to be governed by a bioprospecting agreement.[33] The guidelines make clear that members of BIO should not receive or use any material without undergoing such procedures in advance or accept material when its origin cannot be determined.[34] Though indigenous and local communities are mentioned,[35] BIO Guidelines do not explicitly cover the acquisition of traditional knowledge and the resulting benefit sharing but are confined to the access of genetic resources. Also, it must be highlighted that BIO Guidelines use the term "regulated genetic resources" which limits the range of application of the guidelines to materials which originate in a CBD State party, are to be collected after the entry into force of the Convention, and are subject to national ABS rules.[36] It should be added, that the organization also has elaborated a "suggested model material transfer agreement."[37]

29 www.bio.org/articles/about-bio.
30 www.bio.org/articles/bio-bioprospecting-guidelines.
31 BIO Guidelines, under II. Where samples are to be collected "*in situ*, or from an *ex situ* collection located within the territory of or controlled by [a CBD] *Contracting Party*," this is the focal point identified by that contracting party, see II. A. 1 a of the BIO Guidelines. In case of a collection "from an *ex situ* collection located outside the territory of or not controlled by the *Contracting Party*," a focal point as specified by the custodian of the collection shall be contacted. If the focal point is not known, reasonable steps shall be taken to identify such focal point, see BIO Guidelines, II. A. 1. b.
32 See III. of the BIO Guidelines.
33 IV of the BIO Guidelines deals with benefit sharing and the "sharing of research results" and "intellectual property procurement."
34 See VII of the BIO Guidelines.
35 According to the definitions in I. A. No. 11 of the BIO Guidelines, an "indigenous or local community" may be "providing party" and thus may enjoy "legal authority to grant Prior Informed Consent or authorization to access and use Regulated Genetic Resources" [use of capital letters as in the original].
36 I A No. 13 of the BIO Guidelines reads: " 'Regulated Genetic Resource' means a Genetic Resource in respect of which a Providing Party in a Contracting Party, on or after the date that the Convention on Biological Diversity Party took effect in that Contracting Party, imposes requirements concerning Prior Informed Consent, collection or use."
37 www.bio.org/sites/default/files/BIO_Model_MTA.pdf.

Guidelines of the International Federation of Pharmaceutical Manufacturers and Associations (IFPMA)

Another example of guidelines for the private sector are the "Guidelines for IFPMA Members on Access to Genetic Resources and Equitable Sharing of Benefits Arising out of their Utilization" adopted in 2011.[38] These guidelines (IFPMA Guidelines) cover genetic resources and traditional knowledge and have already taken the Nagoya Protocol into consideration. The short text is of a general nature and defines industry best practices and also lists a number of "enabling steps by government." Regarding industry best practice, PIC and MAT are mentioned. Also, IFPMA Guidelines state that forms of use and commercialization of genetic resources should be avoided if they impede on traditional uses of such genetic resources. Furthermore, it is stated that industry should agree to the settlement of disputes regarding benefit-sharing agreements by means of arbitration under international procedures.

The part on enabling steps by governments includes a call for enacting national legislation to implement the CBD and the Nagoya Protocol and to establish national focal points and competent national authorities – preferably in the form of one single entity. Such entities are called upon to provide for legal certainty for both providers and users of genetic resources through a number of measures, including the determination of indigenous peoples or other stakeholders who have access rights. Furthermore the establishment of fair, transparent, and effective application procedures is mentioned, as well as the function of a checkpoint.

In sum, the document adopted by IFPMA is much less precise and technical than the one by BIO. It is drafted in a more political style. It is worth noting that it focuses on genetic resources just like the BIO Guidelines and does not contain any specific guidance concerning traditional knowledge associated with such resources.

Personal Care Products Council (PCPC): Guidance for the cosmetics/personal care industry

Another example for guidance elaborated from the private sector for its guidance is a document developed by the Personal Care Products Council (PCPC) and named "Access to Genetic Resources and Sharing of Benefits Arising from Their Utilization Guidance for Members of the Personal Care Products Council."[39] According to its website, PCPC has a membership of nearly 30 companies.[40] Its guidance document is structured in a step-by-step mode and addresses prior informed consent and mutually agreed terms and specifically addresses "measures

---

38 www.ifpma.org/fileadmin/content/Innovation/Biodiversity%20and%20Genetic%20 Resources/2013_ IFPMA_Guidelines_Access_to_Genetic_Resources.pdf, published on 6 December 2011.

39 Text made available by the secretariat of the CBD at www.cbd.int/abs/doc/CBDabsGuidance-personalcarecouncil-PublicVersion-Feb2014.pdf.

40 www.personalcarecouncil.org/members.

to protect interests and rights of indigenous or local communities" (para. 7), as well as concerns regarding the conservation and sustainable use of biological diversity (para. 8).

The supplementary instructions of the German Research Foundation (DFG)

Guidelines have sometimes also been developed by science organizations. A well-known example of guidelines defined by research funding organizations are the guidelines adopted by the German Research Foundation (Deutsche Forschungsgemeinschaft, DFG) under the title "Supplementary Instructions for Funding Proposals Concerning Research Projects Within the Scope of the Convention on Biological Diversity (CBD)"[41] (DFG Supplementary Instructions). DFG is the major German research funding institution, is self-governed by scientists, and funds research projects from financial resources provided by the German Federation and the German Länder ("federal states"). It should be noted that the area of activity of DFG contains "basic research" and not applied sciences.

DFG has discussed the implications of ABS for research projects for quite a while. A working group was set up some years ago to discuss the issue. It also has created supplementary instructions. The particular format of this sort of guidelines is due to the specific character of the activity of DFG. As a pure research funding institution, it basically has to do with the evaluation of research proposals and decision making on funding and the subsequent administration of such funds. It should be highlighted that DFG is different from national academies of science which exist in many countries and can be understood as a more general organization for scientists and scientific institutions of a certain country. As a set of "supplementary guidelines," the DFG Supplementary Instructions have to be read in conjunction with the general guidelines for applications concerning the funding of a research project. The DFG Supplementary Instructions contain specific provisions for those applications, which concern research projects that fall into the scope of the Convention on Biological Diversity. In such a case, an applicant has to observe those supplementary instructions in addition to the general guidelines.

The DFG Supplementary Instructions represent a 24-page informative document, which explains the CBD's provisions on access and benefit sharing to researchers while giving guidance to researchers in order to comply with the principles of the CBD and national legislation on the issue. More precisely, the DFG Supplementary Instructions specifically define under VII what a researcher is required to do at the application stage. According to that part of the instructions, a researcher must concretely describe which competent authorities have been or are intended to be contacted and how the access procedure works in the host country. In addition, the applicant must rate the prospects for success. Further, the applicant has to confirm his or her familiarization with these guidelines and

41 www.dfg.de/formulare/1_021e/1_021e.pdf.

the intention to conduct the project according to the principles described in the instructions. Because of this, the researcher is bound by the DFG Supplementary Instructions when receiving funding for the research project. Furthermore, the application may be rejected if the requested information is not provided.

Access and benefit sharing – Good practices for academic research on genetic resources of the Swiss Academy of Sciences (SCNAT)

The Swiss Academy of Sciences, founded in 1815, undertook a large project on ABS after the adoption of the Bonn Guidelines, which were initiated by the Swiss Federal Environment Agency. The project included various activities from research, discussion, awareness raising, development of recommendations for the CBD-ABS process, and importantly involved the elaboration of "Good Practices for Academic Research on Genetic Resources" (SCNAT Good Practice), which were published in 2009.[42] Later on, the project also included the elaboration of model agreements.

The Good Practice project is understood to serve as a tool to assist the Swiss Scientific Community to implement the CBD and the Bonn Guidelines. The SCNAT Good Practice document contains a number of general explanations of the ABS system and case studies to more practically explain the implications. A number of useful tips and a checklist are included to assist researchers.

The MOSAICC and the Belgian Co-ordinated Collections of Micro-Organisms

Guidelines on access and benefit sharing play a prominent role in the area of collections of genetic material, as MOSAICC – the Micro-Organisms Sustainable use and Access regulation International Code of Conduct – may indicate.[43] This code of conduct was developed by BCCM – the Belgian Co-ordinated Collections of Micro-Organisms[44] – together with 11 partners, including other public collections, the private sector, and institutions from the South.[45] The MOSAICC is a voluntary code of conduct which aims at facilitating access to microbial genetic resources (MGRs) and "to help partners to make appropriate agreements when transferring MGRs in the framework of the Convention on Biological Diversity (CBD) and other applicable rules of international and national laws." MOSAICC is understood as "a tool to support the implementation of the CBD at the microbial level." However, in the introductory part of the Code, it is highlighted that it might also serve as a model when dealing with genetic resources other than microbial genetic resources.

---

42 An updated version of 2012 is available at http://abs.scnat.ch/downloads/documents/ABS_GoodPractice_2012.pdf.
43 http://bccm.belspo.be/projects/mosaicc/.
44 http://bccm.belspo.be.
45 See http://bccm.belspo.be/projects/mosaicc/.

The MOSAICC explicitly addresses microbiologists and authorities of countries providing MGRs. It does not specifically cover or address collections and depositories of biological material, such as BCCM itself. However, the Code makes reference to the OECD Best Practice Guidelines for Biological Resource Centres of 2007 and to the World Federation of Culture Collections WFCC Guidelines for the Establishment and Operation of Culture Collections. These two guidelines contain more general rules for the establishment and operation of collections and do not specifically address ABS issues.

The MOSAICC primarily defines methods and formalities for prior informed consent and for mutually agreed terms and contains sample documents in this regard. A model material transfer agreement and a PIC application form as well as a PIC certificate are attached to the MOSAICC.

Guidelines and other instruments for botanical gardens

A number of initiatives have been undertaken by botanical gardens. A major actor in these activities is Botanical Gardens Conservation International (BGCI), an international organization which was established in 1986 to work for the worldwide conservation of threatened plants. Today, BGCI has over 700 members in more than 100 countries. Most of them are botanical gardens. As part of their work, BGCI adopted "Principles on Access to Genetic Resources and Benefit-Sharing"[46] (BGCI Principles). More than 20 botanical gardens around the world have elaborated and endorsed these principles. The two-page document is closely related to the concept of access and benefit sharing in the CBD. Apart from requiring PIC for any acquisition and guiding principles for benefit sharing, the BGCI Principles particularly address the acquisition of genetic resources from *ex situ* collections – a transaction that plays an important role in the activities of botanical gardens. It is highlighted that any acquisition of genetic resources from such *ex situ* sources requires that available documentation is evaluated and that – where necessary – the appropriate steps are taken to ensure that the genetic resources were acquired in accordance with applicable law and best practice. Furthermore, the BGCI Principles state that "when acquiring genetic resources from ex-situ collections (such as botanic gardens), prior informed consent [has to be obtained] from the body governing the ex-situ collection and any additional consent required by that body." The BGCI Principles also address the use and supply of genetic resources and state in general terms that the "use and supply [of] genetic resources and their derivatives [has to be undertaken] on terms and conditions consistent with those under which they were acquired." Also, participating institutions undertake the obligation to "[p]repare a transparent policy on commercialization of genetic resources acquired before and after the CBD entered into force and their derivatives, whether by the participant institution or a recipient third party."

---

46 See www.bgci.org/files/ABS/Principles_English.pdf.

In addition to these principles, a number of botanical gardens have also established an exchange network for the non-commercial exchange of plant material based on the CBD. This network, which is called the International Plant Exchange Network (IPEN)[47] was developed by the German Association of Botanical Gardens and was taken over later on by the European Consortium of Botanic Gardens. It aims at providing a platform for the exchange of plant material between the member gardens in accordance with the ABS regulations of the CBD. Membership in the network requires members to sign and abide by a Code of Conduct[48] (IPEN Code of Conduct) that sets out the responsibilities of participating botanic gardens in view of acquisition, maintenance, and supply of living plant material and benefit sharing. The IPEN Code of Conduct clarifies, that "to the best of its knowledge, the garden will only accept plant material . . . which has been acquired in accordance with the provisions of the CBD and further national and international laws. . . ." Also, "when acquiring plant material from in-situ conditions, the garden shall obtain information on the country of origin's access laws and the procedures for obtaining prior informed consent and relevant permits. . . ." Furthermore, "when acquiring plant material from *ex situ* conditions the PIC will be obtained according to national law from the institution that holds the collection. . . ." Furthermore, the IPEN Code of Conduct specifies the procedure of material entering IPEN, defines material considered unsuitable for IPEN, and addresses the question of "pre- and post-CBD material." Another section of the IPEN Code of Conduct deals with supply and, first of all, – in accordance with the BGCI Principles – states that plant material shall be supplied under the same terms under which it was acquired.[49]

Evaluation

When looking at the documents, a number of differences relating to their origin and context, as well as to their content, become apparent. Apparently, the use of such guidelines is quite common in the area of collections – be it botanical gardens or collections of microorganisms. Also, scientific associations have been active in this field. In other relevant areas, such as in the research community more generally and in industry, only very few initiatives exist. The documents vary also in view of their content and ambition.

Coverage: Rights of indigenous peoples, traditional knowledge, genetic resources

In particular, the documents of SEB and ISE reflect the strong commitment of these associations and their members to indigenous peoples. In more general terms, they express an understanding for the culture and dignity of these peoples

47 www.bgci.org/resources/ipen/.
48 See www.bgci.org/files/ABS/IPEN/ipencodeofconduct.doc.
49 For details see Biber-Klemm et al., Ch. 14 in this volume.

and define obligations for their members. These documents had an impact on the discussion of the issue within the CBD and the implementation of Art. 8(j) of the Convention. However, they do not address access to genetic resources and the sharing of benefits. The contrary is true for the guidelines of the private sector, namely the ones of BIO and IFPMA: They deal with genetic material without also including the issue of traditional knowledge. The same holds true for the initiatives taken by collections of genetic material.

Precision and comprehensiveness

The different guideline projects also vary considerably in view of their precision and comprehensiveness in a technical or legal sense. While some confine themselves to the statement of principles, as is true for instance for the SEB and ISE documents and for IFPMA Guidelines, others contain much more specific guidance, sometimes including model agreements and documents, as is the case of BIO Guidelines, MOSAICC, BGCI Principles, and IPEN Code of Conduct.

Commitment and compliance

In addition to the clarity and precision in legal terms, the aspect of commitment and compliance must be mentioned. SEB and ISE Guidelines allude to professional ethics and reflect a strong moral commitment. Such commitment, however, is only coined into more legal commitment in the case of ISE. On the other hand, the BIO Guidelines give precise guidance but emphasize that such guidance is of a purely voluntary character. The commitment of participating members or institutions is emphasized in the case of MOSAICC and – even more so – in the initiatives of botanical gardens. These clearly spell out that the rules contained in the documents are binding. This degree of commitment is closely related to the structure of these initiatives, which requires members to actively commit to the guidelines. Also, the DFG Supplementary Instructions must be mentioned here, which require researchers to adhere to the guidelines and to demonstrate their willingness to apply them when requesting for research funds. However, the initiatives do not go further to establish specific procedures for cases of noncompliance.

Legitimacy and the participation of providers

The various documents share the fact that they aim at defining the proper conduct in ABS issues. In doing so, they more or less explicitly rely on certain grounds which should add legitimacy to their initiatives. The guidelines are altogether initiated by "users" of genetic resources and – possibly – related traditional knowledge. The question of legitimacy is therefore basically one of the acceptability of the various guidelines for providers. In one particular case, that of BGCI, such legitimacy rests – at least in part – on the participation of providers or provider States respectively. Such direct participation is obviously absent in all other cases. Rather than relying on an active involvement of providers, these initiatives rely on their own judgment on how to best organize ABS. In doing so, they may draw from their particular professional capabilities and responsibilities, as is the case of SEB and ISE, or apply some standard of rationality with special consideration to their particular experiences and expertise, as is the case, for instance, of the BIO and IFPMA guidelines.

Purpose and function

Obviously, the different documents and related activities also serve different aims. SEB and ISE Guidelines define a standard of professional ethics which their members should apply. Besides the desire to spell out such ethics as such and to see their application in research activities, such initiatives may aim at building confidence in the members of the profession and to define the position that the associations are to take in public discourse. A threefold approach becomes apparent at this point, which is reflected more or less by all initiatives mentioned above: They aim at (1) assisting and guiding their members in view of their ABS-related activities and (2) thereby seek to build confidence *vis-à-vis* providers and (3) eventually aim at clarifying their joint positions in public discourse at the international or national level. However, the initiatives taken by collections of genetic material go one step further in (4) aiming at establishing a system for the accession, exchange, and provision of collected materials.

The potential of guidelines and similar instruments under the Nagoya Protocol

Throughout international and national discourse on the implementation of the CBD's ABS provisions, guidelines and similar instruments have played a considerable role. Art. 20 of the Nagoya Protocol calls on parties ". . . to encourage . . . the development . . . of guidelines . . . in relation to access and benefit-sharing." However, when looking closer, it appears that in reality, guidelines have not been used as frequently. With the exception of the case of collections of genetic resources, only a few industry associations, science organizations, and professional societies have undertaken the effort to create such guidelines. The case for the creation of comprehensive guidelines is a compelling one for collections, which rely on confidence and legal security for their operations. In other areas, the need to adopt guidelines seems to be rather remote in terms of assistance, confidence building, and public positioning. The call on States to encourage the development of such instruments as reflected by Art. 20 of the Nagoya Protocol thus has not yet yielded much result.

However, the spirit of the Nagoya Protocol has to be taken into account, which is to foster legal clarity and security on the provider and user side by calling for measures regarding access as well as compliance. Guidelines and similar instruments could become relevant here if they could effectively secure compliance while also offering improved conditions for access. This would probably require interested user groups to design guidelines or related instruments which secure compliance by means of clear rules and a reliable enforcement procedure.

It would, on the other hand, require providers to offer clear advantages in regard to access to those who adhere to such instruments. Both users and providers will carefully consider whether the considerable effort required on both sides and the necessary interaction between them is worthwhile. Stakeholders on both sides might be tempted to rather wait for the full implementation of the Nagoya Protocol by its parties. However, it is not clear when and to what extent the implementation of the Protocol will produce legal certainty and confidence and will render the elaboration of the aforementioned instruments superfluous. Thus, there is still potential for guidelines and similar instruments. However, they need to be far more effective and comprehensive than are the existing ones and require that providers accept them and in turn do something about the facilitation of access.

19 Points to consider for national legislation on access to genetic resources and benefit sharing

Gerd Winter

Introduction

Although there is currently a global trend of states to introduce ABS regimes, states should be aware that their sovereign rights over their GR[1] enable them not to do this (Greiber et al. 2012, 96). States are only obliged – as user states – to establish compliance control.[2]

States which host potentially highly valuable GR would rather opt in favour of an ABS regime. States poor in such resources should weigh the possibly modest benefit expectation against the transaction costs of an ABS regime, which include PIC and contracting procedures, administrative oversight of GR and TK utilization, costs of enforcing contracts in foreign jurisdictions, etc. They might consider desisting from introducing an ABS regime at all, or confine it to a limited list of GR, the compilation of which may be delegated to a competent body.[3] Another reason to desist from an ABS regime can be that a state regards its free access as a service for the global community or that it considers receiving sufficient benefits from the participation in common pools that exchange, study, and develop genetic resources. This attitude explains why only very few industrialized states have introduced ABS regimes after 1993. The exceptions, such as Australia (Burton 2009), may reconsider this.

National legislation on ABS should draw a distinction between rules for access to and utilization of domestic GR and TK on the one hand and rules on the utilization of imported GR and TK on the other. As outlined, states have discretion whether to introduce the first, while if adhering to the NP they are obliged to introduce the second. In the following, we assume that a state wishes to introduce rules in both regards. This would suggest an overall structure of the law as follows:

I   General Provisions
II Access to and Utilization of domestic GR and TK
III Utilization of imported GR and TK

---

1 Art. 15 (1) CBD. States have however an obligation to establish some kind of ABS regime concerning the TK of their indigenous and local communities, see Art. 8 (j) CBD.
2 Arts. 15–19 NP.
3 This is the solution adopted by the Norwegian Nature Diversity Act, section 57, and the Swiss Bundesgesetz über den Natur- und Heimatschutz, as amended on 21 March 2014, section 23q.

We will now discuss these three parts in more detail.

I. General provisions

1. Objectives

The first article of the law will contain the primary objectives of the law. These will be access control and assurance of benefit sharing, with a view to use the benefits for the conservation and sustainable use of biological resources.

2. Legal status of genetic resources and traditional knowledge

It is recommended that the national law clearly determine the legal status of genetic resources and traditional knowledge. In some countries this will already be decided by the constitution, but even then some kind of specification on the level of legislative act may be necessary.

The law should use the notion of property in order to facilitate legal action recovering damage to that property by illegal access and utilization. The damage could then be calculated in analogy to damage recovered by holders of IPRs (Godt 2009).

There are three options of determining property in GRs:

- Private property of the owner of the organism carrying the genetic resource, such as the landowner, owner of *ex situ* collection, etc.,
- Collective property of indigenous or local communities or property of individuals embedded in such communities, and
- State ownership.

We submit that traditional knowledge should be conceived as property either of an indigenous/local community or of an individual belonging to that community subject to the customary rules of the same.[4] The same should apply to landraces[5] cultivated or domesticated by indigenous and local communities. In contrast, genetic resources should in general be regarded as property entrusted to the state as a common good of the entire people.[6] It is true that in some countries genetic resources are deemed to be private property of landowners etc. South Africa appears to be a case in point,[7] but we believe that the property in an

---

4 On the international law status of property in traditional knowledge see Greiber et al. (2012), 101.
5 For the term see *infra* section 3.
6 Cf. the Norwegian Nature Diversity Act, section 57 1st sentence which reads: "Genetic material obtained from the natural environment is a common resource belonging to Norwegian society as a whole and managed by the state."
7 Cf. the National Environmental Management: Biodiversity Act 2004, section 82, which says that a bioprospector needs to enter into a material transfer and benefit-sharing agreement with "a person" "providing or giving access to the indigenous biological resources to which the application relates."

organism does not automatically include property in the genetic potential of the same. The plant grown by a landowner is a specimen which can be sold and consumed, but its genome reaches beyond the specimen; it is not produced by the landowner but used by him or her and thus is a public good.

3. Definitions

Insofar as the terms used in the law are defined in the CBD and the NP, their definitions should be used. However, some of these definitions lack clarity. The law should then step in and clarify the issue. The following terms should be included and defined in the national law:

- "Biological resources," as defined in Art. 2 CBD, "includes genetic resources, organisms or parts thereof, populations, or any other biotic component of ecosystems with actual or potential use or value for humanity."
- "Genetic material," as defined in Art. 2 CBD, means "any material of plant, animal, microbial or other origin containing functional units of heredity."
- "Genetic resources," as equally defined in Art. 2 CBD, means "genetic material of actual or potential value."
- "Traditional knowledge" or "associated TK" is defined neither by the CBD nor by the NP. According to Art. 3 EU-Regulation 511/2014 "traditional knowledge associated with genetic resources" means traditional knowledge held by an indigenous or local community that is relevant for the utilization of genetic resources and that is as such described in the mutually agreed terms applying to the utilization of genetic resources. We suggest that the term should be defined without reference to mutually agreed terms, because if TK exclusively is mutually agreed TK, there cannot be illegal access to TK. Moreover, the definition lacks specification of what indigenous and local community means. It is suggested to follow the Brazilian definition which reads: "traditional peoples and communities are culturally differentiated groups, who identify themselves as such, possess their own forms of social organization, occupy and use territories and natural resources as a condition for their cultural, social, religious, ancestral and economic reproduction, using knowledge, innovations and practices that are generated and transmitted through tradition."[8] In addition, the terms "traditional" and "associated" need to be defined. Once more, the Brazilian terminology may be followed, which defines associated TK as "information on individual or collective knowledge or practice associated to the genetic heritage."[9]
- "Access" to GR or associated TK is defined neither by the CBD nor by the NP. According to Regulation 511/2014/EU, access means "the acquisition of genetic resources or of traditional knowledge associated with genetic resources in a Party to the Nagoya Protocol." This includes a variety of

8 Decreto 6040/2007 Art. 3 (1).
9 Brazilian Medida Provisoria No. 2.186–16 of August 2001, Art. 7 V.

activities including the taking of samples, the purchase of an organism (such as a seed) on a local market, the recording of traditional knowledge, etc. It does not, however, include a situation where someone acquires a biological resource for consumption but later on decides to apply R&D on its genetic potential. Some authors therefore understand access to mean any R&D on the genetic resource (Kamau, Ch. 2 in this volume). This would suggest defining "access" to mean not only the acquisition but also the examination of biological resources in their quality as GR. The legislating state will have to take a position on that difference of understandings. I suggest following the first opinion, because the second appears to deny the term access any function apart from the term utilization. The state may, however, insert a provision stating that PIC shall also be required if R&D on GR or TK is initiated to already accessed biological resources (see *infra*).

- "Utilization of genetic resources," as defined in Art. 2 NP, means "to conduct research and development on the genetic and/or biochemical composition of genetic resources, including through the application of biotechnology."
- "Biotechnology," as defined in Art. 2 NP, means "any technological application that uses biological systems, living organisms, or derivatives thereof, to make or modify products or processes for specific use," while "derivative" means "a naturally occurring biochemical compound resulting from the genetic expression or metabolism of biological or genetic resources, even if it does not contain functional units of heredity." In order to distinguish derivatives from compounds that are not biochemical but just chemical (such as crystallized coral reefs or shells), it should be added that "chemicals which are *in situ* separated from the organic cycle of an organism (such as crystallized corals or shells of snakes) are not considered biochemicals."
- According to Art. 6.1 NP, access to GR is only subject to PIC if it is made "for their utilization," i.e. for R&D on the GR or TK. In order to further clarify what is not meant by R&D, the term "consumption of a biological resource" should be introduced. Consumption might be defined as "the direct or processed use as food, feed, construction material, burning, or similar use, but not, however, for medicinal or cosmetic purposes."
- If the law provides for specific protection of plant or animal varieties that were domesticated or cultivated by or within indigenous or local communities, it may be advisable to introduce the term "landraces." "Landraces" may then be defined as "plant or animal varieties that were domesticated or cultivated by or within indigenous or local communities."
- "*Ex situ* conservation" means the conservation of components of biological diversity outside their natural habitats.
- "*In situ* conditions" means conditions where genetic resources exist within ecosystems and natural habitats, and, in the case of domesticated or cultivated species, in the surroundings where they have developed their distinctive properties.
- "Sustainable use" means the use of components of biological diversity in a way and at a rate that does not lead to the long-term decline of biological

diversity, thereby maintaining its potential to meet the needs and aspirations of present and future generations.

- Some state legislation has definitions of "prior informed consent (PIC)," "mutually agreed terms (MAT)," and "material transfer agreement (MTA)," which are the legal forms used in the NP. It is submitted that national legislation should translate them into the corresponding domestic legal forms. These will be a permit with attached conditions and a contract containing the same and/or additional conditions.

- If the law, following Art. 8 (a) NP, provides different access tracks for non-commercial and commercial research, these terms must be defined. "Commercial" is often regarded as a stage in the R&D process aimed at a marketable product or service, "marketable" including through sales or through IPRs yielding royalties. Such R&D is also called "applied." It produces results which have a market value. In contrast, non-commercial is then understood as "basic," i.e. not meant or not yet ready for the market. The problem of this traditional distinction along market value is the fact that today "basic" research not only generates common taxonomic knowledge (such as about the anatomy or living conditions of an organism) but reaches to the genome of the organism. The new situation is that with the ever-expanding biotechnology, even individual genes whose function has been discovered can be marketable. Sequencing the genome is therefore at the same time "basic" and "applied" research. The discovered gene has a market value. The crucial question is therefore not if there is a market value at all but if the market value is intended to be realized. This depends on whether the R&D result is privatized or made public. Privatization includes keeping it secret, obtaining IPRs and thus establishing exclusive use rights, or manufacturing products the property of which is sold on the market. Privatization is the precondition for bringing a product to the market and generating a price for it. In contrast, publication means to submit R&D results to the public so that anyone can make use of it at no price (or at a low price which reflects the costs of publication (see further von Kries and Winter, Ch. 3 in this volume). The distinction along privatization/publication is also in line with the intention behind Art. 8 (a) NP, which is that the sovereign rights of states should not hinder the enhancement of global biological knowledge which is a prerequisite for the conservation of global biodiversity. In the same vein, the UN Convention on the Law of the Sea (UNCLOS) has established the principle of free marine scientific research and the publication of its results (von Kries and Winter, Ch. 4 in this volume).

Based on these reflections, non-commercial research should be defined as "research aimed at making its results publicly available at not more than incremental costs," incremental cost meaning the cost of publication, copying, etc., but excluding remuneration for the cost of producing the research results and for the market value of the research results. Commercial research would then be "research for proprietary purposes, such as through keeping research results secret, obtaining IPRs, and bringing products and services on the market."

4. Geographical scope of the law

The geographical scope of the ABS regime extends to all organisms found *in situ* or *ex situ* on the territory of the state, including the territorial sea, as well as (if declared) the exclusive economic zone and the continental shelf. It also extends to the associated traditional knowledge of indigenous and local communities living within the territory of the state. In terms of regulatory technique, the geographical scope can be indicated by the term "geographical jurisdiction." The law could read: "The law applies to the GR and associated TK under the geographical jurisdiction of the state. This includes GR found within the territorial sea, the exclusive economic zone, and on the continental shelf of the state."

5. Temporal scope of the law

Provider states have had sovereign rights over their genetic resources and traditional knowledge since the entering into force of the CBD, i.e. December 1993. Since then they have had the possibility of establishing an ABS regime as have done a number of states, but by far not all of them. Those access activities are captured by national laws which were initiated after the entering into force of the same laws, according to their specification of temporal scope. Such specification cannot, however, be retroactive; in other words, it cannot include GR or TK accessed before the date of validity of the law. According to – contested – legal opinion, the law can however extend to new utilizations of GR or TK that were obtained at an earlier date.[10] Of course, proof of that will not be easy so, in realistic terms, we recommend to let the law cover access and benefit sharing concerning only GR and TK accessed after the date of validity of the given law.

6. Material scope of the law

The ABS regime should not be applicable to

- human genetic resources;
- the exchange and use of GR and associated TK within and between indigenous and local communities for their own benefit and based on customary practices;[11]

---

10 Kamau, Fedder, and Winter (2010) 255; in contrast, Regulation (EU) 511/2014, Art. 17, makes its regulation of user countries duties applicable only to GR or TK acquired after the entering into force of the Nagoya Protocol, plus one year for new acquisitions.

11 Cf. the Brazilian Medida Provisoria No. 2.186–16 of August 2001, Art. 4. See also Sect. 3 (a) of the Kenyan ABS Regs 2006: exchange ". . . amongst themselves and for their own consumption."

- access to GR or TK for educational purposes at schools and higher education institutions;[12]
- crops covered by the Multilateral System of the International Treaty on Plant Genetic Resources for Food and Agriculture (ITPGRFA), if they are in the possession of public collections and institutions;
- nonprofit exchange of genetic and biochemical resources and the traditional associated knowledge resulting from the traditional practices of indigenous peoples and local communities.[13]

The legislating state may exclude further kinds of GR that it deems to be organized in a way that ensures adequate benefit sharing. For instance, exchange systems of cattle breeders may be considered beneficial for the participating countries even without a costly ABS system (Louafi & Schloen 2013). Given the fact that in the farm animal sector, germplasm flows from the North to the South rather than its inverse, it can even be counterproductive if a southern state introduces ABS requirements for a transfer from its country because the northern partner may do the same and thus put the southern country in a worse position than it was before.

Considering that Art. 15 CBD relates the sovereign rights of states to "their" genetic resources, it could be discussed whether the legislating state should confine the ABS regime to those GR which have their evolutionary origin within its territory. Some countries indeed speak of "indigenous" genetic resources as objects of their access and benefit-sharing regulation.[14] However, given common migrations and multiple genetic influxes, the evolutionary origin of species is often uncertain and diverse. It is therefore not recommended to introduce limitations as to the origin of genetic resources.

One more problem concerns the fact that traditional knowledge is often shared by multiple communities and may also be disseminated to the modern sector (Kleba 2009). Shared and disseminated knowledge should however not categorically be exempted from the scope of the ABS regime. Rather, in relation to shared knowledge provisions on involving other communities in the PIC procedure could be designed (see *infra* section 15). Concerning disseminated knowledge a distinction could be introduced between TK that can still be traced to a specific community and TK that lost any such connection.

---

12 Cf. the Kenyan Environmental Management and Co-ordination (Conservation of Biological Diversity and Resources, Access to Genetic Resources and Benefit Sharing) Regulations, 2006, section 3 (d) which exempts "approved research activities intended for educational purposes within recognized Kenyan academic and research institutions. . . ."
13 Formulation borrowed from the Costa Rican law.
14 See, e.g. the South African National Environmental Management: Biodiversity Act section 80, according to which the ABS regime applies to "indigenous biological resources" that are specimens and derivatives of "indigenous species" that are in section 1 defined as "a species that occurs, or has historically occurred, naturally in a free state in nature within the borders of the Republic, but excludes a species that has been introduced in the Republic as a result of human activity."

II. Access to and utilization of genetic resources and associated traditional knowledge

The situation of access is the one of which the provider state has the most effective control. The subsequent stages of the handling of the accessed genetic resources are more difficult to control, especially if the material was shipped to and is utilized in other countries. Access regulation must therefore be the starting point of any provider state legislation. Its provisions will cover the following themes:

- the obligation to obtain prior informed consent;
- the competent authority;
- the forms of consent;
- the preconditions and content of consent;
- the application procedure, including the form of applications, and the involvement of other authorities and the public;
- special provisions on access to traditional knowledge;
- special provisions on access to collections.

The provider state should, besides regulating access, also establish self-standing obligations concerning the utilization of genetic resources and traditional knowledge independently of whether access consent was obtained. This has the effect that the obligations under Articles 15–18 NP of user states are reinforced. The appropriate provisions would address topics such as

- duties concerning utilization;
- duties concerning benefit sharing;
- monitoring;
- the legalization of activities violating access conditions;
- sanctions.

7. Obligation of researcher/developer to obtain prior informed consent (PIC) for access

The provision should state that anyone wanting to have access to GR for their utilization (that is, according to Art. 6 NP, research and development on the genetic resource) must obtain the consent of the competent authority. As to access to associated traditional knowledge, the NP does not restrict the PIC requirement to access for utilization. This means that access for other purposes, such as touristic or artistic, could be included into the scope of the law. We are of the opinion, however, that this would extend the scope far beyond the intention of the ABS idea. The broader the scope, the more difficult the supervision of its application would be. We therefore recommend confining the consent requirement to access to TK for utilization.

8. Competent authority

The law should specify what authority is competent to provide the consent. This will normally be an administrative agency, but the competence could also be delegated to other actors such as a university or other trustworthy body.[15]

Besides the authority competent to provide prior consent, a focal point must be designated (which can be identical with the competent authority) that is responsible for informing access seekers about access conditions.[16]

The obligation to obtain PIC should be accompanied by rules on what happens in case of unlawful access. The competent authority should be empowered to issue an enforcement order asking the actor to apply for a permit within a specified term. It should also have the power to stop utilization activities and order the delivery of the material and R&D results, including normal ways of enforcing such orders. Due to the limits of jurisdiction of the provider state, these measures do not, however, have an effect outside its borders. It can nevertheless be provided that the competent authority may send a request to the user state to assist in the prosecution of the order.

9. Form of the access consent

The consent can have the form of an administrative permit or a contract.[17] Permits are administrative acts which in many legal systems imply powers of administrative authorities to enforce them, e.g. by ordering the researcher who does not abide by the permit conditions to act accordingly and, if he/she does not follow suit to impose a fine, stop utilization activities, withdraw the permit, or take other measures.[18] Where administrative agencies have such powers, the permit is more effective than a contract whose enforcement can only be pursued through the courts. The contract is however more effective if the GR or TK is taken to other countries, because contracts can be enforced through foreign courts, while permits are only enforceable within the jurisdiction of the provider state (unless the user state offers administrative enforcement assistance). We therefore suggest that for utilizations of GR and TK within the legislating state, a permit is the best form of consent. If GR or TK shall be transferred to another country, a contract should be concluded in addition or as an alternative to the permit.

---

15 In Costa Rica, for instance, the National Biodiversity Institute was by contract with the Technical Office (the authority competent for access consents) entrusted with such competence. The institute has signed more than 60 bioprospecting contracts. A similar setting has been introduced in Brazil where the National Council for Scientific and Technological Development was endowed with powers to provide consent with access for non-commercial research (Cabrera Medaglia 2012, 346 and 340).

16 See Art. 13 NP.

17 It should be noted that PIC does not mean permit. Also, a contract is a form of consent.

18 In other legal systems the authority must involve a court to impose enforcement measures. For a comparison see Macrory, 79 *et seq.*

10. Preconditions and content of the access consent

No matter if a permit or contract is chosen as the form of consent, the law should specify what the minimum preconditions of the consent and the main content of permit conditions or contract clauses shall be.

There are procedural and material preconditions.

As to procedure, the law will provide that an application must be filed and a procedure followed. This will be addressed below.

The application must include information on the project requesting access and triggering benefit sharing. The scope of information will depend on the conditions/clauses to be negotiated.

As to material preconditions, it should be noted that according to the definition of sovereign rights, these are not unlimited. According to Art. 15.2 CBD, the provider state shall "endeavour to create conditions facilitating access," and according to Art. 8 (a) NP this shall at least be done for non-commercial research. This means that the provider state does not have full discretion whether or not to grant consent. Rather it should fix the preconditions and set a framework for the permit conditions and contract clauses. If these requirements are met, the authority should be obliged to grant consent. Such obligation would also serve to enhance legal certainty as postulated by Art. 6.3 NP and be a means to reduce opportunities for bribery. The preconditions could be

- that the access activities do not cause adverse effects to human health or the environment, and that an environmental impact statement is required if there is indication of such adverse effects.
- in case of access to traditional knowledge and landraces, that the prior consent of the indigenous or local community was obtained; the law should set certain requirements in this regard such as that customary rules on responsibilities of authorities and common ownership are obeyed, possibly based on community protocols in difficult cases.
- if the legislating state so desires, that a foreign researcher or developer may only be granted access if he/she acts in cooperation with an internal researcher/developer; the law may even require that the internal researcher/developer must be the responsible applicant.[19]
- that in case of export of the accessed GR or TK for R&D in foreign countries, a contract must be concluded (rather than only a permit obtained). We suggest that in such cases the consent should only be granted if the user state has appropriate legislation and practices in place implementing the compliance obligations under Art. 15–18 NP.[20]

19 See the Brazilian Medida Provisoria No. 2.186–16 of August 2001, which in Art. 16 para 6 sets out: "The participation of a foreign juridical person in the collection in situ of samples of the genetic patrimonium and in the access to associated traditional knowledge may only be authorized if this is done in combination with a national public institution that is finally responsible for the coordination of the activities and if all involved institutions exercise research and development in biology and related areas" [author's translation].

20 This would also be an incentive for user states to ratify and implement the NP.

As to the permit conditions/contract clauses, the legislating state should set a framework requiring that reasonable agreement should be reached between authority and applicant on the following issues (see further Kamau, Ch. 17 in this volume):

- The geographical site and time frame where and when the sample may be taken or GR/TK may otherwise be acquired.
- The kinds of GR and TK that shall be accessed.
- The allowable research and development: The state must make a decision here whether it aims at predetermining the allowed utilization or opts for free R&D. We suggest that the kinds of R&D (taxonomic, genome sequencing and functional analysis, product development) should not be regulated because otherwise the creative potential of R&D may be lost. Art. 15.2 CBD and Art. 8 (a) NP, which ask for facilitation of access, should be kept in mind in this respect.
- However, determination should indeed be made in relation to whether commercial or only non-commercial R&D shall be allowed, and in the latter case, a new consent must be obtained in case of a change of intention. It should be kept in mind that according to our definition non-commercial/commercial refers to whether the R&D results are put to the public domain or kept private.
- Whether a duplication of the acquired GR or TK shall be sent to a collection to be specified by the law and/or the permit or contract.
- Whether the GR or TK shall be transferable to third parties; it is advisable to require a so-called viral clause in that respect, i.e. a condition/clause obliging the applicant to ensure that the third party signs a commitment to bind herself to the same permit conditions or contract clauses.
- Whether the GR or TK may be moved to other countries; as said in this case a contract must be concluded between the provider state authority and the foreign researcher.
- What non-monetary benefits shall accrue to the state. We suggest that the law should ask for participation of domestic personnel in R&D projects and project publications, albeit only as a principle, not as an absolute requirement, because much depends on the character of the project and the availability of domestic experts. The law should require that obligations and terms for reporting on R&D results shall be determined. It should also require that any publication shall indicate the origin of the GR or TK, and that a copy of the publication itself shall be delivered to the provider state.
- How monetary benefits shall be handled. In case of non-commercial R&D, some revenue may nevertheless be obtained by the researcher/developer for the publication of the R&D results. We suggest that this should not be regarded as monetary benefits that must be shared with the provider state. The phrasing of this issue might be such that any incremental revenue from the publication of R&D results shall not be subject to sharing with the provider state. In contrast, if commercial R&D shall be allowed, then the law might require that a formula for benefit sharing shall be agreed upon

in the contract. The formula will be highly dependent on the contribution the GR or TK is anticipated to make to the final product. If the chain of development is short (e.g. if a drug is made from the extraction of a biochemical from an accessed plant), the percentage of participation in the revenue from sales can be higher than if the chain is long involving many steps and many kinds of intellectual inputs and of GR or TK from other countries. The law should also acknowledge the possibility that the contribution of its GR or TK disappears during the development chain (see further below section 18).

- How the interface between the public domain and commercial use of data should be organized. The underlying problem is that information that was published through print media or stored in open access databases may be used for commercial purposes. This is common allowed practice of the public information domain, but such practice does not reflect the fact that some information may be subject to the benefit-sharing right of provider states of the GR from which the data were derived. For instance, information on a gene of an organism from state A, coding for a certain function (e.g. a commercially interest enzyme), may have been put into an open access database. Some user retrieves the information and uses it for the production of a valuable chemical substance which he or she brings on the market. Benefit sharing can be approached in such cases if the provider state law requires as the content of access contracts:

  - a clause obliging the researcher/developer and, through the viral clause, any third party to ensure that any information that is made public must note the origin of the organism on which it informs, and that commercial use of the information is only allowed upon PIC of the provider state.

This will allow the tracking of the original organism through the chain of R&D and help the provider state to obtain benefit sharing even under conditions of the public domain. However, this is admittedly a very ambitious requirement. It is becoming common practice with regard to standard agreements on the transfer of material,[21] but necessitates fundamental changes of practices with regard to the transfer of data. This is notably the case for databases. They would need to ensure that the origin of the GR travels with the R&D information they store, and they would need to oblige commercial users to respect the rights of the provider state. And even if the databases were prepared to change their practices accordingly, it would still be very difficult for provider states to discover breaches of the rules. They would need to check what databases host what information belonging to them, what users have retrieved such information for commercial purposes, what products have been developed on that basis, and what revenue was obtained from

---

21 See, as an example, the standard material transfer agreement used by the Deutsche Sammlung von mikroorganismen und Zellkulturen (DSMZ) (Fritze and Oumard, Ch. 15 in this volume).

the sales of the product. This is almost impossible for normal provider states. It shows that provider states are in a weak position if they agree to the public domain. But the alternative – tight control of the R&D chain – equally requires enormous effort of administrative supervision. Therefore, the better way out is to introduce the said clause into access contracts and trust that the requested change of practice will take place. For the rest, the problem shows that the best strategy of the provider state is to insist that its scientists are involved in the R&D projects so that the state can develop its own R&D capacity.

- Conditions/clauses should be laid down that allow the authority to withdraw the permit or terminate the contract if they are breached.
- How disputes between the competent authority and the applicant shall be settled. According to customary international law, the courts under jurisdiction of the legislating state will be responsible, if the access and utilization happens within the state's realm, no matter if the researcher/developer is a citizen of the provider state or of a foreign state.

11. The application for access consent

As said, the law will provide that an application must be submitted together with the information the competent authority needs in order to assess if and how the access can be admitted. The information to be submitted may include

- coordinates of the applicant institution;
- outline of the project (what shall be researched and developed, non-commercial and/or commercial intentions);
- partner institutions and their role in the project;
- coordinates of the persons who will perform the access;
- location(s) and time frame of access;
- modality of access (sample, purchase, etc.);
- in case of access to genetic material: description of what species and about how many specimens shall be accessed;
- in case of traditional knowledge: description of its kind and of the community from which it shall be received and an account of steps taken to ensure PIC of the community (customary law, community protocols);
- possible risks of the access for human health or the environment.

The authority should be given a fixed timeline for checking the completeness of the application and be empowered to ask the applicant to complete the required information.

After consultation with other responsible agencies (see No. 9), the competent authority should still be entitled to ask for further information if the information does not suffice to assess whether the requirements for granting the consent have been met. It should also be entitled to hold a meeting of stakeholders in controversial cases.

12. Involving other responsible agencies in the consent procedure

The authority should be required to forward the application to other competent authorities for comment and/or approval. It is recommended that a one-stop shop concept is realized in that regard. Sometimes national legislation requires more permits, such as one for doing research in the country, one (if applicable) for entering a nature reserve, one (if applicable) for doing research in the marine realm, one (if applicable) for entering into and acting within the area of indigenous communities, one (if applicable) for the exportation of the genetic material, one (if applicable) for entering realms of state security, etc. In addition, other agencies may need to be informed about the project and are empowered to intervene if their realm is adversely affected by the project. The access seeker is thus confronted with often lengthy and frustrating procedures in front of many different administrative bodies. A one-stop shop would charge the authority competent for ABS with obtaining consents and comments from the other agencies. The law might even go further and remove one or the other consent requirement considering that the underlying concern can as well be cared for by the ABS authority (Kamau & Winter 2009: 375). This is, for instance, the case with the general research permit and the marine research permit: as the ABS regime has also to do with research and looks even closer at the planned project, the other permit requirements can be waived. Alternatively, the permit requirement could be transformed into a right of the responsible agency to comment on the ABS application. To the extent that the other permit is based on criteria that substantially differ from those of ABS, the ABS authority could be charged to also apply the other criteria. For instance, the ABS authority could be mandated to also protect indigenous communities, check environmental risks, and even see to security concerns. It is true that some agencies wish to keep their competences, not the least if the fees charged flow into their individual budgets, but the thrust for enabling R&D should have priority over such concerns. In the law, the one-stop shop concept could be expressed as follows:

> The competent authority (i.e. the one competent for ABS consent) forwards the application within [. . .] (term to be fixed) after its reception or completion to the authorities responsible for a permit under laws X, Y, Z. These authorities may file their comments within [. . .] (term to be fixed). The competent authority, taking the comments into consideration, assesses if the legal requirements established by the laws X, Y, Z are respected. No additional permit under these laws is required.

13. Involving the public in the consent procedure

The legislating state will have to decide if other private persons or the public at large should be involved in the consent procedure.[22] We suggest that this is not necessary because the ABS regime primarily manages R&D activities which

---

22 See for an example the Kenyan Environmental Management and Co-ordination (Conservation of Biological Diversity and Resources, Access to Genetic Resources and Benefit Sharing) Regulations, 2006, section 10, according to which any application for consent must be published and objections can be made to the competent authority.

hardly affect the individual interests of others. Only competing interests of con-
current researchers and developers may make this request to be informed. But such
interest is hardly well founded, because it is legitimate that a researcher or developer initiates his/her project confidentially in order to prevent the research idea
from being stolen by someone else before it could be elaborated. However, in any
case, a summary of the final decision – the permit and/or contract – should be
made public.

14. Involving the landowner in the consent procedure

The consent of the landowner will have to be obtained in those legal systems
which consider genetic resources to be the property of the landowner. In the other
legal systems, the taking of a sample may be part of common uses of the land. If it
is not covered by common use rights, the consent of the landowner is necessary,
but only for entering the land and taking the specimen, not for the utilization of
the genetic resource.

It is open to question if the ABS legislation needs to deal with the landowners'
rights at all. These rights are ruled by civil law. Their enforcement could be left
to legal interaction between the access seeker and the landowner.

Alternatively, the ABS law could at least provide that the landowner is
informed about the application for access consent. It could also make the consent
of the landowner a precondition of the authority's consent,[23] although this appears
to us to be too much of a public intervention into civil law relationships.

15. Special provisions on access to associated traditional knowledge

If the legislating state acknowledges (as we suggested above sub No. 2) that the
indigenous or local communities and/or individuals of the communities shall be
sui generis proprietors of their traditional knowledge and their landraces, the
provision of consent to the proprietors could be left to them. The law would
then just lay down the condition that such consent must be obtained. However,
considering the possibly weak capacity of indigenous and local communities to
negotiate with well-equipped researchers and developers, the provider state
should put in place some kind of supervision to establish if the consent was
obtained under fair conditions. Therefore, various legal systems have established
that the state must give its consent to the consent of holders of associated TK
and landraces.[24]

In addition, special preconditions of the consent of holders of TK or landraces
should be laid down. Often, it will not be easy to identify them. Customary law
of local authority structures will have to be consulted, which should be made

23 Such is the regulation in South Africa, see National Environmental Management: Biodiversity
   Act 2004, section 82 para. (2). The competent authority must even approve the agreements.
24 See the South African National Environmental Management: Biodiversity Act section 82; also
   the Brazilian Medida Provisoria No. 2.186–16 of August 2001, Art. 12 and Art. 8 § 1°.

obligatory by the law. The researcher or developer, when applying for an access permit or contract, should be asked to explain what steps were taken in identifying and negotiating with the competent local authority. The law should also specify minimum points that any access permit or agreement should contain. These may include those provisions suggested above (No. 10) for the normal access permit and agreement but could be complemented by more specialized points, including, for example:

- that certain non-monetary benefits shall be agreed upon, such as the involvement of locals in the collection and R&D activities;
- the naming of the holder of the TK or landrace in any publication on it;
- transfer of adapted R&D technologies to the indigenous or local community;
- lump-sum payments;
- special reporting obligations;
- obligations to explain R&D results;
- free use of information and products based on the TK or landrace.

Special provision is necessary for TK or landraces that are shared by several indigenous/local communities or by several individuals (such as herbalists) from several communities. We suggest that there is no other way than to let the communities or individuals decide this question themselves. The law might however set certain criteria for these cases, including ancestry in generating the knowledge or landrace, input into its further development, involvement in the planned R&D, etc.

Finally the law should also deal with the problem of disseminated TK and landraces. This is, once more, difficult to solve. The law should accept that widely disseminated TK or landraces are outside the scope of the TK/landraces regime, but that this does not apply if TK/landraces can be traced to identifiable communities and the utilization of TK/landraces is against the intention of the communities or individuals who allow the dissemination to take place.

16. Special provisions on access to collections of genetic resources

States are provider states not only concerning genetic resources they possess in *in situ* conditions, but also insofar as they possess GR in *ex situ* collections. The GR can be indigenous or acquired from other states. In the latter case, the GR must have been obtained in accordance with requirements set by provider states after entering into force of the CBD.[25] The legislating state can decide to regulate access to and utilization of genetic resources held in collections. It may require prior consent of the competent authority, like in the case of access to *in situ* genetic resources. Alternatively, in order not to hinder the exchange of biological

25 Cf. Art. 6.1 NP.

material, the state may desist from a PIC requirement and set rules that the collections must observe by themselves, such as that a material transfer agreement must be concluded with the access seeker restricting any R&D on the genetic resource to non-commercial purposes and requiring prior consent of the host state in case of change of intent to commercial uses. It is also possible to establish a self-standing obligation to that effect which is applicable even if no agreement was signed. Such an example can be found in Norway.[26]

17. Certificate of compliance

According to Art. 17 paragraphs 2–4 NP "a permit or its equivalent issued in accordance with Article 6, paragraph 3 (e) and made available to the Access and Benefit-Sharing Clearing-House, shall constitute an internationally recognized certificate of compliance," which serves as evidence that the provider state requirements were fulfilled. In implementing this provision, the ABS law should contain an article providing that the permit does have the quality of such a certificate. If – as in the case of commercial R&D – an access contract had to be agreed upon, the permit should be amended by a statement declaring that such contract was indeed concluded. If the permit is replaced by a contract, a separate formal statement should be handed out containing the information listed in Art. 17.4 NP, i.e. the issuing authority, date of issuance, the provider, identifier of the certificate, addressee of the consent, genetic resource or TK covered, confirmation that a contract was concluded and prior consent obtained, and the commercial or non-commercial intention of the planned R&D. The law should also provide that the certificate must be forwarded to the Access and Benefit-Sharing Clearing-House.

18. Obligations concerning utilization and benefit sharing

As said above (sub II), the provider state should, besides requiring PIC for access, also establish self-standing obligations concerning the utilization and the commercialization of genetic resources and traditional knowledge independently of whether access consent was obtained or not. This has the effect that a researcher or developer who utilizes or commercializes GR or TK without prior consent, or does this disrespecting permit conditions or contract clauses, acts in violation of the law of the provider state. If the R&D is performed in the provider state, such

---

26 See Nature Diversity Act section 59 paras. 3–5 which read: "Any person that receives genetic material derived from a public collection shall refrain, in Norway or abroad, from claiming intellectual property rights or other rights to the material that would limit use of the material, such as use for food or agriculture, unless the material has been modified in a way that results in a substantial change. If intellectual property rights over genetic material are established contrary to the third paragraph, the competent authorities under the Act shall consider taking measures, including bringing legal action, to ensure promotion of the objective set out in section 57."

"Any person may invoke conditions under the third paragraph, or other conditions that have been set for collection, against any person that, contrary to such conditions, seeks to enforce an intellectual property right."

violation can trigger remedial action by the competent authority. If the R&D is performed in another state, this state may feel obliged to take measures beyond mere control in case access requirements of the provider state were observed. The user state would then also ensure that the utilization and generation of benefits are compliant with the material obligations set by the provider state legislation.

The first material obligation should be that no utilization of GR or TK accessed in the provider state shall be allowed without prior consent of the competent authority, and that if consent was obtained, any utilization must be performed in accordance with the conditions and clauses of ABS permits and contracts.

Another obligation should concern the generation and sharing of benefits. This could be phrased such that any monetary benefit from IPRs on GR or TK accessed in the provider country shall be shared with the same or, in case of associated TK and landraces, with the pertinent indigenous of local community. The precise amount of the share should be the one agreed in a permit or contract. If the commercialization was not allowed or not determined in that way, the law should fix a certain percentage of the revenue from royalties or sales.

The law should also address the possibility that the contribution of the provider state's GR or TK disappears during the chain of R&D. In that case the final product cannot anymore be regarded as "arising from" the GR or TK, as Art. 5.1 and 5.5 NP postulate. For instance, a bioinformatics project may compare genes of organism A with genes of organism B in order to identify functions of those of B. The gene of B and its functions are then used for product development, not that of A. It is true that in very abstract terms the gene of organism A has also contributed to the product, but this appears as very artificial. Another pathway of disappearance of the contribution of the original GR or TK would be that the functional trait taken from the original GR or TK is not anymore identifiable as a distinct feature of the final product. A third pathway would be time related: products arising from an original GR or TK should be freed from monetary benefit sharing after expiry of a certain time. The CBD/NP regime failed to fix such a term, but provider states should fill the gap as an implication of the principle that benefit sharing should be fair and equitable. In analogy to the timelines of patent laws, 20 years might be considered as a fair solution.

19. Monitoring and sanctions

The competent authority should also be mandated to conduct administrative oversight of activities involving access to GR or TK, R&D, publications, IPRs, and the marketing of products based on GR or TK. Such monitoring, of course, is a very demanding task which the law may facilitate by allowing the authority to take action at random or upon notice from other agencies or persons. In order to perform, the authority should be empowered to ask for information, enter premises, and study files. It should also be entitled to issue cease and desist orders and withdraw the permit in case of breaches of permit conditions. It should be mandated to go to court in case of breaches of access contracts.

III. Utilization of imported GR and TK and benefit sharing

If the legislating state is party to the Nagoya Protocol, it bears obligations under Articles 15–18 NP with regard to imported GR and TK. In that regard, the legislating state is acting as the state in whose realm the utilization of GR and TK takes place, hence as a user state. Its legislation as a user state supports the ABS regime of the provider state. As the provider state will have difficulties in monitoring whether its ABS requirements are observed by researchers and developers in the user state, the latter is called to establish its own supervisory regime.

20. *Obligations and administrative checking concerning access, utilization, and benefit generation on GR and TK*

Articles 15–18 NP ask the user state to ensure that for R&D on imported GR or TK conducted within its jurisdiction, prior informed consent of the provider state was obtained. There are different options how to implement this. We suggest six of them in an order of increasing intervention:

1   The researcher and developer are obliged to exercise (and are supervised to have exercised) <u>due diligence by obtaining prior consent for access</u> of the provider state; due diligence means, *inter alia*, that if the legal requirements of the provider state are unclear and the researcher diligently tried to find them out, that he/she is regarded to have complied even if according to thorough analysis prior consent was required. This solution was introduced in the EU.[27]

2   The researcher and developer is <u>obliged to obtain</u> (and is supervised to have obtained) <u>prior consent for access</u> to GR and TK if required by the provider state. This means that the user state must in effect ensure that consent was obtained. This solution was adopted by Norway.[28]

3   The researcher and developer is obliged to apply (and supervised to apply) <u>due diligence</u> to obtain prior consent of the provider state and, <u>when conducting research and development, to comply with any permit and contract conditions</u> if this is required by provider state regulation. This solution was adopted by the EU.[29] It is unclear if Articles 15–18 NP actually require

---

27 See Regulation (EU) 511/2014 which reads: "Users shall exercise due diligence to ascertain that genetic resources and traditional knowledge associated with genetic resources which they utilize have been accessed in accordance with applicable access and benefit-sharing legislation or regulatory requirements, [. . .]."

28 See Nature Diversity Act Art. 60 para. 1 which reads: "The import for utilization in Norway of genetic material from a state that requires consent for collection or export of such material may only take place in accordance with such consent. The person that has control of the material is bound by the conditions that have been set for consent. The state may enforce the conditions by bringing legal action on behalf of the person that set them."

29 See Art. 4.2 Regulation (EU) 511/2014 which reads: "Genetic resources and traditional knowledge associated with genetic resources shall only be transferred and utilized in accordance with mutually agreed terms if they are required by applicable legislation or regulatory requirements." Concerning administrative supervision see Art. 9.4 (b): "The checks referred to in paragraph 1 of this Article may include an examination of:

(a) [. . .]; (b) documentation and records that demonstrate the exercise of due diligence in accordance with Article 4 <u>in relation to specific use activities;</u>" [Emphasis added.].

going that far. Art. 15.1 and 16.1 only require that the GR and TK was accessed in accordance with provider state rules, not that it is also utilized in accordance with such rules and the permit and contract conditions, but the monitoring duties under Art. 17.1 NP[30] appear to extend to the utilization. It is true, though, that according to Art. 18.2 NP dispute resolution must be available concerning mutually agreed terms. But this need not be read to exclude unilateral enforcement action of the user state if due to the ignorance of the provider state no bilateral dispute has emerged.

4   The researcher and developer is obliged to obtain (and supervised to obtain) prior consent of the provider state and, <u>when conducting research and development, to comply with any permit and contract conditions</u> if this is required by the provider state regulation. This would once more be an obligation in effect. Whether it is prescribed by the NP is subject to the same reasoning as above at (4). This solution was also introduced by Norway.[31]

5   Those who draw monetary benefits from GR and TK are obliged to exercise (and are supervised to exercise) <u>due diligence to share the benefits</u> with the provider state upon mutually agreed terms. This solution was introduced in the EU.[32] The NP however does not require contracting states to adopt it.[33]

6   Those who draw monetary benefits from GR and TK are <u>obliged to share</u> (and are supervised to share) <u>the benefits</u> with the provider state upon mutually agreed terms. The Norwegian law has adopted this variant, or could be understood to that effect.[34] Concerning the NP, the considerations under (5) apply.

The ruling interpretation of Art. 6 NP is that the NP only requires a checking by user states if utilized GR and TK was accessed in accordance with provider state

---

30 Art. 17.1 (a) reads at (i): "Designated checkpoints would collect or receive, as appropriate, relevant information related to prior informed consent, to the source of the genetic resource, to the establishment of mutually agreed terms, and/or to the utilization of genetic resources, as appropriate"; and at (iv): "Check points must be effective and should have functions relevant to implementation of this subparagraph (a). They should be relevant to the utilization of genetic resources, or to the collection of relevant information at, *inter alia*, any stage of research, development, innovation, pre-commercialization or commercialization." Why should check points "be relevant to the utilization" if not by ensuring its compliance with provider state requirements?

31 See Art. 60 para. 1 Norwegian Nature Diversity Act.

32 See Regulation (EU) 511/2014 Art. 7.2 which reads: "<u>At the stage of final development of a product</u> developed via the utilization of genetic resources or traditional knowledge associated with such resources, users shall <u>declare to the competent authorities</u> referred to in Article 6(1) that they have fulfilled the obligations under Article 4 [. . .]." Article 4.1 reads: "Users shall <u>exercise due diligence</u> to ascertain that genetic resources and traditional knowledge associated with genetic resources which they utilize have been accessed in accordance with applicable access and benefit-sharing legislation or regulatory requirements, <u>and that benefits are fairly and equitably shared</u> upon mutually agreed terms, in accordance with any applicable legislation or regulatory requirements." Genetic resources and traditional knowledge associated with genetic resources shall only be transferred and utilized in accordance with mutually agreed terms if they are required by applicable legislation or regulatory requirements." [Emphasis added.]

33 For a critique of this reticence see Kamau, Fedder, and Winter (2010).

34 See Art. 60 para. 1 Norwegian Nature Diversity Act.

requirements (above nos. (1) and (2)).[35] No matter what the correct understanding of the NP is, the user state is free to go beyond a minimal reading. For provider states which export more than import GR and TK, it is wise to go beyond and thus demonstrate what they would also expect from user states. Hence, following the Norwegian example, the basic provision might be formulated, for example, as follows:

1   The import into [. . .] (legislating state) of genetic resources and associated traditional knowledge from a state that requires consent for access to such material may only take place if such consent was obtained.
2   The person that utilizes or commercializes the genetic resource or associated traditional knowledge imported from a state that requires consent for access is bound by the conditions that have been set for consent.
3   The person importing genetic resources or associated traditional knowledge for utilization from a state that requires consent for access shall inform the competent authority accordingly and submit the documents containing the consent of the provider state.
4   The person bringing a product based on a genetic resource or associated traditional knowledge imported from a state that requires consent for access to the market or derives monetary benefits from them in other ways (such as through royalties in IPRs) shall inform the competent authority accordingly and submit the documents containing the consent of the provider state.
5   The competent authority shall carry out checks to verify whether persons utilizing or commercializing genetic resources or associated traditional knowledge imported from a state that requires consent for access comply with the conditions set for consent.
6   The competent authority shall serve compliance orders in cases of noncompliance. It shall inform the provider state of cases of alleged significant noncompliance and cooperate with it in taking appropriate measures.

21. Trusted collections

Collections that receive, store, and transfer genetic resources will also be subject to the rules set out under No. 15 above. This means that they need to comply with the ABS regime of provider states if they import genetic resources or receive genetic resources that were imported by other persons. However, the legislating state may wish to desist from supervising collections if they can be trusted to comply by themselves. This presupposes that trusted collections must fulfil certain requirements for being recognized as such. The EU operates such a system.[36] Such a collection must demonstrate its capacity to

---

35 See e.g. Greiber et al. (2012), 163.
36 See Regulation (EU) 511/2014, Art. 5.

- accept samples only with documentation evidencing that they were accessed in compliance with provider state requirements and can be forwarded in compliance with any consent conditions;
- ensure that genetic material is stored with documentation of the provider state where it was acquired;
- supply genetic resources and related information to third persons only in compliance with any conditions set by the provider state consent, such as, for instance, that only non-commercial utilization shall be allowed.

22. Sanctions

Finally, the law will need to lay down rules on penalties applicable to the more serious infringements which were not cured by enforcement orders or which are to be considered severe.

References

Burton, G (2009) "Australian ABS law and administration – A model law and approach?" in: Kamau, EC, Winter, G (eds) *Genetic resources, traditional knowledge and the law. Solutions for access and benefit sharing*, London: Earthscan, pp. 271–308.

Cabrera Medaglia, J (2012) "The Implementation of the Nagoya Protocol in Latin America and the Carribean: Challenges and opportunities" in: Morgera, E, Buck, M, Tsioumani, E (eds) *The 2010 Nagoya Protocol on access and benefit sharing in perspective. Implications for international law and implementation challenges*, Leiden: Nijhoff, pp. 331–368.

Godt, C (2009) "Enforcement of benefit-sharing duties in user countries" in: Kamau, EC, Winter, G (eds) *Genetic resources, traditional knowledge and the law. Solutions for access and benefit sharing*, London: Earthscan, pp. 419–438.

Greiber, T et al. (2012) *An explanatory guide to the Nagoya Protocol on access and benefit-sharing*, IUCN Environmental Policy and Law Paper No. 83.

Kamau, EC, Fedder, B, Winter G (2010) "The Nagoya Protocol on access to genetic resources and benefit sharing: What is new and what are the implications for provider and user countries and the scientific community?", *Law, Environment and Development Journal* 6(3), p. 246, Available online at www.lead-journal.org/content/10246.pdf.

Kamau, EC, Winter, G (2009) "Streamlining access procedures and standards" in: Kamau, EC, Winter, G (eds) *Genetic resources, traditional knowledge and the law: Solutions for access and benefit sharing*, Earthscan, London, pp. 365–380.

Kleba, J (2009) "A Socio-legal inquiry into the protection of disseminated traditional knowledge – learning from Brazilian cases" in: Kamau, EC, Winter, G (eds) *Genetic resources, traditional knowledge and the law: Solutions for access and benefit sharing*, London: Earthscan, pp. 119–142.

Louafi, S, Schloen, M (2013) "Practices of exchanging and utilizing genetic resources for food and agriculture and the access and benefit sharing regime" in: Kamau, EC, Winter, G (eds), *Common pools of genetic resources. Equity and innovation in international biodiversity law*, London: Routledge, pp. 193–223.

Macrory, R (2010) *Regulation, enforcement and governance in environmental law*, Oxford University Press.

20 Micro B3 model agreement on access to marine microorganisms and benefit sharing

Text and commentary

Caroline von Kries, Arianna Broggiato, Tom Dedeurwaerdere, and Gerd Winter

Objectives and legal background of the model agreement

The Micro B3 Project, together with the Ocean Sampling Day Initiative, aims at studying marine microorganisms in different seas (their genetic diversity, their functions, and their ecosystems), producing genomics sequencing to be shared in an open source and open access database, and fostering commercial product development. More specifically, Micro B3 offers improved tools to achieve facilitated access to the research results, including genomic and environmental data, and to integrate data of different marine scientific projects through an innovative and interactive informatics system. Further, the project offers tools for specific capacity building to the research community.

As planned research is based on the taking of samples within internal waters, the territorial sea, and the exclusive economic zone of coastal states, the Convention on Biological Diversity (CBD) applies. According to the CBD the coastal state may, by its national legislation, require its prior consent for the taking and utilization of its genetic resources and ask for the sharing of benefits drawn from the genetic resources. These requirements have been specified by the Nagoya Protocol (NP), which entered into force on 12 October 2014. The conditions of access and benefit sharing (ABS) are normally determined through a contract concluded between a research institution and the coastal state. This Micro B3 Model Agreement on ABS (in the following: Model Agreement) shall be a template for such contract. It is recommended that Micro B3 partners use this Model Agreement, unless the coastal state insists on the use of its own template.

However, neither prior consent nor benefit sharing is required if the Provider State does not make use of its sovereign rights under the CBD and the NP. The Provider State is free to decide not to establish an ABS regime and thus allow for free research and development activities concerning its genetic resources. In this case the Model Agreement does not apply.

Whether a Provider State has established an ABS regime or not can only be determined by examining its domestic legislation and practices. According to upcoming rules of User States, a due diligence obligation applies in such cases. This means that the researcher has to take due care to find out the domestic procedure of the Provider State, if any exists. He/she is not required to carry out an in-depth legal analysis. Rather, it is sufficient diligence if he/she seeks advice at the national focal point on ABS of the Provider State. The latter is bound to notify the CBD Secretariat under Article 13 NP. A list of national focal points is available at the CBD website (www.cbd.int).

Through minor changes in the text the Model Agreement can also be used for other projects, such as those on genetic resources other than marine microorganisms. The aim of the Model Agreement is thus to serve as model contractual clauses for mutually agreed terms according to Article 19 of the Nagoya Protocol. In this way, it hopefully assists in a worldwide harmonization of procedures for access and benefit sharing in international collaboration frameworks for genomics research.

Non-commercial and commercial options within the model agreement

The Model Agreement applies to full commercial, hybrid, and full non-commercial use at the point of access. This agreement can cover three situations:

- PUBLIC DOMAIN: only public domain uses of genetic resources are envisioned when the resource is accessed. Therefore, only conditions for public domain uses are negotiated at the moment of first access (Article 4.2). If desired, commercial uses can be envisioned at a later stage of the research process. Such commercial uses are permitted, but the conditions of this should be negotiated at the point of change of intent (consent clause under Article 4.4).
- (B) HYBRID: public domain uses of some genetic resources/some use of genetic resources are envisioned, and it is clear at the time of access that some potential commercial uses for other genetic resources/other uses of the accessed genetic resource exist.
- (C) PROPRIETARY: commercial uses for all the accessed genetic resources are envisioned. Benefit-sharing conditions for commercial uses will be negotiated at the time of access to the genetic resources. In this case only Article 4.3 applies (Articles 4.2, 4.4 are to be deleted).

The Model Agreement will be commented Article by Article. The Article concerned is set in front, then follows an overview of its content and of its legal background. In a last paragraph the Article is explained in detail.

The preamble to the Model Agreement is not commented. It is an opening paragraph introducing the goals of the Micro B3 Project, the main aspects of ABS regulation in the Model Agreement, and the legal texts that contain provisions on ABS. As such, it does not need to be explained, since later in the commentary the provisions on ABS reappear in the Articles. The preamble has only a declaratory character and its content does not bind the Parties to the agreement.

Preamble

Considering that the European Union–funded research project Micro B3 (hereinafter the "Micro B3 Project") is a scientific research program with the following objectives:

- to cooperatively sample marine microbial biodiversity at various sites, including through global coordinated actions called "Ocean Sampling Days"
- to generate large-scale knowledge on marine microbial genomes in an environmental context and on actual or potential bio-technological applications
- to develop innovative bioinformatics approaches for the large-scale integration of genomic data of marine microbes with environmental and ecosystems data
- to make the resulting knowledge accessible for the research and development community for policy makers and the public at large,

Recalling that access to and utilization of genetic resources taken from the marine internal waters, the territorial sea, the exclusive economic zone, or the continental shelf of coastal states should be consistent with the provisions of the Convention on Biological Diversity (CBD), taking into account their specifications by the Bonn Guidelines on Access to Genetic Resources and the Fair and Equitable Sharing of Benefits arising from their Utilization, and, where appropriate, the Nagoya Protocol on Access to Genetic Resources and the Fair and Equitable Sharing of Benefits arising from their Utilization to the Convention on Biological Diversity, as well as with the United Nations Convention on the Law of the Sea (UNCLOS) and the customary law expressed by UNCLOS,

Recalling that according to these provisions access to and utilization of genetic resources taken from the above-described maritime zones is subject to the prior informed consent of the coastal state and mutually agreed terms if the coastal state so requires,

Recalling that according to these provisions coastal states have the right to regulate, authorize, and conduct marine scientific research in their territorial sea, exclusive economic zone, and on their continental shelf; and that in the case of research undertaken by other states or international organizations the coastal state has the right, if it so desires and if practicable, to participate or be represented in the marine scientific research project and to access data and samples and receive preliminary reports and final results,

Recalling that according to these provisions non-monetary and/or monetary benefits from the utilization of the genetic resources shall be shared with the Provider State if the same so requires and as it is set out in mutually agreed terms,

Recalling that according to these provisions the transfer of genetic resources to third parties shall be set out in a material transfer agreement,

Recalling that according to these provisions measures on access for non-commercial research purposes shall be simplified with a view to contribute to the conservation and sustainable use of biodiversity, and

Acknowledging that research and development on genetic resources can be for the public domain or for proprietary purposes.

Article 1:
Objective of the agreement

1.1 The agreement sets out the terms for the access to genetic resources found in/on the Provider State's marine internal waters, territorial sea, exclusive economic zone, or continental shelf, for the utilization and transfer to third parties of the accessed genetic resources, for the management and transfer to third parties of associated knowledge, and for the sharing of benefits drawn from the same.

1.2 The agreement is part of the Micro B3 Consortium Agreement.[1] Its rights and obligations extend to all Micro B3 partners.

1.3 The Parties agree to release a copy of the agreement to the registered users of the web portal built by the Micro B3 Project.

1. Overview of the Article

The Parties have to fill in their full names, addresses, and contact persons in the head section of the Model Agreement. This initial requirement is necessary for their identification and their definition throughout the agreement ("Provider" and "Recipient").

Article 1.1 introduces Parties to the principal issues addressed by the Model Agreement. These are:

- the access to genetic resources found in/on the Provider State's internal waters, territorial sea, exclusive economic zone, and continental shelf,
- the utilization and the transfer to third parties of the accessed genetic resources,
- the management and the transfer to third parties of associated knowledge, and
- the sharing of benefits drawn from the utilization.

---

1 The Consortium Agreement is publicly accessible at the Micro B3 website www.microb3.eu.

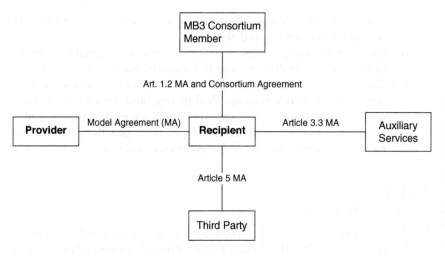

Figure 20.1 Legal relationships between MicroB3 actors
Source: Authors

In Article 1.2 it is set out that the Model Agreement is embedded in the Micro B3 Consortium Agreement. This implies that the Micro B3 Consortium Agreement will be amended by a clause obliging all Micro B3 partners to agree to the terms of the present Model Agreement. In particular, if Micro B3 partners receive genetic resources (GR) from the Recipient researcher they are bound to the pertinent provisions of this Model Agreement when utilizing the GR, reporting on results and generating benefits.

Article 1.3 is a formal publication requirement: the Parties shall provide a copy of the contract to the web portal of the Micro B3 Project. This requirement helps in tracking back the obligations of the initial agreement, if needed.

2. *Legal background*

The Model Agreement is based on Article 15 of the Convention on Biological Diversity (CBD) and the Nagoya Protocol (NP).[2] While Article 15 of the CBD contains the principles of access to genetic resources (GR) and the sharing of benefits drawn from the utilization of the resources (ABS), the NP elaborates the details of the transactions. The NP assumes that negotiations about access and benefit sharing principally take place bilaterally between the "Party providing such (*genetic*) resources" and the "Party that has acquired the genetic resources," e.g. Article 6.1 NP. In the Model Agreement they are referred to as "Provider" and "Recipient."

---

2 Secretariat of the Convention on Biological Diversity, *Nagoya Protocol on Access to Genetic Resources and the Fair and Equitable Sharing of Benefits Arising from their Utilization to the Convention on Biological Diversity*. Montreal: CBD Secretariat, 2011.

Articles 5 and 6 NP are the core provisions of the Protocol since they regulate the principal mutual rights and obligations between the Parties: Article 6.1 requires that the Provider State shall be asked to give prior informed consent to User States seeking access to and utilization of genetic resources; Article 5.1 requires that the benefits arising out of the utilization of genetic resources shall be shared in a fair and equitable way according to mutually agreed terms. In addition, according to Article 6.3 (g) (iii) NP, the Provider State may also require that the provisions of the agreement shall extend to third parties to whom genetic resources are transferred for further use.

The maritime zones are mentioned in Article 1 of the Model Agreement in order to identify those parts of the waters over which the coastal state is entitled to exercise sovereign rights concerning genetic resources. The different zones and their sovereign rights regimes are determined by the UNCLOS. In relation to research and development (R&D) on genetic resources, these determinations largely coincide with those of the CBD and the NP (Articles 4 (a), 22.1 CBD).

Internal waters are subject to the full sovereignty of the coastal state (Article 2.1 UNCLOS), which includes the regulation of R&D activities on genetic resources. With certain exceptions, full sovereignty applies also within the territorial sea which covers a breadth of 12 nm measured from the baseline, i.e. the low-water line. This includes exclusive rights on and the regulation of R&D on genetic resources (Articles 2.1, 3, 245 UNCLOS). Within the exclusive economic zone which forms a belt of 200 nm from the baseline, limited sovereign rights of the coastal states are acknowledged, once again including exclusive rights and the regulation of R&D on genetic resources (Articles 56, 246 UNCLOS). On the continental shelf beyond the 200 nm baseline, reaching a maximum of 350 nm, sovereign rights may also be exercised in the subsoil and on the seabed, but only for the exploration and exploitation of natural resources, i.e. only for commercial R&D (Article 246.6 UNCLOS).

The remaining ocean is made up of the so-called areas beyond national jurisdiction (ABNJ; Article 86 UNCLOS) which break down into the Area and the High Seas. States do not have sovereign rights in these zones. Therefore, the access to and the utilization of genetic resources taken from the ABNJ is free (Articles 87, 256 UNCLOS), but limited by the respect of the conditions laid down by UNCLOS, and by the respect of the interests of other States and of the right under the convention with respect to activities in the Area (Article 87). No access agreement needs to be, nor can be, concluded. Therefore the Model Agreement does not address the taking of samples in the ABNJ.

3. Explanation of the article in detail

The components of the agreement's head section clarify who shall be the Parties to the agreement. They are called the "Provider" and the "Recipient" and are the institutions competent to regulate the subject matter of the agreement. They are the legal persons that bear the rights and duties of the agreement.

The signatory on the Provider side will normally be a governmental authority. The competence may however be delegated to a research institution. This depends on the domestic law of the Provider State. In order to identify who is the competent authority to sign an ABS agreement, the researcher should consult the national focal point on ABS of the Provider State. Further clarity can be obtained from the international ABS Clearing-House which shall be established according to Article 14 NP (not operational as of now). Its mission is to provide information on the national focal point and/or the national authority competent for access and benefit-sharing decisions. At the time of the composition of this commentary (December 2014), the Clearing-House is entering the pilot phase. Meanwhile, however, researchers may directly consult the website of the CBD (www.cbd.int), which provides links to relevant national websites on ABS.

On the Recipient side, the signatory will normally be a legal (public or private) entity such as a research organization or an industrial enterprise. The Recipient shall not be the individual researcher but the institution that employs the researcher. This ensures that the agreement survives changes of personnel and that its implementation is surveyed.

The principal content of the agreement is the regulation of access to genetic resources (Article 3), their utilization (Article 4) and their transfer to third parties (Article 5.1), the management (Article 6 – dissemination of knowledge) and transfer to third parties of associated knowledge (Article 5.2), and the sharing of benefits drawn from the utilization. Benefits are regulated in Article 7 (acknowledgement of the role of scientists), Article 8 (recording and reporting), Article 9 (sharing of information), Article 10 (scientific collaboration with the Provider State and capacity building), and Article 11 (monetary benefits). A detailed analysis follows under the respective Articles.

It is also necessary to define the geographical scope applicable for the Recipient's collection of genetic resources: the Provider State's internal waters, territorial sea, its exclusive economic zone (EEZ), and its continental shelf. It is thus clear that the ABNJ is outside the scope of the agreement.

The geographical scope helps in fencing the realm where the Recipient has to seek PIC before accessing and taking samples from the marine waters. It is not relevant for the other rights and obligations under the Model Agreement. This is due to the fact that the utilization and the benefit-sharing activities usually do not take place on the sea (*in situ*) unless, for example, the genetic material is analyzed in research laboratories on the research vessel directly after taking the sample (utilization) or the User State collaborates with scientists of the Provider State on the expedition boat (benefit sharing). Relevant activities mostly take place outside the Provider State's sovereign realm (*ex situ*, e.g. in the User State).

Article 2: Definition of terms

Article 2 contains the definitions of the key terms used throughout the agreement. The definitions help the contracting Parties to understand the content of the contractual clauses.

The terms and their definitions partially reflect those of the relevant international treaties, especially CBD, NP, and UNCLOS, also including informal texts such as recommendations by the CBD Secretariat. In drafting the Model Agreement, many of the authoritative and widely accepted terms and definitions have been adopted (such as, for example, the definition of genetic resources drawn by the CBD); however, more terms and definitions had to be introduced, taking into account the context and the objectives of the Micro B3 Project.

As used in this agreement, the following terms shall have the meaning provided below:

a) **"Access" means collecting genetic resources from the location where they are found.**

The definition of access focuses on the core activity of sampling. It is clear from the term "collecting" that this may consist of various activities such as surveying and using equipment to search for genetic resources.

b) **"Accessed genetic resources" means the genetic resources collected on the basis of this agreement.**

The term "accessed genetic resources" guarantees the identification of those genetic resources which are subject to the agreement (see Articles 3.1 and 3.2) and thus produces legal certainty for both Provider and Recipient on what shall be the exact objective of utilization, transfer, and – in case of breach of contract (Article 16.4) – destruction.

c) **"Associated genetic knowledge" means any experimental or observational data, information, and other findings on the composition, life conditions, and functions of the accessed genetic resources.**

This is a newly introduced term that is crucial for distinguishing between:

- the knowledge which is directly linked to the accessed genetic resource – then the Provider may claim control of its use, ask for PIC before its transfer, or solicit benefit sharing; and
- the knowledge which is not directly related to the accessed GR but may have been generated with its help (e.g. by comparing genes and functions or by developing a new theory on sleeping genes won at the occasion of research with an accessed GR) – then the Provider is neither entitled to control its use nor to claim benefit sharing.

The latter shall not be the object of the agreement since the Recipient may freely decide on its use.

It is recommended not to list and define "data" and "information" as extra categories but to introduce the umbrella term "knowledge" which is supposed to cover data and information as well as results and other findings.

Scientists normally understand "data" to be the characterization of the genetic resource and its life conditions (which are also called meta-data) referring to the immediate technical description, and "information" as a reference to research results on data. The term knowledge is introduced as a generic term covering both data and information.

d) **"Derivative" means a naturally occurring biochemical compound resulting from the genetic expression or metabolism of biological or genetic resources, even if it does not contain functional units of heredity.**

The definition is taken from Article 2 (e) of the NP. Derivatives are objects of technological applications ("biotechnology") and as such, they are objects of "utilization" as defined in paragraph 1 of the present Article.

e) **"Genetic resources" means any material of plant, animal, microbial, or other origin containing functional units of heredity which is of actual or potential value.**

This definition of genetic resources is a compilation of the definitions of "genetic material" and "genetic resources" in Article 2 CBD. It thus simplifies the use of the term "genetic resource."

f) **"Micro B3 partner" means an institution that is a Party to the Micro B3 Consortium Agreement.**

Micro B3 partners shall have a special status *vis-à-vis* the Parties to the agreement. They are not third parties (see definition i).

As they are Parties to the Micro B3 Consortium Agreement they are bound by the rights and obligations of the Model Agreement as provided in Article 1.2. They may receive genetic resources and associated knowledge from the Recipient without the requirement of PIC from the Provider.

g) **"Ocean Sampling Days" are simultaneous sampling campaigns in the world's oceans, as part of the Micro B3 Project, aiming at providing insights about the microbial diversity and the identification of novel ocean-derived biotechnologies.**

The Model Agreement is principally addressed to the participants and drafted for the objectives of the Ocean Sampling Days that are organized by the Micro B3 Project. The Ocean Sampling Days are aimed to be a worldwide endeavour to take samples of marine microorganisms at various locations, analyze them, and feed the knowledge primarily into the public domain.

h) **"Provider State" means the coastal state from whose marine internal waters, territorial sea, exclusive economic zone, or continental shelf genetic resources are collected in situ.**

The Model Agreement sometimes addresses the "Provider" and sometimes the "Provider State." When the term "Provider" is used it means the Provider as a Party to the agreement ("the authority," see head section of the agreement), being a representative of the Provider State and, according to the Provider State's national law, vested with the power to sign the agreement. By contrast, the term "Provider State" is used

a) when the territory is described (Article 1);
b) when the contribution is acknowledged because there may be more contributing institutions than the authority subscribing to the agreement (Article 7.2);
c) where training and capacity-building shall be agreed (Article 10); and
d) in the clause on the applicable law (Article 14).

i) **"Third party" means any institution other than Micro B3 partners.**

Third parties are relevant in the context of transfer of genetic resources and associated knowledge. They must be distinguished from Micro B3 partners (see Article 1.2). Institutions or individuals that are "contractually bound with the Recipient to provide specified assistance concerning the utilization of the accessed genetic resources" (see Article 3.3) are also not third parties, because they are commissioned to provide specified auxiliary services, but are not entitled to conduct their own R&D activities on the accessed GR.

j) **"Utilization for proprietary purposes" means research and development that aims at protecting the associated knowledge, including products and processes developed, by patent rights, keeping the resulting knowledge secret, making the resulting knowledge accessible at more than incremental costs for dissemination, and/or bringing the products and processes developed from the accessed genetic resources on the market.**

This definition will be explained in conjunction with paragraph k of this Article.

k) **"Utilization for the Public Domain" means research and development that aims at making the associated knowledge, including products and processes developed, publicly available at no more than incremental costs for dissemination, and without being protected by patent rights or further restricted by other intellectual property rights.**

It is a difficult task to define criteria for the distinction of the two forms of utilization, but it is indispensable because different obligations are attached to them.

One may use a substantive criterion that distinguishes between basic research and applied research/development of products. However, results from basic research (such as genes and their function) may already be patented and thus "commercialized." Alternatively, an institutional criterion may be chosen by asking whether the research institution and financial background belong to the public or private sector. But public research institutions are not necessarily confined to non-commercial research while private ones may sometimes work for public benefit.

For the objective of this Model Agreement it is suggested that the question of functionality of the utilization – meaning the dimension of public availability of the associated knowledge – best distinguishes the two realms from each other: If the Recipient intends to make the knowledge publicly available without property protection or further restriction by other intellectual property rights, then the Recipient asks for access to the GR for the purpose of utilizing them for the public domain. If the Recipient's purpose is to protect the knowledge by patent rights or trade secrets and to limit or make costly public availability, it asks for access to the GR with the purpose of utilizing them for proprietary purposes.

1) **"Utilization of genetic resources" means research and development on the genetic and/or biochemical composition of genetic resources, including through the application of biotechnology, which is any technological application that uses biological systems, living organisms, or derivatives thereof, to make or modify products or processes for specific use.**

This is a compilation of the definitions of the terms "utilization of genetic resources" in Article 2 (c) NP and "biotechnology" in Article 2 (d) NP. According to Article 2 (c) NP, utilization means research and development. In other words, applied research and development of products or processes is implied in the term utilization. This is also indicated by the definition of biotechnology which includes the making or modifying of products and processes. Not included in the term is, however, the application and commercialization of developed products (cf. Article 5 NP). R&D can however aim at application and commercialization. This would imply the privatization of R&D results and thus be, in the terminology of this Model Agreement, a case of utilization for proprietary uses.

Article 3: Access to genetic resources

3.1 The Recipient shall be entitled to collect samples as follows:

   a) **Kinds of samples,[3] including the kind of genetic resources,[4] if known:**

---

3 E.g. seawater, sediment.
4 The kind of genetic resources to be extracted from the sample, e.g. virus, bacteria, fungi, microorganisms.

b)   **Number and quantity of samples:**

c)   **Geographical location of collection:**[5]

d)   **Time period for collection:**

3.2 The Recipient shall within . . . [time period to be specified by the Parties] after collection of the samples notify to the Provider the kinds of genetic resources the Recipient intends to utilize. The Provider may, within . . . weeks [to be specified], raise objections in which case the Parties will seek agreement on the kinds of genetic resources allowed to be utilized.

(This clause is to be crossed out if not applicable)[6]

3.3 The Recipient shall be entitled to move the accessed genetic resources to its premises and, subject to Article 1.2 of this agreement, to the premises of other Micro B3 partners, as well as to an institution or individual which is contractually bound with the Recipient to provide specified assistance concerning the utilization of the accessed genetic resources.[7]

3.4 The Recipient shall deliver a portion of the accessed genetic resources to the Provider or an institution designated by the same:

The samples shall be delivered in the following form:

(This clause or part of it is to be crossed out if not applicable)

3.5 The Recipient shall bear all the costs incurred in accessing and delivering the genetic resources.

1. Overview of the article

The objective of Article 3 is the regulation of access to marine genetic resources as agreed by the Provider and the Recipient; it regulates the conditions of access and the rights and obligations of the Parties directly connected with the access.

These rights and obligations may be divided into principal performance obligations (obligation of the Provider to grant access; obligation of the Recipient to access the maritime zones under the agreed parameters: the agreed kind of sample,

---

5 E.g. GPS coordinates.
6 Not applicable if the kind of genetic resources included is known *ex ante* under Article 3.1.a).
7 All other transfers are considered transfers to third parties and bound by the conditions under Article 5.

the agreed number and quantity of the samples, within the agreed geographical area, within the agreed time period) and secondary performance obligations (right of the Recipient to move the genetic resources to the premises of his/her own and to individuals and institutions offering auxiliary services; obligation of the Recipient to send a sample to the Provider State).

2. Legal background

The obligations of the Provider State in relation to the permission of access to its genetic resources are regulated in Article 6 NP. Article 6.1 NP acknowledges the sovereign rights of Provider States to require prior consent and, by implication, to set conditions for the access, such as conditions concerning the sampling and the moving of the sample. If a Provider State has made use of these rights, the Model Agreement serves to specify such conditions in the individual case. Article 6.3 NP strives for legal clarity by requiring State Parties to take the necessary legislative, administrative, and policy measures to "provide for information on how to apply for prior informed consent" (c) and to "set out criteria [. . .] for obtaining prior informed consent" (e). Normally, Provider States ask for both the obtainment of an access permit and the conclusion of an access contract. They may however also simplify procedures by providing the access permit as part of the access contract. This solution is suggested in the Model Agreement: If the Provider signs an agreement, including Article 3 as it is, it thereby grants prior consent to the access. The Model Agreement does not however preclude the Provider State granting a permit in addition to it.

Considering the law of the seas, Articles 245, 246, and 248 UNCLOS acknowledge the same sovereign rights for coastal states as Article 6 NP.

3. Explanation of the article in detail

In Article 3.1 the Parties to the agreement may define, through negotiation, the kinds of samples to be accessed (including the kind of genetic resources if known), the number and quantity of samples, the geographical location of sampling, and the time period for sampling.

See as examples:

a) Kind of sample: *Sediment*
b) Number and quantity of sample: *a minimum of 50 samples of sediment of 50 mL*
c) Geographical location of collection: *GPS coordinates*
d) Time period for collection: *22nd June–29th June 2014*

Submitting this information to the Provider serves the interest of both parties; it provides legal certainty about the limits of the operation regarding the object, the amount of collection, the location, and the time period.

The second paragraph (3.2) was inserted because at the time of conclusion of the agreement the Recipient will not necessarily know which kinds of genetic resource it will actually be able to extract from the sample. In that case, it is sufficient to generally describe the sample (water, sediment, macroorganisms (sponges, algae, etc.)) in Article 3.1; and, as a second step, to specify what kinds of genetic resources (virus, bacteria, prokaryotes, other microbial eukaryotes) shall be utilized as soon as this becomes clear from a screening of the sample. The Provider may in that case raise objections to subsequent utilization.

The third paragraph (3.3) regulates where the samples may be moved: to the premises of the Recipient, to the premises of Micro B3 partners, and to the premises of institutions or individuals that provide auxiliary services such as sequencing etc. These latter transfers do not need a prior informed consent of the Provider for the following reasons: first, Micro B3 Partners are bound by the Consortium Agreement and therefore also bound by the Model Agreement; second, the institutions or individuals are engaged by the Recipient to provide specific technical assistance in the research and development process. This engagement shall not be burdened with too-heavy administrative requirements (e.g. PIC of the Provider) in order not to hamper the research process.

The fourth paragraph (3.4) regulates the obligation of the Recipient to share the collected samples with the Provider. This requirement enables the Provider to supervise the R&D process by tracing the resulting knowledge to the genetic resource. It also enables the Provider to develop its own research activities.

The fifth paragraph (3.5) declares the Recipient responsible for all the costs incurred from accessing and delivering the samples.

Article 4: Utilization of genetic resources

4.1 **The Recipient shall be entitled to the utilization of the accessed genetic resources.**

Specifications, if deemed necessary:

_____

4.2 **The utilization of the accessed genetic resources shall be for the public domain.**

Specifications, if deemed necessary:

_____

(This clause is to be crossed out if not applicable)

4.3 **The Recipient shall be entitled to utilize part/all (please cross out) of the accessed genetic resources for proprietary purposes:**

Specifications, if deemed necessary:

_____

(This clause is to be crossed out if not applicable)

4.4 Should the Recipient, after the conclusion of this agreement, intend to utilize the accessed genetic resources and/or use the associated genetic knowledge for proprietary purposes, the Recipient shall seek the consent of the Provider.

Specifications of the consent procedure, if deemed necessary:

4.5 Should the Provider, after the conclusion of this agreement, intend to utilize the accessed genetic resources and/or use the associated genetic knowledge for proprietary purposes, the Provider shall enter into amicable negotiations with the Recipient on the modification or termination of this agreement.

(This clause is to be crossed out if not applicable)

1. Overview of the article

Article 4 focuses on the steps following access in the chain of valorizing the genetic resources. The Parties may here define the scope of utilization permitted to the Recipient. Basically, the Parties should regulate what kinds of research and development are to be allowed, and whether the utilization shall be exclusively for the public domain or if part or all of it may be carried out for proprietary purposes.

2. Legal background

Article 4 of the Model Agreement is based on Articles 5.1 and 6.1, 6.3 (g) NP which acknowledge the sovereign rights of Provider States to set conditions for access and benefit sharing and thereby prepare the ground for access permits and mutually agreed terms. These conditions may limit the allowed content and purpose of utilization of the accessed genetic resources. Rules similar to this follow from Articles 245, 246, and 248 UNCLOS.

3. Explanation of the article in detail

The Article provides the opportunity to set mutually agreed terms concerning the utilization of the accessed genetic resources. This allows the Parties to individually balance their interests in negotiating special conditions of utilization.

In Article 4.1 the Parties may specify what kinds of research and development activities will exactly be carried out, which research methods may be used, etc. They may however also agree that any R&D shall be allowed and thus leave the space for specifications unfilled.

In Articles 4.2 and 4.3 the Parties shall agree on the functional objective of the utilization activities: Does the Recipient intend to submit the associated knowledge resulting from the utilization of the GR exclusively to the public domain or is its intention to keep (part/all of) the knowledge for proprietary purposes?

The decision pro or contra public domain utilization necessarily entails respective follow-up obligations: the conditions of dissemination of associated knowledge, of reporting and sharing of information, and of benefit sharing may be different in the two cases.

Article 4.4 contains a clause regarding change of intent by the Recipient. If the Recipient, after the conclusion of an agreement that limits all or part of the utilization of the resources to the public domain, decides to utilize the GR (or part of it) or use the associated knowledge for proprietary purposes, it must seek the prior consent of the Provider. Under "specifications" it may be agreed if, in that case, a simple notification is sufficient or if a formal authorization is needed. Other specifications such as benefit-sharing arrangements are regulated under Articles 11.3, 11.4.

A "change of intent" clause for the Provider is introduced by Article 4.5: It might happen that, after the Recipient has shared the sample and the knowledge with the Provider (Articles 3.3, 9.1), the Provider discovers a potential commercial application of the genetic resource or the associated knowledge and would like to prevent the same from being submitted to the public domain. In that case, the Model Agreement does not give the Provider a one-sided right to withdraw its consent, but rather enables it to renegotiate the contract. This solution is mirrored in the case of change of intent of the Recipient in case of which mutual consent must equally be obtained.

As an alternative, the Provider may waive its intention to renegotiate from the onset, for instance in exchange for an upfront payment. In that case Article 4.5 should be disregarded.

Another possibility for the Provider to reserve a share in the commercialization activities *ex ante*, is to use renegotiations according to Article 4.4 to reach conditions on benefit sharing.

Article 5: Transfer of genetic resources to third parties

5.1 The Recipient may transfer to a third party the accessed genetic resources, or parts of them, provided that the third party agrees with the Recipient, to apply to the transferred genetic resources Articles 4 to 16 of this agreement.

5.2 If the Recipient intends to transfer to a third party the associated genetic knowledge which is not yet or shall not be submitted to the public domain according to Article 6, the third party shall agree with the Recipient, to apply to the transferred knowledge Articles 4 to 16 of this agreement.

5.3 In case of transfer to a third party, the Recipient needs the prior informed consent of the Provider, under one of the following modalities:[8]

---

8 NOTE OF CAUTION: The Parties should be aware that too-heavy PIC requirements could significantly complicate the research and development process during the non-commercial stage considered in this contract (defined as public domain). A facilitated PIC procedure for non-commercial use (public domain use) as proposed here would also be to the advantage of the Provider State, because this allows the Recipient to transfer GR or knowledge during the non-commercial stages more easily and thus might lead to increased commercial product development in later stages, in which a new negotiation with the Provider State is initiated according to the renegotiation clause in article 4.4.

- a notification of the transfer to the Provider or an institution designated by the same, along with the sending of a copy of the transfer agreement, will be considered as proof of prior informed consent. The institution shall be the following [if applicable]:

_____

- other [specification of the modality]:

_____

[This clause is to be crossed out upon agreement that the consent is not required]

1. Overview of the article

Article 5 describes the conditions under which the Recipient is allowed to transfer the accessed genetic resources and/or the associated genetic knowledge to third parties. The Article introduces the so called "viral licence clause" for such transfers. The viral licence concept means that the originally signed contract between the Provider and the Recipient travels with the resource and the associated genetic knowledge upon transfer to a second and a third Recipient: that is to say, the subsequent recipients are bound by the same obligations that were imposed on the (first) Recipient in the contract concluded with the Provider. The Provider is therefore reassured that the conditions he/she had negotiated will be respected further down in the transfer chain. This is an important clause given that, usually, Provider States' legislations tends not to facilitate access to genetic resources for research purposes due to legal uncertainty regarding the transfer to third parties and the treatment of materials and knowledge produced out of it by them.

2. Legal background

Article 6.3 (g) (iii) NP acknowledges that the Provider has sovereign rights to establish the conditions for transfer of the GR to third parties. This is commonly implemented by domestic legislation requiring prior consent of the Provider to material transfers to third parties.

The inclusion of the viral licence clause into the Model Agreement was inspired by the experience made with the Material Transfer Agreement used by the European Culture Collections (ECCO MTA). Under this MTA the transfer of the material

a)   between scientists working in the same laboratory,
b)   between partners in different institutions collaborating on a defined joint project for non-commercial purposes, or
c)   between public service culture collections for accession purposes

is allowed provided that the MTA conditions for further distribution are equivalent to those that were agreed upon for the initial transfer of material. Article 5 of the Model Agreement however somehow differs from the ECCO MTA: Scientists working in the same laboratory (above a.) are bound by internal rules of the institution that signs the contract on the Recipient side. And collaborating partners (above b.) are already bound by Article 2.1 of the Model Agreement, because they are Micro B3 partners. Article 5 therefore focuses on transfers to genuine third parties (which may also include culture collections (above c.).

3. Explanation of the article in detail

The Model Agreement offers a viral licence clause in Article 5.

This clause guarantees that all obligations of the initial ABS agreement (Articles 4–16) will be imposed on any third party receiving the material and/or the knowledge associated with the GR (Article 5.1). The Recipient is allowed to transfer the material and/or the knowledge to a third party only under the condition that the third party agrees to respect the conditions of the initial ABS agreement (Article 5.2). This can be implemented by the third party signing an MTA that the initial ABS agreement shall be binding on it.

Article 5.3 provides two modalities of procedures, one of which the parties may choose:

- The Recipient notifies the Provider of any transfer to third parties. In this case the general prior consent the Provider grants by signing the Model Agreement is completed by targeting a specific transfer.
- The Parties introduce additional modalities: they define a period within which the Provider may raise objections or they introduce a requirement that the Provider must give its explicit consent.

It is recommended that the first option shall be chosen for public domain uses in order to avoid too-heavy administrative burdens (see also footnote to Article 5).

A third option which is even less burdensome would be to disregard Article 5.3. In this case the general prior consent would be regarded as sufficient.

Article 6: Dissemination of knowledge

6.1 The Recipient shall make the associated genetic knowledge publicly available at no more than incremental costs of dissemination. The dissemination can be through online media, print media, or delivery upon request. The recommended forums for online dissemination are the Micro B3 Information System (www.microb3.eu) and existing databases and information networks such as the Global Biodiversity Information Facility (GBIF), SeaDataNet, Pangaea, and the International Nucleotide Sequence Database Collaboration (INSDC).

6.2 Such knowledge shall be made available as soon as possible after its generation unless otherwise specified. No embargo period is allowed for the raw sequence data and the oceanographic data associated to the samples collected upon the Ocean Sampling Day.

Specifications if deemed necessary:

6.3 The Recipient shall make reasonable efforts to ensure that the release of associated genetic knowledge through online media, print media, or delivery upon request will be organized such that users are bound not to use the associated genetic knowledge taken from the portals for proprietary purposes unless they have obtained prior informed consent of the Provider.

6.4 Paragraphs 1–3 of this Article do not apply to associated genetic knowledge used for proprietary purposes specified under Articles 4.3 and 4.4.

6.5 The Recipient shall make reasonable efforts to ensure that the users of knowledge accessed from the Micro B3 Information System provide to the System the knowledge from their own research in such form and format as the System will reasonably require in order to promote the objectives of the utilization for the public domain.

1. Overview of the article

The objective of Article 6 is to illustrate the different options for the dissemination policy concerning the associated genetic knowledge and consequently the obligations of the Recipient in that regard. The dissemination policy differs according to the objectives of utilization of the accessed GR that have been agreed upon by the Parties under Article 4. If the utilization is exclusively for the public domain, the Recipient has to make the accessed genetic knowledge available in the public domain as soon as it has been generated. If the utilization is for proprietary purposes, the Recipient is not bound by dissemination obligations under Article 6.

2. Legal background

The legal grounds for establishing such obligations for the Recipient is the principle of mutually agreed terms reaffirmed by Article 6.3 (e) of the NP.

Article 6 addresses issues of data management that have not yet been discussed in-depth in the ABS context. Neither the CBD, the NP nor UNCLOS have specific provisions addressing the way the sovereign rights of Provider States entitle them to monitor and codetermine the processing of knowledge derived from R&D on accessed genetic resources. One important provision framing such rights is Article 5 NP, which ensures that any "benefits arising from the utilization of genetic resources as well as subsequent applications and commercialization" shall be shared with the Provider State. "Arising" also includes processes of knowledge generation from the R&D on the "original" material and for "new" material (such as products). If the phase of knowledge generation involves the submission of results to the public domain, this entails the risk that the Provider State loses track of subsequent steps towards commercialization. It is therefore in the interest of the Provider to control the process to some extent. On the other hand, the Provider State is, according to Article 8 (a) NP, under the duty to facilitate non-commercial research, which is hereby understood as research for the public domain. Article 6 attempts to strike a balance between the freedom of public domain research and the legitimate rights of provider states to control the valorization chain.

3. Explanation of the article in detail

Article 6 illustrates the dissemination obligations of the Recipient in the cases where the genetic resources (or part of them) are accessed for utilization for the public domain as stated in Article 4.2 (or in Article 4.3). In these cases, the Recipient commits itself to make the accessed genetic knowledge publicly available at no more than incremental costs for dissemination and as soon as possible after its generation. The delivery of such knowledge upon request is also considered to be a variant of publication. A fee for access may be included, but this shall not exceed "incremental" costs. This is to be understood as costs for the storage and the technical means of transfer of knowledge.

Several forums for the online dissemination are recommended: the Micro B3 Information System (once it is in place and running) and some existing databases and information networks that have a strong reputation among scientists working on genomics.

Article 6.2 introduces an embargo period for dissemination: The Recipient shall publish the knowledge "as soon as possible" after its generation, but the Parties are free to further specify the embargo period.

No embargo period is allowed for the raw sequence data and oceanographic data associated with the samples collected within the Ocean Sampling Day (OSD) initiative. This aims at ensuring that the pools of data collected through the initiative will be publicly available immediately, as this is one of the main objectives of the initiative. It is also an important step to identify the participants to the OSD initiative and to ensure that the participants respect the OSD data policy.

In Article 6.3, the Model Agreement confers on the Recipient the responsibility to observe third-party use of the knowledge. Users should not take knowledge from the public portal and use it for proprietary purposes unless they have obtained prior informed consent from the Provider. *De facto*, the monitoring of such requirements will however be difficult since the Recipient who has submitted knowledge to a database has no stakes in taking legal action against commercial uses. Nor is it feasible for the database operators to ensure that PIC has been obtained. For this reason databases normally ask users to agree with a disclaimer which frees the database from any liability vis-à-vis a right holder. These disclaimers need to be reconsidered in relation to Provider rights on genetic resources, but this will require more discussion and a longer learning process that cannot be predetermined by strict clauses in the present Model Agreement. Therefore, a goodwill clause rather than an obligation for the Recipient has been drafted using the softer formulation "shall make reasonable efforts to ensure."

However, since the Model Agreement aims at serving as a template also beyond the Micro B3 Project and the Ocean Sampling Days, the proprietary utilization of the GR allowed by Articles 4.3 and 4.4 needs to be granted legal protection by the agreement as well. Therefore, if a respective clause negotiated with the Provider allows for the utilization of part or all of the accessed GR for proprietary purposes, according to Articles 4.3 and 4.4, these public domain dissemination obligations will cover only the associated genetic knowledge produced from the part of GR accessed for the public domain, if any. Otherwise no dissemination obligations bind the Recipient, and Articles 6.1–6.3 do not apply.

The intention of Article 6.5 is that the users of knowledge from the Micro B3 Information System (once in place and running) give knowledge from their own research back to the System in order to promote the objectives of the utilization for the public domain. The Micro B3 Information System will set the forms and formats under which the knowledge is to be provided. Of course, such an obligation is difficult to enforce, both by the database operators and by the Recipient. For this reason the related obligation of the Recipient is framed in soft language.

Article 7: Acknowledging the contribution of the provider state

7.1 When making associated genetic knowledge publicly available, the Recipient shall indicate the country of origin of the utilized genetic resource.

7.2 When making associated genetic knowledge publicly available, the Recipient shall acknowledge the role of scientists from the Provider State, and, where any work, significant advice, or recommendations have been provided by such scientists, their (co-)authorship.

1. Overview of the article

The objective of Article 7 is to acknowledge the contribution of the Provider State when the knowledge is made publicly available. First, it obliges the Recipient to indicate the origin of the accessed genetic resource and thus helps tracking the origin of the associated knowledge. Second, it requires the Recipient to acknowledge the role of scientists, especially in the case of significant contribution to the research results.

These obligations bind the Recipient only in those cases in which the Provider has granted access to its GR allowing their utilization for the public domain.

2. Legal background

The Bonn Guidelines require the users of genetic resources "to maintain all relevant data regarding the genetic resources, especially documentary evidence of the prior informed consent and information concerning the origin and the use of genetic resources and the benefits arising from such use" (paragraph 16 (b) (vi)). Moreover, paragraph 16 (d) (ii) requires the users of GR "to encourage the disclosure of origin of the GR and of traditional knowledge (TK)."

In addition, the list of non-monetary benefits (appearing first as Annex II to the Bonn Guidelines and then repeated in the NP) includes the following benefits to be possibly shared:

- "Collaboration, cooperation and contribution in scientific research and development programmes, particularly biotechnological research activities, where possible in the provider country"
- "Social recognition"
- "Joint ownership of intellectual property rights"

3. *Explanation of the article in detail*

Article 7 is applicable when knowledge generated from the utilization of accessed genetic resources is published. Whether the publication is made as part of a public domain or proprietary track is of no concern. Moreover, publications concerning patented information are subject to the obligation to indicate the country of origin and acknowledge the collaboration of scientists, including co-authorship.

Article 8: Recording and reporting

8.1 The Recipient shall maintain records concerning the storage and transfer of the accessed genetic resources and allow access to such records to the Provider or the authority designated by the same.

_____(insert name and address
       of authority if applicable)

8.2 The Recipient shall report in writing to the Provider or the authority designated by the same every _____ [insert duration] months, beginning _____ and ending _____, providing details of the progress of utilization.

_____ (insert name and address
       of authority if applicable)

8.3 With relation to associated genetic knowledge used for proprietary purposes specified under Articles 4.3 and 4.4, the Recipient shall, when reporting according to paragraph 2 of this Article, also report on any steps taken towards obtaining or implementing intellectual property protection and the selling of products or processes based on this knowledge.[9]

---

9 Subject to negotiation of the Parties, it could be agreed that the consent of the Provider is required for certain steps of commercialization, such as the bringing on the market of the product.

1. Overview of the article

The objective of Article 8 is to keep track of the accessed GR and their utilization and to share this information with the Provider. This obligation helps monitoring the compliance with the mutually agreed terms concluded in the agreement.

2. Legal background

Article 17 of the NP, on "monitoring the utilization of GR," requires each Party to take appropriate measures to monitor and to enhance transparency about the utilization of genetic resources, in order to support compliance. Among these measures each Party shall encourage "users and providers of GR to include provisions in mutually agreed terms to share information on the implementation of such terms, including through reporting requirements" (Article 17.1 (b) NP).

In addition, the obligation to report on the progress of utilization is a possible non-monetary benefit listed in the annex of the Nagoya Protocol which reads as: "sharing of research and development results."

3. Explanation of the article in detail

The Recipient must keep track of the storage and the transfer of the accessed GR and allow access to this information to the Provider upon demand. The Provider can designate the authority competent to ask for access to these records.

Moreover, the Recipient must report in writing to the Provider the details of progress of utilization of the accessed GR. The Recipient and the Provider have to agree on the timeframe for these reporting activities and the Provider can designate the authority competent to receive the reports.

Finally, in the cases of associated genetic knowledge used for proprietary purposes (see Articles 4.3 and 4.4), the Recipient shall also report on any steps taken towards obtaining or implementing intellectual property protection and the selling of products or processes based on this knowledge.

These duties pursue a twofold objective: First, the Provider benefits from the reports related to the content since they may include new scientific findings. Second, the information enables it to regularly monitor if the Recipient complies with the contractual obligations *vis-à-vis* the utilization of the accessed GR.

Article 9: Sharing of knowledge

9.1 **The Recipient shall provide the Provider, or the authority designated by the same, with the associated genetic knowledge and provide assistance in their assessment or interpretation as reasonably requested.**

_____ **(insert name and address of authority if applicable)**

9.2 **Such knowledge shall, at the latest, be provided once it has been made publicly available.**

Specifications if deemed necessary:[10] _____

9.3 The obligation under paragraph 1 of this Article extends to associated genetic knowledge used for proprietary purposes specified under Articles 4.3 and 4.4. When using the knowledge the Provider shall not prejudice any use for proprietary purposes by the Recipient.[11]

Specifications, if deemed necessary:

_____

(This clause is to be crossed out if not applicable)

9.4 The Recipient shall furnish the Provider or the authority designated by the same with _____ (insert number) copies of any publication based on the utilization of the accessed genetic resources.

_____ (insert name and address of authority if applicable)

1. Overview of the article

The objective of Article 9 is to provide for a non-monetary benefit sharing through the sharing of the associated genetic knowledge with the Provider, applicable in the case of public domain agreement as well as in the case of proprietary agreement.

2. Legal background

According to Annex to the NP, No. 2 (a), read together with Article 5 NP, the sharing of research and development results belongs to the (non-monetary) benefits that shall be shared with the Provider State.

Moreover, Article 6.3 (g) (ii) NP acknowledges that the mutually agreed terms might include terms on benefit sharing.

3. Explanation of the article in detail

The Recipient is obliged to share with the Provider the associated genetic knowledge at the latest when it is submitted to the public domain, if public domain is agreed. The Recipient is also obliged to provide assistance in the assessment and interpretation of such knowledge in respect of the needs of the Provider which may vary according to the Provider's scientific capacity.

10 It may be agreed between the Parties that the Provider shall be informed before publication. This may allow the Provider to check if the requirements under Article 7 are fulfilled and/or if there is reason for pursuing proprietary purposes according to Article 4.5. In this case the Provider shall keep the knowledge confidential during the agreed period.

11 This clause will be negotiated along with the benefit-sharing arrangement: a Provider State will prefer to have access to the information (even if the country keeps it confidential as specified under 9.3), but a company might prefer to give a higher upfront benefit sharing under article 11 as a *quid pro quo* for crossing out this article.

If the Model Agreement allows for proprietary uses of the GR (see Article 4.3 and 4.4) the Recipient is still obliged to share such knowledge with the Provider, but in return the Provider commits itself not to prejudice any proprietary use by the Recipient. This means that the Provider shall not obtain intellectual property rights on the knowledge nor publish it but rather treat such knowledge confidentially.

Finally the Recipient is obliged to give to the Provider an agreed number of copies of any publication based on the utilization of the accessed genetic resources. This clause of the Model Agreement applies both to a public domain and to a proprietary agreement. The clause is important from the point of view of scientists: If they publish in academic journals, access to which is subject to a charge, the clause will help scientists negotiate with publishers regarding their right to release their publications for free.

Article 10: Scientific collaboration with the provider state and capacity building

> As part of the Micro B3 Project the Recipient agrees to collaborate with scientists from the Provider State in the utilization activities based on this agreement. Such involvement shall take the following forms:[12]
>
> (to be specified by negotiations)

1. Overview of the article

Article 10 introduces a non-monetary benefit to be shared by the Parties of the agreement. It is a matter of negotiation between the Provider and the Recipient to further specify details of collaboration.

2. Legal background

According to the Bonn Guidelines and the Nagoya Protocol the "cooperation and contribution in scientific research and development programmes, particularly biotechnological research activities" is one of the possible non-monetary benefits to be shared that can be negotiated through mutually agreed terms.

Article 15.6 of the CBD states that "each contracting Party shall endeavour to develop and carry out scientific research based on GR provided by other Contracting Parties with the full participation of, and where possible in, such contracting Parties."

---

12 It should be noted that in the normal case of scientific collaboration the partners conclude a research collaboration contract/project (however, usually the research collaboration is more a project rather than a contract, and it is not legally binding) in which the details of the collaboration are laid out. The ABS agreement should not be overloaded with such details. It will be advisable that the Parties to the ABS agreement make a reference to the research collaboration agreement/project.

Beyond foreseeing collaboration in a mutual relationship, the Parties to the Nagoya Protocol are required, as a general commitment, to engage in collaboration and cooperation in technical and scientific research and development programmes and to promote access to and transfer of technology to countries with less-developed economies (Article 23 of the NP).

3. Explanation of the article in detail

Within the framework of capacity building, the Model Agreement foresees collaboration between the Recipient and scientists from the Provider State. Since the collaboration is related to the utilization activities and given that the definition of utilization (see Article 2) includes research and development, Article 10 implies that the collaboration may extend to all the utilization activities.

The Parties have to indicate the actual level of involvement of the scientists of the Provider State from the sampling activities to the analyzing phase. This is left to the mutually agreed terms of the Model Agreement. However, given the shared research ethos of the Micro B3 Project, it is expected to create the conditions for a strong collaboration between scientists. Moreover, it is important to notice that the Micro B3 Project offers limited possibilities to attend training courses and summer schools on different relevant disciplines. This possibility could also be mentioned in the "specifications" of the Article, if agreed by the Provider and the Recipient.

Article 11: Benefit sharing in case of utilization for proprietary purposes

11.1   The Recipient agrees to pay an up-front compensation of . . . (amount to be specified) to the Provider, if the Recipient utilizes the accessed genetic resources for proprietary purposes. The payment is due to the Provider within . . . months (term to be specified) after consent on the kinds of genetic resources to be utilized has been reached under Article 3.2. The payment shall be transferred to the following account of the Provider:

_____

(This clause is to be crossed out if not applicable)

11.2   If the Recipient utilizes the accessed genetic resources or uses the associated knowledge for proprietary purposes according to Articles 4.3 and 4.4, he/she must fairly and equitably share with the Provider any monetary benefit obtained.

11.3   The share shall be determined by further negotiations between the Parties to this agreement.

11.4.   (Alternatively to 11.3) The share shall be _____ percent of the revenue from sales of the product or process based on the accessed genetic resources. It shall be paid on the basis of a financial report to be sent to the Provider or an authority designated by the same at the end of any year of any revenue generation to the account designated by the same.

(Insert authority and account details if applicable)

11.5 **If the Recipient utilizes the accessed genetic resources or utilizes the associated genetic knowledge for proprietary purposes without being entitled according to Articles 4.3 or 4.4, and therefore in breach of the conditions of this agreement, he/she must share with the Provider any monetary benefit obtained from such utilization or use. The share shall be _____ percent of the revenue from sales of the product or process based on the accessed genetic resources. It shall be paid on the basis of a financial report to be sent to the Provider or an authority designated by the same in due time upon request by the same.**

(Insert authority and account details if applicable)

(This Article or single paragraphs of it are to be crossed out if not applicable)

1. Overview of the article

Article 11 determines the sharing of monetary benefits in cases of proprietary utilization of the accessed genetic resources. It covers those forms of proprietary utilization that were agreed upon between the Parties, and also forms of proprietary utilization that were not agreed and undertaken in breach of Articles 4.3 and 4.4.

2. Legal background

Article 15.7 of the CBD requires the Parties to "take legislative, administrative, or policy measures the goal of which is the fair and equitable sharing of benefits with the Contracting Party providing genetic resources." The determination of benefits that are to be shared is left to the negotiation of mutually agreed terms (Article 15.3). The CBD also foresees different types of benefits to be shared, among which are commercial or other benefits derived from utilizing the genetic resources (Article 15.7). The Nagoya Protocol (in its Article 5.4) expressly recognizes that there may be both monetary and non-monetary benefits derived from the utilization of genetic resources. The Protocol's Annex contains an indicative list of monetary and non-monetary benefits, taken from Annex II of the Bonn Guidelines.

3. Explanation of the article in detail

In cases of utilization of the accessed GR for proprietary purposes, the Recipient has to fairly and equitably share any monetary benefit obtained with the Provider.

Article 11.1 foresees the possibility of an up-front payment. It is suggested that such payment shall preferably not be agreed because at the negotiation stage of the agreement, the economic value of the genetic resources is unknown. While this clause may therefore be crossed out, it is compulsory to regulate an *ex post* compensation. The Parties may either decide to determine *a posteriori* the share of the benefits by further negotiation (11.3) or to determine *a priori* the share (in percentage) of the revenue from the sales of the products or processes based on the accessed GR (11.4). This clause thus establishes the possibility for an *ex ante* compensatory liability scheme.

The Article goes further to impose on the Recipient the share of monetary benefits in cases where proprietary utilization of the accessed GR has been undertaken with no prior informed consent of the Provider (if this would be required according to the Provider's legislation), in breach of the agreement. For such cases of breach the Parties are required to define *a priori* the percentage of the share.

Article 12: Other laws to be respected

The Recipient shall ensure that the collection, storage, transfer, utilization, and exportation of the genetic resources complies with all applicable laws of the Provider State on the protection of human health and the environment, on taxes, on customs and on any other concern.

1. Overview of the article

According to this provision, the Recipient is required to respect the domestic law of the Provider State, especially the law on the protection of health and the environment, on taxes and customs in the course of collecting, storing, transferring, utilizing, and exporting the genetic resources, as long as the activity is carried out in the sovereign realm of the Provider State.

2. Legal background

According to the international customary principle which says that a state has sovereignty over its territory, the Recipient must in any case respect the legal framework of the Provider State. Thus, the contractual clause is only of declaratory importance but it alerts the Recipient of this principle.

3. Explanation of the article in detail

The Article brings attention to the Recipient about the fact that in the course of sampling, utilizing, and moving of the genetic resources it might be confronted with certain domestic legal requirements protecting different public interests such as human health, the environment, or fiscal concerns.

Article 13: Duration of the agreement

The agreement is of unlimited duration, except for the obligations under Articles 8.2 and 10 which shall end on [date to be inserted; e.g. 2 years after the termination of the Micro B3 Project]:

---

1. Overview of the article

The Article specifies the duration of the contract distinguishing between clauses of unlimited and limited duration.

2. Legal background

The Article reflects requirements of general contract law. Any contract must decide on its duration.

3. Explanation of the article in detail

Most of the provisions of the Model Agreement shall be of unlimited duration because the utilization of the accessed genetic resources is of unlimited length. Some of the provisions will however be exhausted after implementation, such as the right to take specific samples under Article 3. Two clauses are limited in time because they are connected to project activities within the Micro B3 framework, i.e. Article 8.2 (Report on steps of utilization) and Article 10 (Scientific collaboration).

In addition, the agreement may terminate under the conditions of Article 16 (termination by mutual agreement and by default). The Parties are required to agree on a time limit for the obligations regulated in these two provisions. A possible time limit would be "two years after the termination of the Micro B3 Project."

Article 14: Applicable law

14.1 The applicable law on any matters relating to the interpretation and the application of the present agreement shall be:

14.2 The competent court for dispute settlement shall be:

---

1. Overview of the article

The provision requires the contracting Parties to choose the applicable law relating to the interpretation and application of the agreement and the place of jurisdiction for disputes arising directly or indirectly out of the agreement.

2. Legal background

The legal background of this Article is Article 18.1 (a), (b) NP. Mutually agreed terms shall include a clause on the jurisdiction to which the Parties will subject for dispute resolution and a clause on the applicable law. For the eventual enforcement of contractual rights and obligations, the Parties shall thus agree in this Article on the applicable law and the place of jurisdiction. This is no obligation, however. In the absence of an agreement, the question would be regulated by international private law and international civil procedural law.

3. Explanation of the article in detail

In the Model Agreement, the Parties are free to determine if the law of the Provider State or the law of the State where the Recipient is based shall be applicable to matters relating to the interpretation and application of the agreement. It is recommended to make use of this choice as part of the negotiation of the mutually agreed terms of the agreement. First, because if the Recipient is willing, for example, to accept the Provider State as the place of jurisdiction, the Provider may possibly partially renounce the benefits to be shared. Second, because regulation by law (see above) and not by the Parties may be necessarily disadvantageous for one of the Parties. Third, the Parties avoid disputes on the interpretation of relevant provisions of international private law.

The place of jurisdiction does not necessarily have to be in the country of the applicable law. However, it would ease proceedings if the judges at court can apply their domestic law and are not constrained to engage in the apprehension of foreign law.

Article 15: Dispute settlement

15.1 No Party shall, in the event of a dispute arising from this agreement, commence court proceedings (except proceedings for urgent interlocutory relief) before searching for an amicable solution according to paragraphs 2 and 3 of this Article.

15.2 A Party to this agreement claiming that a dispute has arisen under or in relation to this agreement must provide the other Party with a written notice specifying the nature of the dispute on receipt of which the dispute resolution shall forthwith begin.

15.3 Any dispute arising from this agreement shall be resolved expeditiously foremost by negotiation in good faith; failure to which the Parties shall engage informal dispute resolution techniques, such as mediation and arbitration or similar techniques, agreed upon by them.

1. Overview of the article

This provision addresses issues of dispute resolution. It strongly supports the idea of finding amicable solutions. The dispute resolution process starts with the Party claiming that a dispute has arisen and providing a written notice to the other

Party. The dispute shall be solved by negotiation, and if negotiation fails the Parties should apply informal dispute resolution techniques such as mediation and arbitration. Court proceedings shall be the last means to the settlement of disputes.

2. Legal background

This Article is inspired by Article 18.1 (c) of the NP. The Parties to the Protocol shall include provisions in mutually agreed terms to cover "options for alternative dispute resolution."

3. Explanation of the article in detail

A dispute may be solved through a sequence of steps, indicating the degree of involvement and engagement of a third party:

a) Written notice by the Party claiming to the other Party that a conflict arose out of the agreement (formal requirement: the notice shall indicate the nature of the conflict)
b) Resolution by alternative dispute settlement

    aa) Resolution by negotiation (no third party involved)
    bb) (if aa is not successful) Resolution by mediation (third party is a bridge between the two parties and assists in the communication between the Parties – more passive role)
    cc) (if bb is not successful) Resolution by arbitration (third party reviews the evidence in the case and imposes a decision that is legally binding for both sides – both Parties must declare beforehand that they agree to be bound by the decision)

c) (if b. is not successful) Jurisdictional proceedings

Article 16: Termination of the agreement

16.1 The agreement may be terminated at any time by mutual agreement in writing.

16.2 The agreement may be terminated by default if the Recipient fails to satisfy any of the following obligations under this agreement: Articles 4.2, 4.3, 4.4, 5.1, 5.2, 5.3, 6.1, 6.3, 7, 8, 9.1 and 9.3, 11.2 and 11.5.

16.3 In the case of default the Provider may immediately terminate this agreement by giving written notice to the Recipient of the termination provided that:

a) the Provider has given prior notice to the Recipient of the alleged default; and
b) the Recipient fails to respond to the Provider within the period specified by the notice (being not less than 20 business days and not

more than 60 business days) to rectify or explain to the satisfaction of the Provider the reasons for the default.

16.4 **If this agreement is terminated under paragraph 2 of this Article the Recipient will not thereafter utilize or transfer the accessed genetic resources or use or transfer associated genetic knowledge; and it will transfer back to the Provider or destroy, at the Provider's discretion, all genetic resources or associated genetic knowledge. The operation of this clause survives the termination of this agreement.**

1. Overview of the article

Article 16 focuses on the forms and conditions of the termination of the agreement before the mutual obligations have been fully implemented. There are two possible forms of termination: termination by mutual agreement and termination by default. In the first case (16.1), the Parties conclude a contract on the termination in which all the obligations that follow from the termination (handling of the GR and the associated knowledge, terms) will be regulated. In the second case the Recipient, in failing to satisfy one of his/her principal contractual obligations listed under 16.2, fulfils the conditions for the termination by default. In consequence, the Provider has the right to terminate the contract unilaterally under the formal conditions of 16.3. The Recipient must immediately stop further utilization of the GR and use of the knowledge (16.4).

2. Legal background

The Article reflects requirements of general contract law. A contract must be clear on its termination.

3. Explanation of the article in detail

Article 16.1 expresses the contractual freedom of the Parties to determine the termination of the contract and the resulting obligations.

Article 16.2 lists the principal obligations of the Recipient the nonfulfillment of which may lead to automatic termination under the formal conditions of 16.3. The relevant obligations are:

- Utilization for the public domain (4.2)
- Utilization for proprietary purposes (4.3)
- Change of intent (4.4)
- Transfer of genetic resources (5.1)
- Transfer of associated knowledge (5.2)
- PIC before transfer (5.3)
- Publication of associated knowledge (6.1)
- Acknowledging the contribution of the Provider State (7)
- Recording and Reporting (8)

- Sharing of knowledge for the public domain (9.1)
- Sharing of knowledge for proprietary purposes (9.3)
- Sharing of monetary benefits (11.2)
- Sharing of monetary benefits in case of breach of Article 4.3 or 4.4 (11.5)

The Provider has to comply, in terminating the contract, with the formal conditions under 16.3: It shall notify the Recipient of the alleged default. Within an agreed period, specified by the Parties, the Recipient may respond to the notice. This reaction may allow for the possibility of finding an amicable solution as an alternative to the termination of the contract. If the Recipient fails to respond within the agreed period, the Provider may, without further delay, terminate the agreement by giving written notice to the Recipient.

No penalty for the Recipient is prescribed for causing the termination of the contract. However, the Recipient is bound by the prohibition to further utilize and transfer the accessed GR or use and transfer the associated knowledge. Eventually, he/she is required to transfer back to the Provider or destroy, at the Provider's discretion, the accessed GR.

Index